A Student Athlete's Guide to College Success

A Student Athlete's Guide to College Success

Peak Performance in Class and Life

Third Edition

Trent A. Petrie

Douglas M. Hankes

Eric L. Denson

WADSWORTH
CENGAGE Learning

Australia • Brazil • Japan • Korea • Mexico • Singapore • Spain • United Kingdom • United States

A Student Athlete's Guide to College Success: Peak Performance in Class and Life, Third Edition
Trent A. Petrie, Douglas M. Hankes, and Eric L. Denson

Senior Publisher: Lyn Uhl

Director of College Success: Annie Todd

Senior Sponsoring Editor: Shani Fisher

Assistant Editor: Daisuke Yasutake

Editorial Assistant: Cat Salerno

Media Editor: Amy Gibbons

Production Manager: Suzanne St. Clair

Manufacturing Manager: Denise Powers

Senior Marketing Manager: Kirsten Stoller

Marketing Coordinator: Ryan Ahern

Marketing Communications Manager: Martha Pfeiffer

Print Buyer: Julio Esperas

Art Director: Hannah Wellman

Senior Rights Acquisition Account Manager: Katie Huha

Permissions Account Manager, Images/Media: Mandy Groszko

Content Project Management: Pre-PressPMG

Production Service: Pre-PressPMG

Cover Designer: Riezebos Holzbaur/ Tim Heraldo

Cover Image: ©Photolibrary/iStockphoto

Library of Congress Control Number: 2009941342

ISBN-13: 978-0-495-57053-0

ISBN-10: 0-495-57053-2

Wadsworth
20 Channel Center Street
Boston, MA 02210
USA

Cengage Learning is a leading provider of customized learning solutions with office locations around the globe, including Singapore, the United Kingdom, Australia, Mexico, Brazil, and Japan. Locate your local office at **www.cengage.com/global**

Cengage Learning products are represented in Canada by Nelson Education, Ltd.

To learn more about Wadsworth, visit **www.cengage.com/wadsworth**

Purchase any of our products at your local college store or at our preferred online store **www.CengageBrain.com**

Printed in the United States of America
1 2 3 4 5 6 7 14 13 12 11 10

Brief Contents

Contents

12 Choosing a Major and a Career: Succeeding in Life and Relationships   269

13 Succeeding on the Field: Becoming a Mentally Tough Athlete   300

Preface

This book is a reflection of our experiences as competitive athletes and our life's work as sport psychologists. As former collegiate athletes, current college teachers, and practicing sport psychologists, we have an intimate understanding of the unique pressures and stressors that college student-athletes experience each day. We know that being a student-athlete means holding down a full-time job, while simultaneously being a full-time student. But, unlike other students who also may work many hours, student-athletes ply their trade in front of hundreds, thousands, even tens of thousands of fans every week. Their every action is subject to a level of scrutiny few others face at any point in their lives, and their academic performance is evaluated weekly to determine if they are in compliance with school, conference, and NCAA requirements. Where other students can underperform in near anonymity, any academic and/or athletic difficulties that student-athletes have may end up under the glare of the media spotlight.

In writing this book, we have taken our understanding of the dual responsibilities of being a high-level sport performer and an accomplished student to create a book that speaks in the language and to the experiences of the college student-athlete. We wanted to provide this unique population of college students with the most relevant and current information and strategies to help them become successful in all areas of their lives. To accomplish that, we have written the book in a form that speaks to the lives and experiences of today's college student-athlete in the following ways:

- The writing style is friendly and conversational, and incorporates real-world examples from the student-athletes with whom we have worked.
- Academic and learning strategies are presented in a straightforward, easy-to-understand manner that provides concrete ideas on how to improve performances.
- Each chapter starts with a "Game Plan" that orients the students to the major topics that will be covered, and then proceeds to a self-assessment (Perceive It!) that provides students with the opportunity to determine their current strengths and areas of growth.
- Throughout each chapter are inspirational quotes from current and past athletic champions that can serve as motivational tools.
- At the beginning of each chapter, a story of a current student-athlete is presented to increase the relevance of the topics that will be covered. These stories speak to the very real issues that collegiate athletes face each day and serve to connect students to the concepts and strategies presented in the chapter.
- Recurring features, such as self-assessments, exercises, special-feature boxes, goal-setting opportunities, and chapter review questions help keep students connected to, focused on, and involved with the material by providing them with active ways to learn.

In this revision, we have kept the best of what was in the previous edition and added material that we know will help you be an even more successful student. From the original book, we maintained the focus on **goals and self-responsibility**. As an athlete, you understand the importance of goals for directing your attention, keeping you motivated, and helping you evaluate your progress; benefits that occur with academic goals as well. But you also know that setting a goal is not enough. You must be willing to put in the effort necessary, each and every day, to make progress. In other words, you must be responsible for your actions and focused in your efforts. No one will do it for you.

We know that students learn in different ways and that these styles do not always match well with how information is presented in college classrooms. Thus, information on **learning styles** again is included in this edition. By identifying the way you learn best, you can adopt strategies that will help you be an efficient and effective learner.

We again provide **self-assessments** at the beginning of each chapter so you can evaluate your knowledge of the current topics and use of relevant strategies. Each chapter is designed to speak to the different areas covered in the self-assessments so you will know, in advance, the topics on which you should focus if you want to improve on your weaknesses and expand your strengths. Each chapter ends with **review questions** so you can determine how well you have learned the material presented.

A key for all students, but student-athletes in particular (who often are kinesthetic learners), is making the material personally meaningful and the learning active. Thus, we have retained the **stories** of student-athletes at the beginning of each chapter and provided **examples** throughout to illustrate key points. We also have included multiple **exercises** within each chapter. These exercises are linked directly to the topics covered in each chapter and give students the opportunity to become more aware of their thoughts and behaviors or to put into practice the information and strategies they are learning. We also included the **feature boxes** in which we presented information on topics of particular relevance to college student-athletes.

Finally, we retained the key topics from the last edition, including **goal setting, learning styles, memory, concentration and motivation, note-taking, test-taking, reading and studying textbooks, choosing a career, stress and coping, health, time management and procrastination,** and **communication**. These topics cover the information, skills, and strategies that provide the foundation for being successful in school, sports, and life.

What's Been Added to the Third Edition of *A Student-Athlete's Guide to College Success?*

First, this edition has been newly designed. The current edition incorporates the best practices in graphic design, producing a cleaner and visually more appealing look. In addition, special design elements have been incorporated to encourage the active involvement of students as they read the material and complete exercises. Elements such as chapter objectives ("Game Plan"), opening photographs of male and female athletes from different college sports that connect the reader to the material, updated opening stories of student-athletes and their experiences concerning the topics covered in the chapter, exercises, feature boxes in which special topics are covered, goal-setting activities, and chapter review questions all increase students motivation and help stimulate learning. In addition, each chapter is organized around three ideas that are salient to athletes—Preparation, Performance, and Post-Game Review. Material presented in the sections designated "Preparation" provide the background information (e.g., theory, definitions) on the topic or concepts covered. In the section designated "Performance," students are introduced to strategies for being a more effective learner. Last, in the section designated "Post-Game Review," students are provided with a summary of the material covered in the chapter, which is an opportunity to consolidate what they have just learned.

Throughout the book, **material has been updated** to reflect the most current information available on the topics presented. For example, new information on motivation, sexual health, setting goals, and finding a career has been added.

Although the twelve chapters from the second edition are also included in the third, they have been reorganized to reflect a more coherent order. The first four chapters—goal setting, learning styles and critical thinking, time management, and motivation—have been grouped together because they represent what we believe are the foundational skills for being successful in anything you do. In other words, whether in the classroom, on the job, in a relationship, or on the playing field, being able to set goals, motivate yourself, learn, and manage your time and not procrastinate are key factors in one's success. The next four chapters—memory, taking notes, reading and studying, and taking exams—represent the information and strategies needed to be successful in the classroom. The next four chapters—stress and coping, heath, communication, and careers—are key topics related to being successful in life and relationships. The final chapter—mental toughness—is a special new addition that addresses student-athletes' desire to be as successful as they can be on the playing field. This new organization will help teachers and students learn and implement the material in the text in a more effective manner.

Because **critical thinking** is cited as one of most important skills college students should develop while involved in higher education, this topic was included in Chapter 2. In addition to introducing students to the topic and giving them a framework for understanding how to think critically, at the end of each chapter is a critical thinking exercise concerning the material in the chapter they just finished. This exercise is designed to help student-athletes evaluate what they know, what they want to learn more about, and what they can reasonably conclude about the topic given the information that has been presented.

We have addressed new topics in the **feature boxes** included in each chapter. In this edition, we have addressed current topics such as managing social networking sites, credit cards, recovery from injury, and acceptable classroom behaviors. In the recurring feature boxes, we have updated them with the most current information available.

Although *A Student-Athlete's Guide* was the most relevant text in addressing the academic and life skills needed for student-athletes to be successful in college, there was one major topic missing—how athletes could improve their sport performances. To correct that, we have added an entirely new chapter on "Becoming a Mentally Tough Athlete." Mental toughness is considered by coaches and athletes to be the most important psychological skill set associated with success in sport. In this chapter, student-athletes will learn what mental toughness is and the characteristics that define a mentally tough performer. They also will be taken through a series of exercises that will help them increase their mental toughness and generalize that to their sport performances. This chapter further distinguishes *A Student-Athlete's Guide* from other study- and life-skill textbooks aimed at college student-athletes.

Finally, the **chapter review questions** have been updated to coincide with the new information in each chapter. These questions will help students assess their learning of chapter material and point them in the direction of areas in need of further study.

A Personal Message from Trent Petrie and Doug Hankes to the Student-Athletes Who Read This Book

About 30 years ago, we started our college careers at the University of Illinois (and later transferred to Ohio State University) and Auburn University. Although we had been in the top 2% of our high school classes, our transitions to college were not smooth. We floundered academically, earning grades far below our potential our first year. As athletes, we were always physically tired and never seemed to have any free time. We always had something scheduled—classes, practices, studying, training room, etc. And when we did have free time, we and our teammates would go out and engage in behaviors that did not always contribute to our being our best academically or athletically. Thankfully, we figured out what we needed to do to be successful. After our first year, we settled down academically, found our rhythm in studying, and chose majors that we enjoyed (which led to our current careers that we love); basically, we started to apply all the ideas that are included in this textbook in the classroom and on the playing field. Although you will likely make many of the same mistakes we did, we hope that, in reading this book, yours will not be as many or as severe. Part of growing up and becoming an adult is recognizing what others have to offer and how they can help you achieve your goals. If your goals are similar to what ours were—being a successful athlete, doing well in classes, learning how to learn, establishing great friendships, finding a major that really fits—then the information in this book can help. We hope you will find it as enjoyable to read as we did to write. If you want to reach Trent or Doug to share your personal success stories, you can do so through the University of North Texas Center for Sport Psychology and Performance Excellence (sportpsych@unt.edu) or Auburn University's Student Counseling Services (scsinfo@auburn.edu).

Ancillaries for Instructors

Assessment Tools: If you're looking for additional ways to assess your students, Cengage Learning has additional resources for you to consider. For more in-depth information on any of these items, talk with your sales rep or visit the website.

College Success Factors Index: This pre- and post-test determines student's strengths and weaknesses in areas proven to be determinants of college success.

CL Assessment and Portfolio Builder: This personal development tool engages students in self-assessment, critical thinking, and goal-setting activities to prepare them for college and the workplace. The access code for this item also provides students access to the Career Resource Center.

Noel-Levitz College Student Inventory: The *Retention Management System™ College Student Inventory* (CSI from Noel-Levitz) is an early-alert, early-intervention program that identifies students with tendencies that contribute to dropping out of school. Students can participate in an integrated, campus-wide program. Cengage Learning offers you three assessment options that evaluate students on nineteen different scales: Form A (194 items); Form B (100 items); or an online e-token (that provides access to either Forms A, B, or C (74 items). Advisors are sent three interpretive reports: The Student's Report, the Advisor/Counselor Report, and The College Summary and Planning Report.

The *Myers-Briggs Type Indicator® (MBTI®) Instrument*[1] is the most widely used personality inventory in history—and it is also available for packaging with *On Course*. The standard Form M self-scorable instrument contains 93 items that determine preferences on four scales: Extraversion-Introversion, Sensing-Intuition, Thinking-Feeling, and Judging-Perceiving.

College Success Planner: Package your textbook with this twelve-month week-at-a-glance academic planner. The College Success Planner assists students in making the best use of their time both on and off campus, and includes additional reading about key learning strategies and life skills for success in college.

Cengage Learning's TeamUP Faculty Program Consultants: An additional service available with this textbook is support from **TeamUP Faculty Program Consultants.** For more than a decade, our consultants have helped faculty reach and engage first-year students by offering peer-to-peer consulting on curriculum and assessment, faculty training,

---

[1] MBTI and Myers-Briggs Type Indicator are registered trademarks of Consulting Psychologists Press, Inc.

and workshops. Our consultants are educators and higher-education professionals who provide full-time support helping educators establish and maintain effective student success programs. They are available to help you to establish or improve your student success program and provide training on the implementation of our textbooks and technology. To connect with your TeamUP Faculty Program Consultant, call 1-800-528-8323 or visit www.cengage.com/teamup.

For Students

A Student-Athlete's Guide to College Success **Companion Website**
www.cengage.com/success/Petrie/StudentAthlete3e
     A companion website provides students with the option to complete exercises online and to either print or e-mail the completed exercise to their instructor.

Acknowledgments

I want to thank my family and friends for their support during the writing of this revision. To my children, Kyla and Braeden, who as they grow continue to teach me about what is most important in life. As they have now become successful students and athletes in their own rights, I am reminded on a daily basis of just how salient the strategies and information in this text are. A special thank you to Dr. Doug Hankes, a former student and now respected colleague and friend. I have enjoyed all of our work together over the years and the opportunity to collaborate on this third edition has been special. I also want to thank and acknowledge the hundreds of student-athletes and coaches with whom I have worked over the decades. These shared experiences have shaped me in wonderful ways and have given me the opportunity to continue to learn and grow as a sport psychologist, teacher, and person. Finally, thank you to the Psychology Department at the University of North Texas. To my colleagues who support the work I do through the Center for Sport Psychology, you have my complete gratitude.
                                                            —Trent A. Petrie

I also want to thank my family, colleagues, and friends for their support during the writing of this revision of *A Student-Athlete's Guide to College Success.* To my wife, Shannon, and son, Keegan (a freshman at the University of Chicago), thank you for your support and understanding as I headed to the office on weekends to write and left the yard work and vegetable garden to you! You guys are the best. I reserve a special thank you for Trent Petrie who had enough confidence in me to ask if I would serve as his co-author for this third revision. I also have had the privilege of working with hundreds of student-athletes and coaches while I've been at Auburn University's Student Counseling Services and athletic department. Over the years, I've been lucky to hear, "Thank you, Dr. Doug" many times, but truly, I've gotten far more than I've given. I get excited thinking about the opportunity to continue working as a sport psychologist for many years at the university.

It's a great gig. Finally, thank you to Auburn University's Division of Student Affairs and the OPS (Optimal Performance and Support) Team within the athletic department. Without their support, I couldn't do the work that I do.

—Douglas M. Hankes

To all the professionals at Cengage who have been part of this project—Shani Fischer, Cat Salerno, Daisuke Yasutake, the production team—we offer our deepest gratitude. A project such as this requires a diverse set of skills and we are grateful that you were able to bring together such a talented group to assist us. Thank you for all your efforts and support in helping us create a book about which we can all be proud.

We also want to thank the reviewers who provided us with insightful, cogent comments that guided us in this revision: Kristy Belden at the University of Central Florida, Tamara Drummond at the University of Massachusetts—Amherst, Dr. Joe Luckey at the University of Memphis, and Maria Tyson at North Carolina State University.

Chapter 1 | Establishing the Foundation of Success

Setting and Achieving Your Goals

Game Plan:

In this chapter, you will learn:

- About the challenges and stressors you will face during your transition to college

- About the value of a college education

- What a syllabus and course handbook are

- What goals are and how to set them effectively

- How to identify and implement goal-achievement strategies

- How to identify and overcome potential obstacles to attaining your goals

- How self-responsibility plays a major role in achieving your goals and thereby increasing your self-efficacy

© Jerry Zitterman, 2009 / Used under license from Shutterstock.com

"I am a member of a team, and I rely on the team, I defer to it and sacrifice for it, because the team, not the individual, is the ultimate champion."

MIA HAMM
U.S. Olympic Gold Medalist, Soccer

Self-Assessment—Perceive It!

Read the following statements and place a checkmark next to each one you generally do. For you to change and develop new and effective academic, athletic, and personal strategies, you must be accurate in your self-perception. So, be honest in how you answer each question.

1. I have made new friends on my team and in my classes.   _____

2. I have reviewed my course syllabi and know what is expected of me in each class.   _____

3. I have gotten involved in school activities other than my sport.   _____

4. I know where important student services, such as the libraries, computer labs,
   and counseling center, are located on my campus.   _____

5. Whenever possible, I use the skills I have developed in sports, such as being able
   to concentrate under pressure and motivate myself to work hard, to be successful in school.   _____

6. I have made an effort to meet and get to know my instructors.   _____

7. I am financially responsible. I stay within my budget, pay my bills in full, and save some
   money each month.   _____

8. When I make a plan to do something, I follow through.   _____

9. When I set a goal, I also identify the strategies or behaviors I will need to implement in order
   to reach my goal.   _____

10. When I do not reach my goals, I determine why and make the necessary changes so I can
    be more successful the next time.   _____

11. At the beginning of the school term, I set a goal for my academic performance.   _____

12. At the beginning of my sport season, I set goals for my performance and development
    as an athlete.   _____

13. Whenever I set a long-term goal, I break it down into smaller tasks that I can accomplish
    along the way.   _____

Take a moment to review your responses. How many items did you check? Each one you checked represents a current strength. Now consider the items you did not check…these represent areas where focus and growth are needed. Now, to summarize your self-perception, complete the following statements:

1. My areas of strength are:

_____

2. The areas I need to improve are:

_____

As you read this chapter and participate in your classes, keep your strengths and areas of improvement in mind. At the end of the chapter, you will have the chance to set a goal related to the topics covered in this chapter. Achieving these goals will help you become a more effective student and athlete.

Going to a Four-Year University

Introduction

During high school, Makesha played setter for her school's volleyball team. As a senior, she helped her team earn a third-place finish at state while earning all-tournament honors. She received a scholarship offer from the state's major university and was expected to quickly move that program forward to national prominence.

As soon as practice started, her teammates saw how gifted she was. Makesha earned the starting setter position and took charge of the team's offense. The team was playing far better than it had in the past five years and had even beaten their top conference rivals. Makesha worked hard during practice and got along well with the other players. Unfortunately, about two months into the season, she suffered a sprained ankle that forced her to miss over a week of practice and matches.

To regain strength and flexibility in her ankle and to return to play as soon as she could, Makesha spent additional time in the training room.

Although a "B" student in high school, Makesha was overwhelmed by college academics. She often did not see the relevance of her classes—general electives—and had a hard time focusing on the lectures. When she studied at night, she was usually so tired from practice that she fell asleep. In addition, she missed classes because of the team's travel schedule. When exams rolled around, Makesha was so far behind that she had to cram the night before. Although she earned a couple of "Bs" with this approach, her overall average was a "C–." Makesha was motivated and able to focus on her sport, yet she wondered whether she had the ability to be as successful academically as she was athletically.

Attending a Community College

Chris wanted to attend a four-year school, but he knew with his grades he would not qualify, so he decided to attend a community college in another state that had offered him a basketball scholarship. He knew that if he continued to play well on the court and improved his grades, he could transfer after his second year. He thought going out of state was just what he needed—some time away from his family and the chance to prove himself to his new coach and teammates. He was excited about this new chapter in his life.

At first, Chris was so busy with basketball and school he did not miss being away from home. As the semester progressed, though, and the pressures of school and basketball intensified, he became increasingly stressed. Because his friendships were primarily with teammates and other student-athletes at the school, he did not feel he could talk about the pressures he was experiencing. He did not want to burden them, and he certainly did not want to tell his coach (he was afraid his coach would think he had made a mistake in recruiting him and pull his scholarship). He was able to keep himself together while playing and practicing, but not so much in the classroom. He did talk with his academic advisor, but other than recommending Chris spend more time in study hall, nothing really changed. At that point, he decided that he needed to deal with the situation himself, as he had dealt with most other things in his life.

Because games were just starting and they had an out-of-town tournament that weekend, Chris was unable to go home for Thanksgiving. Instead, he stayed on campus with the team, practicing and then traveling to the games. Even though being out of state had seemed like a great idea at the beginning of the semester, the longer he stayed at school, the more he missed his family. He knew he needed to get it together and do well in school, but he felt stressed and unable to perform in the classroom. By the time the semester ended, all he wanted to do was go home and escape the academic and athletic pressures he had been facing.

As these stories illustrate, the transition to college and college athletics—whether played at a two- or four-year institution—has potential challenges and stressors. By following the ideas and strategies in this book, though, you should be able to increase your chances of adjusting positively in your new school and being successful as a student and athlete.

In this chapter, we identify some of these challenges and stressors, and then offer strategies for coping effectively and becoming more involved on your campus. We also discuss the importance of understanding and living consistently with your values. Next, we introduce and define three important psychological processes—goal setting, self-responsibility, and self-efficacy—and present a straightforward and effective system for setting and achieving your goals. Understanding your values and the ability to set and achieve your goals are, without a doubt, the foundation of success in school, sports, and life.

Preparation: Challenges During the Transition to College

Some student-athletes make a smooth transition to college, but others run into difficulties along the way, never reaching their potential in the classroom nor on the playing field. Certainly intelligence, previous education and schooling, and athletic ability are important, but college can overwhelm even the most "prepared" student-athlete.

Other factors, such as your attitude and your expectations, also play a role in determining how successfully you navigate this transition. Do you view college as an opportunity to learn and grow personally, academically, and athletically? Do you resent the expectations and required work, or do you relish the opportunity to push yourself beyond your current capabilities? Do you see college primarily as a place to socialize, have fun, and play your sport, or do you take a more balanced view, where athletics and meeting people are balanced against gaining an education and preparing for career? Your expectations and how you perceive your college experiences will strongly influence what you do and your potential for success. To help you become more aware of how your current transition to college is going, you may want to complete Exercise 1.1.

Being aware of the challenges and situations you may face can help you cope more effectively. In this section, we identify some of these.

Where You Live

Depending on your school and your personal situation, you may live at home, in a campus residence hall, or in an off-campus apartment. All of these situations have positives and negatives. For example, living

---

Exercise 1.1   Your Transition to College

1. What did you expect, academically, athletically, and socially, in college? How do your current experiences compare with your expectations?

2. Describe the thoughts and feelings you had during your first full day of classes. How do you feel now about your classes and the academic expectations that exist for you?

3. If your season has started, describe your thoughts and experiences from the first day of training/practice. How do you feel about your sport now?

4. Describe the friendships you have made since you started school. How satisfying have these been?

5. Overall, what has been the biggest surprise to you as you've navigated the transition from high school to college?

at home may be comfortable, but you may chafe at having to abide by your parents' rules. Living in the residence halls may provide you with more personal freedom and the chance to develop new friendships, but may be stressful because of the small, shared living space, the potentially unappetizing food, and the hall's rules and regulations that you have to follow. Wherever you live, take advantage of the opportunities each situation provides (e.g., being centrally located on campus, opportunities to meet students from all walks of life). And, if you experience problems, then work proactively to resolve them. For example, if you live in the residence halls, you are likely to have a resident advisor (RA) living on your floor who can provide support and guidance, and is someone who can help you with negotiating your living situation.

Roommates

With the exception of living at home, at some point during your college career, you are likely to have a roommate. Although there are many reasons for having a roommate, such as friendship, a primary one for most students is to share living expenses. Even college graduates have roommates—it just makes financial sense.

Roommates can be a great source of support and friendship, but they also can be a source of frustration, stress, and discomfort. Your roommate may be disrespectful, violate your privacy, ignore you and your wishes, have different living habits, and just not be very nice.

College Instructors

There are three major types of instructors at colleges and universities:

- *Professors*—these individuals usually hold doctoral degrees and are considered experts in their fields of study. They are full-time employees and will differ in rank, ranging from assistant (lowest) to associate to full (highest). They also conduct research and provide service to the school and the community. They form the core of the school's instructional and research staff. Because of their research responsibilities, especially at larger universities, they may teach less than other staff. Because professors are producing knowledge, it means that you will be exposed to the very latest discoveries in the field, especially in upper-level classes.

- *Lecturers*—these individuals often hold a doctorate in their field and have been hired primarily to teach courses within that area. They may be full-time employees but generally are not required to conduct research, nor do they qualify for the tenure system in which most professors operate.

- *Teaching Fellows*—these individuals are graduate students who are teaching in their field of study. Though new to their field and teaching itself, most are highly enthusiastic and motivated to be excellent instructors. They teach many introductory and mid-level undergraduate courses and assist professors and lecturers with their classes. In many cases, today's teaching fellows are tomorrow's college professors.

© Dmitry Nikolaev, 2009 / Used under license from Shutterstock.com

If you have a chance to choose your roommate, then do so carefully! You will want to learn how to effectively communicate with your roommate early in the relationship, so you can avoid some of the issues that may come up during the term.

Classes

A major difference between high school and college or between a two-year and four-year institution is the manner in which classes are taught and their degree of difficulty. Even if you have taken AP (advanced placement) classes in high school, college-level courses can be challenging because they require you, not your instructor, to be responsible for what is learned. You are responsible for attending classes, turning in your assignments on time, and adequately preparing yourself for exams. Do not expect your teachers to hold your hand because very few will.

Lack of Academic Skills

Unfortunately, some student-athletes, like students in general, enter college lacking solid academic strategies for being successful in the classroom. It is not that they are unintelligent or don't have the ability to succeed; they just have not learned skills and strategies for being an effective student. Consider a sport, basketball, as a parallel. If you were big enough and participating at a less competitive level, then you could be successful against weaker opponents even if your basic skills, such as dribbling, passing, and defensive positioning, were not well developed. If you tried to play at a more competitive level, however, and still lacked the fundamental skills, then you would likely experience considerable frustration and minimal success. The same is true of schoolwork. If you have not learned the fundamentals, such as how to take notes or prepare for exams, but are a relatively bright person, then you may be able to achieve some success in a less challenging environment, such as high school. However, if you enter college without these basic skills, then your chances of success diminish considerably. To help you evaluate your current academic skills, you may want to complete Exercise 1.2.

Eating

Whether you live at home, in the residence halls, or in an off-campus apartment, eating nutritiously is a challenge for all students, but especially student-athletes. Busy schedules, unappetizing food, and insufficient funds all can play a role. Many students fail to eat healthy, balanced, nutritious meals. Instead, they eat snacks and fast food, both of which can be high in fats and low in nutritional value. As an athlete, eating well is a key to performing successfully in practices and competitions (see Chapter 10 for more information), so don't sell yourself short in this area because it is important in your academic success too.

Exercise 1.2 Academic Self-Confidence

Assuming that you are motivated to do your best, rate your confidence in your ability to successfully complete each academic behavior, using the scale below (1, *not at all confident*, to 10, *totally confident*). Be honest in your responses and rate yourself as you currently are, not as you would like to be.

1	2	3	4	5	6	7	8	9	10
Not at all Confident				**Moderately Confident**					**Totally Confident**

1. I can attend every class, every day. _____
2. I can always complete my textbook assignments before they are due. _____
3. I can understand everything I read in my textbooks. _____
4. I can take thorough and understandable notes in all my classes. _____
5. I can study for at least two hours every day. _____
6. I can stay focused and concentrate throughout every class. _____
7. I can understand and memorize all the material that will be covered on any test. _____
8. I can stay focused and concentrate throughout every exam. _____
9. I can ask questions of my instructor whenever I do not understand something. _____
10. During lectures or while reading textbooks, I can identify and understand all the important concepts that are presented. _____
11. I can set and follow through on all my academic goals. _____
12. I can prioritize my academic tasks and set aside sufficient time to complete them by the time they are due. _____

Add up all your confidence ratings across the items and then divide by 12. This value represents your initial confidence level with respect to behaviors associated with academic success. The higher this value, the more confidence you have in yourself. If you find that your overall confidence score is somewhat low, or your scores for some items are low, say a 7 or less, then you may want to focus on that area to develop the skills and confidence to be successful.

Student-Athlete Stressors

In addition to these general school stressors, as a high-level athlete, you may face additional pressures, including:

- *Balancing School, Athletics, and Relationships*. Practice, studying, travel, academic advisors, conditioning, training room, study hall, spending time with friends, etc., sometimes it will seem like you just don't have enough time to do it all.
- *Physical Problems*. Injuries, whether chronic or acute, can interfere with your mobility and require substantial time and effort to heal.
- *Public Visibility*. As an athlete, particularly in "revenue" sports, such as football and men's and women's basketball, your actions will be closely scrutinized.
- *Performance Expectations*. Public, familial, and personal, there will be many expectations that you always perform your best on and off the court.
- *Additional Rules or Expectations*. In addition to the general university rules and policies, you will have to follow those of your team, athletic department, conference, and NCAA.

© Ken Inness, 2009 / Used under license from Shutterstock.com

- *Athletic Termination.* You will not be able to compete forever and, depending on injuries, grades, or other personal reasons, you may experience a transition out of your sport during college and before you intended.
- *Financial Pressures.* Even if you have an athletic scholarship, you still may have little discretionary income and have a hard time making ends meet.

Given these general and unique challenges, just how well do student-athletes cope? For the most part, student-athletes are healthy, motivated individuals who can handle most obstacles and challenges. Even so, these and other stressors can affect even the most resilient athletes, resulting in poor academic performance, interpersonal problems, or not reaching their athletic potential.

> "If you worried about falling off the bike, you'd never get on."
>
> LANCE ARMSTRONG
> *7-Time Winner,*
> *Tour de France*

Performance: Coping with the Transition to College

Whether you attend a two- or a four-year university, there are some fundamental things that every student-athlete can do to make a positive transition to school. In this section, we discuss various strategies to help you cope more effectively with the challenges you may face and illustrate them in relation to Makesha and Chris, athletes we introduced at the beginning of the chapter.

Establish New Social Support Networks

For many student-athletes, attending college means moving away from friends, family, teammates, and coaches who have been long-standing sources of support. Although being on your own may be exciting, without a support system, the transition to school can be difficult. As Chris found during his first semester, you are often so busy competing and trying to keep up academically that you don't have time to develop a close and extensive network of friends. Teammates are one source of friendship, but their support may be limited because they are experiencing many of the same stressors as you. Chris wanted to talk with someone, but was reluctant to do so with his teammates because they were stressed, and he did not think they would want to hear about his problems.

Roommates can be a source of support but, as mentioned previously, they also can be a source of stress. To increase your chances of having a positive living situation with a roommate, if possible, meet the person before you live together. If you cannot meet face-to-face, then contact the person by phone, e-mail, text, or Facebook. When you talk, discuss what each person's expectations are for sharing space together and come to an agreement ("contract") about basic living arrangements. Although this idea may seem extreme, it will help you avoid problems during the semester and will allow you to maintain a respectful and peaceful environment. To help you do that, you may want to complete Exercise 1.3.

To have a successful relationship with a roommate, it is important to be respectful of your roommate's thoughts, feelings, and behaviors. If their values, beliefs, or attitudes are different from yours, then view the situation as one where you can learn from each other, not one where you are right and they are wrong. Also, talk about problems as they arise. Although the socially expected response may be to "let things slide," this approach often leads to anger and resentment. But, you also need to be flexible. You are sharing a room, so you cannot have everything your way. Relax and accept how other people do things. Finally, don't focus solely on your roommate as a source of support; develop friendships with other students as well. Although it is nice when your roommate turns out to be your best friend, this is a rare occurance. Therefore, it is important to work proactively to create a positive living situation so you can get along together.

Classmates are another possible source of support, though busy schedules and large classes may require you to make extra efforts to establish such friendships. Faculty and staff represent a third potential support network, and it's a mistake not to take advantage of this resource because you believe the services and support provided by your athletic department are sufficient. Always make connections beyond your team and athletic department. Sometimes, it's beneficial to have individuals outside your usual support system. They can offer a different perspective that you might not have considered. These individuals—classmates, teachers, etc.—can offer valuable support, encouragement, direction, and advice. Listed here are a variety of ways to become involved in and connected to your school, its faculty and staff, and your fellow students.

- Form study groups.
- Come to class with questions and ask them before, during, or after class.
- Talk with and get to know your instructors—visit during office hours or after class or send them e-mails to make contact.

Exercise 1.3 Roommate Agreement

Consider the following areas when discussing living arrangements with your new roommate. In each area, specify the rules to which you and your roommate agree.

1. Cleaning and Other Chores (e.g., When will the room be cleaned? Who will do it?).

2. Quiet Time (e.g., When will we know it will be quiet in our room...no TV, friends, etc.).

3. Overnight Guests (e.g., Can we have overnight guests? Same or opposite sex? When?).

4. Food (e.g., Who will buy the food? Will we share?).

5. Bills (phone, utilities, etc.) (e.g., Split basic costs? Responsible for our own use?).

6. Room Decorations (e.g., In our own bedrooms? In the common areas?).

7. Borrowing Each Other's Property (e.g., Is it OK? Do we need permission?).

8. Other Areas Not Covered Above.

- Join a student organization.
- Attend campus events or activities with your roommate or classmates.
- Walk around campus with another student so you can learn more about your school's history and where services are located.
- If you are able to work, then consider part-time employment on campus or in the local community.
- Hang out at the student union and talk with other students.

So, make time to become involved in an activity with the purpose of meeting new people.

Use Student Services

As a student-athlete, many of your needs will be met within the athletic department (e.g., academic advising, registration). However, your athletic department cannot meet all your needs. Universities have well-established support services for all students, including you.

Let's consider Makesha. During her first semester, she felt overwhelmed by school and athletics. The athletic department provided her with academic support and the medical staff helped her recover from her ankle sprain, but she really needed someone to talk to about all the stress she was feeling. She did not want to talk to anyone in the athletic department, because she did not want information getting back to her coach. What she needed was a counselor who was trained to assist students in coping with stressors like the ones she was experiencing. Unfortunately, she did not know about the university's counseling center and the services they provided. If she had, then she could have taken advantage of it and received the help she needed.

Be proactive and become aware of the wide variety of services available to you. Athletic departments generally focus on your academic performance and your physical health, not on other areas of your life, such as your relationships or your personal adjustment. Don't wait for your coach, an academic advisor, or a teammate to introduce you to your school. Instead, do it yourself. To help you become more aware of the services available on your campus, you may want to complete Exercise 1.4.

> "I was told over and over again that I would never be successful, that I was not going to be competitive and the technique was simply not going to work. All I could do was shrug and say 'We'll just have to see.'"
>
> DICK FOSBURY
> *Olympic Gold Medalist, Inventor of the "Fosbury Flop" High-Jump Technique*

Exercise 1.4 Student Services

There are many services or offices on campus whose purpose is to assist students. Although their names may differ across schools, they often include: Dean of Students' Office, Career Services and Placement, Counseling Center, Women's Services Center, Multicultural Affairs, Disability Services, Student Legal Affairs, Residence Life, International Studies, and Student Employment.

1. Select a student service at your school, and then call that office to arrange an informational interview with a professional staff member. At that interview, you may want to ask the following questions (and develop some of your own):
   a. Name, location, phone number, and hours of operation of the student service.
   b. Name, title, and job responsibilities of the staff member.
   c. What is the primary purpose or function of your office/program? What services do you provide for students?
   d. How does a student get access to the services provided by your office?
   e. When should students use the services provided by this office?
   f. Who staffs this office? What are the staff's qualifications?

You may want to share the information you obtained with your fellow student-athletes. Doing so will help everyone learn about the services that are available on your campus.

Become an "Active" Learner

As an elite athlete, you probably already have developed the ability to regulate your performances, whether in practice or competition. You have learned to manage your feelings, thoughts, behaviors, and motivation to maximize your athletic experiences. Remember Makesha? When she became injured, she motivated herself to spend additional time in the training room for rehab so she could return to play as soon as possible. Although she was frustrated by her injury, she remained positive and focused because she knew that would be most helpful. Like most successful athletes, she determined what she needed to do and then did it.

Such abilities also are an excellent predictor of academic success. Student-athletes who are able to regulate their behaviors and motivation, putting forth the necessary effort to study and remaining focused on their academics despite distractions, are the ones who earn the highest grades. Although it is easy to say that you just aren't a "good" student and thus don't have to put forth effort, the reality is that you can learn to be a better student, no matter your current level of intelligence or ability. By following the strategies outlined in this book, you can become a more active and involved learner, one who consistently puts forth the effort needed to be successful.

Transfer Athletic Skills to Academics

Before you read any further, you may want to complete Exercise 1.5.

Do you see any overlap in the two categories you developed in Exercise 1.5? Being able to persist despite obstacles, concentrate under pressure, and set and reach goals could just as easily characterize a successful athlete as an effective student. Most student-athletes have developed these important skills through years of sports participation. The key, then, is to learn about the skills you already possess and apply them to nonsport areas of your life, such as academics.

Makesha obviously had many important skills that contributed to her athletic success. She was highly motivated, worked hard, set goals, and knew how to manage her time. Unfortunately, she did not always transfer these skills to her classwork. This "lack of transfer" is not uncommon for student-athletes because often they do not see the connection between preparing for an exam and preparing for a competition. Yet these activities are very similar. For example, Bill, a baseball player, applied many of the same skills he used in athletics to his academics. He developed a pre-performance routine that helped him get focused and ready to compete,

> "The quality of a person's life is in direct proportion to their commitment to excellence, regardless of their chosen field of endeavor."
>
> VINCE LOMBARDI
> *NFL Hall of Fame Football Coach*

Exercise 1.5   Athletic Skills

1. Think about your own sport performances and about the skills and personal attributes that have helped you be successful. List as many as you can think of, such as "concentrate under pressure" or "work hard."

2. Think about the skills and personal attributes that go into being a successful student. List as many as you can, such as "get work done ahead of time" or "prepared for class."

3. Look at the two lists. What similarities and differences are there between the skills and attributes that you listed for the two categories, athlete and student?

4. Which of your sports-related skills can you apply in the classroom to help you be a more successful student?

whether for a game or an exam. He also used goal setting to motivate himself and measure his progress. Although your skills may differ from those of Bill, the connection remains the same. Become aware of the skills you have and then transfer them to other areas of your life. Remember, these skills can help you excel personally, academically, and professionally if you apply them.

Understand Why You Are in College

As a student-athlete, a primary reason you are in school is to compete in your sport. But why else did you decide to go to college? Was it to prepare for a career as a professional athlete? Obtain a degree? Train for a nonathletic career? Appease your parents? Or make friends and party? Regardless of the reason, if you do not know why you are here, then the transition may be more difficult, and your motivation diminished (you can't play your sport or socialize 24 hours every day).

Thus, understanding why you are in school is important. Although the reasons may change over time, knowing them now can increase your motivation, make the college experience more meaningful, and help you prioritize your daily behaviors to make them consistent with your short- and long-term goals. To help you evaluate why you are in college, you may want to complete Exercise 1.6.

Manage Your Money

College is a time for fiscal responsibility and, possibly, financial independence. It may be your first time to open a checking account, regularly pay bills, or have a credit card. Unfortunately, some students make poor decisions about money and spending, such as accumulating considerable credit card debt, which can ruin their financial status. Good money management begins with understanding your financial goals. To define what your short- and long-term goals are, you may want to complete Exercise 1.7.

Even if you consider yourself a responsible money manager, the following strategies can help make your transition to financial independence and responsibility a smooth one.

- *Spend only what you have*—with easy credit, many people live beyond their means. So, monitor how you spend money for a one- or two-month period and see where your money goes.
- *Do not buy on impulse*—even for small items, like a magazine or a CD. Instead, take a few days to consider whether you want (need) the item. If you still do after that time, then see if this purchase fits into your budget. If not, then don't buy it.
- *Always pay your credit card bill in full each month*—a credit card offers you a free, short-term loan if you pay off your balance

Exercise 1.6   Why Are You In College?

Think about why you decided to come to college. Although playing your sport may be the number one reason, list 5–10 other reasons you are enrolled at your current school.

Exercise 1.7   Financial Goals

1. Think about your financial goals for the next six to nine months. What are you saving for? What financial obligations will you have? Although you may not have not given much consideration to this idea before, it is never too early to begin addressing your financial goals.

2. Think about your financial goals over the next five years and then list them on a sheet of paper. What will you be saving for, such as going on a post-graduation trip or buying a car? If you do not think you'll be able to save much during this time, have

you developed a plan for any student loan debt you may acquire while in college?

3. Now, think about where you want to be financially in the next 30 years and write these goals on a sheet of paper. Think about the kind of lifestyle you want to have. What assets do you hope to have acquired? What expenses (e.g., child's education) will you have?

Now, with these short- and long-term goals in mind, you can begin planning how you are going to earn, spend, and save money.

---

each month. When you do not make full payment, you pay interest and many companies charge 18 to 20 percent, which can add up quickly if you only pay the minimum each month. Use no-fee credit cards and limit yourself to one or, at most, two cards. If you can't stay within your budget, then only use a debit card, which immediately deducts expenditures from your bank account.

- *Buy sale items and shop discount stores*—most products go on sale, you just have to wait and watch. Also, buy in bulk if it's a good price, particularly for items that do not have expiration dates, such as toiletries, dry or canned foods, and some frozen foods.
- *Have your paycheck directly deposited*—direct deposit saves time and gives you the security of knowing your money will be there each month.
- *Pay by check, debit card, or credit card*—these forms of payment, as opposed to cash, provide a record of your expenditures that you can track month to month. Consider destroying your ATM cards, because such easy access to cash can be a downfall. If you use an ATM, then be aware of any fees so you can limit these unnecessary expenses.
- *Start a savings plan*—in college? Absolutely! With compound interest, you should begin saving as early in life as possible. And, if you develop the habit of saving now, then it will be that much easier to do when you have a "real" job and a salary to match. If your job allows 401k–type contributions, then take advantage of these or the many other Individual Retirement Account (IRA) options that currently exist.
- *Use a semester-by-semester budget*—by developing a budget, you will know how much money can be spent on fixed and essential costs (e.g., tuition, food) and how much for nonessential items (e.g., entertainment). Always budget enough to pay your required bills first. To help you develop a budget, you may want to complete Exercise 1.8.

Maintain Your Health

Eating nutritiously, exercising regularly, drinking alcohol moderately (if at all), and sleeping consistently each night are essential behaviors for maintaining a healthy life (we discuss these topics in more detail in

---

Exercise 1.8   Setting a Budget

1. For the next month, monitor how you spend your money. At the end of each day, record the money you spent, no matter how small the amount, by placing it in the category that best fits the expense, such as rent, food, cell phone, Internet, utilities, auto (including gas, insurance), clothing, school supplies, and entertainment. Be as specific in describing each expense, such as $4.00 (entertainment—DVD purchased).

2. Once you have finished your month, calculate the total amount you spent in each category. Now you have an idea of how much you spend in each area during an average month. Are there any categories in which you spent more than you expected?

3. Identify the sources and amounts of all income you receive each month. List them on a piece of paper and then total. For example, you might receive $100.00 from your parents and a scholarship check of $650.00 each month, so your list would include two items: Family ($100.00) plus Scholarship ($650.00) equals $750.00.

4. Compare your monthly income and expenses. Ideally, your income would exceed your expenses, leaving you with a balance at the end of each month. If so, what might you do with this surplus (e.g., put it in savings). If your expenses exceed your income, then what do you need to change (e.g., increase income, decrease expenditures) to reach a place of balance?

Chapter 10). Unfortunately, many student-athletes abuse their bodies by not following these simple guidelines. Although being young may provide some protection from unhealthy behaviors, by not taking care of yourself you increase the chances of performing below your potential, both in the classroom and in your sport. So, make every effort to maintain a healthy, balanced lifestyle that provides you with the energy and focus you need to succeed in your classes, your relationships, your sport, and your life.

Discover the Library

The library is the primary information resource at your school, housing books, journals, magazines, newspapers, videos, audiotapes, electronic databases, and other technologies. Whether you access this information on-site or through remote, Internet-based search engines, it is important to know what is available to you, particularly as you move into your upper-level classes. Libraries also are key locations for studying since they have quiet areas, such as tables or carrels. Many campuses may have more than one library, so become familiar with all those at your school. To help you learn more, you may want to complete Exercise 1.9.

Exercise 1.9   Learning about Your Library

Either via a library tour, the library's website, or by talking to one of the librarians, find the answers to the following questions:

1. How many libraries are on your campus? What are their names and what subjects does each one cover? Which one contains materials that are most relevant to your major?

2. Where are your libraries located and what are the hours of operation?

3. When is a reference librarian available for assistance?

4. Where are the computers for doing electronic searches located?

5. Where is the circulation desk? How many books can a student check out at one time, and for how long can they have them?

6. What is an interlibrary loan and where can you access this service?

7. Where are the books, journals, magazines, films, etc., housed in your library?

8. What is one service or fact about your school's library that is special or unique?

Preparation: The Importance of Values

Values are your foundational beliefs. They are the beliefs that most strongly influence your decisions, your goals, and your life's direction—they provide purpose and meaning in your life. Because one's values generally develop through personal experiences and family influences, they are likely to vary from person to person. For example, Jamie believes that a person should not engage in sexual intercourse until marriage, whereas Phyllis believes sex is part of being in love and should not be limited in that way. Clearly, these two hold different values concerning this important topic.

Understanding your values is essential to success, be it academic, athletic, or personal, because your values provide meaning and direction in life. They can promote reflection and action, and bring about strong emotions. If you are unclear as to your values, then you are like a ship without a rudder. You will likely be in motion, but without a clear direction or sense of purpose.

As you experience the diversity that defines the college experience, your values are likely to be challenged. Although not always comfortable, such challenges generally lead to positive growth, either in terms of solidifying your current beliefs, adopting new, more personally congruent values, or modifying existing ones to make them more realistic. Whatever the case, the beginning of college is an important time to define your current value system. So, what is most important to you? To help you begin to examine your values and determine how you want to live your life, you may want to complete Exercise 1.10.

As foundational beliefs, your values should have a strong influence on your priorities in school, sports, and life, and on the goals you set for yourself. For example, if one of your values is education, then you might set the goal of obtaining a bachelor's and master's degree. When your priorities and goals are consistent with your values, then your life is likely to have balance and meaning. However, during college, students may question their value system or be swayed by their friends, such that their priorities and goals become inconsistent with what they think is most important. For example, Kanye believes that getting an education is important, but his friends are more focused on socializing and partying. As a result, he often finds himself spending time at parties (instead of studying) and drinking far more than he knows he should. Thus, it is important to know what you believe is most important and what your priorites are for college. To help you accomplish that, you may want to complete Exercise 1.11.

Exercise 1.10 Understanding Your Values

1. List 5–10 important values in your life. For example, some important values might include honesty, fidelity, perseverance, or financial security.

2. For each one, discuss how it was formed and came to hold a central place in your life.

Exercise 1.11   What Are Your Priorities?

Listed here are some priorities that emerge from fundamental values individuals hold. For each one, rate how important that priority is to you using the scale provided.

For example, if "Being athletically successful" is important to you, you might score yourself as a 5 or a 6. Be honest with yourself in terms of how important each area is to you.

1. Being academically successful

Not at All Important   1   2   3   4   5   6   7   Extremely Important

2. Being athletically successful

Not at All Important   1   2   3   4   5   6   7   Extremely Important

3. Developing a career

Not at All Important   1   2   3   4   5   6   7   Extremely Important

4. Being socially connected/involved

Not at All Important   1   2   3   4   5   6   7   Extremely Important

5. Being financially secure

Not at All Important   1   2   3   4   5   6   7   Extremely Important

6. Having a positive and supportive relationship with your family

Not at All Important   1   2   3   4   5   6   7   Extremely Important

7. Having a positive and supportive relationship with your boyfriend/girlfriend

Not at All Important   1   2   3   4   5   6   7   Extremely Important

8. Being physically healthy

Not at All Important   1   2   3   4   5   6   7   Extremely Important

9. Being well rested

Not at All Important   1   2   3   4   5   6   7   Extremely Important

10. Eating nutritiously

Not at All Important   1   2   3   4   5   6   7   Extremely Important

11. Being spiritually or religiously grounded

Not at All Important   1   2   3   4   5   6   7   Extremely Important

12. Being connected to and involved in your community

Not at All Important   1   2   3   4   5   6   7   Extremely Important

13. Being politically active and informed about national events

Not at All Important   1   2   3   4   5   6   7   Extremely Important

14. Other areas of importance/value to you (please list and rate each one)

Not at All Important   1   2   3   4   5   6   7   Extremely Important

Keep these priorities in mind as you make your day-to-day decisions about your goals and how you will manage your time. In Chapter 2, we will have you revisit these.

Performance: Setting Goals and Achieving Success

What Is a Goal?

As an athlete, you have likely set goals, either individually or as part of a team. A goal is something you work toward, something you attain, an endpoint you want to reach. A goal provides you with a direction for your effort and energy and can help you persevere even when you are tired and unsure as to which way to go. Although your experience with setting goals may be primarily in the athletic domain, goals can be set in all areas of life, such as academics (e.g., earning a 3.3 semester GPA), finances (e.g., saving $1,000.00 within a year), and relationships (e.g., establishing two new friendships the first semester), to name just a few.

There are many benefits to setting goals, not the least of which is improved performances in whatever domain the goal has been established. For example, a swim team may set the goal of shaving two seconds off their 4 X 100 freestyle relay time and, over the course of their season, they saw improvements in their performances, culminating in reaching their goal at the conference meet.

Setting goals also can lead to improvements in your ability to focus your attention. Goals help you direct your attention to the task at hand and to avoid being distracted by less important things in your environment. For example, Frieda had identified earning a "B" on her music

history paper as her goal. Therefore, she was more focused on going to the library every night than on socializing with her friends. If she had not had her goal, then she might have been easily distracted by her friends.

Goals can help increase motivation and the effort you put into the task at hand. Goals act as markers against which you gauge your progress. Such performance feedback can motivate you to maintain your current level of effort if you find that you are doing well or to make a greater effort if your initial attempts fall short. In other words, goals can help you persist even when you have not been as successful as you initially planned.

Goals also are associated with increases in confidence, something we will discuss in more detail later in the chapter. When you set and reach your goals, you generally feel more confident about your abilities, and less anxious about the task you are doing. For example, Kaycee, a gymnast, had never performed a high-difficulty vault that her coach wanted her to do in competition and was quite anxious. There was, however, a vault that was less difficult but consisted of similar moves, so she set the goal of learning the easier vault first. As she worked on and mastered the easier vault, she grew more confident in herself. She then began to practice the more difficult vault during each training session, as well as working on learning it through visualization. By her first competition, she knew she could perform the more difficult vault.

Setting SMART Goals

Goal setting can improve your performances in all areas of life. However, not all approaches to goal setting are equally effective. In fact, there are certain guidelines to follow when setting goals (Kyllo and Landers, 1995; Locke and Latham, 1985; Weinberg, 1996). From our perspective, these guidelines are best summarized using the acronym SMART. That's right! When you set goals, set SMART ones:

S   Short- and Long-Term
M   Measurable
A   Attainment Strategies
R   Realistic
T   Target Obstacles

By using this system, you increase your chances of setting goals that provide direction and challenge, and identify the specific behaviors you will need to implement to actually reach your goals. In the remainder of this section, we discuss each guideline in detail and illustrate each one with a story of two student-athletes, Terrence and Laura, who have set goals for themselves. Terrence, who is a football player, wants "to do well" in school. Laura is a softball player who has set the goal of "being a better hitter" on her team.

When you are setting goals, the first thing you need to do is decide what you want to achieve and then set that as your goal. Terrence and Laura have each identified a goal, which is a good first step. They can make their goals even better, though, by making them SMART.

S: Short- and Long-Term

Long-term goals are critical. They are what you ultimately want to accomplish in school, in your sport, in your relationships, in your career, or in any other area of your life. They provide the direction for your energies over time and should be consistent with your values and priorities. Even so, remaining motivated and focused on something that is months or even years in the future can be very difficult—this is where short-term goals play an important role.

Short-term goals act as the bridges or stepping-stones to your long-term goal. They are signposts on the journey toward your long-term goal that let you know whether you are on course or need to change direction. They provide feedback that lets you gauge your progress. Such feedback can help you remain motivated over the long haul and allow you to modify your goals or efforts as needed to keep you on track. Imagine if your goal were to make the 2012 Summer Olympic Team or to play professional sports when you graduate from college. Top-level, elite athletes with such long-term ambitions set weekly, monthly, and yearly goals to help them stay motivated and focused and to provide themselves with feedback about their progress. Short- and long-term goals go hand in hand. Setting one without the other is insufficient for consistently improving your performance.

Terrence's and Laura's goals, as initially stated, can be considered long term. Thus, they need to set short-term goals to help them along the way. Terrence's short-term goals might include doing well on his midterm exams, finishing his English paper before it is due, and attending every scheduled chemistry lab. Laura's short-term goals could include making contact with the ball more often or improving the mechanics of her swing. Whatever they identify as their short-term goals, it is important that these goals move them toward their long-term goals.

Whenever you set goals, think about the following questions:

1. Are your long-term goals consistent with your values and your priorities?
2. Do your short-term goals, if reached, move you closer to attaining your long-term goal?

If you answer "No" to either question, then revisit your goals and modify them accordingly. In doing so, make sure that (a) you identify all relevant short-term goals and (b) these goals help you make progress toward what you want to accomplish in your life.

M: Measurable

Measurable and specific goals, as opposed to general "do your best" goals, provide markers against which you can gauge your progress and are associated with better and more consistent performances. Vague goals, such as "to try harder" or "to be the best," make it difficult to evaluate performances because no one knows what those terms mean or when you've achieved your goal.

Terrence and Laura need to change their initial goals to make them more measurable and specific. Wanting "to do well" in school or be "a better hitter" provide no specific outcome against which to measure

> "Take small steps. Don't let anything trip you up. All those steps are like pieces of a puzzle. They come together to form a picture. When it's complete, you've reached your ultimate goal, step by step. I can't see any other way of accomplishing anything."
>
> MICHAEL JORDAN
> *NBA Superstar*

Why Is a College Education Important?

A university is not just a group of buildings, nor just a place where people come to work or study. A university, in many ways, is an ideal. It is defined by the people who come together because of their interest in and their pursuit of knowledge. Universities are places where men and women meet to discuss and debate issues, to consider new ideas, and to challenge old ways of thinking. They are places to interact with people who have backgrounds and histories different from your own. Such experiences allow you to learn not only about your field of study, but about yourself and your relationships to others. Knowledge of yourself and of other people is as central to your education as anything you will learn from a textbook.

Whether or not you will be able to realize this ideal, however, is up to you. For some student-athletes, a university is nothing more than a training ground for a future career in professional sports. For others, it is an opportunity to pursue an education, a chance they might not have received if it were not for athletics. You have the choice as to how you will experience your college career. Do you want college to be a place where you find personal, athletic, educational, cultural, and intellectual growth and excellence, or do you simply want it to be a place where you put in some time before you move on to the next stage of your life?

Although a primary focus for many student-athletes is their sports participation, the value of college extends far beyond the playing field. Universities offer great opportunities for intellectual and personal growth, and for many student-athletes, it is these opportunities that motivate them to attend. They are interested in learning to think and critically evaluate information; in being exposed to people with different backgrounds, values, and worldviews; and in being introduced to new ideas. For others, though, the value of pursuing a college degree is more practical: A university education is an investment in future earning potential. Although a few student-athletes will make the "pros," signing lucrative contracts and receiving product endorsements, *the overwhelming majority will not*. Most college student-athletes will earn their livings in other ways and, as more and more careers require higher levels of education and training, a college degree is becoming a passport to the upper levels of the world of work.

Even among those student-athletes who make the "pros," most will last only a few years in their chosen sports. Thus, all student-athletes, even those who later succeed in professional sports, will still spend 30 to 40 years pursuing another career. Recent census information on full-time workers between 25 and 64 suggests that college graduates, on the average, will earn considerably more than those who have only a high school diploma. Given these facts, one motivation for earning a college degree is financial. However, if you do not learn basic skills in college (such as how to read and integrate information from various sources, do basic math, be responsible, manage your time, think critically, and communicate clearly), then you may have a difficult time obtaining and keeping a financially and socially rewarding job.

their performance and determine their progress. Instead, Terrence might set as his goal "earning a 3.2 GPA for the term," whereas Laura might change her goal to "batting .375." For their short-term goals, Terrence could choose earning at least a "B" on all his midterms and finishing his paper five days before it is due, whereas Laura could choose making contact with the ball, whether it is fair or foul, during each at-bat. Such changes make their goals more precise and provide markers against which they can evaluate their progress.

Whenever you set goals, think about the following questions:

1. Would another person know if you had reached your goal?
2. What specific measures would this person use to gauge your progress? Are these measures clearly stated in your goal?

If you would answer "No" to either question or could not identify specific measures of outcome, then you might want to modify your goals to make them more measurable and specific.

A: Attainment Strategies

Unless you identify (and implement) attainment strategies, a goal is almost worthless. Unfortunately, many people fail to determine what they need to do to actually reach their goals. They do not clarify the behaviors they need to implement if they are ultimately going to succeed. Remember, a goal only provides the direction for your effort and energies; you still have to determine, and follow through on, the behaviors that will get you there.

Terrence's long-term goal is to earn a 3.2 GPA during the upcoming academic term; one of his short-term goals is to earn at least a "B" on each exam he takes. To achieve these goals, he will need to identify specifically what he has to do to achieve success. For example, to earn a "B" on each exam, he could review his notes within 24 hours after each class, complete his textbook readings in advance, study in the library four evenings a week, begin his pre-exam review at least five days in advance, attend every class, and meet weekly with a study group. For Laura to reach her goal, she could receive individualized instruction from the head coach, stay after practice with one of the pitchers to hit extra balls at least twice a week, work out in the weight room three times a week to increase her arm strength, and schedule an appointment with the school's sport psychologist to fine tune her pre-batting routine. Remember, though, that even the best-formulated attainment strategies will be of no value if you do not take the *responsibility* to follow through and implement what you have planned.

Whenever you set goals, think about the following questions:

1. Have you identified the behaviors you need to implement to actually reach your goal?
2. If so, are your attainment strategies sound, and are you following through on them?

If you would answer "No" to either question, then think about other things you could do to help ensure that you reach your goal. Remember, a goal without a plan of action is like a car without an engine! You may look good sitting in it, but you'll be stuck in one place.

R: Realistic Goals

Your goals should be challenging, yet realistic. If you set goals that are too difficult, then you may consistently fail to attain them and therefore feel unmotivated and lack confidence. If you set goals that are too

> "Setting a goal is not the main thing. It is deciding how you will go about achieving it and staying with that plan."
>
> Tom Landry
> *NFL Hall of Fame Football Coach*

easy, then you may not sufficiently challenge yourself to reach your potential, improve your performance, or do your best. Unchallenged, you may settle for mediocrity. To avoid these extremes, make sure that your goals are challenging, but that you have a realistic chance of reaching them if you work hard and implement your attainment strategies.

To determine how realistic Terrence's and Laura's goals are, we need to consider other factors in their lives, such as his high school grades and her past batting performances. Terrence was a "B" student in high school. Thus, his goal of earning a 3.2 semester GPA seems to be realistic but challenging. Lori's batting average during the previous season was .275 and she struck out twice in every five at-bats. Thus, her goal, as currently stated, may be unrealistic. Instead, she may want to revise her goal to hitting .325 or striking out only once in every six at-bats. Such changes would make them challenging but attainable, and thus maximize the effort she would put forth.

Whenever you set goals, think about the following questions:

1. Does your goal challenge you to work beyond your current capabilities?
2. What percentage chance of success do you associate with reaching your goal?

If you would answer "No" to question 1, then your goal may not be sufficiently challenging. If you would indicate a low percentage chance of

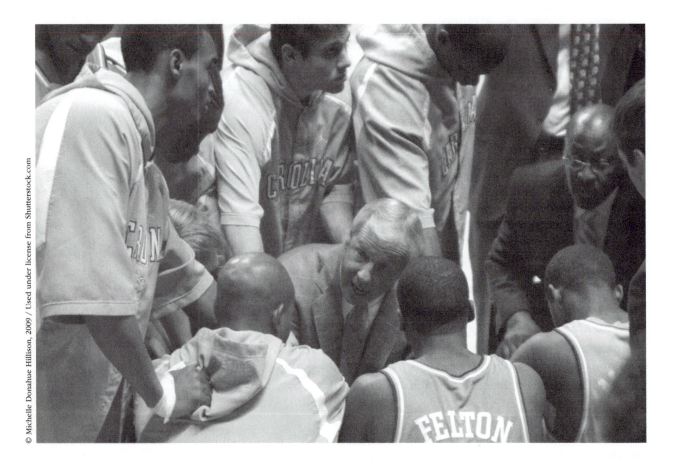

success, then your goal may be unrealistic. In either case, modify your goals to make them more consistent with your current capabilities.

T: Target Obstacles to Achieve Your Goals

Even in the best circumstances, obstacles may arise, which can shift your energy and effort away from your goal. Although some obstacles cannot be anticipated (e.g., someone in your family becomes ill, your car breaks down, you become injured), others (e.g., your team has an away game the weekend before an important political science midterm) can be identified in advance and potential strategies for handling them developed so they do not become problems. So, when you set your goals, think through the possible obstacles you may face while working toward them. With each obstacle you identify, consider the

> ❝Setting goals for your game is an art. The trick is in setting them at the right level— neither too low or too high.❞
>
> GREG NORMAN
> *PGA Champion*

Tips for Effectively Using Team Travel Time

Traveling with your team will present many special challenges and unique opportunities. Here are some suggestions for getting the most out of your time on the road.

1. Before leaving, review your syllabi so you know what assignments need to be finished. Make sure you have the books, notes, and computer supplies you'll need, and notify your instructors in advance of your upcoming absence to arrange to complete assignments (especially tests) before, during, or after your trip.

2. Take care of errands and other small tasks, such as paying bills and doing laundry, before you leave so that you won't be overloaded upon your return.

3. Consider exploring the cities you visit (with your coach's permission), especially if there are attractions different from your hometown or the area where your school is located.

4. If you study en route, then work on tasks that don't require concentrated, uninterrupted thought, such as making flash cards or recopying notes. For other tasks, such as reading or studying your notes for an exam, wait until you arrive at your destination and have a quiet place where you can focus.

5. Make sure you set aside time to study, whether on your own or at an organized study table (if your team offers one while it is on the road). Don't fall behind!

6. If you can, choose a roommate whose lifestyle and study habits are similar to your own. If you are placed with someone who is incompatible, then talk with your coach to see if a change can be made or find other places that are quiet and conducive to studying.

7. Check your e-mail and stay up to date with Web-based assignments, communication with your instructors, and submitting work online.

8. Traveling can be tiring and can throw you off balance, so make sure you get as much rest as possible and eat healthfully to minimize the physical and psychological effects.

ways that you can cope most effectively by either avoiding the obstacle altogether or minimizing its impact.

To illustrate the importance of identifying obstacles, let's examine Terrene's situation. His team had a long weekend tournament (Wednesday through Sunday) just before his last chemistry exam was to be given and an English paper was due. To reduce his anxiety and increase his focus on his sport, he planned to complete the first draft of his paper before his team left for the tournament and then to take it with him to get some feedback from a teammate who was an English major. For the chemistry exam, he planned to bring his notes and book and make flash cards while he was on the bus to the tournament. He also intended to study each evening in the hotel room or another quiet location. Such advance planning ensured that he would be able to keep working toward his academic goal and perform without worry in his sport.

Whenever you set goals, think about the following questions:

1. What potential obstacles exist for each of your goals?
2. What advance plans can you make to handle them effectively?

Remember, planning in advance can actually save you time. Invest now by planning for those obstacles you can foresee and save yourself from headaches and wasted time later.

Other Considerations When Setting Goals

By setting SMART goals, you increase your chances of accomplishing what you want, whether in athletics, academics, and other key areas of life. Whenever you set goals, apply the five SMART guidelines and ask yourself the questions we provided at the end of each guideline.

Even when you have set a SMART goal, there are a few other things you should take into account. First, goals can be forgotten, pushed aside, and not followed through. To minimize the likelihood of these problems occurring, you should: (a) make your goals visible in some way (Figure 1.1), such as taping them to your mirror or listing them on your screensaver; seeing your goals every day is a stark reminder of what you need to be doing to actually attain them; (b) tell a friend, teammate, coach, teacher, or family member about what you are trying to accomplish; these individuals can help you stay honest with yourself and accountable to what you are trying to accomplish; and (c) establish a time frame in which you want to achieve your goal; goals that have no defined "due" date can be pushed off into the future and/or easily forgotten.

Second, consider setting both performance and outcome goals. A performance goal is one in which you use yourself and your past behaviors as the comparison. For example, an athlete who sets the goal of increasing her squat max by 10% has set a performance goal. Performance goals have the advantage of being independent of others' achievements; they are *under your control.* As a result, they allow you to better gauge your performances and the improvements you are making. Such feedback is crucial if you are to ultimately reach your goal. With outcome goals, on the other hand, you use some external standard or your performance against others as the comparison. For example, the goals of winning the game or placing second in the meet are outcome-based because they are determined relative to other performers. Outcome-based

Figure 1.1 Making Your Goals Visible

goals may be better than performance-based goals for improving performances, because some people become highly motivated and focused when they are competing against others. Thus, it may be useful to consider a combination of outcome- and performance-based goals, possibly focusing on performance goals for improving your skills in practices and outcome goals with respect to competitions.

Third, when setting goals, especially when not skilled at doing so, student-athletes may experience several common problems, including: (a) setting goals that are too vague and general (e.g., "I want to do well in the game") and thus do not provide the needed motivation or accountability; (b) not monitoring progress toward their goals, which can undermine motivation and interfere with their ability to receive important feedback about the progress they are (or are not) making; and (c) setting too many goals and thus not being able to follow through on all of them. So, when setting goals, make sure they are specific and measurable, you carefully track your progress toward your goal, and focus on only one or two key goals at a time, particularly when you are just getting started in the process of setting goals.

Self-Responsibility and Achieving Your Goals

Self-responsibility is a key factor in attaining your goals and is defined as

- being in control of your life and making decisions for yourself,
- knowing what you can and cannot alter in your life and focusing on that which you can change,

- following through on the commitments you have made to yourself and others,
- investing yourself fully in each experience, relationship, or situation,
- being able to delay immediate or short-term gratification for long-term gain,
- being accountable for your actions and not blaming others for what has happened, and
- being open to feedback from others so you can learn how to improve yourself.

Being self-responsible gives you the best opportunity to learn and be successful.

Goals and self-responsibility are inextricably linked. Goals provide the direction, and self-responsibility the follow through. Without self-responsibility

- you will not commit to and actually implement your attainment strategies,
- you will not follow through on the feedback you receive regarding your progress and make the needed changes in what you are doing, and
- life will simply happen to you.

Be self-responsible and become an active change agent in your life, charting your own success and living life to the fullest. To help you begin thinking about the role self-responsibility currently plays in your life, you may want to complete Exercise 1.12.

Self-Efficacy and Setting Goals

Self-efficacy, along with goal setting and self-responsibility, helps regulate motivation. Self-efficacy is your belief in your ability to organize and execute courses of action required to attain a specific, desired outcome (Bandura, 1977, 1982, 1986). Self-efficacy is how confident you are in your ability to perform certain behaviors that will lead to desired outcomes; they are specific to a situation and normally do not generalize to different circumstances. For example, Chris had high self-efficacy when it came to her math class; she was confident she could solve any of the problems that her instructor gave—whether on homework or on an exam. Thus, she attended every math class, did all the assigned problems (regardless of whether they were to be turned in), and visited her instructor once a week to clarify any questions she had. With respect to her English class, though, Chris's self-efficacy was quite low. She did not believe she could extract the main ideas from the stories she read nor understand the important supporting details. As a result, she tended to put off her readings until the last minute, if she did them at all.

Self-efficacy beliefs influence what you choose to do, the effort you put forth, and your level of persistence (Bandura, 1977). People participate in activities in which they feel efficacious and avoid those in which they don't, which may be why students procrastinate on

Exercise 1.12 Self-Responsibility

Read the following statements, and, using the scoring system provided, rate yourself as you currently are (not how you would like to be) with respect to self-responsibility.

Not at all	Sometimes	Always	Self-Assessment
1	2	3	I know what I can and cannot change in my life, and I act in those areas to make improvements.
1	2	3	I actively participate in all my classes.
1	2	3	When I have difficulty doing my work, I determine what is interfering and make the necessary adjustments.
1	2	3	When I receive a grade that is lower than I expected, I use the feedback to make positive changes in how I study so I can increase my chances of future success.
1	2	3	I am open to the feedback I receive from others.
1	2	3	My success in school or athletics is under my control and determined by how much time and effort I invest.
1	2	3	I follow through and complete my academic commitments on time.
1	2	3	I follow through and complete my work/job commitments on time.
1	2	3	I follow through and complete my personal commitments on time.
1	2	3	I recognize when I need help on something and take the initiative to find it.
1	2	3	I invest myself fully in and try to get the most out of whatever I do.
1	2	3	When I experience obstacles in reaching my goal, I modify my behaviors as needed and then keep trying.
1	2	3	I delay doing "fun things" when I know they will interfere with my reaching my goals.

Take a moment to review your responses. Items you rated "3" are strengths. Next, consider the items rated 1 or 2. Some of these, particularly those you rated 1, represent areas of focus. Keep these areas in mind and think about how you can increase your level of self-responsibility.

certain academic tasks. For example, Erin loved her communication and English classes and always did that homework first. Although she sometimes earned a "B" in those classes, she started each semester with the belief that he could earn an "A" in that type of class. Math, on the other hand, was another story entirely. She hated those classes because she could never seem to understand how to solve the problems. As a result, she avoided doing her homework, often putting it off until the absolute last minute. In which class/activity do you think Erin had the highest self-efficacy?

High self-efficacy also increases the chances that you will put forth considerable effort and persevere, even when faced with considerable obstacles. For example, Clarisse had high self-efficacy regarding cars—building them, repairing them, or just knowing about them. In fact, when rebuilding an engine, she would work for hours on end, even when things were not going well and she was frustrated. As a student-athlete, it is likely that your efficacy is very high in your sport and that you are motivated to excel in this area, no matter how difficult it is.

Self-efficacy can be increased in any given area and there are several ways to accomplish that end (Bandura, 1986). The primary way to increase your self-efficacy is to be successful in something you are doing. That is, setting a goal, working toward it, and then attaining it can increase your efficacy in that area. Once self-efficacy develops, failure does not usually have negative effects because you are more likely to persist in the face of obstacles. Perhaps Nike had the right idea—"just doing it" can lead to higher self-efficacy if what you are attempting is challenging, but realistic and within your capabilities.

You also can increase your efficacy by watching someone who is similar to you engage in a successful performance. This "vicarious" experience teaches you that you can do it too. For example, watching an older, more experienced teammate execute a sport skill can help you develop the belief that you can do that skill as well. Being encouraged or persuaded by others with statements such as, "I know you can do it," or "Let's go; you're the one," or "You're smart; you can pass this test," also can increase self-efficacy levels. Self-efficacy beliefs that result from encouragement generally are not very stable unless they are followed by performance successes. Encouragement may be what is needed to get you started, but you need to follow through and gain success for you to see changes in your efficacy beliefs.

Although self-efficacy is important in determining whether a person is likely to engage in a specific behavior, there are other factors that affect the actual performance outcome. Yes, you must be confident in your abilities, but to be successful you must actually have the necessary skills and value the outcome that may result from your behaviors. For example, if Rick does not have the academic skills to prepare for his statistics test, even a high level of confidence is not likely to make him successful. Furthermore, how individuals interpret their successes determines whether self-efficacy beliefs increase (Schunk, 1991). If you attribute your successes (earning an "A" on your first midterm) to events or people outside of you, such as the test being easy, the instructor helping you, or luck, then your self-efficacy will likely remain unchanged. If, however, you attribute your success to internal factors, such as effort, hard work, and/or skill, then you will probably experience an increase in your self-efficacy beliefs. The attributions you make for the successes and failures in your life will strongly influence your self-efficacy beliefs and ultimately your ability to regulate your motivation. In Chapter 4 we discuss attributions and their influence on motivation.

> "Success is a journey, not a destination. The doing is usually more important than the outcome. Not everyone can be Number 1."
>
> ARTHUR ASHE
> *Tennis Champion*

Performance: The Relationship of Goals, Self-Responsibility, and Self-Efficacy

Goal setting, self-responsibility, and self-efficacy are part of an integrated self-regulatory process that can profoundly influence motivation and performance success (Figure 1.2). Reaching your goals, which takes self-responsibility, can lead to higher levels of self-efficacy. With higher levels of self-efficacy, you may set more challenging goals, which then can increase your self-efficacy even further. Unfortunately, this cycle can also move in the opposite direction. If you set goals that are too challenging and unrealistic and cannot be reached, then your self-efficacy may decrease and you may be less able to put forth the needed effort on future goals.

> "It's a lack of faith that makes people afraid of meeting challenges, so I believe in myself."
>
> MUHAMMAD ALI
> *World Heavyweight and Olympic Boxing Champion*

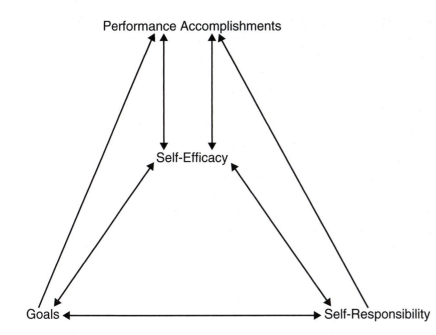

Figure 1.2   The Interrelationship Between Goals, Self-Responsibility, and Self-Efficacy

Student Handbook and Course Syllabi

The student handbook (sometimes referred to as the undergraduate catalogue) contains just about everything you need to know about being a student at your school. Not only does it give an overview of the rules that apply to all students, but it usually provides an introduction to your school, highlighting important services and historical information. Obtain a copy (or find it in your school's website) and become familiar with the information it contains.

Most of your instructors will provide you with a class syllabus, which is an outline or overview of the main areas or topics that will be covered. Most universities require that all instructors provide a syllabus. Generally, the syllabus contains the following:

- Name, office, phone, e-mail and, perhaps, the website of your instructor
- Office hours
- Textbooks or other readings used in the class
- Instructor's expectations for students, such as attending class and participating
- Description of assignments, often including point values for each
- How grades will be determined
- Schedule of topics to be covered
- Assigned readings
- Schedule of examinations and dates when assignments are due

In essence, the syllabus is your "map" for that course. You can also view the syllabus as a "contract." It contains the ojectives, requirements, and methods of evaluation for the course, and instructors are responsible for following what they have written in the syllabus. So, review each syllabus as soon as you receive it to familiarize yourself with course expectations, readings, exams and/or assignments, and the way grades will be determined and plan your schedule for each academic term.

Post-Game Review

Although the focus of this book is helping you become academically successful, self-responsibility and goals can also help you improve as an athlete. One thing that underlies all high-level performers, be they athletes, musicians, or actors, is their ability to set and follow through on their goals. Although these strategies may seem simple and straightforward, integrating them into your life will take time, effort, and commitment. Through this book, you have the opportunity to systematically evaluate yourself and your behaviors to determine if you are living how you want, making the choices you desire, and reaching the goals you set. You also have the chance to adopt a new approach to life, one based on choice, goals, and self-responsibility.

Thinking Critically about Goal Setting, Self-Responsibility, and Self-Efficacy

1. Summarize what you now know about the transition to college, setting goals, self-responsibility, and self-efficacy based on the information presented in this chapter.

_____

_____

_____

2. What additional questions do you have about these topics and how to use these skills?

_____

_____

_____

3. What conclusions can you draw about these topics and how they, in particular goal setting and self-responsibility, might help you be a more effective and successful student and athlete?

_____

_____

_____

Achieve IT! Setting an Academic Goal

1. Choose the academic goal that is most important to you—one you are truly invested in and want to attain this term.

Academic Goal I Want to Achieve This Term: _____

2. Now identify three short-term goals that will help you reach your goal this term. For example, if you put earning a "B" in your economics class as your term goal, then you might list earning at least "Bs" on all midterms and earning an "A" average on your two group projects.

3. For the short-term goals, identify the attainment strategies you will need to reach them. For example, to increase your chances of earning at least a "B" on all your exams, you could attend all your classes, conduct daily and weekly reviews of all your class notes, join a study group, talk with your instructors each week to discuss any questions you have, and begin studying for each exam at least five days in advance.

4. List any obstacles you might face in trying to reach these goals and identify your plan for overcoming each one.

5. Don't forget to make your goal visible and tell others about them so they can keep you accountable regarding what you want to achieve.

Setting an Athletic Goal

1. Choose the athletic goal that is most important to you—one you are truly invested in and want to attain this term.

Athletic Goal I Want to Achieve This Term: _____

2. Now identify three short-term goals that will help you reach your goal this season. For example, if you set increasing your vertical jump by five inches as your goal, then you might list increasing your leg strength by 20% as one of your short-term goals.

3. For the short-term goals, identify the attainment strategies you will need to reach them. For example, to increase your leg strength 20%, you could do squats three times a week in the weight room, run four sets of stadium stairs three times a week, and do plyometrics twice a week.

4. List any obstacles you might face in trying to reach these goals and identify your plan for overcoming each one.

5. Don't forget to make your goal visible and tell others about them so they can keep you accountable regarding what you want to achieve.

Chapter 1 Review Questions

1. You possess many skills developed through sports that can be transferred to other areas of life, such as academics and relationships, and can help you be successful. (True or False)

2. By the second month of her freshman year, Tanya was broke. To avoid future financial troubles she might:

   a. Only put as much on her credit cards as she can pay each month.
   b. Buy things when they are on sale.
   c. Stop carrying so much cash in her wallet.
   d. All of the above.

3. Dr. Lambert is a full-time employee of the college who has been hired primarily to teach. He does not have any research responsibilities, and he does not qualify for the tenure system. He is likely a(n):

   a. Assistant professor.   **b.** Lecturer.
   c. Teaching fellow.   **d.** Emeritus teacher.

4. To increase the chances of living satisfactorily with a roommate, you should:

   a. Develop a "how to live together" agreement.
   b. Do whatever you want, particularly if you are paying most of the bills.
   c. Keep your frustrations to yourself.
   d. Focus your energies on making your roommate your best friend.

5. A syllabus provides all the rules and regulations about being a student at your school. (True or False)

6. According to the SMART system, you should

   a. Make very challenging goals.
   b. Make "do your best" goals.
   c. Make measurable goals.
   d. All of the above.

7. Setting performance goals is always the best approach for improving athletic performance. (True or False)

8. Celeste set the goal of improving her free throw shooting during the season. What common problems might she experience with trying to attain this goal?

   a. She may develop a level of efficacy that is too high.
   b. She may fail to monitor her progress while she works toward her goal.
   c. She may attribute her success to the extra time and effort she is putting forth in practices.
   d. All of the above.

9. Discuss the advantages of making your goals visible.

10. "Winning the meet" is an example of

   a. A performance goal.
   b. An outcome goal.
   c. A goal obstacle.
   d. A realistic goal.

11. Explain the relationship between goals, self-responsibility, and self-efficacy.

12. Gordon believes that he can be successful in any math class he takes. Gordon has a high level of

   a. Self-responsibility.
   b. Self-regulation.
   c. Self-control.
   d. Self-efficacy.

Chapter 2 | Establishing the Foundation for Success

Learning Styles and Critical Thinking

Game Plan:

In this chapter, you will learn:

- What your learning styles are

- How to capitalize on your learning style to be a more successful student and athlete

- What critical and creative thinking are

- How to think critically in your classes

© James M Phelps, Jr, 2009 / Used under license from Shutterstock.com

"I think that everything is possible as long as you put your mind to it and you put the work and time into it. I think your mind really controls everything."

MICHAEL PHELPS
Olympic Gold Medalist, Swimming

Self-Assessment—Perceive It!

Read the following statements and place a checkmark next to each one you generally do. For you to change and develop new and effective academic, athletic, and personal strategies, you must be accurate in your self-perception. So, be honest in how you answer each question.

1. When I study, I try to involve as many of my senses as I can.   _____

2. I construct personal examples of the concepts in my courses to make the material more meaningful and my learning easier.   _____

3. Whenever appropriate, I visually represent my notes and my textbook readings by making graphic organizers or using different colored highlighters.   _____

4. In class, when I am confused, I ask my instructors to explain or present the material in another way to help me understand it better.   _____

5. Regardless of how my friends take notes or read their textbooks, I study in the ways that I know work best for me.   _____

6. I respect people who can actually get things done as opposed to just talking about them.   _____

7. I know when I need to understand the "big picture" and when I need to break a problem down into its parts.   _____

8. I always ask questions about information that is being presented to me, such as in class, from news sites, or from friends.   _____

9. When new information is presented to me, such as in class or on a website, I independently evaluate its validity before accepting it.   _____

10. When I become aware of them, I look at my assumptions and biases and challenge those of others.   _____

Take a moment to review your responses. How many items did you check? Each one you checked represents a current strength. Now consider the items you did not check; these represent areas where focus and growth are needed. Now, to summarize your self-perception, complete the following statements:

1. My areas of strength are:

_____

2. The areas I need to improve are:

_____

As you read this chapter and participate in your classes, keep your strengths and areas of improvement in mind. At the end of the chapter, you will have the chance to set a goal related to these areas. Achieving these goals will help you become a more effective student and athlete.

Introduction

Mike was a starting lacrosse player on his team and second team all-conference last season. Despite his outward success, it always took Mike a long time to learn new plays and understand the coaches' strategies. His coaches always talked through strategies and rarely diagrammed plays, an approach that left Mike out in the cold. It was only when he got on the field and started to execute the plays that he fully understood what the coach was saying. In fact, he seemed at his best in games when he had to improvise, such as when a play was broken. He learned best by doing and getting his body involved in the situation.

Tony was bright and inquisitive, but he always felt like a fish out of water when he read his textbooks. He did great in lectures, listening to his instructors; in fact that was when he understood things best. He preferred to have things explained to him by another person and dreaded reading things on his own. He tended to avoid reading his textbook, which did not help his grades in classes, and this problem was only getting worse. In his upper-level classes there was lots of reading, most of which was not discussed in class but was part of his exams. He had to find some way to talk about what he was learning if he expected to pass his classes and graduate from college.

For as long as she could remember, Elle had found it easiest to learn new things when information was represented visually. In fact, until she could "see" the material, she often felt lost and unsure of herself. Once she saw a new play diagrammed by her coaches or saw one of her teammates execute the play in real-time, something "clicked," and she was able to do it herself. Schoolwork was no different. When taking notes, she used different colored pens to highlight information to make it easier to discern. When reading her textbooks, she tended to pay more attention to the graphs and illustrations than the written words. Until she could "see" the material, she was often lost.

Martina loved to write. In classes, she looked forward to taking notes—it was the process of writing down information that helped her understand what the instructor was saying. If all she did was listen, then she often ended up confused or barely remembered what was said. When she read her textbooks, she often took notes, writing out questions and answers about the material. When she was done with her readings, she only studied the notes she had taken. In her sport, she kept a journal in which she wrote notes to herself about meetings with her coaches, new strategies and plays she was trying to learn, and anything else that seemed relevant. Writing the information in the notebook and reviewing it later helped her learn the material and excel at her sport.

Can you relate to Mike, Tony, Elle, or Martina? Are you like one of them or perhaps some combination of all four? Everyone learns in different ways. Some do best by reading, whereas others learn by listening to what their instructors or coaches say. Some only "get it" when they can be active and "do."

In this chapter, we introduce the concepts of learning styles and critical and creative thinking. First, we provide you with the opportunity to understand your strengths in learning and how to improve in the areas where you are weakest. Next, we define critical thinking and discuss how you can be more creative in your learning and problem solving.

Preparation: Learning Styles

A "learning style" is the preferred ways people have for learning, or taking in, new material. Although learning styles have been thought of and assessed in different ways, we will focus on only one in this section. To help you determine your preferred way for learning, you may want to complete Exercise 2.1.

Exercise 2.1   Your Preferred Learning Style

Circle the letter next to the answer that best matches your preference. If a single answer does not match your preference, then circle the best two choices. Leave blank any question that does not apply.

1. I learn best in courses where there are:
   R. Handouts, printed notes, and/or a textbook.
   K. Field trips, labs, internships.
   V. Flow charts, diagrams, slides, videos.
   A. Discussion sections, question-and-answer sessions, guest speakers.

2. You want to go to a club that your friends have been telling you about. The club, however, is hard to find. How would you prefer your friend help you get there?
   V. Draw you a map or give you a website link to a map.
   K. Take you to the club earlier in the day, so you can find your way later that night.
   A. Give you verbal directions on how to get to the club.
   R. Give you written directions, but no visual map to look at.

3. In which type of "new student" orientation program would you most prefer to participate?
   K. Walk around campus and be shown the sights by a guide.
   V. Watch a video that shows you the different parts of the campus.
   R. Read a brochure and other related materials (e.g., undergraduate catalog) about your college.
   A. Have a junior or senior talk to you about the college experience, without a tour.

4. You are thinking about buying a laptop computer. Assuming cost is not an issue, what would most influence your decision?
   A. Hearing about the capabilities of the laptop from someone.
   R. Reading about the laptop's specifications and features in a consumer magazine.
   K. Trying one out at the computer store or borrowing your friend's for a day.
   V. How it looks.

5. Which of the following would be most helpful to you when studying for a final exam in a class such as Human Anatomy?
   V. View pictures of the bones and their positions in a textbook or on a computer.
   A. In a study group, talk with your friends about the bones and their position in the body.
   K. Go to a lab to actually pick up and manipulate the bones.
   R. Read written descriptions about the bones and their positions in the body.

6. You have just purchased something that requires you to assemble it. How would you proceed to put it together?
   V. Look at and follow the pictures, diagrams, or charts that come with it without reading the instructions.

R. Carefully read the assembly instructions before starting.
A. Ask a friend who just purchased the same thing to tell you how to put it together.
K. Just do it without looking at pictures or reading directions.

7. You have been assigned the task of learning a new computer program in your class. When you open the program, you would most likely:
   K. Just start experimenting with the program and learning through trial and error.
   A. Talk with the teaching assistant about how to operate the program.
   R. Read the instructions which you received from your teacher.
   V. Watch what a classmate at the computer next to you is doing.

8. You are not sure how to spell a word. You:
   R. Look it up in a dictionary or on a dictionary website.
   V. See the word in your mind and choose what "looks" best.
   K. Write down several versions of the word to see which one seems best.
   A. Say the word to yourself under your breath so you can hear it.

9. You have become interested in learning about a religion other than your own. You would most likely:
   K. Go to services in the new religion to experience it as it is practiced.
   A. Have someone in that religion tell you about it.
   V. Watch a documentary or Web video on the religion.
   R. Read about the religion in a blog or book.

10. What do you most like to do in your free time?
    K. Exercise, play sports, or do some other physical activity.
    R. Read a book or magazine.
    A. Listen to music.
    V. Watch television or videos on the web.

Now total how many times you listed each "letter code" across the 12 questions. Write the totals in the spaces provided:
Visual: _____
Aural: _____
Reading/Writing: _____
Kinesthetic: _____
Circle your top two learning styles.

In our conception of learning styles, there are four primary modalities through which individuals take in information: Aural (learn through hearing), Visual (learn through seeing), Reading/Writing (learn through reading or writing about material), and Bodily-Kinesthetic (learn through doing). Although individuals are likely to have a preferred modality for learning—one that is the primary means through which they take in information—in most learning situations, using more than one modality can facilitate understanding and later recall of information. So, it is in your best interests to develop multiple ways to successfully take in information.

In college, most material will be presented either verbally through lectures and discussion sections (which benefit aural learners) or in

---

Types of College Classes

There are four types of class formats that you likely will experience while in college:

- *Lecture.* The instructor, assumed to be an expert, shares information about the subject with students. The instructor is responsible for organizing the class material, determining how the students will be evaluated, and selecting the topics to be covered. This format is the most typical in U.S. colleges, particularly for introductory courses that are often held in large lecture halls. In general, this type of format does not lend itself to detailed discussions of topics, though there may be websites associated with the class in which more information is presented and students have opportunities to interact with the instructors in more depth. This format may be ideal for auditory and reading/writing learners.

- *Recitation/discussion.* Recitation/discussion classes often accompany larger lecture classes, particularly those in mathematics and the physical sciences. Classes are generally small (around 20 students) and are often taught by upper-level undergraduates or graduate students from that discipline. Instructors lead in-depth discussions on the material from the previous lecture or assist students in working through homework problems. This type of class may be ideal for aural learners and provides an excellent opportunity to clarify material that was discussed in the lecture.

- *Lab/activity.* Lab/activity classes focus on hands-on learning. These classes are often found in various science disciplines and in physical fitness and health. These classes give students the opportunity to see how the theories, concepts, and processes they are studying actually work. These classes are ideal for kinesthetic learners.

- *Seminar.* In seminars, the focus is on in-depth discussion of the subject matter, with the responsibility for learning being shared by instructors and students. Generally, seminars have fewer students than other classes and are used for upper-level undergraduate and graduate courses. In seminars, instructors and students read about the subject through journal articles, books, blogs, textbooks, and other written materials, and come to class prepared to discuss the readings. Students may be responsible for organizing and delivering presentations about different topics in the course. This format is ideal for aural and reading/writing learners.

written form through textbooks, website pages, and other materials (which benefit reading/writing learners). Research (Petrie & Petrie, 1999), though, indicates that students prefer bodily-kinesthetic and visual modalities when learning:

- 48% were bodily-kinesthetic.
- 22% were visual.
- 18% were aural.
- 12% were reading/writing.

And, for student-athletes, it is likely that there is an even higher percentage whose primary modality is bodily-kinesthetic. These findings suggest that students' preferred learning styles often do not coincide with the primary teaching modalities. If you find yourself in a similar position, then it will be important for you to strengthen your less developed learning styles and to learn how to effectively translate verbal and written material into forms that are most useful for you. Otherwise, learning in college classes may be difficult.

Performance: How to Use Your Learning Style

Now let's think about your learning style with respect to three important academic behaviors—what you do in class, what you do when you are studying, and what you do during exams—and your involvement in your sport. How might you capitalize on your learning style?

Visual Learners

In Class. You might underline important points or highlight them to make them more pronounced when you are taking notes in class. For example, you could use different color pens or symbols, charts, and graphs to represent different points made during the lecture. Also, make sure that you record any information that the instructor presents that already is in a visual form. You can also use a note-taking form, such as a concept map, that is visually appealing to help you better understand the material.

When Studying. When studying and reading your textbooks, continue to use all the strategies you do when taking notes. In particular, pay attention to visual materials, such as graphs, illustrations, tables, bold-faced or italicized words, and summary information. When you are reading, underline and highlight important text (though don't overdo it). When reviewing your notes, you may want to use graphic organizers (see Chapter 6), in particular information matrices, to represent material. These organizers are excellent for producing concise summaries of the material.

During Exams. When taking exams, recall the "pictures" of your note and textbook pages that you created while studying to find the specific information you need to answer a question. Once you have recalled these pictures, you can put them into words to answer the question. Before beginning any type of exam, you might write important diagrams and formulae on your test to help you remember. For essay or short-answer questions, you might use graphic organizers, such as Pro-Con T's or concept maps to organize your ideas before you begin to write.

In Your Sport. When practicing and learning new skills, techniques, strategies, and/or game plans, pay particular attention to visual diagrams your coaches present to you (e.g., on a white board, in a play book). If your coaches tend to rely on talking to communicate information, then either ask them to work with you to make that information visual in some form or learn to do so yourself. If you can, watch video of your practices and competitions so you can "see" how you are performing. Dartfish is a good example of an advanced video technology that can assist you with technical and tactical analysis. You also may want to use psychological strategies, such as mental imagery, to help you learn new plays and improve your performances (see Chapters 11 and 13 for more information).

Aural Learners

In Class. Make sure you attend all lectures, discussions, and tutorials because hearing material discussed by instructors, classmates, and tutors is beneficial to you. When you are taking notes, listen first and then write the information in your own words. If it's allowed by your instructor, then you also might record the lecture for later study and review (such as listening to a lecture on your iPod when you are traveling to away competitions). If you have questions after you have listened to a recording of a lecture, discuss them with your instructor the next time you are in class. Some instructors also make their lectures available in podcasts.

When Studying. You will benefit from discussing material with classmates, such as in a study group, so consider joining one or visiting with your instructors during office hours. Being able to explain class material, including the overheads, pictures, and other visuals you saw in class, is a good way to cement your knowledge. Consider summarizing notes or textbook readings and then reading them out loud to yourself. Recording this information and listening to it later also is a good way to review. Also, do not be afraid to talk to yourself when working through problems or difficult information. Sometimes the act of talking it through is exactly what an aural learner needs to better understand the material.

During Exams. When taking exams, listen to the voice in your head and write down what it says. You have learned the information aurally, so you may benefit from trying to recall it in a similar manner. If you are stuck or unsure, then talk out the question and possible answers under your breath before responding.

In Your Sport. Talk with your teammates and coaches to make sure that you understand what is being taught. If you are unsure, ask questions (at the appropriate time). Also, don't be afraid to talk something through with yourself if you are not sure. How many times have you watched NBA players talking to themselves on the free throw line, or a professional tennis player before she hits a serve? Although the idea of talking to yourself might seem silly, it's much less so than making a mistake or not being able to execute a skill because you did not understand what the coaches were trying to teach you.

Reading and Writing Learners

In Class. Make sure you attend every lecture, not so much to hear the instructor but to give you the chance to write down what he says

---

Words to Live By

What senior student-athletes have told us about making it in college:

- Don't let your sport interfere too much with your studies. Talk with your coaches and athletic department academic advisors if there is a conflict.
- Get off to a good start academically: earn good grades your first semester or quarter. It is hard to raise your GPA when you are a junior or a senior.
- Get to practice early.
- Attend all your classes, even the ones at 8:00 A.M.
- Develop effective academic skills; these will help you in all your classes.
- Always turn in your work on time. Don't put things off!
- Don't let socializing or relationships interfere with your studies.
- Be interested in your classes: ask questions, sit in the front, read your assignments in advance.
- Get to know your instructors: talk with them after class, see them during their office hours, e-mail them with questions.
- Make consistent progress toward your degree. Don't put off your hardest classes until your senior year.
- As in sports, never give up. Rise to the challenges you face in your classes.
- Be positive about all your classes, even the "boring" ones.
- Be positive about practices, even when you are physically and mentally exhausted.
- Learn how to communicate effectively, both verbally and in writing.
- Be open to learning about yourself.
- Set goals, both in classes and in sports, and always try to attain them.
- Think about what you are learning, be inquisitive, ask questions. Don't just accept what you are told.
- Learn to manage and use your time effectively.
- Be responsible with your money.
- Accept you are responsible for what you get out of your education and your success in sports.
- Get to know people, such as faculty or students, who are outside the athletic department.

and create a set of notes that you can use for future review. Make sure that you write your notes in your own words as opposed to simply writing exactly what the instructor says. If you receive handouts or other written materials in class, then carefully review these and write a summary of each one. Use dictionaries and linguistic definitions to be sure you understand new terms. Identify keywords in your notes and readings and associate those with the details by writing them out together.

When Studying. Reread your notes and readings and summarize them in writing using your own words. The act of writing down the information is important for you. When reading a chapter, you might write notes to yourself in the margin that summarize sections and highlight main points of the assignment. You also might try translating visual information, such as graphs and charts, into words and statements. When studying for an exam, reread the summaries. If possible, use old tests to practice answering questions. If old tests are not available, then answer review questions in textbooks by writing out your responses.

During Exams. Write out important lists at the beginning of an exam. Use keywords in the questions to trigger your memory and provide you with complete answers. For essay questions, write your thesis statement and develop an outline. Consider constructing an information matrix that will help you organize and construct a more complete answer. Like aural learners, don't be afraid to "talk" to yourself during an exam. In this case, though, the "talking" will take the form of writing out information on the back of the exam or on scratch paper. Doing so may facilitate recall of information.

In Your Sport. During practices and competitions, it would be difficult, if not impossible, to take notes about what you are learning and experiencing, so you will have to utilize this learning style only during appropriate times. For example, you might keep a journal, and after practices and competitions you could record your ideas, reactions, plays, new skills you are learning, etc. If you watch video of games or your play, then take notes, writing out (in your own words) what you want to learn. During meetings with your coaches, don't just listen to what they say; write it down in your own words so it is more meaningful to you. You also might translate visual diagrams into words that describe the play or skill that has been outlined.

Kinesthetic Learners

In Class. Try to use all of your senses while in class. Labs and real-life learning opportunities, such as field trips, can be particularly important for you. For example, if studying art history, then you might benefit from going to a museum to view some of the works. Also, trial-and-error learning is acceptable. Do not be afraid to try something new—you can learn from your mistakes. Whenever possible, use a hands-on approach to learning any material. In addition, make sure you write down all the examples provided by your instructors. These

> **"The glory of sport comes from dedication, determination, and desire."**
>
> JACKIE JOYNER-KERSEE
> *Olympic Gold Medalist, Track and Field*

examples serve as real-life illustrations and may substitute for live learning experiences.

When Studying. Notes may seem irrelevant, but they are not, particularly the detailed examples instructors usually provide. In addition to instructor-provided examples, you should create personal examples to make the material more meaningful and easier to learn. If applicable, then use pictures and photos to illustrate your notes. For example, a basketball player could diagram class material in the form of basketball plays. When studying the diagrams at home, he could actually run the plays to get more physically involved. Also, talk with classmates to see how they have related the material to their own lives. If sitting for long periods of time is difficult, then you may want to stand, move around, or walk when studying. When you are preparing for an exam, practice answers to likely questions, but do so in an environment that simulates exam situations (e.g., quiet, with a time limit).

During Exams. When you are taking an exam, try to remember instructor-provided or personal examples you created and the hands-on learning situations you have had. Do not be afraid to jump right into the exam—get started and get involved. If you become restless during the exam, then stretching or moving around a bit might help to jog your memory.

© Laurence Gough, 2009 / Used under license from Shutterstock.com

In Your Sport. Because your learning occurs primarily through doing, you initially may make mistakes as you try new skills or execute new plays. But that is part of your learning process. Make sure you have time, either in structured practices or on your own, to get lots of repetitions of the skill or strategy you are trying to perfect. When coaches are giving you instructions, translate that into the actual movements that underlie the skill/technique. Ask your coaches to be "hands on" with you, helping you physically move your body in the right way for that skill, technique, or play.

Although these ideas are presented to help you maximize your learning style strengths, in the end, you also must adapt to the teaching styles of your instructors and coaches. By knowing how you learn best, you are in the position to do that. To help you begin to make better use of your learning style(s), you may want to complete Exercise 2.2.

Exercise 2.2   Using Your Learning Style(s)

Reflect on your favored learning style(s)—reading/writing, aural, visual, or kinesthetic. List two things that you could do to make better use of this style:

- While in class
- While studying
- During exams
- In your sport

Preparation: Critical Thinking

To begin this section, you may want to complete Exercise 2.3.

Critical thinking has long been noted as an essential skill for success in higher education as well as life. If you asked college-level instructors to identify a skill they want their students to develop, then critical thinking would be at the top of the list. Many universities cite critical thinking as one of the primary objectives of earning a college degree.

Wade and Tavris (2003) defined critical thinking as "...the ability and willingness to assess claims and make objective judgments on the basis of well supported reasons and evidence rather than simply relying on emotion and anecdote (p. 7)." Thinking critically does not mean tearing down or criticizing ideas and/or people, it is about examining the data, opinions, and information that are presented to determine its merit and to draw a logical and supported conclusion. In this definition, there are three important points to consider:

Ability—critical thinking is a skill that can be learned. There are specific tools and guidelines that can help you improve your ability to think critically (we introduce these later in the chapter).

Willingness—you have the choice whether or not you examine things from different perspectives, consider the validity of the ideas that are being presented, and/or draw an unsupported or emotionally based conclusion. Are you willing to do so? Unfortunately, not all individuals are. For example, how often do you question (or think critically about) claims made by the media, whether in a commercial for a product or in a news story about a person or situation? Do you formulate your own ideas based on consideration of different viewpoints, or do you just "listen and absorb" what you hear and see on TV and through the Internet? It takes time, energy, and consistent effort to think critically about all the different information to which you are exposed each day, which may be why some people are not willing to do so.

Assess claims—the cornerstone of critical thinking is the evaluation of the data, opinions, points of view, etc., to which you are exposed each day. In critical thinking, you assess the merit and veracity of the information and then make a judgment that is based on your objective evaluation. In this assessment process, it is important to remain open to the different perspectives, opinions, and ideas that will be part of any discussion or debate. Being open-minded does not mean accepting everything as stated or that all opinions are created

---

Exercise 2.3   Defining Critical Thinking

1. Define critical thinking. What does it mean to you?

2. Once you have read the definition provided in this chapter, compare and contrast your original view with it. That is, discuss how similar and different these two definitions are from one another.

3. Which definition of critical thinking makes more sense to you? Why?

> "Strength does not come from physical capacity. It comes from an indomitable will."
>
> MAHATMA GANDHI

equally…they are NOT. Being open-minded involves the ability and willingness to weigh and evaluate several disparate pieces of information before drawing a conclusion.

Performance: Guidelines for Thinking Critically

Critical thinking is a skill that can be learned and one you should develop during your time in college. Critical thinking is not just about answering questions, though it is essential for doing that. It also is the basis for making decisions in all areas of your life, such as what should my major be, and solving problems, such as should I live in the residence halls or get a place off-campus. In this section, we present guidelines for how you can become a more effective and involved critical thinker (Wade & Tavris, 2003):

Ask Questions—asking questions indicates that you are interested, curious, and wondering about what is going on around you and in your life. Obviously, it helps you gather more information, but it also assists you in framing your thoughts and putting you in the position to evaluate the merits of people's positions. Questions represent the first and, perhaps, most crucial, step in critical thinking. For example, what questions did you ask when you were deciding on which college to attend? Did you ask "Where will I fit in best? Where is the best academic program? Am I too close or too far from home? Where are my friends going? What scholarship money will I receive? How much playing time will I get? Why do I want to play for this coach and team?" The questions you ask influence the conclusions you eventually draw. So, ask thoughtful and thorough questions so you have the information you need to adequately evaluate situations, make effective decisions, and find workable solutions to problems.

Define Terms—when asking questions, you have to make sure that your terminology is clearly defined (and thus are unambiguous), or you will have difficulty finding an answer or your answers will be incomplete or even incorrect. For example, the questions "Will an educated person earn the most money over a lifetime?" or "What makes a person intelligent?" or "Are male athletes better than female athletes in a similar sport?" can only be answered if "educated," "intelligent," and "better" are defined. In science, researchers are very specific when defining their terms. If they weren't, then they could not effectively evaluate and draw conclusions from their data. So, when asking questions and thinking critically, always be sure to define your terms and make sure you understand how others are defining theirs. Never be afraid to ask, "What do you mean by that term?" or "How are you defining that word in this context?" Asking these questions helps you to be clear about what others mean.

Examine Evidence—do not take the information that is presented to you or the answers to your questions at face value. Instead, weigh the evidence of the pros and cons to the position being presented.

"Winning" Classroom Behavior

Dr. Bill Buskist is the Distinguished Professor in the Teaching of Psychology and a Faculty Fellow at Auburn University. He's also an Ironman Triathalon competitor and a "cool dude." He has spent his academic life researching how teachers can be most effective in the classroom, and in the process, has learned a great deal about how students can contribute to that process.

Similar to your goals and values, Dr. Buskist has developed his own teaching philosophy. He emphasizes that teaching is about opportunity. Effective teachers create opportunities for students to gain knowledge and new skills in an academic domain and within the larger framework of life. To encourage these opportunities, a teacher needs three things: a deep and abiding knowledge of their own discipline, effective communication skills, and a keen sense of the context in which teaching occurs.

It is this keen sense of context that is particularly important to classroom behavior. Students and teachers bring many different variables to a learning situation that influence how well teachers teach and students learn. Teachers enter the classroom with varying levels of knowledge, communication skills, interest in teaching, concern for students and their learning, and their willingness to make themselves available to students outside of class. Students bring into the classroom different levels of intelligence, learning histories, motivational levels, willingness to change, personal and social distractions, and the values they place on becoming educated individuals. These variables (and others) converge in the classroom to create a dynamic and emotionally charged playing field. In Dr. Buskist's and our eyes, the classroom is a "sacred" place where ideas are exchanged freely in a mutually respectful and supportive environment. And although this idea might seem a bit esoteric (definition: understood by or meant for only the select few who have special knowledge or interest), education is the starting point for the examined life. Only people who examine their lives stand any real chance of genuine and enduring personal growth.

Listed below are guidelines to assist you in bringing your "A" game to the classroom and putting yourself in the position to be an involved learner and to start on the road to having a life full of personal growth:

1. Be on time to class. As one weight and conditioning coach reminds his football players, "Fifteen minutes early is on time. On time is late. Fifteen minutes late is 5 A.M. conditioning with me." If you are late (and we suggest that never happens), then take your seat quickly and quietly.

2. If there is an assignment due in class, then it should be completed before you get to the classroom, preferably a day or two before. Do not do assignments just before the class begins or try to complete it during class.

3. Unless you have made other arrangements with the instructor, stay until the class is finished. Do not close notebooks, click your pen, pack your backpack, look at your cell phone, etc., before the instructor ends class. You would NEVER do that in a practice.

4. Sit in the first two rows of the classroom. Many coaches and athletic academic advisors mandate it, but it is a good idea regardless. There are fewer distractions in the front of class, and you can focus on the instructor, lecture, and discussion.

(continued)

5. Turn off your cell phone or mobile device before entering the classroom and keep them off until the class is over. Do not text, tweet, social network, or communicate technologically with anyone other than the instructor during class.

6. iPods, iPhones, MP3 players, or other musical implements disrupt your opportunity to learn and should be placed in the same compartment of your backpack as your cell phone or mobile device…hidden from the world.

7. If you bring your laptop to class, then use it only for the purpose of the class. Do not surf the Web, answer e-mail, blog, etc., unless the instructor gives you explicit permission to do so.

8. Pay attention to what is being taught in the class. It is disrespectful to everyone if you are reading the newspaper, talking to the person sitting next to you, or studying for other classes.

9. Do not monopolize class discussion. Avoid talking over other people during classroom discussions. Only one person should have the floor and everyone's attention, so stay quiet and focused until it's your turn to talk.

10. Do not be a passive receptacle of information, sitting quietly as if the lecture is "poured" into you. Engage your instructors and classmates in discussion in an appropriate manner (e.g., ask questions, make observations, etc.). Be an active learner!

11. Do not use language that may be offensive to others. Avoid racist and sexist comments, cursing, or any other type of language that may be considered offensive.

In particular, consider ideas that are contrary and may refute what is being expressed. Although you may tend to be more accepting of ideas and information that are consistent with your own opinions, keep an open mind so you can consider other points of view before you make your decision. Being able to thoughtfully, objectively, and without bias examine the information and evidence before you, will lead you to make sound, rational, logical, and well-supported decisions and conclusions.

One way to help you examine both sides of an argument or position is to take on both "doubting" and "believing" perspectives. Traditional conceptions of critical thinking can be viewed as "doubting." That is, ideas and proposals are immediately subjected to doubts to see if they can withstand scrutiny; what is wrong, faulty, invalid, etc., with the position being expressed. For example, if a book came out advertising a simple diet that would make all athletes faster and stronger, and perform better in their sports, then you might be skeptical and doubt the truthfulness of these claims. You might ask "What scientific data support the claims made?" or "What are the harmful side effects?" or "How will the diet affect the results of any sanctioned drug tests?" But you also would want to ask other questions, ones that emanate from a "believing" perspective. From this viewpoint, you try to empathize, that is, understand the situation from the other perspective. In other

---

Exercise 2.4 Taking a Doubting and Believing Perspective

With a small group of classmates or just with a partner, divide into two groups. Select any one of a number of issues that exist, such as "racial profiling," limiting civil liberties in order to prevent terrorist attacks, use of race/ethnicity in making decisions about admission to college, the United States as world peacekeeper (e.g., sending troops to other countries to end violent uprisings), or deregulation of college tuition (i.e., state legislatures allowing universities to

independently set tuition and fee rates), or paying athletes to participate in their sports during college, to name just a few. Once you have selected an issue, have each group take a perspective, either as "doubters" or "believers." Then develop questions from that perspective. After doing so, share your questions with each other to see the different perspectives that you took. Once you have discussed the issue, select another and then switch the perspective you take.

---

words, what might be correct, useful, or helpful? For the simple diet, you might ask "What are examples of athletes who already have been helped by this diet?" or "In what ways can I expect my performance to improve when on the diet?" By considering both sides of the position being expressed or the information being presented, you can more thoroughly, thoughtfully, and accurately evaluate the evidence. To practice using these two different perspectives, you may want to complete Exercise 2.4.

Analyze and Challenge Assumptions and Bias—assumptions are beliefs that are thought to be true, but for which there is little proof or evidence. For example, instructors might hold the assumption that a current student-athlete is not very smart, because a past student-athlete did not pass their class. Assumptions influence your thinking, often in ways that are limiting. So, it is important to acknowledge your assumptions (everyone has them) and make those of others explicit so you can directly address and consider them. When an assumption is so entrenched that it limits your ability to consider other ideas, opinions, or points of view, it has become a bias. To be an effective critical thinker, you must be willing to examine and challenge your assumptions and biases, which can be an emotionally uncomfortable process to endure. When you move beyond your assumptions and biases, you open yourself to new ideas, positions, and points of views, which can make you a more effective critical thinker. To begin learning more about your assumptions and biases, you may want to complete Exercise 2.5.

> ❝I believe the reason you go to college is to get your degree. It's not a minor league or an audition for the pros.❞
>
> REBECCA LOBO
> *WNBA All Star*

Exercise 2.5 Uncovering Your Assumptions and Biases

College is a time when ideas and beliefs are challenged because you are exposed, perhaps for the first time in your life, to people who hold different opinions and have different life experiences than you do. Through formal and informal discussions and by interacting with other people, you will have the opportunity to become aware of some of your assumptions and biases. In fact, you may have done so since you entered college. Have you ever reacted strongly (i.e., emotionally) to what others were saying about a topic or situation, such as interracial dating, stem-cell research, sexual orientation, religion in politics, the BCS, or the use of performance enhancing drugs? If you did, then

you likely were having some of your assumptions and biases challenged or questioned, perhaps without you even knowing it.

1. Based on these and other experiences you may have had in your life, list some of the biases and assumptions you hold.

2. Discuss how these assumptions or biases developed (e.g., what was their source).

3. How do these biases limit your thinking and influence your behaviors?

4. How might you change these assumptions/biases?

Don't oversimplify—in the complex world in which you live, rarely is anything as simple or straightforward as others might suggest or argue (e.g., "you can lose weight by taking one CarbX pill, one time per day"). Instead of accepting generalizations or anecdotes as fact, critical thinkers are comfortable with the complexity that underlies most situations and seek out more information. In taking this approach, critical thinkers acknowledge that there might not be an easy answer, or that there may be limited evidence regarding a situation or point of view. In other words, they are able to tolerate the uncertainty of not knowing or not having an answer right at that time. When you feel this uncertainty, avoid the temptation to oversimplify. Although simplifying things might make you "feel" better in the moment, it will not help you in your search for a well-reasoned answer.

Creativity plays an important role in critical thinking. But what is creativity? Many students believe that they are not creative, that creativity is limited to those who are artistic in some way. But if you think about creativity as the ability to transcend traditional ideas, rules, patterns, and relationships and to develop meaningful new ways to dealing with the world (Random House Dictionary, 1993), you will see that you have the potential to be creative. Thus, thinking creatively means going beyond how you normally view situations and problems so new ideas and solutions can be generated. And, when you think critically, being creative can be a real advantage. For example, if you were thinking creatively about a situation or information, you would be able to consider other's perspectives, diverse opinions, and possible solutions. You could take the believing perspective and flesh out both sides of an argument or position.

Thinking critically is a life skill, one that you should hone while in college and then use during the rest of your life. Whether in personal relationships, on a team, or in your career, you always will face situations in which your ability to think critically will play a prominent role in the outcome you achieve. To help you start the process of becoming a better critical thinker, you may want to complete Exercise 2.6.

Exercise 2.6   Thinking Critically about the World in Which You Live

Find an opinion piece on a current topic (e.g., politics, war, health care). Such pieces may be found in magazines, news organization websites, newspapers (or their Internet equivalent), blogs, or on TV news shows (e.g., CNN, Fox News, MSNBC). Carefully read or listen to the piece and then answer the following questions:

1. What is the main point(s) being made by the author/newscaster/blog?

2. What evidence does he/she provide in support of his/her position?

3. What assumptions/biases are present in the author's argument/position/evidence?

4. Of the evidence presented, what seems questionable or what might you want to check to determine its validity? Why or why not? What evidence seems truthful? Why or why not? (You may want to check these facts through reliable and valid Internet sources.)

5. How well, in your opinion, does the author support his/her point of view with the evidence provided? What other information might the author provide to better support his/her point of view?

6. Has the author oversimplified any of the evidence or his/her point of view? If so, what?

Post-Game Review

In this chapter, we introduced the idea of learning styles, which are your preferred ways of taking in and learning new material. Now that you know your learning style, you can determine how closely it matches the traditional teaching modalities used in higher education. Thus, you may need to develop your weaker learning styles and adopt strategies for working in class, studying, and taking exams that maximize your strengths.

We also discussed critical thinking, an essential skill for being successful in college, your future career, and in your life in general. We introduced several guidelines to follow when thinking critically, including asking questions, examining evidence, and challenging assumptions and biases. If you follow these guidelines and apply them to the information you receive, then you put yourself in the position to be truly engaged and in control of what you learn. Don't just accept what you are told, whether by your instructors, your parents, or your coaches. Ask questions, gather information, weigh the evidence, and then make your own reasoned judgments.

Thinking Critically about Learning Styles

1. Summarize what you now know about learning styles based on the information presented in this chapter.

_____

_____

_____

2. What additional questions do you have about these topics and how to use the skills introduced in this chapter?

_____

_____

_____

3. What conclusions can you draw about this topic and how it might help you be a more effective and successful student and athlete?

_____

_____

_____

Achieve IT! Setting a Learning Style Goal

1. Based on your self-assessment and your responses to "thinking critically," select a goal in relationship to implementing your learning style that you would like to achieve this term.

2. Now identify three short-term goals that will help you reach your goal this term.

3. For the short-term goals, identify the attainment strategies you will need to reach them.

4. List any obstacles you might face in trying to reach these goals and identify your plan for overcoming each one.

Don't forget to make your goal visible and tell others about them, so they can keep you accountable regarding what you want to achieve.

Chapter 2 Review Questions

1. When studying, visual learners benefit from

  a. Tape-recording lectures.
  b. Rereading the textbook.
  c. Using graphic organizers.
  d. None of the above.

2. Aural learners will particularly be helped by

  a. Creating charts of material in lectures.
  b. Participating in study groups.
  c. Rereading old exams.
  d. All of the above.

3. List several study methods that a bodily-kinesthetic learner might use.

4. Given your learning style, what are three things you can do in your sport to help you improve and perform better?

5. Critical thinking involves criticizing other's perspectives and forming simple solutions. (True or False)

6. To think critically, you should:

  a. Question everything.
  b. Examine different perspectives.
  c. Recognize that there is not always going to be a simple answer.
  d. A and B.
  e. All of the above.

7. Your assumptions and biases can act as blinders, keeping you from considering other perspectives and different evidence. (True or False)

8. In the classroom, you should:

  a. Arrive early to class every day.
  b. Study notes from other classes when the instructor is talking about something unimportant.
  c. Listen and simply accept everything your instructors tell you because they are smarter than you are.
  d. All of the above.

Chapter 3 | Developing the Foundation for Success

Managing Your Time

Game Plan:

In this chapter, you will learn:

- How to manage your time effectively and reach your goals

- The importance of using the limited time you have to your advantage

- How to plan, organize, and manage your time day-to-day as well as over the long term

- How to prioritize your daily schedule so it is consistent with your goals and values

- To recognize how being self-responsible helps you successfully manage your time

- To understand your procrastination patterns

- To minimize the times you procrastinate

© Richard Paul Kane, 2009 / Used under license from Shutterstock.com

"The mental approach to things is what separates players at every level."

LISA LESLIE
WNBA Superstar

Self-Assessment—Perceive It!

Read the following statements and place a checkmark next to each one you generally do with respect to time management. For you to change and develop new and effective academic, athletic, and personal strategies, you must be accurate in your self-perception. So, be honest in how you answer each question.

1. I plan specific times for studying, such as reading textbooks, each week. _____

2. At the beginning of each academic term, I make a master schedule that shows when everything is due in all my classes. _____

3. I follow a daily schedule, such as a day planner, or use a "to-do" list to make sure I complete what I intend to do each day. _____

4. During any week, I know approximately how much time I spend on different activities, such as sleeping, practicing, or studying. _____

5. I schedule my time to get my work done in advance so I can avoid the anxiety of doing things at the last minute. _____

6. When I have several things to do, I prioritize them and focus my attention on the most important tasks first. _____

7. I am in control of my time. _____

8. How I use my time each day helps me reach my goals. _____

9. I plan my schedule so I have sufficient time to focus on one task at a time. _____

10. I am on time for classes, meetings, practices, appointments, and so on. _____

11. I maintain the necessary balance in the time I spend on my sport, my classes, and my personal life. _____

12. I schedule my study time to minimize distractions or disruptions by others. _____

13. I know why I procrastinate. _____

14. Once I become aware that I am procrastinating, I am able to stop and get started on the work I have been avoiding. _____

Take a moment to review your responses. How many items did you check? Each one you checked represents a current strength. Now consider the items you did not check…these represent areas where focus and growth are needed. Now, to summarize your self-perception, complete the following statements:

1. My areas of strength in time management are:

_____

2. The time-management areas I need to improve are:

_____

As you read this chapter and participate in your classes, keep your strengths and areas of improvement in mind. At the end of the chapter, you will have the chance to set a goal related to how you use your time. Achieving that goal will help you become a more effective time manager.

Introduction

Sonya was a freshman swimmer at a Division I university. Given that it was her first semester in college, she wanted to get off to a good start personally, academically, and athletically. Although her coach and advisor urged her to wait, she decided to rush a sorority and take a full class load. A solid "B" student in high school, Sonya had always been involved in school social organizations, so she was not too worried about her schedule or the extra time her sorority would take. Initially, things worked out well. She was able to manage her time and meet all her social, academic, and athletic obligations. She was able to schedule her studying and her sorority meetings around her workouts and training room requirements. By about the seventh week of the semester, though, she began to feel overwhelmed. She was busy all the time, with her sport, her classes, and her sorority. She was behind in all her class readings and had two exams and a major paper coming up the following week. In addition, swimming was taking up more time as her coach added dry land and circuit training workouts. Although she wanted to succeed both academically and athletically, she was not doing as well as she wanted. She tried to manage her time—going to every class, arriving early for workouts, and attending all her sorority obligations—but she never seemed to have enough time to get everything done. To cope, she began to stay up later and to sleep fewer hours. Unfortunately, this made her consistently more tired and less able to function effectively. Things would be better if she could just find more time in each day to get her work done.

As a student-athlete, you will find that your life often seems not to be your own. You will be expected to balance the basically full-time job of being an elite-level athlete with being a full-time student. This balance also will be affected by the level at which you compete in your sport, and your goals to pursue post-collegiate opportunities (e.g., professional leagues, Olympics, etc.). Maintaining this balance is a very challenging task, particularly with respect to effectively managing your time. "What time?!?" We have heard many student-athletes respond that way, particularly when their sport is in-season. Although it may not seem that you have any time to manage, in fact you do. Becoming aware of the way you use your "free time" is even more important for student-athletes who have schedules as busy as yours. To help you make wise time choices and accomplish tasks important to you, in this chapter we:

- introduce the concept of time and time management
- discuss time planning and task management
- define procrastination, identify the different reasons why students might do so, and offer strategies for minimizing your procrastination

In discussing these topics, our message is clear—decide how to make the best use of your time and then be self-responsible and follow through. At its essence, time management is self-management. Although scheduling your time (self) may seem rigid and take away your spontaneity, student-athletes frequently find that a good time-management system actually has the opposite effect. Life becomes more productive and fun, and filled with more "free" time to do what you want.

Preparation: Getting Ready to Manage Your Time

What do President Barak Obama, the president of the NCAA, Bill Gates, your coach, you, and Sonya all have in common? Time. Each person, regardless of gender, race, sexual orientation, job, or socioeconomic status, has just 60 seconds in each minute, 60 minutes in each hour, 24 hours in each day, 7 days in each week, and 52 weeks in each year. We all have to make do with the same allotment—24 hours

"Time is at once
the most valuable
and the most
perishable of our
possessions."

JOHN RANDOLPH
*Former Member of the
United States Congress*

a day and 168 hours a week—just like everyone else. Time levels the playing field.

Time is dispassionate. It doesn't care who you are or what you do...time moves forward without pause or end. Your time is finite. Thus, the goal of time management is to learn to make better use of what you have. Just as a basketball coach must learn to effectively manage the 40-minute game clock if her team is going to win, you must learn how to manage the time you have in your life. And because we do not know how long we will live, a sense of urgency to use our time wisely is important. Instead of asking yourself, "How can I find more time?" or worrying about how long you will live, you might want to reflect on, "How can I effectively use the time I do have to achieve my goals and create a well-lived life?"

To answer these questions, you have to know what is important to you and that is where your values and goals come into play (see Chapter 1). Once you have established your values and set your goals, how you prioritize the use of your time should be easy to determine. For example, if you and your family value learning and you have the goal of being an "A" student, studying should be such a high enough priority that you would put off going out with your friends or miss a big party so you could finish a paper that was due the following week. On the other hand, if you value being socially connected and making lots of new friendships as one of your goals while in college, then a time priority likely will be going out to parties, spending time on Facebook (or other social networking sites), or just talking with your roommates. To help you determine if your daily use of time is consistent with your values and goals, you may want to complete Exercise 3.1.

Exercise 3.1 Determining Your Time Priorities

1. Listed are the values that we introduced to you in Chapter 1 (see Exercise 1.11). In Chapter 1, you rated how important each value was to you. In this exercise, using the scale associated with each item, we'd like you to indicate whether you are spending too little or too much time in the activities that underlie that value. For each value, we have listed specific behaviors you might be doing that are associated with that value. For example, under "Being academically successful," we have listed the behaviors "attending classes" and "studying each day." So, if you are not spending enough time in those behaviors, then you might score yourself as a −3 or a −2. If you are spending too much time, then you might rate yourself a +2 or a +3. A score of zero (0) means that you are spending just the right amount of time on those behaviors/activities. Please be honest with yourself in terms of how much time you are spending in each area.

Being academically successful (e.g., attending all your classes, studying each day and in advance for exams, working with a tutor)

Too Little Time	−3	−2	−1	0	+1	+2	+3	Too Much Time

Being athletically successful (e.g., getting to practices early, spending extra time in physical conditioning, reviewing game film, meeting with your coaches to learn new skills/strategies)

Too Little Time	−3	−2	−1	0	+1	+2	+3	Too Much Time

Developing a career (e.g., taking necessary classes, doing a summer internship)

Too Little Time	−3	−2	−1	0	+1	+2	+3	Too Much Time

Being socially connected/involved (e.g., joining student organizations/clubs, developing new friendships, spending time on social networking)

Too Little Time	−3	−2	−1	0	+1	+2	+3	Too Much Time

Being financially secure (e.g., getting a job to pay your bills, obtaining financial aid, earning an athletic/academic scholarship)

Too Little Time   −3   −2   −1   0   +1   +2   +3   Too Much Time

Having a positive and supportive relationship with your family (e.g., contacting them regularly through e-mail, texts, or phone calls; having them visit you on campus; going home over holiday breaks when possible)

Too Little Time   −3   −2   −1   0   +1   +2   +3   Too Much Time

Having a positive and supportive relationship with your boyfriend/girlfriend (e.g., spending time together each week, planning surprises for him/her)

Too Little Time   −3   −2   −1   0   +1   +2   +3   Too Much Time

Being physically healthy (e.g., getting care from medical staff when needed, working out during breaks as prescribed by coaching staff)

Too Little Time   −3   −2   −1   0   +1   +2   +3   Too Much Time

Being well rested (e.g., getting sufficient sleep each night)

Too Little Time   −3   −2   −1   0   +1   +2   +3   Too Much Time

Eating nutritiously (e.g., eating sufficient amounts of fruits/vegetables, carbohydrates, proteins; drinking enough water/sport drinks to maintain adequate hydration)

Too Little Time   −3   −2   −1   0   +1   +2   +3   Too Much Time

Being spiritually or religiously grounded (e.g., attending religious ceremonies, praying)

Too Little Time   −3   −2   −1   0   +1   +2   +3   Too Much Time

Being connected to and involved in your community (e.g., volunteering, such as reading to children in schools, working Habitat for Humanity)

Too Little Time   −3   −2   −1   0   +1   +2   +3   Too Much Time

Being politically active and informed about national events (e.g., reading newspapers/blogs/websites or listening to the news each day, volunteering for a political candidate, voting each election)

Too Little Time   −3   −2   −1   0   +1   +2   +3   Too Much Time

Other areas of importance/value to you (Include what you listed in Exercise 1.10 here and then rate your time use in these areas.):

Too Little Time   −3   −2   −1   0   +1   +2   +3   Too Much Time

2. Now, review Exercise 1.11 and identify those values you rated 5, 6, or 7. These are values you indicated were extremely important to you (they are a "High Priority"). Also, identify those values you rated as 1, 2, or 3. These are less important to you (they are a "Low Priority"). In this section, list your five highest-priority values and your five lowest-priority values. Then, next to each one, write in the time ratings from Question 1 of this exercise.

High Priority Value/Time	Low Priority Value/Time
_____	_____
_____	_____
_____	_____
_____	_____
_____	_____

3. Are you spending enough time on your high-priority activities? Ideally, your time expenditure would be consistent with the importance of the value (i.e., rated 0). If you are not spending enough time on the values that you consider important, then you may want to consider changing the way you allocate your time on a day-to-day basis. For example, if you rated Being Academically Successful a 6 but indicated that you were spending too little time on it (e.g., rated it −2), then you may want to schedule more time each day for studying.

4. Are you spending too much time on any of these low-priority activities? Ideally, your time expenditure would be consistent with the importance of the value (i.e., rated 0). If you are spending too much time in areas that you consider unimportant, then you may want to consider changing the way you allocate your time on a day-to-day basis.

5. Based on this exercise, what is the one thing you could do more of or change that would make a significant difference in your use of time and is consistent with your personal values and the way you want to lead your life?

© Michaeljung, 2009 / Used under license from Shutterstock.com

By encouraging you to reflect on your values, goals, and how you use your time, we are not saying you have to work actively toward your goals every minute of every day. What we are saying is to make conscious, deliberate choices about the way you spend your time. Does your use of time reflect what you say is important in your life and goals you want to attain? For example, suppose your coach gave you an "off day." No practice, no weight room, no athletic responsibilities. With that extra time, you could do lots of different things, such as study, work on a paper, do your laundry, go out with friends, download music, log on to Facebook, watch TV, text on your cell phone, or go to the bank. What you choose to do, however, should be guided by your values and goals…what you think is most important in your life and what you want to accomplish. Thus, always keep your values and goals in mind when making decisions about how to use your time. Doing so puts you in the position to manage your time most effectively and, if you do, you are likely to experience many of the following benefits:

- decrease procrastination,
- accomplish more during each day,
- feel more in control of your life,
- enjoy your free time because you have more of your work completed,
- earn higher grades, and
- feel less stressed by the constant demands you face as a student-athlete.

In the next section, we introduce you to the "how to" in managing your time.

Performance: Managing Your Time

So what is time management? In reality, it involves the following (Britton & Tesser, 1991; Macan, Shahani, Dipboye, & Phillips, 1990):

- *Short- and long-range planning*. Successful time management involves paying attention to your immediate time use and what you want to accomplish in the future. You cannot focus solely on today or next week and expect to be consistently successful. You also need to know your commitments months in advance. Planning for today requires you to know what is expected of you tomorrow.
- *Being organized*. Although there are many ways to be organized, minimizing distractions and disruptions and focusing on the tasks to be accomplished are common to all. Being organized underlies your successes in athletics, academics, and life.
- *Taking action*. This is where the rubber meets the road. Taking action is the actual commitment to overtly changing your

behavior...doing things differently than you have done before. To make your dreams, goals, desires, etc., a reality, you have to take action; if you don't, then you are just sitting on the sideline and not getting into the game.

As we discussed earlier in this chapter, time management is most effective when planned and implemented with your values, goals, and priorities in mind. If your time use is not matched to what is important in your life, no matter how good you are at managing it, then you will fall short of your goals. Always remember to spend your time in ways that are consistent with your values, goals, and priorities.

Despite the obvious advantages of this skill, many student-athletes do not use it to its full potential. With your mostly inflexible schedules, it is tempting just to follow what others tell you to do: go to practice at this time, training room at that time, classes in the morning, study sessions at night. Don't become complacent by allowing others (coaches, academic advisors, etc.) to schedule your time. If you do, then you've missed an opportunity to take responsibility for your own life. Like motivation, time management is not biologically determined, so you, like everyone else, have the chance to become a more skilled and effective time manager. Time management can benefit you throughout your life, so take advantage of the opportunity you have now to develop these strategies.

Long- and Short-Range Planning

Long-range planning can help you put together the "big picture" of your time demands, whereas short-term planning, which is based on your long-term plans, guides your week-to-week and day-to-day use of time. In this section, we illustrate each approach by examining the time demands and schedule of a freshman wrestler, Jorge.

Ways to Make the Best Use of Your Time

Listed below are different general strategies for using your time most efficiently.

1. Use short- and long-term schedules.

2. Use a to-do list and prioritize your activities each day.

3. Focus on top-priority items on your to-do list.

4. Plan your day so you study when you are most alert and attentive.

5. Build two or three 3-hour blocks of study time into your weekly schedule and commit to those study blocks just like you would attending a practice.

6. Set clear stop and start times for studying.

7. Use 10–15-minute blocks of time you have throughout each day to accomplish a task (e.g., review your notes, create flash cards) or make progress on a larger project (e.g., read a journal article for a research paper, e-mail or call group members to discuss progress on a group presentation).

(continued)

8. Use travel time efficiently and productively. For example, if you learn best by listening/hearing (i.e., an aural learner) and you tape lectures or are able to download podcasts, then you might listen to these tapes or podcasts when you are commuting to school or traveling to and from competitions with your team.

9. Make sure your notes and study materials are organized and easily accessible.

10. Begin projects with the intention of completing them. If you are unable to complete the project, then make a note as to your progress so you do not have to start from the beginning.

11. Study where you are less likely to be interrupted or distracted, such as in the library, an empty classroom on campus, or an off-the-beaten-path coffee house.

12. Complete your low-priority tasks when you are least alert and attentive.

13. TiVo your favorite TV shows so you can watch them at a later time and fast-forward through the commercials.

14. Use relaxation and enjoyable activities (e.g., watching TV, going out, social networking) as rewards for accomplishing your tasks.

15. Whenever possible, handle business on your cell phone or through the Internet.

16. Learn to stay focused and attentive so you do not have to repeat tasks.

17. Run errands efficiently—do not make multiple or special trips. Instead, tack errands onto trips that are already planned, or try to do as many as possible when they are located in the same part of town or your campus.

18. Delegate tasks and responsibilities whenever possible. You do not have to do everything.

19. Prepare the night before for the next day. For example, you might set out your clothes, pack food for a snack or lunch, or get your notebooks and class materials in order.

20. Wait to get a pet until you graduate and are settled in a career. Although dogs are man's (and woman's) best friend, they are extremely time intensive and complicate your life immensely.

21. Use weekends to study. Although Fridays and Saturdays seem to automatically become social times, they can be a secret weapon and a source of pride for those committed to academic success.

Long-Term Scheduling

In any given athletic season, whether you realize it or not, you are engaging in long-range planning. When you start pre-season practice, you know who you will play, where you will play, and when the competitions will take place. You have the season mapped out in advance and have a good idea what you need to do to succeed in each competition. If your sport requires multiple games or matches over several days, then you know this in advance and can adjust your training and preparation to be successful. Unfortunately, long-range planning skills do not automatically transfer to other areas of life, such as academics. When we ask student-athletes when their exams are scheduled, many respond, "I'm not sure. I think I have one in a week or two." These are the same student-athletes who can recite the who, what, where, and when of their competitive schedules. This is a potential problem.

Whether in academics, athletics, or your personal life, you need to know what's due in two months as well as next week. Without long-term planning, you have nothing to guide your week-to-week or day-to-day scheduling. As with goals, your long-range schedule guides your short-term planning, providing direction for how and on what you will spend your time. To use an athletic analogy, long-range planning parallels your overall game plan for competition. It is the basic strategy you want to use against your opponent, such as establishing the run in football, "seven seconds or less" offense in basketball, or running as a pack during the first half of a cross-country meet. Short-term planning is similar to calling the individual plays that are part of the game plan. One without the other decreases your chances of success.

The academic term provides a good framework in which to engage in long-range planning. At the start of each term, it is important to identify the major athletic, academic, family, social, and work responsibilities that you will encounter during that time frame. A long-range planner is not for scheduling your daily responsibilities, such as going to practice or reviewing your class notes, but rather for the events that are not part of your regular routine, such as examinations, athletic competitions, or family commitments. Identifying and scheduling these types of tasks and obligations gives you a "big picture" of your time demands and allows you to better plan each week and each day.

In Figure 3.1, we present an example of Jorge's completed academic planner. Jorge is taking five classes: College Algebra, English, Introduction to Sociology, American History, and Health and Fitness. Your course syllabi will provide you with the important dates specific to your academic requirements. On the planner, Jorge has listed all of his athletic, class, and social responsibilities for the upcoming term. Most of his requirements are spread out over the term, though there are a few weeks (5, 6, 9, and 13) where he has significantly increased academic responsibilities. His athletic competitions do not start until near the end of the term, so until then, he has only practices and conditioning to do. He will, however, be going home on the weekend before his second sociology exam. During final exam week, he has two tests on Monday and one test on each of the next three days. To avoid becoming overwhelmed during these busy times, Jorge will need to schedule extra time during the preceding weeks to study and finish his papers.

The type of long-term planning illustrated by Jorge's schedule offers many benefits, including:

1. You can literally "see" your obligations and responsibilities over the next few months, which is a particular benefit to visual learners. In this case, bigger is better. Your long-term semester schedule can be put on large poster boards or newsprint paper and posted in a conspicuous place (e.g., a bedroom wall), so you can't avoid seeing it.
2. It is organized and provides an easy reference for all your responsibilities. As a result, you are less likely to "forget" about something or let an event/obligation sneak up on you.

"We all have dreams. But in order to make dreams into reality, it takes an awful lot of determination, dedication, self-discipline, and effort."

JESSE OWENS
Olympic Gold Medalist

WEEK	MON.	TUES.	WED.	THURS.	FRI.	SAT.	SUN.
FALL TERM							
1					Sociol. Quiz 1		
2		English Paper 1					
3					Sociol. Quiz 2		
4			Sociol. Exam 1				
5	Algebra Exam 1	History Exam 1			Sociol. Quiz 3		
6			English Paper 2	Racquet. Exam 1			
7					Sociol. Quiz 4		
8			English Exam 1				Trip home to see family
9	Sociol. Exam 2				Algebra Exam 2		
10	Sociol. Quiz 5			History Exam 2			
11			English Paper 3		Sociol. Quiz 6		
12				Thanksgiving Holiday	First wrestling meet (home)		
13		History Paper	Sociol. Exam 3		Algebra Exam 3		
14		Racquet. Practical Exam		History Exam 3	Second wrest. meet (away) Sociol. Quiz 7		
15	English Paper 4			Home Meet			
16	Eng./Sociol. Finals	Racquet. Final	Algebra Final	History Final			

Figure 3.1 Jorge's Academic Planner

3. You know when there are "busy" and "relaxed" times each month, allowing you to plan in advance and always be prepared when an event is planned or an assignment is due.
4. You can use it to better organize your weeks, planning time so you can accomplish your long-term objectives.

To give you the opportunity to begin planning your academic term, you may want to complete Exercise 3.2. Doing this exercise will help you determine the what, when, and where of your academic, athletic, and personal obligations for the upcoming term. Getting a "big-picture"

Exercise 3.2   Planning Your Academic Term

On the blank academic planner (Figure 3.2), list all your major class assignments, athletic responsibilities (such as competitions), family or social obligations, and work responsibilities for the current academic term. If you would prefer to complete this exercise in a less "old-school" manner, then you can use Google Calendar or iCal, a powerful Apple desktop calendar application. Regardless of the technology you use, do not leave anything out. Mapping out your responsibilities in this way will give you a "big picture" of when all these things will occur in relation to one another. If other obligations arise later, then simply add them to the planner when they do. Use Figure 3.1 as an example of how a completed academic planner might look.

			FALL TERM				
WEEK	MON.	TUES.	WED.	THURS.	FRI.	SAT.	SUN.
_/_/_							
_/_/_							
_/_/_							
_/_/_							
_/_/_							
_/_/_							
_/_/_							
_/_/_							
_/_/_							
_/_/_							
_/_/_							
_/_/_							
_/_/_							
_/_/_							
_/_/_							
_/_/_							

Figure 3.2 Blank Academic Planner Form

view of your academic term will put you ahead of the game when it comes to short-term planning.

Short-Term Scheduling

Alone, the academic planner is insufficient for helping you effectively plan your time. You also need a mechanism for translating the information from the academic planner into a format that can help guide your activities week to week and day to day. For example, it is not enough to know that you have two exams and a paper due during the tenth week of the term. You must also be able to schedule the days during the week before the exams and the paper's due date so that you have sufficient time to study, write, review, and revise. You need to know what hours of each day are taken by recurrent activities, such as classes and practice, and where you have blocks of "free time" in which you can spend extra time studying. This is where scheduling your time on a weekly basis can help. Again, an application such as Apple's iCal can easily remind you of upcoming events or exams and allow you to choose the type and time of notification you want from an alarm pop-up menu.

A weekly schedule, regardless of the technology you use, allows you to plan each hour of each day during each week of the term based on your upcoming obligations (and you know what these are from your academic planner!). To most effectively use a weekly schedule, you should plan your time at least a week or two in advance—for example, plan your schedule for the sixth week of school at the beginning of the fourth or fifth week. This approach will ensure that you always have two consecutive weeks scheduled so that no obligation goes unnoticed or unmet. Remember, a weekly schedule will have a limited benefit if you do not look at it each day. In other words, after scheduling your time for the week, let it be the guide for what you do day to day.

To complete the weekly schedule, fill in those activities that generally occur at the same times each day or week, such as practice, classes, fixed study blocks you have identified, or religious commitments. Next, write in the other activities that generally happen each week but may occur at different times, such as eating, study table, or athletic department events (e.g., volunteer activities, CHAMPS/Life Skills presentation). Once you have filled in these times, you should have an idea of your preset commitments for the week. In the remaining time, fill in the tasks that you want to complete for that week. For example, if you have a paper due on Friday, you may want to schedule four hours on the preceding Saturday and Sunday, two hours on Monday, three hours on Tuesday, and two hours on Thursday to write and revise the paper. Whenever you fill out a weekly schedule, make sure you do it in conjunction with your academic planner so you do not forget any obligations.

As an illustration, we present an example of Jorge's schedule for the fourth week of the academic term (Figure 3.3). Before completing this schedule, Jorge reviewed his academic planner to find out what his upcoming obligations were. Because he had an exam during the fourth week (sociology, on Wednesday) and two exams during the fifth week, he had to schedule sufficient time to study. To begin, Jorge wrote in all his academic and athletic responsibilities, specifically classes, practices (including training room time), and study table. (As you can see, these activities take up a considerable amount of time each day.) Next, he filled in his other activities, such as eating, studying, laundry, and meetings. In doing so, he made sure he had planned enough time to study for his three exams. During this week, he scheduled eight hours for history, seven hours for sociology, and five hours for algebra. For

TIME	FALL TERM - WEEK 4						
	MON.	TUES.	WED.	THURS.	FRI.	SAT.	SUN.
6 am	Weight Room	Running	Weight Room	Running	Weight Room	Sleep	Sleep
7 am	Shower Breakfast	Shower Breakfast	Shower Breakfast	Shower Breakfast	Shower Breakfast	Sleep	Sleep
8 am	Review Eng. notes	Read History	Study Sociology	Read History	Review Eng. notes	Breakfast	Sleep
9 am	Eng.	History	Eng.	History	Eng.	Laundry	Study History
10 am	Sociology	History	Sociology Exam	History	Sociology	Laundry	Study History
11 am	See Advisor	Racquetball	Talk/w Coach	Racquetball	Lunch	Relax	Lunch
Noon	Lunch	Lunch	Lunch	Lunch	Study Algebra	Lunch	Watch TV (football)
1 pm	Algebra	Relax	Algebra	Bank	Algebra	Study Algebra	football
2 pm	Training Room	Training Room	Training Room	Training Room	Training Room	Study Algebra	football
3 pm	Practice	Practice	Practice	Practice	Practice	Study Algebra	Study History
4 pm	Practice	Practice	Practice	Practice	Practice	Relax	Study History
5 pm	Practice Train. Rm.	Practice Train. Rm.	Practice Train. Rm.	Practice Train. Rm.	Practice Train. Rm.	Call Home	Study Talk w friends
6 pm	Dinner	Dinner	Dinner	Dinner	Dinner	Watch TV.	Dinner
7 pm	Relax Study	Relax Study	Relax Study	Relax Study	Relax Study	Go out on date	Socialize w/friends
8 pm	Study Sociology	Study Sociology	Study Eng.	Study History	Study History	Date	Study Algebra
9 pm	Study Sociology	Study Sociology	Watch TV	Watch TV	Go out - party	Date	Watch TV.
10 pm	Study Sociology	Study Sociology	Sleep	Sleep	Party	Date	Sleep
11 pm	Sleep	Sleep	Sleep	Sleep	Party	Date	Sleep
12 pm	Sleep	Sleep	Sleep	Sleep	Sleep	Date	Sleep

Figure 3.3 Jorge's Weekly Schedule

his history and algebra exams, he would study even more during the fifth week. Even with this amount of study time scheduled, he still had plenty of time to socialize, eat, sleep, do his laundry, hang out, e-mail, text, watch TV, play Wii, etc. Because he planned in advance, Jorge was able to fit into his schedule everything that he needed or wanted to do.

Managing Your Time through Technology

The number of ways that you can manage and organize your time through technology has increased exponentially in recent years, and there is no reason to believe there will be a decline in these types of options anytime soon. In fact, there have likely been improvements in technology since we wrote this section. In general, mobile devices (e.g., BlackBerry Smartphones, iPhones, etc.) offer tremendous organizational power. The calendar feature includes interconnected daily, weekly, and monthly schedules. The daily calendar breaks down days by the hour, and an item written on the daily calendar is automatically transferred to the weekly and monthly calendar. Recurring events can be programmed into your calendar so they automatically show up in your schedule at the correct time each week, month, or year. The mobile devices interface easily with your computer. Mobile devices and your computer can also provide an alarm function that will remind you of important upcoming events. To complement your calendars, mobile devices include a prioritized to-do list to help you focus on important activities. After writing in your tasks, indicate if it is a 1, 2, or 3 priority, then check off the accompanying box when it's completed. There are even applications that allow users to share notes by e-mail and sync notes between your mobile device and computer.

Mobile devices and wireless technologies also allow you to transfer information to and from your computer, updating the information on either device. With your mobile device, you also can take along electronic files, such as an upcoming English paper, wherever you go. With the aid of some specific applications, you can download the file from your computer onto your mobile device and work on it whenever you have spare time. Spreadsheets, presentations, music, video clips, podcasts, and many other files can be transferred to your mobile device as well, giving you the power to take your work with you anywhere you go. If your university participates, then iTunes U will allow you to listen to your professor's lectures and view digital lessons. Mobile learning and constant access to information is a permanent part of the academic landscape.

Mobile devices offer other convenient capabilities such as a contact list, memo files, e-mail, GPS tracking, Web applications, social networking, and personal finance management. With the capability of storing hundreds of contacts, you can easily edit and search for phone numbers, e-mail addresses, and street directions. You can send and receive e-mail on your mobile devices. Personal finance applications can help you track your spending by allowing you to self-monitor your expenditures as you make them. Mobile devices and applications offer an endless array of options to assist with time management.

Before purchasing a mobile device, carefully assess your needs. What will you use it for? What capabilities will you need? What is your price range? Then talk to someone who owns one and have him or her show you how it works. Further, you may want to consult independent sources, such as *Wired* magazine or Digg, a social news website, that provide information and reviews on different mobile devices. When you have identified the mobile device that is right for you, research how much it costs through retail outlets and Web-based sources to find the lowest price possible.

Whether you choose a mobile device or a more traditional paper-and-pencil organizer, find a time-planning system that works for you so you'll use it on a regular basis. Used correctly, any organizational system not only will help you develop an orderly schedule but will also help you stay on track so you can be successful and attain your goals.

The mechanism that you use to schedule your time each week can vary. Some people prefer "day planners" or "personal calendars," which can be purchased from your school's bookstore. Some will gravitate toward high-tech options (see "Managing Your Time through Technology"). Others prefer something old-school like the blank weekly schedules provided here (Figure 3.4). Choose the system that fits your personality and will work best for you, and then USE IT!

In working with student-athletes on time management, we have heard many say that a weekly schedule is too rigid and too hard to follow hour to hour: "Things come up." "Schedules need to be changed." "Interruptions occur." True, these things do happen! When they do, adjust your schedule as needed. Do not, however, let interruptions become an excuse not to schedule your time, focus on your work, or put in the time needed to reach your goals. Like goal setting, managing your time each week and each day requires self-responsibility. Again, ask yourself whether your use of time reflects what you have stated is important to you. If you have scheduled time to work on your paper or study for an exam, then don't put yourself in a position where you can be disturbed or distracted by the TV, your cell phone, or your Facebook home page. Even though you may be interrupted on occasion, it is still important to have an idea of how you want to spend the time you have each day. Without such planning, you will be more likely to procrastinate and fail to get done what you need to do.

To-Do Lists

A *to-do list* is another type of short-term planner that can remind you of what you want to accomplish in a given day. These lists can be used by themselves or in conjunction with weekly schedules. For example, some student-athletes develop weekly schedules, but only carry a to-do list of the things they want to accomplish on a given day. If you use a mobile device, then there are many to-do applications that can be easily utilized (see "Managing Your Time through Technology" for more information). To-do lists can be very useful for individuals who have fairly fluid schedules and are able to structure their days without having each hour pre-planned.

On your to-do list, prioritize the tasks you want to complete. Prioritizing your tasks reminds you of what is important and helps you stay focused on what you need to accomplish. Without prioritizing, you may work on tasks that are relatively easy, such as making a phone call or getting your hair cut, but not crucial to reaching your goals. It is funny how entertaining and important cleaning out the refrigerator becomes during the study week prior to final exams. Carrying out low-priority tasks gives you a temporary feeling of satisfaction because you can cross many tasks off your list. In the end, though, this approach will leave you feeling frustrated when you fail to finish high-priority items that are related to achieving your goals. Below, we offer a straightforward system for prioritizing your tasks:

1. A very important task; I must get it done.
2. A somewhat important task; I should attend to it soon.
3. A not very important task; I can let it go for now.

> "Only a man who knows what it is like to be defeated can reach down to the bottom of his soul and come up with the extra ounce of power it takes to win when the match is even."
>
> MUHAMMAD ALI
> *World Champion, Boxing*

    A Student Athlete's Guide to College Success

TIME	WEEKLY SCHEDULE						
	MON.	TUES.	WED.	THURS.	FRI.	SAT.	SUN.
6 am							
7 am							
8 am							
9 am							
10 am							
11 am							
Noon							
1 pm							
2 pm							
3 pm							
4 pm							
5 pm							
6 pm							
7 pm							
8 pm							
9 pm							
10 pm							
11 pm							
12 pm							

Figure 3.4 Blank Weekly Schedule Form **(Photocopy this page for use again later)**

Assign a priority number to each task on your to-do list. Priority 1 tasks are those that are crucial to your success and play an integral part in your reaching your goals. These are tasks that you must complete; that generally take focused, intense time; and/or that need to be attended to immediately. Examples of Priority 1 tasks might be studying for your math exam, finishing your biology lab paper, or paying your rent on time so you are not evicted. Always focus your time and energy on these Priority 1 tasks. If you assign a task a 3, you are, in essence, saying that it is not crucial at this time—that leaving it uncompleted will not make a difference. If you give a task a 3 rating, then do not spend time on it until your higher-priority tasks are completed. Remember, your priority ratings can change from day to day. What you rated as a 3 on Monday may become a 1 by the end of the week. What is important is that your ratings reflect the priority of each task in relation to your long-range plans and weekly schedule. For example, if you have an exam on Thursday, and one of your goals is to earn at least a "B" in that class, then you will likely want to give studying for that test a priority of 1.

In Figure 3.5, we present an example of Jorge's to-do list for the Tuesday of the eleventh week of the academic term. On this day, he has his regular classes, practices, and study table. His third English paper is due the next day, so he needs to revise his first draft, type the revised draft, and print out the final version. He also wants to talk with his coach about how he has been practicing, go to the bank, register for next term, read his sociology assignment, and spend some time with his girlfriend. Although there is a lot he wants to accomplish, his number-1 priority is to finish his English paper. After that, he has listed talking with his coach and spending time with his girlfriend as his next most important tasks. He has rated the remaining items as 3s because they are not crucial at this time.

To Do List......

Revise paper in the morning (1)

○ *Type final draft of paper at night (1)*

Read sociology (3)

Attend all classes (1)

○ *Register for classes (3)*

Talk with coach (2)

Go to bank (3)

○ *See girlfriend (2)*

Practice (1)

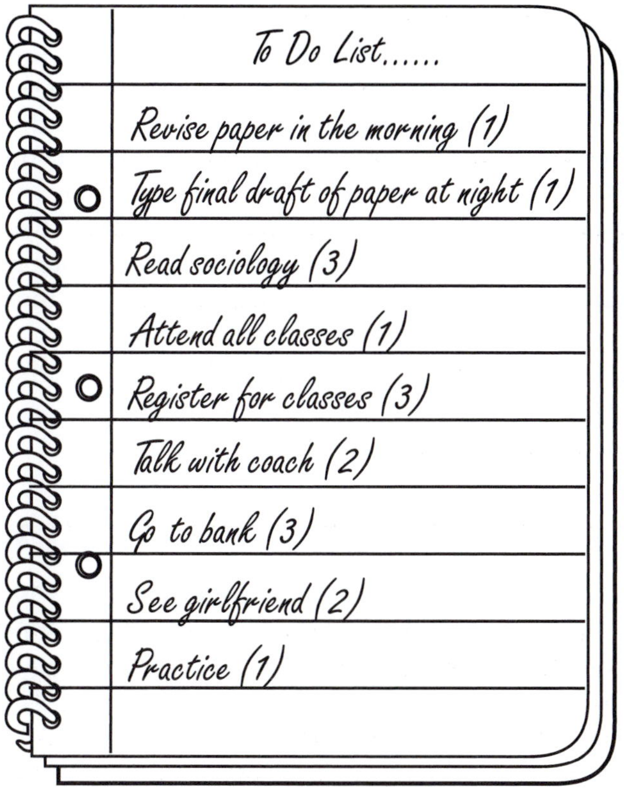

Figure 3.5 Jorge's 'To Do' List for Tuesday

Being Organized

Although not as concrete as making a scheduling or a to-do list, being organized is a key part of successful time management. In fact, your organization is intimately tied to the effectiveness of your scheduling. For example, if you are not organized and fail to load all of your events, activities, and obligations into your calendars, then your schedules will be severely limited. To avoid this problem, as soon you become aware of any new events, put them into your scheduling system (both long- and short-term plans). If the event/obligation is far in the future, then put it on your academic planner. If it is in the next couple of weeks, make sure it gets onto your weekly schedules or to-do lists. Do not put off scheduling these new tasks, because if you do, you may forget them or not be able to allocate enough time to complete them when they come around.

Taking Action

Having schedules and being organized are necessary but not sufficient strategies to successfully manage your time...you also must implement your plans. No matter how elaborate or organized your schedule, if you do not put it into practice, then you will not complete your tasks and accomplish your goals.

© Nicholas Moore, 2009 / Used under license from Shutterstock.com

In order to get started, your intentions need to move from the hopeful or wishful sounding (e.g., "I'm thinking about making some changes soon in the way I use my time.") to the more obligatory or "ought-to" sounding ("I intend to start my time-management plan immediately because it is clear if I don't, then I won't be very successful academically while I'm in college."). If this sounds a lot like our earlier mention of Nike's old advertisement campaign, "Just do it," then you're right. The message that underlies that ad campaign was that once you did it, then you felt better. And in the case of time management, we're offering you the same message. If you'll get started, then you'll feel more empowered and intentional about your approach to school. Those feelings in turn will lead to increased self-confidence and motivation. Later in the chapter, we provide some additional suggestions for how to stop procrastinating and take action.

Preparation: What Is Procrastination?

Procrastination is engaging in something other than what you need to be doing to reach your goals or to accomplish an important task. Procrastination is not the same as doing nothing. It is simply doing things other than what is needed. Thus, procrastination is not defined by your behavior at a given time, but by the *purpose* of the behavior at that time. If your intent is to delay working on your business class project that will highly influence your final grade, then doing your laundry (an important task in its own right) could be procrastination. Everyone procrastinates to some extent, and research indicates that up to 70% of students are chronic procrastinators (Schouwenburg, 2004). A common characteristic of procrastinators is poor time-management skills and, not surprisingly, students who report higher levels of procrastination also tend to have lower grades (Beswick, Rothblum, & Mann, 1988).

In our work with student-athletes, we have noted some common behaviors or activities that are forms of procrastination. Do you use any of these to procrastinate?

- Watch TV, listen to your iPod, text or talk on the cell phone
- Relax at the student union—talk with friends, play pool, people watch, be seen
- Hang out in the training room
- Surf the Internet, download music
- Visit a friend, wander around a store, such as Target or Wal-Mart
- Do laundry
- Twitter, check your e-mail, update your Facebook profile
- Read *ESPN The Magazine,* fan blogs
- Play video games (e.g., Guitar Hero, Madden NFL, Nintendo Wii)
- Do extra workouts
- Go out with friends
- Sit in the dining hall and visit with friends
- Watch extra game film or visit your coaches

Are these behaviors bad? Not necessarily. They become problematic when they interfere with your working toward and achieving your goals. You don't have to eliminate them from your life. Instead, increase your awareness of why you engage in the behaviors you do so you can make good choices about how you are going to spend your time.

Prepare: Why Do People Procrastinate?

People procrastinate for many reasons, including:

- *Fear of failure*: "If I try to take this exam, then I am going to do terribly, and I'll probably get an F."
- *Fear of the unknown*: "I have no idea what the instructor wants for this paper."
- *The task is overwhelming*: "I don't know where to start. I have a ten-page paper for my English class due next week and two exams this week. I don't know how I am going to find the time to get organized, let alone write and study."
- *Fear of looking foolish*: "What if I work really hard on improving my play but still perform poorly in competition?"
- *Perfectionism*: "I have to make an "A" on the chemistry lab, but it's going to take so much time to do it right I don't even know if I want to start."

"Procrastination is like masturbation. At first it feels good, but in the end, you are only screwing yourself."

AUTHOR UNKNOWN

- *Rebelliousness*: "This world history class is boring and has nothing to do with my life or career goals. Why should I have to take it?"
- *Fear of success*: "If I earn an 'A' on this paper, then are others always going to expect me to maintain this level of performance?"
- *Don't know how to do the task*: "I've never written a college paper before, and my instructor didn't give any guidelines except to go to the library. I have no idea how to research a paper at a university library."
- *Low self-efficacy*: "It takes me a long time and a lot of effort to read. I'm just not very good at it so why even bother trying— I just never seem to understand."
- *Just being lazy*: "I just don't want to do the work."

Why do you procrastinate? To determine why, you have to look inside and be honest with yourself to recognize the reasons. Are you afraid? Do you feel overwhelmed? Do you feel conflicted? Is your self-efficacy low? Are you just being lazy? Whatever the reason, acknowledge it and get started. And if you can't identify the reason, then you still need to get started. There are times when finding out "why" we do or don't do something has minimal impact on whether we make the change or not. Sometimes you can eliminate the procrastination through good planning and self-responsibility. For example, if you fear failure, then there are many strategies that would decrease the likelihood of your failing, such as setting goals, starting and following a study schedule, getting a tutor, or requesting help from the instructor. With each success you have, your reasons for procrastinating are likely to diminish. Overcoming your procrastination, though, means making the decision to directly confront what you are avoiding, whether it is fear, conflict, or not having enough information. To help you become more aware of your procrastination patterns, you may want to complete Exercise 3.3.

Exercise 3.3   *Procrastination Patterns*

1. Identify and list the top three areas/activities in your life in which you procrastinate (that is, the areas in which you put off doing work, such as studying).

_____

_____

_____

_____

_____

2. For each area you identified in question 1, list what you do when you procrastinate.

_____

_____

_____

_____

_____

3. For each area you identified in question 1, identify possible reasons for your procrastination.

_____

_____

_____

_____

_____

4. Finally, think about why and how you procrastinate (from questions 2 and 3) and then identify possible solutions for overcoming your procrastination.

_____

_____

_____

_____

_____

Perform: Strategies for Defeating Procrastination

Like in sports, where there can be many different game plans that can lead to success, there is no single way to overcome and defeat procrastination. By completing Exercise 3.3, you now have some ideas of how and why you procrastinate. The key now is selecting and implementing strategies that may work for you. In this section, we offer some general strategies, many of which involve managing your time effectively.

- *Learn to say "No."* Delaying gratification is a key to success in all areas of life. Because you cannot do everything you want, you have to be self-responsible and make time choices that will help you reach your goals.
- *Take responsibility for yourself, your behaviors, and your thoughts.* Don't let procrastination rob you of your goals by learning to control your thoughts, feelings, and behaviors to maximize your success. Successful people have a habit of doing the things that people who fail don't like to do, like getting up early to finish a reading assignment.
- *Do "boring" and challenging schoolwork when your attention is best.* Tackle your highest-priority tasks when you are most alert and can maintain your focus and concentration.
- *Don't overplan.* Scheduling too many activities can be overwhelming and can make it hard to stick to your time plan. Maintain a schedule that is realistic and manageable.
- *Refocus when interrupted.* Life happens, and when it does, you will need to refocus on your plans and not allow a disruption to become an excuse not to do your work.
- *Practice, practice, practice.* With each success sticking to a schedule, saying "No" to others, and handling distractions comes increased confidence in your ability to control your time.
- *Develop a study routine.* Establish times in your schedule when you study every week because, like any other routine or habit, once developed it can be hard to break. (Think about your practice schedule.) Also, study in places that are generally free from distractions and conducive to learning, like your school's library or your athletic department's academic center. Studying in the same location creates a mental and physical association that being in this place means it is time to study.
- *Continually ask yourself, "What is the best use of my time right now?"* This question, developed by noted time expert Alan Lakein (1973), can help you remain focused and make sure you accomplish your tasks.
- *Get enough sleep.* Intelligent athletes know the importance of recovery from intense training, and its impact on overall performance. Sleep is a big part of it. The same is true regarding a student's ability to study for and perform on exams. If you are tired, then you are less likely to put forth the effort needed to be a successful student.
- *Face your fears.* There are many reasons why people procrastinate, and it may be to your advantage to discuss these fears with a trusted teacher, academic advisor, or one of the counselors at your school. These professionals can help you resolve your fears and thus stop procrastinating.

- *Use effective long- and short-term time-management strategies.* As we have discussed, find the ones that work for you and then implement them on a daily basis.
- *Just do it. Stop whining.* The more you put things off, the greater the task seems, the more your anxiety increases, and the more you have to deal with deadline pressures. Sometimes you simply have to fight every impulse you have to avoid your work and get started on the task at hand. Once you do, you may find it easier to get started in the future.

Post-Game Review

Whether you consider yourself a bad time manager or even a procrastinator, you can improve your ability to control your time (and your life) if you implement the ideas discussed in this chapter. As you successfully complete academic, athletic, or personal tasks, your confidence in your ability to manage your time and reach your goals will likely increase. By developing your confidence and your time-management skills while in college, you increase your chances for success throughout your life, because so much depends on the ability to use time effectively.

Thinking Critically about Time Management

1. Summarize what you now know about time management and procrastination based on the information presented in this chapter.

_____

_____

_____

2. What additional questions do you have about time management and procrastination and how to use these skills?

_____

_____

_____

Exercise 3.4   Monitoring Your Time

To become more effective in managing your time, you must first increase your awareness of the way you spend it. In general, many students underestimate the time they spend on leisure activities, such as watching TV or going out with friends, and overestimate the time they devote to studying. Although as a student-athlete you may have a good idea of where your time goes, in this exercise you can determine exactly how much time you spend on any given activity during a week of your life. Using the Time Awareness Form (Figure 3.6), keep track of the way you use your time each day during a one-week period. Although it is difficult to account for every minute of every single day, it is possible to obtain an overall picture of the way you use your time. Thus, as accurately as you can, record how you spend each 30-minute period of each day for the next week. Ideally, it would be even better to keep track of your day in 15-minute intervals since we've already stated that these small chunks of time can be important when used conscientiously. At the end of the week, add up the time you spent on each activity and record those amounts on the Time Awareness Summary Form (Figure 3.7). Remember, there are 168 hours in a week, so account for them all.

3. What conclusions can you draw about time management and procrastination, and how they might help you be a more effective and successful student and athlete?

_____

_____

_____

TIME	TIME AWARENESS FORM						
	MON.	TUES.	WED.	THURS.	FRI.	SAT.	SUN.
6:00 - 6:30 6:30 - 7:00							
7:00 - 7:30 7:30 - 8:00							
8:00 - 8:30 8:30 - 9:00							
9:00 - 9:30 9:30 - 10:00							
10:00 - 10:30 10:30 - 11:00							
11:00 - 11:30 11:30 - NOON							
NOON - 12:30 12:30 - 1:00							
1:00 - 1:30 1:30 - 2:00							
2:00 - 2:30 2:30 - 3:00							
3:00 - 3:30 3:30 - 4:00							
4:00 - 4:30 4:30 - 5:00							
5:00 - 5:30 5:30 - 6:00							
6:00 - 6:30 6:30 - 7:00							
7:00 - 7:30 7:30 - 8:00							
8:00 - 8:30 8:30 - 9:00							
9:00 - 9:30 9:30 - 10:00							
10:00 - 10:30 10:30 - 11:00							
11:00 - 11:30 11:30 - 12:00							

Figure 3.6 Blank Time Awareness Form **(Photocopy this page for use again later)**

| TIME AWARENESS SUMMARY FORM ||
ACTIVITY	HOURS SPENT
School (Classes)	
Studying	
Practices	
Competitions	
Training Room	
Watch TV	
Eating	
Sleeping	
TOTAL	*168*

Figure 3.7 Blank Time
Awareness Summary Form
**(Photocopy this page for use
again later)**

Achieve IT! Setting Time Goals

1. From the results of Exercise 3.4 and your Thinking Critically responses you
have a better idea of the way you spend your time in a given week. Discuss
your reactions to what you learned about how you spend your time.

2a. Based on your time-awareness results, choose one area in which you
would like to change the way you spend your time. For example, you may
have discovered that you spent only 6 hours studying, but 25 hours relaxing,
going out, and watching TV. Or you may have found that you sleep 75 hours

per week, but do most of it on the weekend and end up feeling tired much of the time. Indicate the area(s) you would like to change.

2b. From this list, choose the area that you would most like to change. For example, you may have decided that increasing your study time and decreasing your leisure time would help you to be more successful academically. Indicate below your goal for the coming week in terms of the time you will spend in the area you identified as most important. Remember, your goal should be specific and measurable.

Short-Term Goal: _____

Long-Term Goal: _____

2c. Indicate what you will have to do to reach this goal. For example, if your goal is to increase the number of hours you study to 15 per week, your behavioral strategy may be to study at the library, find a serious study partner, schedule time to study on Sunday afternoons, and/or unplug your TV.

Goal attainment strategy: _____

_____

2d. What obstacles might you face as you work toward this goal? What strategies might you implement to either keep these obstacles from occurring in the first place or minimize their effect when they do occur?

Obstacles: _____

Strategies: _____

3. With your goal attainment strategy and obstacles in mind, schedule your time for the next week using either a weekly schedule (electronic or paper), a day planner, or a series of to-do lists. If you use a weekly schedule or a day planner, then begin by filling in all your fixed tasks, such as classes and practices, and then put in any other responsibilities that you have for that week. With the remaining "free time," schedule each day so you can reach the goal you wrote in above. If you use a to-do list, then list and prioritize the tasks you want to complete each day. During the next week, use either your weekly schedule or your to-do lists to guide you as to how you will spend your time each day. Pay attention to how well you are able to follow your time-management strategies.

4. When you have finished the week of scheduling your time, determine whether or not you were able to meet your time goal. Did you change the way you use your time? Why or why not? If you were not successful, then what might you need to do differently to make sure you are using your time as you want?

Chapter 3 Review Questions

1. Learning to manage your time can help you to

   a. Feel more relaxed and in control of your life.
   b. Enjoy your "free time" more.
   c. Reduce your procrastination.
   d. A and C.
   e. All of the above.

2. Time management involves

   a. Long-range scheduling.
   b. Being organized.
   c. Having low self-efficacy.
   d. A and B.
   e. All of the above.

3. List three priorities in your life and discuss the ways in which you are working toward them.

4. Each day that you use a to-do list, your goal should be to complete as many number-1 tasks as possible. (True or False)

5. Which of the following is *not* a potential form of procrastination?

   a. Doing the laundry.
   b. Talking with your coaches.
   c. Doing "research" on the Internet.
   d. B and C.
   e. All are potential forms of procrastination.

6. A primary reason that students cite for their being unsuccessful academically is

   a. Not being smart enough.
   b. Having ineffective teachers.
   c. Not using their time well (procrastinating).
   d. Not using study groups.

7. When you are using a weekly schedule or a day planner, the first thing you should do is to fill in your preset time demands. (True or False)

8. List three reasons that people procrastinate.

9. Before making any changes in how you actually use your time, you should

   a. Buy a mobile device and get organized.
   b. Talk with your academic advisor about your semester schedule.
   c. Monitor your time for a week or two to determine how you actually spend your time.
   d. Increase your self-efficacy.

10. You should schedule your studying at different times each day and each week so you don't fall into the rut of a set routine. (True or False)

11. In general, students who procrastinate earn grades that are

   a. Lower than students who do not procrastinate.
   b. Higher than students who do not procrastinate.
   c. The same as students who do not procrastinate.

12. To reduce procrastination, student-athletes might

   a. Learn to say "No" to time requests from others.
   b. Schedule time for only the most important tasks each day.
   c. Just get started on the task, even if they do not feel motivated.
   d. All of the above.

4 | Establishing the Foundation for Success

Motivation and the Process of Change

Game Plan:

n this chapter, you will earn:

- About the social, emotional, and cognitive factors that affect motivation

- How optimism and pessimism influence your motivation

- To recognize what motivates you

- How to increase your motivation

- About the stages of change and that you can make positive changes in your life

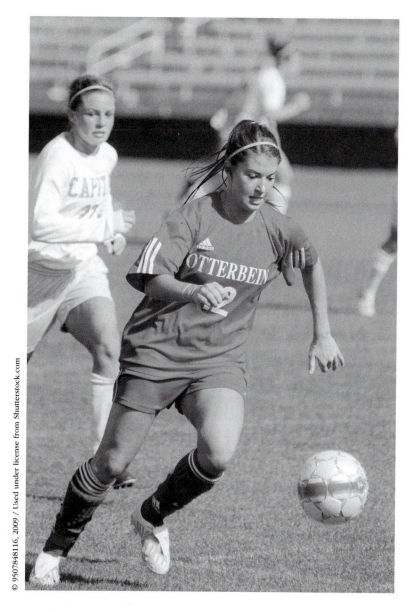

"There is no shoulda, coulda, woulda. If you shoulda and coulda, you woulda."

PAT RILEY
Basketball Coach

Self-Assessment—Perceive It!

Read the following statements and place a checkmark next to each one you generally do. For you to change and develop new and effective academic, athletic, and personal strategies, you must be accurate in your self-perception. So, be honest in how you answer each question.

1. I usually start a task right away, even if I'm not sure how well I'll perform. _____

2. When I am successful at something, I don't become stressed or upset when others expect me to do even better in the future. _____

3. I can meet the expectations of others and still be independent. _____

4. The effort I put into anything I do is more important than the outcome I achieve. _____

5. If I fail at something, then it is easy for me to try it again. _____

6. I usually know the steps to take in beginning a major task, such as breaking it down into smaller steps. _____

7. I usually know why I act or behave the way I do. _____

8. I usually do things because I want to, not because someone else expects me to or is going to reward me in some way. _____

9. My motivation is under my control. _____

10. When I want to make changes in my behavior, I usually plan my actions first. _____

Take a moment to review your responses. How many items did you check? Each one you checked represents a current strength. Now consider the items you did not check. These represent areas where focus and growth are needed. Now, to summarize your self-perception, complete the following statements:

1. My areas of strength are:

_____

2. The areas I need to improve are:

_____

As you read this chapter and participate in your classes, keep your strengths and areas of improvement in mind. At the end of the chapter, you will have the chance to set a goal related to these areas. Achieving these goals will help you become a more effective student and athlete.

Introduction

Dante, a sophomore sprinter on the track team, was—in the eyes of his coaches—the embodiment of unfulfilled potential as a student and as an athlete. Dante was enormously talented, setting the state record in the 100 meters in high school and demonstrating occasional flashes of that same brilliance in college. Likewise, as a student, his college entrance exam scores were high enough to gain admission into many select schools in the country, but so far in college, he has struggled to maintain his eligibility. Frequently late for classes and practice, Dante had a habit of waiting until the very last minute to complete any task and always complained that he was just not that motivated about his schoolwork and practices. Dante had some vague long-term goals that he wanted to get a college degree and run track professionally, but he had a difficult time seeing how the monotonous day-to-day tasks of practice and studying were going to get him there. He wanted to simply fast forward and get on with what he viewed as the more exciting stage of his life, the future. It didn't seem to matter that what others asked him to do was for his own benefit or that he usually knew perfectly well what he needed to do. To everyone around him, Dante seemed to be a lazy, unmotivated young man who would never achieve what his abilities suggested he could. In fact, his coaches were so frustrated with him they decided against making him a captain on the team and to not let him run in the upcoming conference championships. Dante's struggles with motivation were clearly quite costly.

For many students, motivation is a mysterious, ephemeral concept; it's either present or it's gone. Although motivation may seem to be an external force that you have no ability to harness, that isn't the case at all. Learning to regulate your motivation is under your control and will be a key to your success in school, sports, and life. We begin this chapter by defining motivation, exploring its role in your life, and offering strategies to help you increase it in academics and other realms. As you will see, motivation is not something that magically appears out of the blue. It is something you can actually influence and regulate! Later, we introduce a model for how people make decisions about changing behaviors in their lives. Through this model, you can determine why you are or are not making and maintaining the changes you want in key areas of your life.

Preparation: Motivation

A primary reason students give for their academic difficulties (and athletes give for poor sport performances) is lack of or less than an optimal level of motivation. Although most students and athletes know when they are motivated, it is still an elusive concept to accurately describe. Its definition also is complicated by the fact that motivation can be viewed from several different perspectives. The definition of motivation can be framed by asking three fundamental questions (Finch, 2002). First, what causes or initiates behavior? In other words, why do some individuals willingly and passionately engage in their classes specifically (and the learning process in general) and others do not? Or, for example, in a family that values athletics, why does one child choose to specialize and excel in a particular sport and other children choose a completely different sport, activity, or nothing at all? The second question relates to intensity. Why do students study hard some days or for some classes and not others? Athletically, why do some individuals work hard in practice some days but go through the motions on others? The third question addresses individual differences in motivation. Why do some students and athletes embrace and seek out challenging tasks, whereas others avoid or look for easier paths or endeavors? Why do students and athletes respond differently to the same motivational techniques employed by coaches and professors? For example, why does one defensive lineman put forth more effort when he is yelled (and occasionally cursed) at whereas another lineman shuts down and gives less effort? In addition to these questions, it is important to consider the role context (or the environment) plays in understanding motivation. For example, why is it accepted for coaches to yell at their athletes on the playing field (athletic context) to motivate them, but instructors cannot do the same with their students in the classroom (academic context)? Clearly, motivation is a complex concept and not simply something we have or don't have!

In order to increase or maintain your motivation, you must take into account: 1) what initiates motivation; 2) what regulates its intensity; 3) what are your individual differences; and 4) how your environment influences it. In this section, we introduce three areas of motivation—social, emotional, and cognitive—that incorporate these

"The best motivation always comes from within."

MICHAEL JOHNSON
Olympic Gold Medalist

four aspects of motivation and discuss how these factors have relevance in your life (Bernstein, Penner, Clarke-Stewart, & Roy, 2007). We present each one separately, but these factors often overlap and interact with one another. This is the simplest place to begin the complicated process of exploring what motivates you. Without an understanding of motivation, you may remain stuck at the starting line, athletically and academically.

Social Factors

Because human beings are social creatures, it is not surprising that social factors are highly motivational. The ways people, such as friends, family members, and coaches, react toward you and feel about you can be influential in determining your actions. The fear of disappointing others often has a significant impact on our behavior. Thus, we are motivated to behave in ways that are pleasing to others, that gain us social status or acceptance, and that emulate our role models. Conversely, we also are motivated to avoid unpleasant outcomes, not upset people who are important to us, and not be perceived negatively. In addition, the media can strongly influence your motivation and what you choose to do. For example, no one questions the power and appeal of athletic shoe or sport drink commercials to motivate you to pursue excellence in your sport or to purchase and use their products. Family and cultural norms and values, such as the importance of education, religion, or extended family, can be social motivators as well. Some student-athletes may attend an in-state college because their families expect them to remain close to home. Others may choose to cut classes because they believe they want to spend time with their friends and that is a rewarding experience. Social motivators come in many forms and are all around you.

Emotional Factors

Positive and negative emotions can also be sources of motivation. Your emotions can prompt you to move forward with your plans and try to attain your goals, such as when feeling confident or happy helps you start studying a week before an exam because you want to earn an "A" on it. But, they also can limit or restrict you, such as when fear keeps you from working on a paper because you are unsure how to do it. Sport psychologists have identified emotional states and reactions that are associated with optimal athletic performance. Although there are obviously individual differences among athletes, some states are consistently related to peak performance or being "in the zone," including: feelings of confidence, high energy, low anxiety, an immersion in the present, total concentration on the task at hand, a sense of control, a loss of self-consciousness, and an altered sense of time (things slow down). Sport psychologists can help athletes identify their optimal emotions and how to maintain them in order to increase the chances of a successful performance. We explore some of these concepts in more detail in Chapter 13.

Cognitive Factors

Cognitions, or how and what we think about, are the final source of motivation. Cognitive motivators are the thoughts and expectations that you have about achievement-related situations, which then define how you behave. There are a number of theories that describe how athletes think about competitive situations, including achievement motivation theory (Nichols, 1992). Simply put, this theory suggests that people think about and are motivated within competitive, performance situations along two dimensions (or they hold two different "goal orientations": task, or mastery, and ego, or performance). Individuals who hold a task or mastery goal orientation are motivated in achievement situations (e.g., practices, competitions, exams) by mastery and improvement of skills in relation to their own past performances. In other words, their goals and thus their motivation is self-referenced. They want to learn and master skills for the sake of self-improvement; their success is defined relative to themselves. They are willing to put themselves in a position to risk "failure" if they think it will help them improve their play or learn. They are motivated by intrinsic factors, such as enjoyment and satisfaction with the effort they put forth. They are willing to be challenged, because they are not afraid of failing, and they value feedback from others because they know that can help them improve their performance. In comparison, students with an ego or performance goal orientation are motivated by performing better than others, by showing mastery (not over a skill) but in competition with someone else. They want to improve because it will allow them to be better than their competitors; their success is defined relative to others. They put forth effort in areas where they know they will "win" and are less likely to risk doing something in which they might "fail." For example, a performance-oriented student would be motivated by the idea of earning the highest grade in the class or scoring the most points on her team.

Your achievement goal orientation determines what motivates you, what you focus on in achievement settings, and how you evaluate your success. For example, if you are task- or mastery-oriented, then your final course grade might not be as important or as motivating to you compared to whether you believe that you conquered the subject material and can apply it in a real-world setting. Similarly, a task- or mastery-oriented student might be disappointed by an "A" grade if she did not believe she was pushed in the class or she had not learned anything. If you are an ego- or performance-oriented student, then you might struggle with your motivation in a class where the final grade was Pass/Fail rather than receiving a letter grade, or if you did not receive any feedback in comparison to your classroom peers.

Each goal orientation has its benefits. A task/mastery orientation can be very helpful in terms of putting forth effort in practices, wanting to learn new skills and improve performances, being willing to take risks for improvement, and being open to feedback that can guide your learning. An ego/performance orientation, on the other hand, might help athletes put forth their best effort in competitions, trying to win the game or beat their opponents. In fact, sport psychologists generally view having both orientations as important in determining an athlete's success. To help you determine your goal orientation, you may want to complete Exercise 4.1.

Now that you understand how social, emotional, and cognitive factors can motivate you, complete Exercise 4.2 to learn more about what specific things motivate you in your life.

Exercise 4.1   Determining Your Goal Orientation

Sport psychologist Dr. Joan Duda and her colleagues developed a questionnaire to measure athletes' goal orientations (Duda, 1989). For each question, circle the number that describes how strongly you agree or disagree with the statement. For example, if you "strongly disagreed" with the second question, then you would circle "1." There are no right or wrong answers, so be honest and respond as it applies directly to you.

	Strongly Disagree	Disagree	Neutral	Agree	Strongly Agree
1. I feel most successful in a sport when I'm the only one who can do the play or skill.	1	2	3	4	5
2. I feel most successful in a sport when I learn a new skill and it makes me want to practice more.	1	2	3	4	5
3. I feel most successful in a sport when I can do better than my friends.	1	2	3	4	5
4. I feel most successful in a sport when others can't do as well as me.	1	2	3	4	5
5. I feel most successful in a sport when I learn something that is fun to do.	1	2	3	4	5
6. I feel most successful in a sport when others mess up and I don't.	1	2	3	4	5
7. I feel most successful in a sport when I learn a new skill by trying hard.	1	2	3	4	5
8. I feel most successful in a sport when I work really hard.	1	2	3	4	5
9. I feel most successful in a sport when I score the most points/goals, etc.	1	2	3	4	5
10. I feel most successful in a sport when something I learn makes me want to go and practice more.	1	2	3	4	5
11. I feel most successful in a sport when I'm the best.	1	2	3	4	5
12. I feel most successful in a sport when a skill I learn really feels right.	1	2	3	4	5
13. I feel most successful in a sport when I do my very best.	1	2	3	4	5

Now, you need to determine your Task and Ego scores by summing up the items associated with each goal orientation and then dividing by the number of items.

Task—Add together items #2, 5, 7–8, 10, and 12–13 and then divide by 7

Ego—Add together items #1, 3–4, 6, 9, and 11 and then divide by 6

Your score for each goal orientation should range from 1 to 5. The closer you are to 5 the more strongly you hold that goal orientation. If you are high in Task, then you likely will be motivated by achievement situations that allow you to learn new skills, improve your performance, challenge you to be your best, provide you with feedback on how to improve, etc. You are likely to be willing to try new things if they might help you learn. If you are high in Ego, then you likely will be motivated by achievement situations where you can demonstrate your ability and superiority over others. You may be hesitant to try anything new, particularly if you are unsure if you will be able to be the best when doing it. Use this information to better understand how you respond in your practices, competitions, studying, and taking exams.

Exercise 4.2 Your Personal Motivators

Take a moment to think about what motivates you in your life. For example, it might be "earning good grades," "having lots of friends," "being happy," or "earning all-conference honors." List motivators in each of the following areas:

a. Academics
b. Relationships
c. Athletics

Next to each motivator you listed, indicate whether it is a social, emotional, or cognitive factor. For some motivators, as we discussed before, you may find that more than one factor applies to it. Once you are done, determine which source of motivation is strongest in your life.

Perform: Motivation and Optimism

Like it or not, most universities look at high school grades and College Board scores (ACT and SAT) as the primary factors in determining admission to their freshmen class. The common belief is that higher high school grades and College Board scores will predict academic success in college. Yet, deans of admissions are well aware that relying so heavily on these data is flawed. Grades and test scores do not perfectly predict academic performance during one's first semester in college. In fact, some students do much worse than would be expected. These are the academic "all-stars" who failed their college courses and were kicked off the team (suspended from the university). There is also a second, even larger, group of students who do much better than the selection process would predict. These students are the equivalent of walk-ons who beat out scholarship athletes for starting positions. So, if grades and test scores are not such great predictors, then what factor could explain the performances of the former academic all-stars and the overachieving walk-ons? Optimism! Those students who did much worse than expected, on average, were much more pessimistic (Seligman, 1991).

According to Seligman, optimists are characterized by their ability to believe that setbacks and defeats are temporary and are confined to that specific situation or case. They look for alternative explanations for setbacks and defeats, such as believing circumstances, bad luck, or other people are the cause. They simply are not fazed by defeat. If they are confronted with a bad situation, then they just look at it as a challenge and try harder. In comparison, pessimists tend to believe bad events last a long time, sometimes forever. These bad events affect all parts of their life and undermine everything they do. Pessimists blame themselves for defeats and believe everything is their own fault. Although it might sound like pessimists take more responsibility for what goes wrong in their lives, unfortunately, that doesn't translate into more effort. They simply give up because they don't believe they can change their circumstances or have the ability escape their misfortune.

There are very few situations in life where being an optimist does not pay off. Optimists get depressed less and recover more quickly if they do. They achieve more than their talent and ability would predict. They enjoy greater physical and emotional health. They experience less stress and get more joy out of life. Research indicates that optimists even live longer. In contrast, pessimism is associated with

Motivational Conflict

Motivational conflict (Lewin, 1948) is probably an experience that is familiar to you. When you find yourself stuck between two or more competing desires or motives and you are unable to make a satisfactory choice, you are experiencing motivational conflict. Student-athletes sometimes say they are unmotivated when they are actually caught between competing motives. Motivational conflict is often stressful and frequently prevents us from taking any action at all. Motivational conflict can take several forms:

1. *Approach-approach* conflicts occur when you are pulled in different directions by opposing goals or desires. Pursuing one goal prevents you from pursuing another (and you would like to pursue both). The process you went through in choosing a college could be an example of an approach-approach conflict. Casey, a basketball player, was heavily recruited by several schools, two of which were very appealing to him. College A offered the prospect of a lot of playing time in his first year, whereas College B had just won the conference championship and was expected to win it again. Both schools were good options, but he could choose only one. Approach-approach conflicts generally become harder to resolve as the importance of the decision increases.

2. *Avoidance-avoidance* conflicts arise when you are faced with two unattractive options. By avoiding one undesirable option, you are forced to choose the other unattractive one. These are among the most difficult conflicts to resolve. Julie, a softball player, faced such a conflict after transferring from a community college to a university. She hated science and foreign-language classes. If she chose a major that did not require her to take many science classes, then she would have to take two years of a foreign language. Because Julie was motivated to avoid both science and foreign languages, she faced a difficult and painful dilemma that had no completely satisfying solution.

3. *Approach-avoidance* conflicts are also quite difficult to resolve because they involve activities that are simultaneously attractive and unattractive. Dante, our sprinter from earlier in this chapter, faced such a conflict in dealing with his coach. On the one hand, he wanted to talk to his coach to find out why he was running in fewer events. On the other hand, Dante was intimidated by his coach, and their interactions were usually stressful and unpleasant for him. Dante was motivated to find answers to his questions, which could only be provided by the coach. Yet, at the same time, he was motivated to avoid the anxiety he experienced when they talked. He could not get the answers to his questions and still avoid contact with his coach. Although sometimes painful or uncomfortable, deciding to approach, rather than to avoid, can lead to personal growth and achievement. You can give your self-confidence an important boost by successfully taking on the challenges presented by tasks you have avoided in the past.

becoming depressed more easily and frequently, achieving less than talent and ability would predict, having more physical health problems and a lowered immune system, finding life less pleasurable, giving up more easily (especially in times of stress or crisis), and converting small setbacks into disasters or catastrophes. Perhaps, when you're sitting at a railroad crossing and a speeding train is approaching rapidly, it's better to quiet your optimism, "Yeah, that train sure is coming fast, but I feel totally positive and confident I can beat that train across the track! This will be a great opportunity to see if I've really learned how to drive using a clutch!" At the railroad crossing, be a pessimist, but in the academic realm (and almost all areas of life), there is every reason to be the optimist.

How do the defining characteristics of optimism play out in an academic setting? We know that optimists believe defeats and bad events are temporary setbacks. An "F" on an English composition paper is bad, but it is not catastrophic. Failures and setbacks are confined to one case or life area. That "F," for example, does not affect how optimists feel about their performance in their other classes. It also doesn't affect their effort in the swimming pool, their relationship with their partner, or their overall mood. It's simply an "F" on a specific paper. Optimists also don't believe that the failure or defeat is entirely their fault. In making this statement, we are not advocating that you solely rely on blaming others or external factors for your poor grades. Optimists look for situational explanations and changeable factors. They steer away from attributing failure to fixed or stable personal factors in themselves that they cannot change. We are suggesting that you look for additional or alternative explanations for your setback. Telling yourself, "I'm stupid" or "I never do well in English" does not enhance your motivation for your next English assignment. Accepting the "F" and seeking other less permanent explanations for the poor performance does increase motivation and the effort you are willing to put forth. "If the due date of the English Comp assignment hadn't changed and landed on the same day as our home invitational track meet, then I probably would've been a bit more focused on the paper."

So, what if you are a pessimist? Are you stuck with that as another obstacle to overcome in your pursuit of a college degree? Absolutely not! The good news is that if you are a pessimist, then you can learn to become more optimistic. An individual's level of optimism and pessimism is not fixed. At the heart of changing pessimistic to optimistic thinking is learning how to argue with yourself more effectively. Dr. Seligman refers to this self-argument as your "explanatory style," which is the way you characteristically explain why events (good and bad) happen. When a good or bad event happens, do you point to internal or external factors to explain what happened? For example, if you set a personal record (PR) and broke your school's record in the shot put, do you explain this good event as having occurred because you got lucky and the weather conditions were favorable (external, uncontrollable factors)? Or, do you explain the PR by thinking that your hard work, total commitment to training, and embracing your coach's suggestions for changes in technique (all internal, controllable factors) were responsible for the breakthrough performance? When something good or bad happens, do you make universal or specific explanations for what occurred? This is referred to as the pervasiveness of an event. In other words, how much of your life is affected by the bad or good event? For example, let's say you have been secretively attracted to a guy in another sport at your school. You've finally worked up your nerve over several months to ask him if he would like to hang out with you, and he just laughs at you. Not only does he laugh at you, he posts his rejection on his Facebook page. If you explained this rejection universally, then you might say to yourself, "I guess I really am ugly. I was so stupid to think he would hang out with me." A more specific and effective explanation might be, "I guess he doesn't have good taste in women. That's his loss." Obviously, if you believed the universal explanation, then this rejection might affect the way you felt about other areas of your life, such as influencing how you feel about your classes ("I can't get this assignment done. I'm just too stupid.") or the likelihood that you might ask anyone else out ("If he rejected me, I'm sure everyone else will, too. Why even try?"). With the specific explanation, you would likely be initially upset by the rejection but be able to move on quickly without it affecting other areas of your life.

Finally, when a good or bad event occurs in your life, how long does it influence you? The optimistic student believes setbacks (e.g., a failing exam grade) are due to external factors, only affect their feelings about that class, and won't permanently affect their ability to be academically successful. Successes and good events, for the optimist, are caused by internal factors, affect other areas of their life in a positive way, and are long lasting. For example, if you make the Dean's List for the first time, then the optimist would allow this successful event to positively influence their feelings (e.g., increased confidence) about the next term. For the optimist, the good feelings associated with making the Dean's List might also positively affect how you train for your sport, interact with your teammates, and treat your partner. As you can clearly see, whether you are an optimist or pessimist has a profound effect on how you engage the world and feel about your place in it; it affects your motivation. To begin to explore optimism and its role in motivation in your life, you may want to complete Exercise 4.3. As odd as it might seem, many individuals do not accurately assess whether they are an optimist or pessimist, so it is important first to get an objective measure.

Although your goal orientation and level of optimism, as well as if you are experiencing motivational conflicts, may influence your level of motivation toward school and your academic performance, there

---

Exercise 4.3   Your Optimism and Motivation Profile

1. Go to *www.authentichappiness.org* and take the Optimism Test that is located in the center panel of the Authentic Happiness home page under Engagement Questionnaires. You will be required to register on the website, but it's a simple and confidential process. After completing the test, you will be provided with results that compare your level of optimism to other college students.

2. In which areas on the Optimism Test were you most optimistic? Pessimistic? Did any of your scores surprise you?

3. Pick two areas in your life, such as relationships, athletics, academics, health, and spirituality, in which you have been particularly pessimistic. In each area, identify the situation about which you have been thinking pessimistically and describe it and your thoughts (explanatory style). Then, for each area, discuss how you can think more optimistically (specifically identifying how you would change your explanatory style).

are other factors to consider as well. In the next section, we introduce you to some potential motivators that may increase your interest and effort in school.

Performance: Motivation and School

Many student-athletes were recruited for college based on their athletic ability, and you may be in school primarily as a way of enhancing your professional prospects in your sport. That is certainly a valid reason to attend college; however, it may not provide you with sufficient motivation to tackle your academic challenges with the same energy you put into athletics.

Many student-athletes claim to be unmotivated in their college classes. Sustaining effort and energy throughout a long academic term can be difficult. Having a clear understanding of why you are in school, and of its benefits, can help you remain motivated. To help you clarify the reasons why *you* are in school, you may want to complete Exercise 4.4.

In addition to the reasons you generated in Exercise 4.4, we provide you with several important reasons why students, in general, would attend college, including life, social, and job skills; knowledge; enjoyment; and self-responsibility. As you read through them, think about why you are in school and how you can benefit from the college experience. The more varied the reasons you can identify for attending

---

Exercise 4.4 Why Are You in School?

1. Think about the top five reasons you decided to attend the school in which you are currently enrolled.

   _____

   _____

   _____

   _____

   _____

2. Now consider your current behaviors as they apply to the reasons you listed in question 1. Are your behaviors consistent with the reasons why you decided to attend college? For each reason, give an example of a behavior you currently engage in that supports that reason. For example, you might have listed "to help me get to the pros in my sport" as a reason for attending college. "Spending extra time watching game or practice films" is a behavior you engage in to support that reason.

   _____

   _____

   _____

   _____

   _____

3. Identify behaviors you engage in that conflict with the reasons you gave for attending school. For example, you may have listed "getting a degree" as a reason, but you may not spend much time studying.

   _____

   _____

   _____

   _____

   _____

4. Before continuing, review your answers to questions 2 and 3. Overall, are your behaviors supporting or conflicting with the goals that brought you to college? If your behaviors tend to hold you back, what can you change to make sure they are more consistent with your educational goals?

   _____

   _____

   _____

   _____

© Andresr, 2009 / Used under license from Shutterstock.com

> "Money was never a big motivation for me, except as a way to keep score. The real excitement is playing the game."
>
> DONALD TRUMP

college, the more motivation you are likely to have to succeed academically.

Life Skills

In college, you will have the opportunity to learn important skills, such as organization, time management, and goal setting, which will benefit you throughout your life. We try to emphasize this crossover of skills throughout the book. Take advantage of all the opportunities you have to learn. Don't shy away from challenges! Remember, you can learn from your mistakes as well as your successes. If you're not failing occasionally, then you're probably not challenging yourself enough or getting outside of your comfort zone.

Social and Interpersonal Skills

In school you will meet a number of people whose backgrounds are very different from yours, which can be fun, interesting, informative, and challenging. Through these relationships, you will have the opportunity to learn how to communicate effectively (see Chapter 9 for more information) and to become more skilled in social situations. You will also have the opportunity to learn how to negotiate with people whose opinions, perspectives, and backgrounds are different from yours. Interpersonal skills are often cited as a major factor in an employer's decision making when choosing from job applicants (see Chapter 12 for key skills that employers are looking for).

Career Skills

Many students assume they will learn career skills only in their major courses. Wrong! Certainly these courses provide you with the vocabulary and basic information that are part of your chosen field; however, the skills you acquire in becoming a successful student—communication, leadership, initiative, and logical thinking—often come from outside your major and will be important in your profession. In some cases, it is the ability to succeed in areas outside of your main interests that shows the self-discipline and persistence that employers value in the workplace. Never lose sight of the fact that employers hire *people*, not majors and degrees, so be sure to take advantage of all the ways you can acquire a wide range of career skills.

Knowledge

There is an important difference between earning a degree and gaining knowledge. You can earn a degree by fulfilling the requirements of your college, but unless you make an effort to immerse yourself in your education, your degree will not be worth the piece of paper it is printed on. The real value of your college degree comes from what you learn and apply in your life.

Enjoyment

College can and should be fun. For some students, however, fun becomes the sole reason for being in school. Who hasn't heard that college is supposed to be the best time of your life? Participating in extracurricular activities (besides athletics), such as joining campus organizations and attending cultural events, is one way to have fun. Your classes, if you approach them with an open mind, can also be interesting and fun. All of these can provide great opportunities to learn about yourself, which can be helpful in choosing a satisfying career. Students often determine that certain classes, books, or fields of study will be boring before they have any contact with them. Instead, be open-minded and you will see that life is full of new experiences and opportunities for self-discovery. For many, college will be a great time your life, but let's hope the best time of your life is always what's happening in the present!

Community Involvement

Another benefit of college is the opportunity it provides to become active in the local community. Many college athletic departments have established programs that make it easy to serve the community in which the school is located. Some colleges have internships and service learning programs in which you can earn course credit for community service. Such activities often provide student-athletes with valuable career development experiences and help them establish a network of influential persons they can turn to when looking for a job. Many student-athletes find these experiences to be among the highlights of their collegiate years. By taking advantage of these programs, you can have experiences that provide personal and academic rewards while you provide important services to others.

Self-Responsibility

College is one of the primary involvements through which student-athletes learn to be self-responsible. Although your coaches, academic advisors, and family will be watching your progress, no one will be there to monitor all your activities and decisions or to bail you out of all your difficulties. You will have to take increasing amounts of responsibility for the consequences of your decisions and actions. You will also have to take responsibility for motivating yourself. Although others can provide some external motivation, external motivators are usually less powerful than internal ones, and their impact tends to diminish when they are no longer present. Internal motivators have a more lasting impact on your behavior and will lead to greater persistence. Learn what works for you and what keeps your motivation strong through difficult times. This means remaining interested and confident when others doubt you, or not letting a difficult class or instructor prevent you from pursuing something that interests you.

"Being a professional is doing all the things you love to do on the days you don't feel like doing them."

JULIUS ERVING (DR. J)
NBA Hall of Famer

Post-Game Review: A Final Word on Motivation

Motivation does not suddenly appear out of the blue; it is an end result of hard work and self-responsibility. The relationship between motivation and hard work is not a one-way street; that is, motivation does not simply lead to hard work, as many people assume. Rather, the relationship is reciprocal: Motivation and hard work increase one another. Working harder increases motivation, and increased motivation leads to greater effort. You have probably noticed that your motivation at the beginning of practices or workouts is not constant. Some days you are "flat" and just have a hard time getting energized. Yet somehow you manage to get started, and you force yourself to push on and work hard anyway. As you do, you may find that your energy and motivation come back. This happens in part because you recognize that you were able to persist and accomplish something despite low motivation. Your hard work led to greater motivation. The same is true in academics. Often, the harder you work in your classes, the more motivated you will be to succeed. Remember when we discussed self-efficacy and goals at the beginning of this book? That is what we are talking about here. You will not always feel confident about a task or motivated to perform it. Instead, you will just need to set a goal and work toward it, letting the motivation *follow* your behavior. Sometimes, the solution to low motivation is "just do it!"—your behavior (hard work) will then take care of your attitude (motivation). This important idea applies to your academics, athletics, and career. If you always wait for motivation to come to you, then you will be spending a lot of time waiting to become successful in life.

Preparation: Understanding the Behavior Change Process

You should now have a better understanding of motivation, but there is another question to address: What prevents students from making changes in their lives? The reality is that change does not just happen. Rather there is a process or stages of change that people go through. From this perspective, when we say that people are not making changes, we mean that they are in the earliest *stages of change*.

Most people focus on the highly visible aspects of behavior when they speak of change. As you will see, change is a complex process that involves a number of stages, some highly visible, others much more subtle, but all necessary for making meaningful, lasting changes. Thus, it may be more accurate to say that someone is in the early stages of the process than to say he is not changing at all. Let's take a brief look at the overall *process* of change. Discussing the stages of the change process will provide a framework within which you can put together the ideas we have explored in this chapter. It will also help you to see where you might be stuck as you try to make changes in your life.

"Know yourself and you will win all battles."

SUN TZU
Chinese Philosopher

To make changes in your life, you need to understand the process of change—that is, the stages people progress through in making change. Prochaska, Norcross, and DiClemente (1994) have suggested a multistage model of the change process, which can be a useful guide. Once you understand the process of change, you will be better equipped to make behavioral changes that can help your academic, athletic, and interpersonal performances. As you read about these stages, you may notice the many parallels between the change process and the stages you progress through in your sport. You may also notice that actually engaging in new behaviors—what we typically think

of as change—is one of the *last* stages of the process. Engaging in new behaviors and sticking with them is a product of new attitudes and beliefs—in short, it results from the preparation you do before you change.

Pre-Contemplation: I Don't Have a Problem

Although it may not seem to be, this is the first stage of the change process. *Pre-contemplation* is the stage where others are more interested in changing your behavior than you are. Not only is it difficult for you to see that there is a problem, but you are also likely to feel resentment when others attempt to point one out to you. At this stage, the primary motivation for considering change is to reduce external pressure. At this point, you may not have been able to develop any positive internalized reasons for changing.

Jerry is a student-athlete who struggled throughout his first term on campus. He came to school somewhat reluctantly, because he had never been a strong student in high school, and he missed being with his girlfriend back home. Early in the term, he began missing classes and tutoring sessions and did not complete his assignments. When confronted by his academic advisor and by his coaches, Jerry denied any problems with his behavior, claiming that "everything was cool" and that he was in control of his academic situation. He told everyone to back off and became angry if anyone suggested that he needed to take a different approach to his academics. He saw nothing wrong with his behavior and was clearly not ready to change at this point.

Contemplation: Maybe There Is Something Wrong

The second stage is *contemplation*. Although you may not understand the nature of the problem, its causes, or how to resolve it, you are aware that there is a problem. When you have reached the contemplation stage, you have accepted responsibility for changing the problematic behavior and are actively engaged in thinking about the problem and identifying a goal. Although you recognize the problem and have some idea of how to resolve it, at this stage you are not truly ready to make the necessary changes. Change involves risk: the risk of giving up problematic, but familiar, behaviors in exchange for new behaviors that offer the hope of improvement but lack the comfort of familiarity. The good news is that you can see the problem. Unfortunately, new behaviors that are implemented during the contemplation stage rarely last.

Laura, a basketball player, understood that she had some academic difficulties that stood between her and graduation. Unlike Jerry, she was willing to acknowledge that there were problems she needed to face. She was able to see some of the causes of the problems and had a good sense of what she needed to change in order to be successful. For Laura, however, making the necessary changes in her behavior meant that she could no longer act in ways that were comfortable and familiar. Cramming the night before an exam and relying on her boyfriend to complete her assignments no longer seemed to be acceptable options. Despite her understanding of the need for change, Laura was not quite ready to take the next steps.

Preparation: Time to Get Busy

In the third stage, *preparation*, you have decided that change is essential, desirable, and not far off. You know what you need to do, you've let others know that you honestly intend to make changes, and you may even have made some smaller, related behavioral changes. Preparation is the stage at which you put together your "game plan" for change, just as your coaches do before competition. Here you work out your plan for what you will do and how you will do it. You gather the necessary resources, decide how you will monitor your progress, and try to get the support of others. The preparation stage is also where you develop strategies for dealing with potential setbacks or disruptions to your plans for change. Preparation is the stage where you finalize your resolution to change, so it is a critically important stage. Just as success in athletics usually depends on a solid game plan and good practices, making successful changes in other areas of your life require preparation.

Pete is a student-athlete in the preparation stage. Like Jerry and Laura, he needed to make changes in his academic habits in order to reach his academic goals. Pete, however, was ready to make plans to change his behaviors. He spent some time examining his situation and figured out specifically what he needed to do differently. With help from his academic advisor, he determined that he had to reduce some of his socializing, attend classes regularly, and meet each week with his advisor to discuss his progress. He also enlisted the support of his advisor, tutors, coaches, and instructors to help him make the changes. In other words, he used sound goal-setting strategies to help his plan succeed.

Action: Go for It

This stage is the most visible. It is the stage where you actually begin doing differently those things you've committed yourself to change and where others take notice of the changes you are making. Although the *action* stage is a visible and necessary part of the change process, it is no more important than the stages before and after it. The relationship between the "pre-action" stages (pre-contemplation, contemplation, and preparation) and action is similar to that between practice and competition. Lack of attention to practice often leads to poor performance in competition; lack of attention to the pre-action stages usually leads to difficulty in the action and maintenance stages.

Megan presents a good example of the action stage. Like the other student-athletes described in this section, Megan had initially resisted the idea that there was a problem with her behavior. She later realized that she needed to make changes and eventually mapped out a plan for change before she took action. To improve her academic performance, she had already committed herself to making a number of changes: meeting regularly with her advisor to discuss her progress; attending her instructors' office hours; studying her notes and readings in smaller chunks, but more frequently; and establishing a regular study schedule. In this stage, she began to make these behaviors part of her daily routine. She also started receiving positive feedback from others who noticed the changes she made.

Maintenance: Keeping It Going

True to its name, this stage involves maintaining and strengthening the gains you made in the previous stages so that the changes become part of the person you are. *Maintenance* involves developing strategies to fight the temptation to return to earlier, problematic ways of functioning. Maintenance also involves periodic reassessment of how you are doing with regard to the behaviors you chose to change. Success during the maintenance phase means recognizing that change is an ongoing *process*, rather than an *event*. The way it works is similar to the way that post-season conditioning and workouts reinforce the skills you developed and the progress you made during the competitive season. Just as you monitor your progress with workouts and conditioning and make any necessary adjustments in your routine, you engage in the same kind of reevaluation and adjustment process when changing your behavior in other areas.

Lamar is a student-athlete in the maintenance stage. During his years in college, Lamar implemented a number of changes in his academic behaviors, and he continued engaging in these behaviors well after initially implementing them. Over time, the behaviors, which had once been new to him, became second nature. In fact, they became so strongly ingrained that he could hardly remember behaving in any other way. For the times when he began to waver, however, Lamar used his support system, including his advisor, to help him get back on track.

If you want to improve your academic performance by changing your academic habits, you now know the major stages of the change process. This knowledge should make it easier to understand the steps you'll need to take and should reduce the likelihood of failure when you attempt to make changes. The process we have outlined here can be applied just as well to other areas, including athletics and your personal

66**Success breeds** success.99

MIA HAMM
Olympic Gold Medalist and World Champion, Soccer

Exercise 4.5   Identifying Stages of Change

You probably have several areas in your life in which you would like to make changes, such as in your relationships, how you approach your academics, or the level at which you invest yourself in athletics, but have not yet done so (or maybe you have tried, but relapsed). Pick two areas and then answer the following:

1. Describe each life area in which you want to make a change.

2. For each area, discuss where you are in terms of the stages of change model introduced in this chapter. Specifically, identify the stage you are in.

3. For each area (and stage), discuss what you could do to move yourself forward to the next stage. For example, if you are in contemplation in one life area, what do you need to do to move to preparation?

---

life. Although we have discussed five stages of change, it is important to understand that change is rarely a linear process, nor does it always follow a smooth trajectory. In reality, as you make changes, you sometimes will cycle back through earlier stages you thought you had moved beyond. Some stages also take longer to go through than others. Understanding the nature of change is an important tool you can use to increase your level of motivation and decrease your tendencies to procrastinate.

To identify the stage you are in for each area in your life where you would like to make changes, you may want to complete Exercise 4.5. If you are in the "pre-action" stages—pre-contemplation, contemplation, or preparation—with regard to a problem, then you are probably not ready to take the plunge just yet. Instead, focus your efforts on making steady progress through those stages. You need to have a solid foundation in place. If you do, you have a much greater chance of making meaningful, lasting changes. For those behavioral changes that are in the action stage, you can feel good about the work you have done. Try to build on the momentum you have established. Finally, for the changes that are in the maintenance stage, congratulations! Your focus will be on creating a supportive environment that allows you to sustain the gains you've made while you turn your attention to other areas of growth and change. This approach is particularly important because the natural external support that comes immediately after someone makes a change will lessen as time passes and others become used to you behaving in this new way.

Post-Game Review

We have discussed two closely related topics in this chapter: motivation and the process of change. Both of these topics are also related to the main theme of this book: setting goals and being self-responsible. Understanding what motivates your behavior is a crucial aspect of being successful in all areas of your life. It will be difficult to monitor and manage your behavior if you don't understand the factors that motivate it. Self-responsibility and the process of behavior change are also intertwined. Preparing for and then making changes in your life can't happen in a meaningful way without self-responsibility. Being aware of what motivates you and the possible motivational conflicts that are present and knowing how the process of change works should help you to achieve the success you seek in academics, in athletics, and in life.

Thinking Critically about Motivation and Change

1. Summarize what you now know about motivation and the process of change based on the information presented in this chapter.

_____

_____

_____

2. What additional questions do you have about these topics and how to use the skills introduced in this chapter?

_____

_____

_____

3. What conclusions can you draw about this topic and how it might help you be a more effective and successful student and athlete?

_____

_____

_____

Achieve IT! Setting a Motivation Goal

1. Based on your self-assessment and your responses to Thinking Critically, select a goal in relationship to becoming more motivated or changing a behavior that you would like to achieve this term.

2. Now identify three short-term goals that will help you reach your goal this term.

3. For the short-term goals, identify the attainment strategies you will need to reach them.

4. List any obstacles you might face in trying to reach these goals and identify your plan for overcoming each one.

Don't forget to make your goal visible and tell others about them, so they can keep you accountable regarding what you want to achieve.

Chapter 4 Review Questions

1. According to Seligman, which of the following factors can serve as an important predictor of academic success?

    a. Locus of causality.
    b. Optimism.
    c. Interpersonal skills.
    d. All of the above.
    e. None of the above.

2. Which of the following are types of motivators?

   a. What others expect of us.
   b. Our thoughts about a situation.
   c. Our feelings about something or someone.
   d. All of the above.

3. List and define the three types of motivational conflict described in this chapter.

4. Motivation always is a precursor to hard work. (True or False)

5. Action is the most important stage of the change process. (True or False)

6. Boris is considering changing his studying habits. He has become aware that studying the night before his exams is not an effective approach and is considering trying to start studying in the week beforehand. It is likely that Boris is in what stage of change?

   a. Contemplation.
   b. Preparation.
   c. Maintenance.
   d. Action.
   e. None of the above.

7. The process of change is

   a. Linear (i.e., we pass through each stage only once).
   b. Circular (i.e., we may cycle back through earlier stages).
   c. All about taking action.
   d. All of the above.

8. Identify four motives for attending school discussed in this chapter.

9. Which of the following is true of an individual who is a pessimist?

   a. Good events last a long time.
   b. Bad events are caused by others.
   c. Good events positively influence other areas of life.
   d. A and C.
   e. None of the above is true of a pessimist.

10. A task- or mastery-oriented student-athlete would be highly motivated by an academic environment that emphasized competition between groups on class projects.

Succeeding in the Classroom
Memory and Concentration

Game Plan:

In this chapter, you will learn:

How the information processing system works, including sensory, working, and long-term memory

Strategies for improving memory and concentration

About types of attentional focus and how to use them effectively to improve your performances

© Nicholas Moore, 2009 / Used under license from Shutterstock.com

"Throughout my life, I have always had the ability to concentrate on what has to be done and not worry about things I can't do anything about."

JOE PATERNO
College Football Coaching Legend

Self-Assessment—Perceive It!

Read the following statements and place a checkmark next to each one you generally do. For you to change and develop new and effective academic, athletic, and personal strategies, you must be accurate in your self-perception. So, be honest in how you answer each question.

1. After studying, I can remember the main concepts and important details of the material I have covered. _____

2. I know what type of studying environment is best for me and seek it out when I study. _____

3. I am not easily distracted when studying my textbook and/or my notes. _____

4. I am familiar with and use memory enhancement techniques to help me better remember course material. _____

5. I involve multiple senses, including seeing and hearing, in learning and studying. _____

6. I can tailor my attentional focus to the demands of a given situation or environment. _____

7. I can identify the primary reasons why I forget information. _____

8. I understand how sensory, working, and long-term memory interact with one another. _____

Take a moment to review your responses. How many items did you check? Each one you checked represents a current strength. Now consider the items you did not check. These represent areas where focus and growth are needed. Now, to summarize your self-perception, complete the following statements:

1. My areas of strength are:

_____

2. The areas I need to improve are:

_____

As you read this chapter and participate in your classes, keep your strengths and areas of improvement in mind. At the end of the chapter, you will have the chance to set a goal related to these areas. Achieving these goals will help you become a more effective student and athlete.

Introduction

Amber was a freshman. Although it was her first extended time away from home, she was excited to be at school playing on the volleyball team. For fall practice, she reported several weeks before most of the other students on campus, which gave her a chance to adjust to campus. During this time, she also took advantage of the college's "summer start" program, which was designed to provide new students with an overview of college life and academics. Along with her freshman teammates, Amber was able to earn college credits by participating in the program during the morning and working out with her team in the afternoon. Academics in high school had not been easy for her, and she welcomed the opportunity to make a fresh start in college. Amber was confident that she would be able to avoid the pitfalls she had experienced in high school. She had made a commitment to stay on top of her studies and pay more attention in class. During the first few days of the "summer start" program, she lived up to her commitment, reading the assignments and taking notes in the class. However, as the pace picked up, both in her "summer start" classes and in workouts, she soon found herself struggling to keep up with her assignments. In addition, the physical fatigue from the increased intensity of the pre-season workouts made it difficult to concentrate during class or to study at night. She soon found herself unable to remember much of what she studied.

Amber managed to make it through the program, but she had the same problems during the fall term, and now they were worse. She didn't like her classes very much; she was traveling to competitions; and her roommates, who were not student-athletes, were noisy, so it was difficult for her to focus on studying. Soon she was overwhelmed. She was behind in every class and could not keep straight what she learned in her different classes. She found herself bored and easily distracted in class. The excitement of the late summer was gone, and she contemplated giving up. Amber reasoned that if she couldn't remember concepts and facts or pay attention to her work, she just wasn't cut out to be a college student.

Amber's situation is not unusual for student-athletes. During each term, you will be expected to learn and recall vast amounts of information, such as theories, concepts, and new terminology. Many instructors will act as if their classes are the only ones you are taking and give you plenty of work! Your professors are experts in their fields, and they will want to share their knowledge with you, whether or not you are interested in the subject. Therefore, you will often have lengthy reading assignments in several classes at the same time. Nor is it unusual to have classes that meet for an hour and a half or longer. Lengthy reading assignments and extended class periods can test the organizational, attentional, and memory skills of the most dedicated student.

In addition to these academic challenges, as a student-athlete you will be responsible for learning an increased number of sophisticated plays, techniques, and strategies in your sport. All of these changes can tax your memory and ability to focus. In this chapter, we discuss concentration and offer strategies for how you can improve your attentional focus, both in classes and competitions. We also introduce memory through the Information Processing System (IPS). Through this system, you will understand how memory works and what strategies you need to use to enhance your ability to retain and recall information. By using the strategies presented in this chapter, you will be better prepared to avoid some of the pitfalls Amber experienced when she entered college.

Preparation: Concentration

Concentration is an essential skill for learning, remembering, and being academically successful. In our years working with student-athletes, many of them have told us that it is difficult to concentrate on school. Interestingly, we have observed that many of these same student-athletes have shown a remarkable ability to focus on sport-related tasks and not be distracted by other external stimuli. You may find this to be true of yourself. This observation suggests that the ability to concentrate often has as much to do with your interest and motivation in the activity as it does with an innate ability. It also suggests that an important part of improving concentration is finding ways to make the material more interesting; that is, you must take responsibility for helping to make the material personally meaningful. By connecting the material you are studying to your life, you will find it much easier to remain attentive and to retain the information.

In addition to making your course work personally meaningful, there are other ways to strengthen your concentration that we discuss later in this chapter. To begin, though, you may want to complete Exercise 5.1 to evaluate your current concentration abilities.

Exercise 5.1   Focus and Concentration

Sit quietly, close your eyes, and see how long you can focus on a single thought. When you are finished, answer the following questions:

1. What was the single thought that you chose?

_____

2. How long were you able to remain focused on this thought?

_____

3. If you were only able to stay focused on it for a short period of time, what distracted you?

_____

4. If you were distracted, then were you able to go back to focusing on your thought? If not, why?

_____

_____

Look at an object or action photo from your sport. If distracting thoughts enter your mind, then bring your attention back to the object or photo. Don't try to actively ignore the distractions or focus on them. Instead, just gently bring your attention back to your task.

1. What was this experience like for you? Describe your thoughts, your feelings, and any physical sensations you experienced.

_____

_____

2. How well were you able to stay focused?

_____

3. If you were distracted, were you able to restore your focus easily? If not, why?

_____

_____

Attentional Focus

Have you ever had a coach yell at you to "focus!"? Most athletes have had this experience. But what do coaches really want when they yell that? Although this type of comment suggests that focus is a unidimensional phenomenon, with one correct way to achieve it, in fact it is not. There are several different types of focus, all of which are important in performance success. Sport psychologists (i.e., Nideffer, 1986) have suggested that attentional focus is based on two dimensions: *broad-narrow* and *internal-external*. The broad-narrow dimension concerns the *range* of informational cues to which you pay attention when you are performing a specific task. In some situations, you need a *broad* focus for success—that is, you must scan the environment and be attuned to a lot of information all at once. At other times, a *narrow* focus is required. A narrow focus involves paying attention to a limited number of informational cues, or in some situations, a single cue. The second dimension, *internal-external*, concerns the *source* of information and the *direction* of your attention. At times, to succeed you must attend to your own feelings, thoughts, and internal states. In other situations, you have to focus externally, on things that are outside of yourself.

Taken together, these dimensions interact to form four different types of attentional focus (see Figure 5.1). Each one, which we describe in the subsequent sections, has its strengths and, if applied correctly, can help you achieve the focus you need to be successful in anything you do. No one type of attentional focus is better than another and, in any given performance, you are likely to switch between the four types. In fact, your ability to focus is determined by how well you apply the attentional type that is needed at that moment. When you are unable to focus or find your attention drifting, generally that means that your attentional focus is wrong for the needs of the performance

66 **Without the concentration of the mind and the will, performance would not result.** 99

ROGER BANNISTER
First Man to Break the 4-Minute Mile

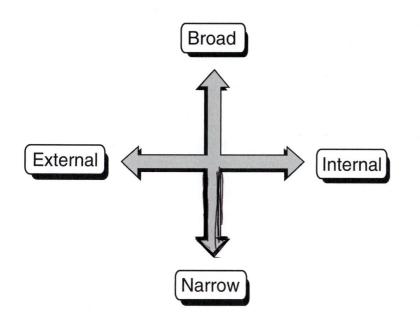

Figure 5.1   Dimensions of
Attentional Focus

at that time. As we describe each type of attentional focus, it will become clear how your focus needs to match the demands of the performance situation.

Broad-External. Broad-external focus is used in situations where rapid assessment and decision making are required. Broad-external focusing involves the ability to quickly and completely scan the environment for relevant information and then use that information to make a decision. This type of focus is in play when you attend to several external stimuli at once. For example, when a point guard sees the entire court while running a fast break in basketball or a quarterback reads a defense before changing a play at the line of scrimmage, a broad-external focus is being used. As you can see from these examples, the ability to take in and process large amounts of rapidly changing information is quite different from the type of focusing involved in situations where your task is to concentrate on small amounts of information or to focus in greater depth.

Broad-Internal. With a broad-internal focus you attend to lots of information, but the information is within you as opposed to in your outer environment. You use a broad-internal focus when you analyze situations and develop strategies. It involves considering and using a wide variety of cues and information in order to develop a plan. A baseball or softball pitcher uses broad-internal focusing when deciding how to pitch to a certain hitter. The pitcher needs to consider factors such as how she did against this batter previously and which pitches she has been able to throw for strikes during the game. Your coaches use broad-internal focusing when they develop a game plan. They have to consider scouting reports on the opposition, the skills of their own athletes, the playing conditions, and their gut feelings. In both examples, paying attention to external stimuli would probably be distracting and disruptive.

Narrow-External. A narrow-external focus is when you pay attention to only a few specific environmental cues. The ability to narrow your focus to only the most important information is crucial so that you are acutely aware of the smallest details and the subtlest changes in the stimulus. Hitting a baseball or golf ball, judging the position of an opponent, or finding your spot during a reverse two-and-a-half off the 3-meter springboard are situations in which a narrow-external focus is helpful. Focusing on other stimuli, such as the butterflies in your stomach or what the fans in the stands are screaming, would be counterproductive.

Narrow-Internal. The fourth type of attentional focus—narrow-internal focusing—is used for mental rehearsal of a specific performance situation, and to monitor and control internal arousal and anxiety. For narrow-internal focusing, you have to shut out external distractions and concentrate only on the information that is relevant to your mental and physical state as you complete a task. Relaxation and mentally practicing the necessary skills for success in a situation involve narrow-internal focusing. In basketball, you would use this type of focusing as you prepared to shoot a free throw. A golfer preparing to putt or a batter preparing to hit a softball would also use narrow-internal focusing. In each case, your attention is on your mental and physical state as you get ready to complete the task. Worrying about girlfriends, boyfriends, or what your coach is yelling at you would interfere with getting the job done. To assess the roles of various attentional foci in your sport, you may want to complete Exercise 5.2.

This model of attentional focus applies to almost all performance domains, including taking exams and studying. For example, suppose you are getting ready to take the final exam in your political science class. The test will be given in a large lecture hall in a building where you have never been. Initially, your attention is likely to be broad and external as you look for the room and check out the seats, the lighting, and the general environment.

Next, in the minutes before the instructor arrives, your focus becomes broad and internal as you plan your approach to taking the test. You decide your strategy will be to answer the objective questions first, focusing on the ones you definitely know. You will make outlines for the essay questions before writing your answers. Once your "game plan" is in place, you might shift to a narrow-external focus as you receive the exam form. With the narrow-external focus, you carefully look over the exam to make sure that all the pages are in order, see if the exam format is what you expected, and look at your watch or the clock to note the time when you are starting. Finally, as you begin the exam, your attention shifts to a narrow-internal focus as you think about yourself confidently taking the test, feeling relaxed and ready to

---

Exercise 5.2   Attentional Focus in Your Sport

Although one type of attentional focus may predominate in your sport, in most performances you are likely to use all four at different points in time to be successful. For each type of focus, describe situations in your sport where you are most likely to use each type of attentional focus.

a. Broad-External:

_____

b. Broad-Internal:

_____

c. Narrow-External:

_____

d. Narrow-Internal:

_____

Mississippi State University
75 BS Hood Dr., Cullis
Wade Depot
Mississippi State, MS 39762
662-325-1576

Barnes & Noble @
Mississippi State

STORE:02040   REG:003   TRAN#:2546
CASHIER:JAMES S

PETRIE/STUDENT ATH
USED
2900495570539   N
(1 @ 107.25)
06NONCOMMISSIONABLE PR 10% (10.73)
(1 @ 96.52)   96.52
    APPROVED FINANC   96.52

TOTAL   96.52
FINANCIAL AID   96.52

******** FINANCIAL AID DETAIL ********
ITEM   EVENT   AMOUNT
PETRIE/STUDENT ATH   000001 96.52 N
******* FINANCIAL AID SUMMARY *******
AMOUNT DESCRIPTION   BALANCE   EXEMPT
96.52 30 MSU MEN S   903.48

MARIO   KEGLER

ACCT #   XXXXXXX05

Amount Saved   10.73

All Textbook sales are Final.

   00   06/01/2016 03:01PM

CUSTOMER COPY

- No refunds on Digital Content once accessed.
- Textbooks must be in original condition.
- No refunds or exchanges without original receipt.

General reading books, NOOK® devices, software, audio, video and small electronics

- A full refund will be given in your original form of payment if merchandise is returned within 14 days of purchase with original receipt in original packaging.
- Opened software, audio books, DVDs, CDs, music, and small electronics may not be returned. They can be exchanged for the same item if defective.
- Merchandise must be in original condition.
- No refunds or exchanges without original receipt.

All other merchandise

- A full refund will be given in your original form of payment with original receipt.
- Without a receipt, a store credit will be issued at the current selling price.
- Cash back on merchandise credits or gift cards will not exceed $1.
- No refunds on gift cards, prepaid cards, phone cards, newspapers, or magazines.
- Merchandise must be in original condition.

Fair pricing policy

Barnes & Noble College Booksellers comply with local weights and measures requirements. If the price on your receipt is above the advertised or posted price, please alert a bookseller and we will gladly refund the difference.

NOOK® is a registered trademark of barnesandnoble.com llc or its affiliates.

REFUND POLICY

Textbooks

- A full refund will be given in your original form of payment if textbooks are returned during the first week of classes with original receipt.
- With proof of a schedule change and original receipt, a full refund will be given in your original form of payment during the first 30 days of classes.
- No refunds on unwrapped loose-leaf books or shrink-wrapped titles which do not have the wrapping intact.
- No refunds on Digital Content once accessed.
- Textbooks must be in original condition.
- No refunds or exchanges without original receipt.

General reading books, NOOK® devices, software, audio, video and small electronics

- A full refund will be given in your original form of payment if merchandise is returned within 14 days of purchase with original receipt in original packaging.
- Opened software, audio books, DVDs, CDs, music, and s
  may not be returned. They can be exchanged for the
- Merchandise must be in original condition
- No refunds or exchanges without or

All other merchand

- A full refund will be given in y
  original receipt.
- Without a receipt, a store credit w
- Cash back on merchandise credit
- No refunds on gift cards, prepaid
  magazines.
- Merchandise must be in original con

Fair pricing policy

go. As you begin to answer the questions, your attention is likely to shift between narrow-external (as you read a question), broad-internal (as you consider all the material you have learned to determine the correct answer), narrow-internal (as you determine the correct answer), and then back to narrow-external (as you write your answer on the exam).

To be successful in your performances, whether they are in academics or athletics, you need to be able to shift your attentional focus to meet the demands of the situation. For example, if you were a basketball player bringing the ball up the court, your attentional focus might be broad-external as you scan the court and determine how you will attack the defense. However, if your coach calls out your name because she wants to give you a play, then your attention will need to shift to narrow-external as you focus on what she is saying. To help you think about how your attentional focus naturally shifts, you may want to complete Exercise 5.3.

Performance: Concentration Distractions and Solutions

Concentration is a complex, but critically important part of your academic success. If you cannot concentrate on what you are studying, then you likely will not learn it and then be unable to recall it when you need to, such as during an exam. Although a mismatch between your attentional style and the demands of the situation is one reason for concentration disruptions, there are others as well. We discuss these reasons here and offer some strategies you can use to overcome them:

Physical discomfort and fatigue. We often hear students say, "I try to sit and study, but it's just hard to sit for very long. My back starts to hurt and my eyes get tired." Finding a place to study that has sufficient workspace and a comfortable chair can go a long way toward improving

---

Exercise 5.3   Natural Shifts in Attentional Focus

1. Think about different performance situations in your life. For example, playing your sport, studying in your room, taking an exam, going out to dinner with your parents, or going to a party. Pick one that has happened recently and that you remember well. Briefly describe this situation/performance.

_____

_____

_____

_____

_____

2. Now, deconstruct this situation and give an example to illustrate each type of attentional focus. For instance, if you choose "going to a party," you might use "when I arrived at the party I checked out everyone who was there and looked to see where the food

and drink were located" to illustrate a broad-external focus.

a. Broad-External:

_____

b. Broad-Internal:

_____

c. Narrow-External:

_____

d. Narrow-Internal:

_____

3. After illustrating each attentional focus with your situation/performance, which focus did you find yourself in most often?

_____

concentration. If you are uncomfortable, then you won't be focusing on what you are studying. Be sure that there is adequate lighting and you are wearing any corrective lenses you may need. If you find yourself fatigued, then stand up and stretch or go for a short walk. Although we do not recommend it as a common practice, in moderation, you also may want to drink a caffeinated beverage. Keep your study sessions to no more than three hours. Beyond that time, you will likely become much less efficient in your learning. Do not read in bed or in a reclined position. Instead, sit upright when you study. If, despite adequate sleep, good exercise, and healthy eating, you are still fatigued, then you may want to consult your team trainer or physician.

Disruptions and temptations. Disruptions to concentration often come in the form of roommates, friends, and family members. Temptations such as television, the Internet, cell phones, iPods, or getting something to eat can all interfere with your ability to concentrate. Although social networks and being "plugged-in" may be important to you, they are not conducive to staying focused while you study. To counteract and minimize disruptions and temptations, study in an environment free of these distractions. If you have a roommate, then you may need to study elsewhere if others are disrupting you. Try the library or the study hall in your dorm, but be careful these locations are frequently sources of social interactions, too. Tell your friends and family your study schedule: "From 7 until 10 P.M. on weekdays, I will be studying." They may be better able to respect your need to study when they know when you will be available for them. Use a signal, such as closing the door to your room or a sign stating "Distracters Will be Severely Punished," that indicates when you are studying and cannot be disturbed.

Personal problems. Student-athletes, like other students, struggle with personal problems that are unrelated to school but still affect their concentration. Directly addressing your stress and anxiety on a regular basis is the best way to combat this form of distraction. Take care of yourself by setting aside time to do things that are relaxing and attend to your personal problems as they arise. It may help to keep a journal or talk to a friend or family member about your feelings. If you are still bothered by stress, anxiety, or sadness, then take advantage of your school's counseling center, which is an excellent resource to facilitate personal excellence.

Deadlines and pressure. At times, you may believe there is so much work to do and so little time that you feel so stressed it interferes with your concentration. During such times, it is easy to spend your energy worrying about the deadlines and not working on the task at hand. To reduce deadline pressure, follow academic term and weekly schedules so that no commitments or projects catch you off guard (see Chapter 3). Break your projects down into manageable tasks and work on them one step at a time. Use a prioritized to-do list and work through the list one job at a time from most important to least.

Daydreaming. When your mind begins to drift from your studying or you become bored, make a note of it. What types of things were you thinking about? Is there a pattern as to when your mind wanders? If you keep track of the times when your attention wanders, then you will get a better idea of how to structure your study time. If you can't get your mind off one thing in particular, then you may need to stop what you are doing and deal with it. Also, spread out your studying and don't extend beyond your ability to concentrate effectively. When you do study for longer periods of time, include short breaks to help maintain your concentration.

Next, we examine some other ways of improving your focus and concentration that are not tied to specific distracters.

Set realistic expectations. Many student-athletes try to do too much at one time… across athletics, academics, and their personal lives. If, however, you are realistic and schedule your time based on your priorities, then you generally will have sufficient time to successfully meet your school and sport obligations. When you don't schedule sufficient time in advance, you often will feel overloaded and stressed when deadlines arrive. You will then spend more time worrying about what you have to do than actually doing it.

Being realistic also involves understanding when you are mentally at your best each day. Identify the times when you are most effective and try to do as much of your work as possible during those times. If you are most alert in the morning, then waiting until late at night to study is probably not the best idea. Because you have different types of academic obligations, such as typing the final draft of a paper (a relatively mechanical task) or studying a week's worth of notes (a task that requires high levels of concentration), you will also want to find out which types of academic work you do best at certain times. If you are sharpest in the morning, then it will be easier to focus on thought-intensive tasks at that time; save the mechanical tasks for later, when it's not quite as easy for you to focus.

Be consistent. Self-responsible learners know that consistency in their work routine and work environment maximizes their ability to concentrate. Consider how your concentration before a competition is affected when you find out that there is a time or venue change, or you experience an injury during warm-ups. You do need some variety in your life to function at your best, but too much variety is stressful and keeps you from developing a sense of continuity. With poorly established routines, you are not efficient with your time because you are distracted and off-task. Your coaches understand this idea, which is why they establish routines for practice, travel, and competition—to let you focus as much as possible on what you need to do to succeed in your sport. The same is true for academics. You will find it much easier to concentrate on completing your work if you can study at approximately the same time and place each day; distractions will be less noticeable and disruptive. Establishing a set study location also sends a message to your mind and body that it's time to get serious about studying, which is the attitude you bring to practice and competition when you reach the field, pitch, or arena.

Active learning. You are responsible for being an active participant in your learning, so work to make the material interesting and personally meaningful. No one else can do that for you, and you cannot blame anyone else if you don't. Your instructors will vary in their ability to make course content interesting and bring it to life; some do a better job than others. Regardless of what your instructors do, it is important for you to listen (or read) actively, ask questions, engage the instructor, look for common themes, and explore the relationship of the material to experiences in your life. When you get good at this, you will begin to have "Aha!" moments, as previously dissimilar courses and material are connected in ways you would not have guessed possible. By becoming an active learner, you are much more likely to concentrate on what you are doing. In your sport, you probably learn the most in situations where you participate, ask questions, and work to understand your role within your team, so do the same in your classes.

Momentum. Finally, you can improve your focus by taking advantage of those times when you are "on a roll" to keep working on the task at hand. If you find yourself engrossed in what you are reading or studying, then keep going. When you are involved in your sport—in a "zone"—you stay with what's working for you, using the momentum to your advantage. You might even lose awareness of time because you are so involved and focused. It may be surprising to hear, but you can have the same experience with academics, if you're open to letting it happen.

Concentration: Some Final Thoughts

Your ability to concentrate and focus can be developed, just like writing, playing a musical instrument, or performing in your sport. It does not come out of the blue, nor is it something that is innate. Learning to maintain your concentration requires the proper environment, the right mental attitude, the proper physical approach, and, above all, a commitment to practice. If you create the kinds of environmental conditions we have outlined and if you are willing to be actively involved, then you will likely see improvement in your ability to concentrate, learn, and remember.

Preparation: Memory

In general, memory can be defined as the mental ability to recall or recognize experiences or information that you have been exposed to in the past. However, as you might suspect, memory is more complex than that, and understanding some of the intricacies of memory will be vital to improving your ability to learn and remember. In this section, we introduce an Information Processing System (IPS) model (Letteri, 1985; Schunk, 2000) to help you understand how individuals attend to, select and process, encode, store, and then retrieve information in memory. In other words, how do individuals learn new information and then later recall it when needed.

The IPS model conceptualizes memory and learning through three independent, but interrelated systems: (1) sensory memory; (2) working memory (also referred to as short-term memory), and (3) long-term memory. The IPS model assumes that all information enters through our basic senses, such as hearing and vision, with the possibility of being acted on and then transferred to long-term memory. Clearly, though, not all information to which you are exposed makes it to your long-term memory, and you could never possibly attend to everything you are exposed to in your environment. In the next sections, we elaborate on each memory system in the IPS (Figure 5.2).

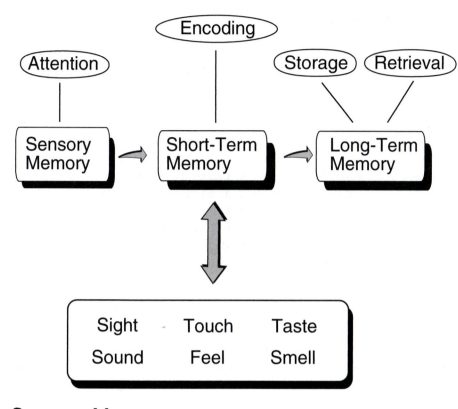

Figure 5.2   Memory, Cognitive
Processes, and Sensory Channels

Sensory Memory

Memory and learning begin when something stimulates one of the
sensory systems, such as sight, sound, or touch. According to Schunk
(2000), each sense has a register that receives and briefly holds sensory input. While in the register, the input is matched to information
that is already stored in long-term memory, a process known as perception. Sensory memories are brief in duration and will rapidly decay
or be pushed out by new stimuli unless attended to and processed in
working memory. At any given time there is far more sensory information available than you can attend to or process. A good example of
sensory memory is the way you can remember the first few letters of a
word long enough to combine them with the last letters and recognize
the entire word (Hamachek, 1995).

Another example is remembering the beginning part of a play while
the quarterback calls the rest of it. Once that information is recognized
(or matched to existing information in long-term memory) it is moved
to working memory where it can be processed. Sensory memory is the
gateway through which all information enters our memory system.

Can You Read This?

"Aoccdrnig to rscheearch at an Elngsh uinervtsy, it deoesn't mttaer in what order
the ltteers ina word are, the only iprmoetnt thing is that frist and lsat ltteers are
in the rghit pclae. The rset can be a total mses and you can still raed it wouthit a
porbelm. This is bcuseae we do not raed ervey lteter by itself but the word as a
wlohe. Initsereg, ins't it."

Attention. Attention is the key cognitive process associated with sensory memory—you can't remember something you don't notice or pay attention to! Attention means being aware of what is in your environment. Some stimuli are more important than others, and of course there is much more information in your environment than you need (or can use effectively) to carry out an activity at any one time. Therefore, part of the attentional process involves making decisions about what to focus on and what to ignore. In other words, you must pay attention to all the information that is "task-relevant," while ignoring what is irrelevant or interferes with getting the job done. Obviously, you engage in this process all the time when you participate in your sport. A basketball point guard, for example, like a quarterback in football, is exposed to a lot of information from the environment. Teammates, opposing players, defensive formations, and so on are stimuli that have a significant impact on completion of the task—that is, running the play successfully. At the same time, crowd noise and playing conditions are also stimuli, but they are likely to become distractions if they are the focus of attention. When they pay attention to what the defense is doing, point guards and quarterbacks take in what they see for future reference. Thus, the first step in forming memories is deciding what information is worth processing further so you can transfer it to working memory.

Working Memory

Working memory (WM) is the active or conscious part of the IPS (like the working memory—RAM—of a computer system). Sensory information that has been selected and attended to moves to WM, which is limited by capacity and duration (Schunk, 2000). The limits on capacity have to do with the amount of information that a person can hold at any one time. Generally, this capacity is defined as 7 ± 2 units of information (Miller, 1956), although the size of the unit can be expanded through a variety of strategies that we will discuss later in the chapter. Expansion can increase the overall amount of information held in WM, but the amount is small compared to the capacity of long-term memory (LTM). Duration has to do with how long information will remain in WM if not acted on in some way. Although information lasts longer than in the sensory memory, if not processed quickly, it will decay. Thus, you need to either actively rehearse (i.e., recite) the information to keep it fresh in WM, or apply deep-level processing strategies to facilitate transfer to LTM.

As a result of these limits, one of three things generally happens to information that is transferred to WM (Dembo, 2000; Eggen & Kauchak, 1997):

- Information is lost if it is not acted on in some way (e.g., rehearsed). For example, you meet several people when you come to a party but then a minute or two later cannot remember the names because you did not practice them.
- Information is "kept alive" in WM for a period of time when it is actively repeated. For example, when a football coach gives a player a play on the sideline, the player must keep that information active in WM until he gets to the huddle and can communicate it to the

quarterback. Obviously, holding information in WM requires constant attention or the information will fade in about 15–20 seconds.
- Information is transferred to LTM when it is processed using deep-level strategies, such as elaboration or creating associations. For example, when you study your textbook by asking questions, discuss topics with a study group, and relate material to information you already have learned, you are transferring information to LTM.

Although each outcome has benefits, the key is to make sure that information you want to learn is attended to and acted on using deep-level processing strategies to facilitate transfer.

Encoding. Paying attention to environmental stimuli is the key for determining what information will enter the IPS, but once done, information must be *encoded*. Encoding is the process of changing the raw information into a mental representation that can be stored in memory. In theory, information can be encoded using any or all of your physical senses or by its meaning (semantics). Most college classes require you to look and listen, so you need to concentrate on both. In contrast, in sports, the way things feel to the touch and the internal body sensations that movements create also are often important ways of encoding information. The methods you use to encode information can have a significant impact on what you remember and how you recall it. In general, the more ways you use to encode information, the better your recall will be.

Sensory channels. There is a parallel between how you take in information and how memories are formed. You can process information by seeing (visual channel), hearing (auditory), feeling (tactile), tasting (gustatory), smelling (olfactory), or through the bodily sensations the information creates (kinesthetic). Each channel provides you with unique and rich information about environmental stimuli, and different people emphasize different channels for gathering, processing, and recalling information. For most people, the development and use of the channels is somewhat uneven; that is, some rely more on seeing, whereas others rely more on hearing or touching—clearly this will be influenced by your learning style (see Chapter 2).

Different activities and tasks may call on different channels as well. Thus, it is important to involve as many senses as possible to improve your memory. Although each person has preferred channels for processing information, using multiple channels may help you improve your ability to retain information. Athletics often require you to process information through touch and feel, as well as sight and sound. In contrast, because most academic tasks involve reading, writing, and listening, the ability to process information in the visual and auditory channels is important.

Visual—in college, much of your learning involves seeing the information that is presented, such as reading books and papers, going over notes, and looking at diagrams. For this reason, you want to be sure to encode information visually, which often is a strength for student-athletes. In fact, it would be difficult to succeed in most sports if you could not process and recall information visually. You can incorporate visual processing by creating graphic organizers (see Chapter 6) and diagrams of the material you are learning, much as a play book uses diagrams to illustrate the formations or plays to be run.

Auditory—listening is also a major way in which information is processed. Much of your time in classes is spent listening, just as you spend a lot of time listening to instructions from your coaches. In athletics, the instructions are often fairly short—so as not to overload you with too much information at once—and frequently repeated. For some students, what they hear is more likely to capture their attention than what they see. If you are one of these students, then you will want to practice repeating—in your own words—information presented to you in class, especially if you want to understand and master the material. This is a form of semantic encoding—representing information by what it means—and best promotes learning and understanding. Encoding information in different ways can facilitate storage in and recall from long-term memory. Thus, make sure you represent new information semantically, particularly information you want to understand and be able to apply.

Other Channels—the remaining channels—kinesthetic, tactile, olfactory, and gustatory—are not as likely to be used in your classes. These channels are likely to play a bigger role in your processing of information in other areas of your life, such as athletics. Nevertheless, we mention them briefly because they can serve as ways to strengthen your memory, if you choose to use them. For example, you might create associations between certain information and certain bodily sensations, even if the information is not presented through that particular channel. In some classes, such as laboratories in the physical or biological sciences, you may actually have opportunities to use these channels more directly by touching specimens or smelling chemical reactions. Although these sensory channels are not traditionally used in your classes, they are still valuable. If it helps you to process information by the way it feels, smells, or tastes, or by its texture, go for it! We have known student-athletes who study more effectively if they do it standing, or as they move around the room. This seems to tap into student-athlete's kinesthetic sense since they tend to be more in-tune with their bodies. Remember, the more senses you involve and the more active you are in the learning process, the more successful you will be.

To illustrate the interaction between encoding and sensory channels, consider the following example. In a class, you are given three terms to remember. If you encode them by sight or by sound, then you will probably remember how to list them, but you may not remember their meaning (which requires semantic encoding). Another example of the way this process works can be seen in many sports. You can encode your actions in your sport by seeing how and in what sequence they are to be performed; you can encode them based on the sounds associated with them and perhaps by their semantic meaning. However, it is also likely you would want to recall them based on the tactile and kinesthetic sensations they generate—that is, by the way they feel when you perform them correctly. A baseball pitcher uses kinesthetic and tactile encoding to recall how it feels to throw a curve ball properly, as does a golfer on her drive or a basketball player shooting free throws, or a crew member feathering their oar. If you use multiple sensory channels during the encoding process, then you can compensate if one of them fails you during recall.

Long-Term Memory

Long-term memory, the third type of memory, is the permanent storage place for all that you have learned but are not currently using, like the hard drive on a computer. With theoretically unlimited capacity and duration, long-term memory is an important part of what makes you human. Without the ability to store information indefinitely, you would not be able to function on a daily basis, nor would you have successful relationships or much of a personality, since there would be little or no consistency in your behavior. Continuing with our football example, long-term memory would be represented by the ability to retain the team play book in your memory, so that you know all the formations and plays that can be run. Thus, when the quarterback calls the play, you know what you are supposed to do because you have stored the play in memory and can access it when necessary. Long-term memory for large amounts of information, such as a play book, often involves creating associations, a topic we will discuss later when we introduce memory enhancement techniques.

Storage. Storage is the process of holding encoded information in memory over an extended period of time. Working and long-term memories have to do with differences in storage. Working memory is relatively brief, lasting just long enough to complete the task at hand. Once that task is completed, the information essentially disappears from memory—it is not truly stored. In long-term memory, on the other hand, information is stored and can be accessed at any time. Such information is initially treated as a short-term memory until you decide it should be stored in long-term memory. Repetition of information is one way to move it from short- to long-term memory. For example, think of learning the plays and formations that are part of certain sports, such as soccer, basketball, or football. Practicing plays is, in essence, repeating information (plays, formations) until it becomes deeply embedded and available for recall and execution at some point in the future, for instance during competition. The first time you are exposed to an individual play or formation, it goes into working memory: You remember it just long enough to execute it, but without rehearsal or practice, it is soon lost.

Information in long-term memory is stored not in complete sentences or as exact words, but rather as general units of knowledge or meaning (Schunk, 2000). These basic units of information are organized and stored in long-term memory through associations, with related concepts being connected to one another (Ormrod, 1999). Elaboration is a mechanism whereby you create associations between something you are trying to learn and things you already know, and thus is another way to move information to long-term memory. Related material from long-term memory is activated and pulled into working memory to be integrated with the new ("to be learned") information (Schunk, 2000). As the associations between new and

© Monkey Business Images, 2009 / Used under license from Shutterstock.com

old are made, the information is re-stored in long-term memory. (It has been learned.) Again, to use an example from sports, plays and formations are often given certain colors or names associated with famous teams that also run them. This is not a coincidence. Not only does this strategy use shorthand to make recall easier, it also takes advantage of the fact that it is simpler to remember something when it is connected to something else that is familiar and grabs your attention. Effective storage is promoted when you represent the new information in ways that are personally meaningful.

Retrieval. The last aspect of the memory process is retrieval, or the act of remembering something when you need to. You cannot retrieve information that you have not previously paid attention to, encoded, and stored in some way. Yet even if you have done these things, it does not guarantee that you will be able to retrieve what you need to remember. However, the way you store information strongly influences the retrieval process. When information stored in long-term memory is well organized, encoded in multiple forms (e.g., visual and semantic), and correctly specified or classified, then retrieval is easier. If this is not the case, then the information may be "misfiled" and you risk losing it.

The "tip-of-the-tongue" phenomenon is an example of a breakdown in the retrieval process, and occurs when you are sure you recognize a word or a name, but you can't quite recall it. You have paid attention to, encoded, and stored the information, but you cannot access it, which is much like locking up a prized possession in a safe and knowing where the safe is located, but losing the key. Encoding information using various channels is like having spare keys to the safe. Retrieval is affected not only by encoding but also by storage, especially if you use elaboration to increase the amount of information you associate with what you are trying to learn.

In the next section, we discuss techniques to improve your memory for the things you need to remember in school and in other areas of your life.

Performance: Memory Enhancement Techniques

Understanding how the memory system works sets the stage for knowing what strategies to apply when learning college level material. Generally, we can think about learning as occurring at two levels: surface and deep. *Surface-level* approaches focus on taking in information at a superficial level, with minimal or no effort to integrate or connect it with other existing information. These approaches emphasize memorization and rehearsal. Rehearsal, recitation, acronyms, mnemonic devices, and the like are essentially surface-level approaches. Although surface-level techniques are quite useful in certain circumstances, they are not best for facilitating learning in college classes. *Deep-level* approaches use techniques involving organizing information, elaborating upon it, and making it personally meaningful. Creating associations and categorizing are examples of deeper-level strategies that actively involve you, the learner. We now present some techniques and strategies you can use to strengthen your memory.

Rehearsal and Recitation

An important surface-level approach is recitation (Pauk & Owens, 2007). Recitation and rehearsal involve three basic processes: reading the material in small segments, converting it into your own words, and testing yourself for recall. Some students make the mistake of simply reading and rereading their textbook or notes, which gives them a false sense of confidence in their ability to recall the material. It intuitively feels like a good strategy, but it's not. You must work with the material in an effortful way in order to consistently recall it. You can recite by simply restating material from memory in your own words. Another technique is to convert what you have read into questions, read your questions, and then answer them. This can be done either verbally or in writing, because the memory processes are similar for both methods.

Create Associations

Connecting a new idea to one that is already familiar to you is a deep-level strategy for learning material. Associations occur naturally in many instances, but it is important not to leave this process to chance. Instead, actively link new material to what you have already stored in your memory. According to Pauk and Owens (2007), associations can be categorized as either logical or artificial. In the case of logical associations, memory is strengthened by (1) building on your basic background and knowledge of the topic, and (2) using images to support what you are trying to remember.

To build on your basic background, you need a solid understanding of the introductory material in your courses. Although you may not always enjoy such courses, they often serve as building blocks for more advanced courses and concepts. If your basic background in a subject is poor, then it will be difficult, if not impossible, to form meaningful logical associations.

Artificial associations are connections that you create, and may or may not make sense to anyone but you. Because such associations are yours alone, you are free to make them as wild as you like. Have some fun with them! The more vivid and unique, the more meaningful and useful they will be to you. For example, what if you were asked to define the word *chimera*? In common usage, it means an illusion or fabrication of the mind; especially an unrealizable dream. In Greek mythology, a chimera is also a fire-breathing monster with a lion's head, a goat's body, and a serpent's tail. An artificial association might be to picture the word *fabrication* tangled in the lion's head; a "mind" added to the goat's body; and the words *unrealizable dream* tattooed on the serpent's tail. Ridiculous? Of course, but those artificial associations would likely help you remember the two different definitions for chimera. To give you the chance to practice creating associations, you may want to complete Exercise 5.4.

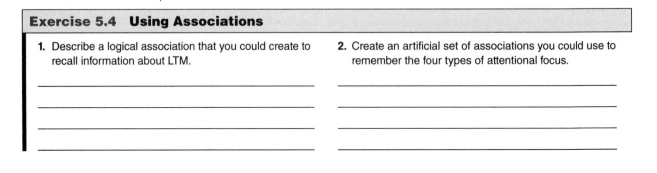

1. Describe a logical association that you could create to recall information about LTM.

2. Create an artificial set of associations you could use to remember the four types of attentional focus.

Categorizing

In categorizing, or grouping, the main idea is to find some concept, theme, or feature that pulls together the terms or items you need to remember (Hamachek, 2006). What do the items or ideas have in common? As with association, the unifying concept can be whatever makes the most sense to you. For example, you might see the following list of classes:

Psychology	Sociology	Anthropology
Biology	Chemistry	Physics
English	Spanish	French
Economics	Algebra	Statistics

These classes can be categorized in a variety of ways. You might group them by discipline (e.g., social sciences, natural sciences, languages, and mathematics), or perhaps by their format (e.g., lecture or seminar), or by size (large or small), or even according to whether they end in *-ology* or not! Not only can this process make it easier to remember the items, the process of creating categories can help you to better understand the relationships among the concepts or items.

Chunking

Chunking is a natural process that occurs when you take many individual bits of information and combine them into larger units, or chunks (Hamachek, 2006). Each chunk can contain approximately seven items, which is roughly the capacity of working memory. With chunking, you boost your ability to remember by decreasing the *number* of individual items you are remembering, but increasing the *size* of the items. Phone numbers and social security numbers are often recalled in chunks. It is far easier for most people to learn a phone number as three chunks, 206-555-5849, rather than trying to learn ten separate numbers, 2 0 6 5 5 5 5 8 4 9. Another way to think of chunks is to look at them as categories, themes, or patterns. The key with chunking is to make sure you do not put too much information into each chunk.

Acronyms

Acronyms are words formed by using the beginning letters of several words that you are trying to remember to form a new word. These new words can be an excellent device to help you remember material.

Acronyms can be actual words or nonsensical ones; no matter which type they are, acronyms take advantage of your brain's natural tendency to remember whole items better than fragmented ones. A clever advertising campaign by a major athletic shoe and clothing manufacturer used the acronym PLAY (Participate in the Lives of American Youth) to convey a community service message, promote sports, and sell shoes in the process! The NCAA uses the acronym CHAMPS (CHallenging Athletes' Minds for Personal Success) for its life skills program.

Another example comes from an article in the *Chronicle of Higher Education* that discussed why college students do not study as much as in the past and how that affected grades. In the article, there were six ways that researchers have recommended to encourage more or better studying by students:

1. Require students to take study-skills courses or to attend orientation sessions that emphasize time management.
2. Involve faculty members in campus tours for prospective freshmen, to emphasize the importance of academics.
3. Better reward faculty members for teaching and spending time with undergraduates.
4. Provide more financial aid or otherwise encourage students to work fewer hours in jobs to allow more time for studies.
5. Create "learning communities," in which students are placed in groups of about 25 and share a set of classes to build a better sense of connection to the university and to academic work.
6. Take steps to halt grade inflation.

So, how could you create an acronym to remember these six statements? First, select the main idea for each statement:

1. time management
2. faculty tours
3. reward
4. aid
5. learning communities
6. grade inflation

Second, identify the first letter (T, F, R, A, L, G) of each main idea, and then reorder these to form different words, such as LG FART, which can help you remember the six recommendations. Although a bit crass, we bet you would be able to remember the acronym and what it stands for! To practice using categories, chunks, and acronyms, you may want to complete Exercise 5.5.

Pictures

Memories can also be strengthened by the use of visual aids, such as graphic organizers (see Chapter 6), which are a form of deep-level processing. As Pauk (1997) notes, pictures can be drawn or can just be visualized in your mind. The process of generating pictures and images is just a way of organizing information that involves you as an active participant. Generating mental images is a useful technique because almost any memory can be transformed into a visual image for later recall, and you need no artistic talent to do it. Using pictures and

> "To succeed...
> You need to find
> something to hold
> on to, something
> to motivate you,
> something to
> inspire you."
>
> TONY DORSETT
> *NFL Hall of Fame*

Exercise 5.5   Categories, Chunks, and Acronyms

1. Think about material you are learning in one or more of your classes; generate a category, a chunk, and an acronym that you can use to better remember the material.

   a. What is the category and all of its elements?

   _____

   _____

   b. What is the chunk?

   _____

   _____

   c. What is the acronym and the words for which it stands?

   _____

   _____

2. Repeat the processes used above, but use material you need to remember for your sport.

   a. What is the category and all of its elements?

   _____

   _____

   b. What is the chunk?

   _____

   _____

   c. What is the acronym and the words for which it stands?

   _____

   _____

---

images to encode and recall information allows you to use more of your brain's capacity for information processing. In fact, your brain has one center for processing language, and another for processing images and pictures. You can enhance your ability to remember by maximizing the number of processing centers and senses you use to encode information. For example, you might draw a picture of a plant or a tree, labeling the parts you need to remember for your botany class. We have had student-athletes draw diagrams using academic material in the form of a sport diagram to visually make connections between material and aid in memorizing. Combining words and pictures will give you a clearer understanding of the topic than using words alone.

Analogies

In developing analogies, you relate new material, particularly that which is abstract and unfamiliar, to common concepts and situations (Ormrod, 1999). Analogies provide a basis for understanding something new because that new material is directly related to what you already know. Analogies take the abstract and help make it concrete and understandable. For example, relating how a computer's RAM is similar to the working memory is an analogy. Analogies are useful, but taking an analogy too far can lead to you to misunderstand the material and make mistakes when recalling the information from memory. Consider again the computer-memory system analogy, which is useful for understanding how long-term memory functions. If this analogy is applied to forgetting, though, it might lead you to draw the conclusion that information never decays, which is incorrect.

Distribute to Consolidate

This last suggestion is more of an approach to learning than a specific technique, but we include it here because it is a way to practice good self-care and it is crucial to memory enhancement. Learning occurs over time. Thus, the best approach to learning involves practice that is spread out, rather than done all at one time. You might, for example, study your notes in botany for half an hour each evening. After studying botany, you take a 10-minute break before spending the next 30 minutes of each evening studying political science. Following another short break, you read a short story for English. You have spread out your studying for each class over each night, so that you don't have too much to learn at any one time. You have also given yourself time between subjects to recover before taking on new material and given your memory a chance to consolidate what you've just learned. Not only does this approach lessen the chance of being overloaded, it also reduces the possibility that you will become bored. Taking short breaks during the times when you are rehearsing material also keeps you fresh, much as breaks at practice allow you to catch your breath before the next drill.

Post-Game Review: Some Final Thoughts on Memory

In the preceding sections of this chapter, we pointed out just how important memory is to your academic success. We also introduced the IPS model and described the three types of memory—sensory, working, and long-term memory—and their relationship to the processes involved in memory formation and recall. Attention, encoding, storage, and retrieval are integral processes involved in memory. Breakdowns in any of these processes can make it difficult to learn information and may cause you to forget what you have already learned. Fortunately, there are a number of strategies you can use to maximize retention and recall of information. Although these strategies are quite different, ranging from acronyms to pictures, they all share a common principle: involving as many processing centers and senses as possible. The memory enhancement strategies we discussed also draw on two other themes we have repeated throughout this book: being an active learner and practicing the skills you want to improve. These are keys to success in athletics as well as academics.

Performance: Forgetting

We all forget things or only remember bits and pieces of what we thought we knew. Even young, healthy individuals can forget. Some forgetting is simply annoying, such as when you forget the name of a classmate, but other forgetting has more consequences, such as when you forget key information on an exam.

Why do people forget? There are several different ways that people's memory fails them, what Daniel Schacter (1999), a Harvard cognitive psychologist, calls "sins of memory." In this section, we introduce three of these sins and present ways that you can minimize each type of forgetting.

Sin #1: Absentmindedness. In the sin of absentmindedness, you have failed to adequately encode new information. This type of forgetting represents the memory failures people experience every day, such as not remembering where they put their keys or not remembering a play in their sport. When your attention is divided (e.g., when students try to study and watch TV at the same time) or focused elsewhere, you encode information superficially if at all.

Attention is the key for avoiding this memory sin. You must focus your attention on what you are doing so you can adequately encode the information and process it deeply for transfer to LTM. When studying, make sure you do not engage in other activities, such as watching TV, checking your Facebook page, or talking with friends. If your attention is wandering, then take a brief break and come back to focus on the task at hand—studying.

Absentmindedness also occurs during retrieval, such as when you fail to carry out a required task or function at a certain time or when a certain event occurs. For example, Martin failed to turn in his paper when he went to class even though he had reminded himself to do so (an event-based retrieval error). Jamie, on the other hand, forgot to call her sister on Friday night when she had planned (a time-based retrieval error). In Chapter 3, we discuss time-management strategies that can help you avoid this type of forgetting.

Sin #2: Transience. The sin of transience involves a LTM storage failure. Psychologists know that memories decay over time, with forgetting occurring most quickly immediately following learning and then slowing with the passage of time. You are most at risk of forgetting during the time immediately following learning (often within the first 24 hours). Thus, if you do not think about the material during this key time period, the likelihood of transfer to LTM (i.e., learning) is significantly decreased. In Chapters 6, 7, and 8, we discuss the importance of daily and weekly reviews in learning.

But forgetting old, irrelevant information, such as old offensive plays, is adaptive. It allows new, more relevant information to be focused on and learned. By thinking about what you need to remember, you keep only the most important information accessible.

Sin #3: Blocking. The sin of blocking involves a failure to retrieve memories that are in LTM. Even well-encoded, frequently used information may be difficult to recall. When this occurs, you are likely to be aware that it is happening, such as when you "just know" but cannot recall the chemistry formula that will help you solve an exam question. This is also referred to as the "tip-of-the-tongue" phenomenon.

© KennStilger47, 2009 / Used under license from Shutterstock.com

"Blocking" may occur because, during retrieval, similar but incorrect information may be accessed and this interferes with the individual's ability to recall the correct information. Psychologists generally refer to two types of interference:

- *Proactive.* With proactive interference, something learned earlier interferes with the retrieval of something learned later. For example, Wanda studied her French in the morning and her art appreciation in the evening and then had trouble on her art test (which emphasized the French Romantic period) the next day because she kept recalling information from her French assignment. If information is well organized when you learn it, then you decrease the chances of this type of interference occurring. Thus, when you are learning, carefully organize information in a meaningful fashion and distinguish between related, but different, material.

• *Retroactive.* Retroactive interference occurs when currently learned information interferes with your ability to recall previous information. For example, you learn new offensive plays, but then have trouble remembering plays from last season that are still part of your offense. To reduce this type of interference, minimize what happens following learning. When you are studying, one strategy is to study up to an hour or so prior to going to sleep every night.

Learning and Attentional Disorders

Sometimes problems with concentration and memory arise from more than just deficits in academic and study skills. Some students, including student-athletes, may have Attention Deficit/Hyperactivity Disorder (ADHD) or a learning disorder. If you have been diagnosed, then inform you academic advisor so that you can begin receiving the accommodations that you are legally entitled to. Not infrequently, though, ADHD and learning disorders go undetected for many years and are sometimes not accurately diagnosed until a student enters college. If you have struggled academically despite being a motivated and well-prepared student, then it is important to be able to recognize the indicators of ADHD and learning disorders.

Symptoms of Learning Disorders

Learning disorders are diagnosed when there is a significant discrepancy between a person's level of academic achievement and what would be expected based on his or her age, education, and general level of intelligence. These disorders interfere significantly with academic achievement and daily activities that require reading, mathematical, or writing skills and affect between 5 percent and 10 percent of all students. Symptoms of learning disorders include (American Psychiatric Association, 2000):

• Slowness in reading and reading comprehension errors
• Distortions, substitutions, or omissions in oral reading
• Difficulty decoding written math problems into mathematical symbols
• Impaired ability to organize objects into groups
• Difficulty recognizing mathematical symbols and arithmetic signs
• Problems copying numbers or figures correctly
• Difficulty following sequences of mathematical steps
• Frequent grammatical or punctuation errors in writing
• Poor organization of paragraphs
• Multiple spelling errors
• Excessively poor handwriting skills

(continued)

Symptoms of Attention Deficit/Hyperactivity Disorder

The essential feature of ADHD is a persistent pattern of inattention and/or hyperactivity-impulsivity that causes significant impairment; the symptoms were present before age 7 years. ADHD affects between 3–7 percent of students. Symptoms of ADHD include (American Psychiatric Association, 2000):

- Failure to pay close attention to details, leading to careless mistakes in school or other activities
- Shifting from one uncompleted task to another
- Difficulty following through on instructions
- Persistent difficulty organizing tasks and activities
- Forgetfulness in daily activities
- Being easily distracted
- Avoiding tasks that require sustained mental effort
- Fidgeting with hands or feet
- Persistent feelings of restlessness
- Interrupting or intruding upon others
- Impulsive behavior, especially risk taking, without considering consequences

If you suspect you may be suffering from either of these disorders, then talk with your academic advisor to get a referral to your school's counseling and testing center for a thorough evaluation. If you are diagnosed, then you likely will receive special assistance and accommodations to facilitate your learning.

This memory sin is adaptive because it keeps some information out of consciousness. Imagine taking an exam and accessing all possible information with any given retrieval cue (not just the information you needed to answer the questions!). You would be overwhelmed and would spend untold amounts of time trying to determine which of the recalled information was relevant for the task at hand.

There are many explanations for why people forget important information. Although finding out why we forget can be satisfying, we are still left with the problem and what to do about it. So for you, the committed student-athlete, the most critical thing to remember is there are also many strategies for improving concentration and memory. And, if you apply what has been discussed in this chapter, you will make the improvements you want.

Post-Game Review

As we close this chapter, it is important to reiterate—as we have done throughout this book—that to concentrate effectively and learn and recall information, you must apply effective study strategies and be self-responsible. Improving your memory and concentration is first of all a matter of taking responsibility. If you don't acknowledge the problems you have in these areas and commit yourself to improving, then you will not be successful. Although others may point out deficiencies to you, only you have the power to take action to correct them. Making such a commitment will pay big dividends for you in all the major areas in your life: academics, athletics, and personal development.

Thinking Critically about Memory and Concentration

1. Summarize what you now know about memory and concentration based on the information presented in this chapter.

_____

_____

_____

2. What additional questions do you have about these topics and how to use the skills introduced in this chapter?

_____

_____

_____

3. What conclusions can you draw about this topic and how it might help you be a more effective and successful student and athlete?

_____

_____

_____

Achieve IT! Setting an Attentional Focus or Memory Goal

1. Based on your self-assessment and your responses to Thinking Critically, select a goal in relationship to improving your focus or your memory that you would like to achieve this term.

2. Now identify three short-term goals that will help you reach your goal this term.

3. For the short-term goals, identify the attainment strategies you will need to reach them.

4. List any obstacles you might face in trying to reach these goals and identify your plan for overcoming each one.

Don't forget to make your goal visible and tell others about them, so they can keep you accountable regarding what you want to achieve.

Chapter 5 Review Questions

1. Within the IPS model, which memory is the "gateway" for information entering the system?

   a. Sensory.   **b.** Working.

   c. Encoding.   **d.** Storage.

2. Long-term memory is limited by

    a. Duration.   **b.** Capacity.
    c. Retrieval.   **d.** None of the above.

3. When Sarah studied for her exam, she was watching TV and talking with her friends. During the exam, she was unable to remember key bits of information. This type of forgetting is called

    a. Transience.   **b.** Misattribution.
    c. Low self-efficacy.   **d.** Absentmindedness.

4. Once information is learned and transferred to LTM,

    a. It can be retrieved at a moment's notice.
    b. It can be stored only in a semantic form.
    c. It can decay over time if not used.
    d. All of the above.

5. Difficulty in concentrating can be reduced by:

    a. Being an active learner.
    b. Developing and maintaining a consistent work routine.
    c. Studying in realistically scheduled blocks of time.
    d. All of the above.

6. You are getting ready to take a test. Your attention is directed toward monitoring your own tension and mentally rehearsing the steps necessary for success on the test. You are most likely using what type of attentional focus?

    a. Broad-external.   **b.** Narrow-internal.
    c. Narrow-external.   **d.** Broad-internal.
    e. Internal-external.

7. A learning disorder may exist when there is a significant gap in a student's general level of intelligence and academic achievement. (True or False)

8. Attention Deficit/Hyperactivity Disorder (ADHD) is a medical condition in which the following symptoms may be present:

    a. Careless mistakes caused by lack of attention to detail.
    b. Frequent shifting from uncompleted tasks.
    c. Difficulty organizing tasks and activities.
    d. Impulsive behavior and feelings of restlessness.
    e. All of the above.

9. The memory technique of relating new material to information you already know is called?

    a. Chunking.   **b.** Acronyms.
    c. Association.   **d.** Encoding.

10. Deep-level learning techniques are most effective in facilitating learning. (True or False)

Game Plan:

In this chapter, you will learn:

- How to develop positive and respectful classroom behaviors

- How to listen attentively, identify main points in lectures, and take useful notes

- How to understand the connection between reviewing class notes and learning class material

- How to get to know your instructors

- How to use learning aids, such as creating personal examples and graphic organizers

© Brandon_Parry, 2009 / Used under license from Shutterstock.com

"Pain is temporary. Quitting lasts forever."

LANCE ARMSTRONG
Seven-Time Winner, Tour de France

Self-Assessment—Perceive It!

Read the following statements and place a checkmark next to each one you generally do. For you to change and develop new and effective academic, athletic, and personal strategies, you must be accurate in your self-perception. So, be honest in how you answer each question.

1. I take organized and thorough notes during every class lecture.　　＿＿＿＿

2. Before class starts, I review my notes from the previous lecture.　　＿＿＿＿

3. I read the assigned textbook chapters ahead of time so I am better able to understand the lecture and take effective notes.　　＿＿＿＿

4. During lectures, I ask questions when I am unclear about something and when I want additional information on the topic.　　＿＿＿＿

5. When I take notes, I pay particular attention to information the instructor writes on the board or displays on a screen.　　＿＿＿＿

6. I try to review my notes as soon after class as possible, but always within 24 hours of taking them.　　＿＿＿＿

7. I use a note-taking system that is organized and easy to read and understand.　　＿＿＿＿

8. I sit in the front and center of all my classes.　　＿＿＿＿

9. Each semester, I take the time to meet with and get to know all my instructors.　　＿＿＿＿

10. Before I write my notes, I think about what the instructor is saying and try to understand the information in my own words.　　＿＿＿＿

11. When I listen to a lecture and take notes, I can understand the main points the instructor is trying to communicate.　　＿＿＿＿

12. When I study, I make connections between what I am learning and what I already know.　　＿＿＿＿

13. Whenever possible, I create personal examples to help illustrate the material I am trying to learn.　　＿＿＿＿

Take a moment to review your responses. How many items did you check? Each one you checked represents a current strength. Now consider the items you did not check. These represent areas where focus and growth are needed. Now, to summarize your self-perception, complete the following statements:

1. My areas of strength are:

＿＿＿＿＿＿＿＿＿＿＿＿＿＿＿＿＿＿＿＿＿

2. The areas I need to improve are:

＿＿＿＿＿＿＿＿＿＿＿＿＿＿＿＿＿＿＿＿＿

As you read this chapter and participate in your classes, keep your strengths and areas of improvement in mind. At the end of the chapter, you will have the chance to set a goal related to these areas. Achieving these goals will help you become a more effective student and athlete.

Introduction

Marcus was a sprinter who had recently transferred to his current school after attending an out-of-state junior college for one year. At the JC, classes were small, and instructors put all their lectures on their Web sites so students could have PowerPoint handouts prior to each class. Thus, Marcus didn't think he had to take notes during class because he had the slides. Instead, he would just try to listen as best he could. Even so, his mind would wander because he knew that the important information on the topic was included on the slides. He thought that if he had any questions, he could always ask his teachers after class.

Marcus had a rude awakening when he began attending classes at his current school. Most of his classes were in large lecture halls with 300 or more students, so there was much less individual attention. In addition, only two of his instructors provided access to their lectures through their Web sites. The other instructors expected students to listen to the lecture and discern for themselves what was important. Although Marcus tried to listen and take good notes during classes, he was floundering after only a week of school. Because he did not know with any certainty what the most important points of each lecture were, he just tried to write down everything his instructors said. This approach did not work because most of them talked too fast for him to keep up. He knew he needed help, but he did not know where to go to get it. He wanted to talk with his instructors, but he could not make it to their office hours, and they always seemed busy after class. After a while, he stopped taking notes altogether. He thought he would be better off just listening to the lecture and trying to memorize it than becoming frustrated with his inability to take good notes. Needless to say, this approach was an epic failure. Marcus became painfully aware of how much he did not remember when he tried to study for his first set of midterms. Although the material seemed fairly clear when he heard it during lectures, he remembered very little at exam time and, because he had not taken notes, he had no record of what had been covered. Thus, he had to focus on his textbook, which, unfortunately, only included a portion of the material that was covered on the exams. If he was going to be successful in school, then he would have to learn a better system for taking notes!

Like Marcus, many students experience difficulties when it comes to getting the most out of their classroom experiences and taking notes that actually help them learn the material and do well on exams. Although the reasons for these difficulties are varied, ranging from not being prepared when they enter the classroom to using ineffective note-taking systems, the end result is usually the same: Students do not create organized and accurate records of the material that is covered in their classes. Without such records—for this is what class notes are—students do not have the information they need to study for their exams.

In college, taking notes represents one of the two major ways in which you will be exposed to, and have the opportunity to learn, course material; the other is reading your textbooks, which we cover in Chapter 7. Although in some introductory classes there may be overlap between lectures and assigned textbook readings, in most (and certainly in upper-level classes), instructors will introduce original material during lectures and class discussions. If you don't take notes, then you will miss out on a substantial amount of material for which you are responsible.

So, note-taking serves two primary purposes (Kiewra, 1989). First, as mentioned previously, the notes you take are a permanent record of each lecture, a form of external storage. As such, they provide you with a way to review and study the material after the class is over. Because college classes will include material that is not in your assigned textbook, you may miss out on important information if you do not take detailed notes. By studying notes after class, you put yourself in the position of learning the class material. In fact, it is through the review of notes that most learning occurs.

Second, taking notes helps you encode lecture material and other class information in a meaningful, organized form. During note taking, you have to focus your attention on the lecture material, organize the information in your notebooks, and begin to make associations between the new material and what you already know (which is a deep-level learning strategy). By taking this approach, you are engaging in what Wittrock (1990) called generative learning. Specifically, generative learning involves developing connections among the topics covered in the lectures and between new and previously learned material. Both of these processes help you create associations, organize the material, and make it more meaningful. For example, as she listened to the lecture on the information processing system, Juanita (who was on her school's field hockey team) began to make connections between working memory and the transfer of information to long-term memory. As her instructor continued to discuss the memory system and how it provided the foundation for effective learning, she began to relate that material to what she already knew about forgetting, something she had learned in her introductory psychology class. She began to make connections between learning and forgetting as well as developing examples from her own life to illustrate how the memory system worked.

These generative approaches allow you to take "ownership" of what you are learning. Generative strategies help you better organize information presented in lecture, put it in your own words (e.g., create personal examples, which will be discussed later in this chapter), and construct new, deeper meanings from the material. The two prominent strategies you can use to facilitate generative learning are (1) developing and answering questions related to lecture material (which will be discussed in more detail later in this chapter) and (2) writing summaries for each set of lecture notes. Developing and answering questions is a particularly effective approach because it allows you to self-monitor your comprehension and retention during test preparation and adjust your learning strategies as necessary to maximize comprehension.

In this chapter, we begin by discussing what you can do to prepare in advance for taking organized notes and how you can be actively involved in your classes. Next, we introduce an effective three-step process for taking notes. Although you may believe that taking notes begins and ends in the classroom, there are many things you can do before and after class that will help you be more successful academically. Finally, we present two important learning aids—personal examples and graphic organizers—and discuss how you can use these to organize class material and make it more personally meaningful.

To become aware of your present note-taking behaviors and be in a better position to make decisions about whether (and how) you want to modify what you currently do, you may want to complete Exercise 6.1.

Exercise 6.1 Your Typical Note-Taking Routine

1. Describe how you typically take notes during a lecture. For example, where do you sit? What format do you use for your notes? What types of information do you pay attention to and record in your notes?

2. What are the strengths or positive characteristics of your current approach to taking notes? For example, your current approach may be well organized so that your notes are easy to read.

3. What are the limitations or weak points of your current approach to taking notes? For example, your current approach may focus too much on main points and leave out important details.

4. Based on the strengths and weaknesses of your current note-taking system, what changes might you make in the way you currently take notes so you can be even more successful in the classroom?

Note taking is an essential part of your learning experience. Don't try to fool yourself into believing that listening will be enough or that you will make a summary of the lecture after class. Such a summary will likely be insufficient and perhaps even inaccurate. Remember, too, that to take notes you must attend class. Just as you would never miss practice, at least not without your coach's permission, you should never miss class. If you have to miss a class due to being ill or travel for your sport, then talk with your instructors about your absence and find out what you must do to catch up. *Never ask your instructor whether you "missed anything important."* To many instructors, such a question is insulting and communicates disrespect for them personally and professionally. Instead, assume that the material covered during your absence was important and that you are now responsible for catching up. To do so, you might say, "I know I missed an important lecture. I've already gotten a classmate's notes, but I wanted to know if there is anything else I might do to make sure I understand the material that was covered." Being respectful and demonstrating a high level of self-responsibility should characterize any communication you have with your instructors.

> **Genius without education is like silver in the mine.**
>
> BENJAMIN FRANKLIN

Preparation: Taking Effective Notes

Effective note taking involves three important steps:

1. Prepare in advance, or set the stage, to be a good note taker. This first step parallels your preparation for competitions.
2. Use an organized note-taking system when listening to class lectures and trying to determine the important points to record in your notes. This second step parallels having a game plan for competition, which gives you some direction and structure.
3. Review your notes so you can understand and master the class material. You can think of this step as being similar to post-competition debriefings or viewing of game tapes. Real learning and improvements in performance occur as a result of carefully studying past performance.

We discuss these three steps in more detail here.

Step 1: Setting the Stage

Note taking is not only about what you do during a lecture. There are things you can do before the lecture that will help you take more organized and accurate notes:

1. *Read outside assignments.* As we discussed in Chapter 7, it is essential that you complete your textbook readings before they are covered in class. Instructors assign readings for each lecture topic because the textbook material will be similar to, or will provide the necessary background for, what will be discussed in class. Thus, completing the assigned readings provides you with a context in which to better understand the lecture material and

take more organized and accurate notes—it gives you an advantage when you enter the classroom. It also helps you engage in generative learning; that is, creating associations between what you already learned in your textbook with what the instructor is discussing in class.

2. *Review course notes before coming to class.* Like reading outside assignments, reviewing the previous day's class notes provides the background for understanding what will be covered. In particular, reviewing your notes in this way can help you begin to see the connections among topics covered from one class to the next.

3. *Have a separate notebook for each class.* To keep your class notes organized and separated, have a different loose-leaf notebook for each class. Spiral notebooks may seem appealing, but they are limited by a finite number of pages and by the fact that once you tear out a page you can't easily (or securely) put it back. Spiral notebooks also may get misplaced or lost more easily.

4. *Arrive at classes early and be prepared.* Use the time before the lecture begins to prepare yourself to be an active participant in class. Do you have the pen and notebook you need? Have you reviewed your notes from the previous class? Have you reviewed the questions you had about the last lecture so you can ask them today? Remember, too, that being an active learner is a state of mind. When you get to class, are you there to "kill another hour," or are you there to actively participate and learn about a new topic? Just as you want to be in the right frame of mind when you practice or compete, you want to do the same for classes.

5. *Be well rested and properly fed.* Being tired or hungry are distracters, and they make it difficult to concentrate during the lecture. Always make sure you have had plenty of sleep and are fueled with nutritious food so your awareness will be at its peak.

Step 2: Taking Organized Notes

There are three key factors in taking organized notes.

Listen Actively in Class

Listening actively during class means focusing on, attending to, and thinking about what is being said. Instead of sitting back and letting the instructor's words wash over you like waves on a beach, be self-responsible and actively involve yourself in the lecture. The following strategies may help you listen actively in your classes:

1. *Sit in the front and center of the classroom.* Sitting in this position, particularly in a large lecture hall, can minimize distractions, whereas sitting in the back often is associated with not paying attention, falling asleep, and/or talking or texting with friends. By sitting in the front you can see the instructor and the board (or screen) more clearly, which is important particularly for visual learners. Also, the instructor can see you, which is a good thing. Getting to know your instructors can be an important part of your academic and personal success. If your instructors see you in class every day, then they will not only get to know you faster, but will likely form a positive impression of you. As a result,

you will probably feel more comfortable asking questions about the class, seeking out independent study opportunities, getting a letter of recommendation for a job or graduate school, or just receiving support during your time in college.

So why do so few students take advantage of the opportunity to get to know their instructors? Student-athletes tell us that with their busy schedules, they just don't have the time to get to an instructor's office hours or stay after class. Although this may be true for some, the majority of student-athletes could find the time if they made a commitment to do it. So what else might be stopping them? In our experience, the true reason usually is fear. Many student-athletes, like students in general, feel intimidated by and afraid of faculty members. They may be afraid that the instructor will not have time for them, will think that they are stupid, or will make fun of them in some way. Further, they may be afraid that if they introduce themselves as student-athletes, the instructor will not be able to see them as anything but athletes. Although we would like to guarantee that none of these things will happen, we can't. We can say, though, that most faculty members respect their students and do want to get to know them. Unfortunately, few students visit faculty members during their office hours. To help you get to know your instructor, you may want to complete Exercise 6.2.

2. *Prepare in advance.* By following all the suggestions we made during Step 1 of the note-taking process, you increase your chances of actively listening during classes because you will have a context in which to follow and understand the current lecture. This framework is like an outline; it will keep you on track and focused while you listen.

3. *Think about what the instructor is saying and write it in your own words.* Although there will be times to write down exactly what the instructor has said, such as a definition of a concept, in most

---

Exercise 6.2   Getting to Know Your Instructor

Here are a series of questions you may want to ask your instructors. In addition to these, think of three to five more you could ask, or think of some things you want to share about yourself. Once you have all your questions together, schedule a 15- to 20-minute meeting with your instructor. When you set up the meeting, make sure you tell him/her that you are interested in learning about him/her and his/her work and would like to ask him/her some questions. Although some instructors may be reticent, most are likely to welcome the opportunity to interact with their students, talk about their work, and share what they believe will lead to success in their classes.

Instructor's Name: _____

Title (or rank): _____

1. What schools did you attend and in what areas did you receive your degrees?

2. What are your areas of expertise in your field of study?

3. How did you become interested in your field of study?

4. In addition to teaching, what other work do you do at the university/college?

5. a. Besides the class I am taking with you, what other courses do you teach?

   b. What interests you most about these classes?

6. What are three of the most important ideas (in the course that I am taking) that you would like students to take with them?

7. As a teacher, what advice would you give a student to help him succeed academically in all his classes?

8. Outside of your involvements at school, what do you like to do in your free time?

Remember to come with 3–4 additional questions or things you want to share about yourself.

9. _____

10. _____

11. _____

12. _____

cases it will be important to think about the material being presented before you write it down in your own words. Even during unorganized or fast-paced lectures, make an extra effort to think about what the instructor is trying to communicate and then try to organize the information in some coherent manner. Doing so will benefit you when it comes time to review for exams. If the lecture is so confusing that you are having a hard time discerning its structure, stay relaxed, because you will have time afterward to review your notes and organize them better. If you have any questions after your review, then bring them to your next class and talk to the instructor. If you have instructors who talk too fast, then you might privately ask them if they could slow down or if they have any suggestions as to how you might better follow their lectures. If you miss something during a lecture, don't panic. Instead, make a note about it in your notebook, such as "missed this point," and then follow up with a classmate or with the instructor after class.

4. *Ask questions.* Asking questions in class is another way to facilitate active listening and comprehension. If you are thinking about the material that the instructor is presenting, then you are likely going to have questions, which is part of being an active learner. Write down your questions as they come to you and then, when there is an opportunity during class, respectfully ask the instructor.

There are four types of questions that you might ask:

1. *Factual questions.* Factual questions represent verifiable hard data. Such questions address the who, what, where, and when of the matter. They are usually answered with a list of particular items. For example, "Who developed the theory of multiple intelligences?" or "When did the great depression occur?" Factual questions also can be complicated, such as "What were the causes of World War II?" If you do not understand or are missing some important facts from a lecture, then these are the types of questions to ask.

© Yuri Arcurs, 2009 / Used under license from Shutterstock.com

2. *Conceptual questions.* Conceptual questions use information obtained from asking factual questions to begin to explore the structures, relationships, functions, and contexts in which the material is to be understood. Conceptual questions address issues of description, discussion, explanation, comparison, and contrast. For example, "Discuss the historical factors that contributed to Gardner developing his theory of multiple intelligences." "Describe how cells function." To answer conceptual questions, you must use general concepts that relate and integrate your data.

3. *"What if" questions.* "What if" questions are concerned with options, innovations, and new possibilities. Through these questions you demonstrate your understanding by applying the facts and concepts to novel situations, which is a true indication of understanding and learning. In college, simple memorization of factual material will be insufficient to pass your courses. Example questions include "How would multiple intelligences be used to explain how

individuals without college degrees have been successful in business and other fields?" or "How might the information processing system work if long-term memory was limited in terms of capacity?"

4. *Evaluation and judgment questions.* After having learned the facts and concepts of a subject and explored the alternatives and application to new situations, students are often asked to pass critical judgments on what they are learning. These questions do not simply call for an expression of your likes and dislikes or your feelings or unexamined preferences. Instead, they require a reasoned and critical examination of the material and a judgment based on evidence and argument; that is, they require that you engage in critical thinking (see Chapter 2). Examples of such questions are "Which theory/approach to intelligence best explains moral reasoning and why?" or "Evaluate the role of religion in modern-day politics."

Do not ask only factual or conceptual questions. Yes, understanding the facts and concepts is critical, but if you limit yourself to these types of questions, you will likely not do well on exams that include "what if" and evaluation/judgment questions. Make sure you understand the course material at all four levels of questions.

Many students refrain from asking questions during class, possibly because they are shy or simply intimidated. For these students, writing questions in their lecture notes and then asking their instructors might be a viable solution. To give you the opportunity to practice formulating and feeling more comfortable asking questions in class, you may want to complete Exercise 6.3.

Have a Note-Taking System

The second key factor in Step 2, Taking Organized Notes, is having a structured system for organizing and recording your notes. Although there are many such systems, we offer one that is straightforward and easy to implement. For this system, we suggest you:

1. Use loose-leaf paper and write on only one side of the paper.
2. Have a separate folder (e.g., three-ring binder) for each class and always make sure you date, label, and number your pages. The folder also is where you may keep your syllabus and all handouts from the class.
3. Before you begin taking notes, draw a vertical line about two inches from the left-hand side of your paper (some notebook

---

Exercise 6.3 Asking Questions in Class

During a two-week period, ask at least one question during every class you attend. Whether you come to class with a prepared question or make one up during the lecture, make sure you have it answered that day. Although it may not be comfortable at first, try to ask your question during the lecture (as opposed to waiting until after class to talk privately with your instructor). Doing so may help you get more involved in the class material. After your two weeks of asking questions, answer the following:

1. How did you feel initially when you asked questions in class? How were you feeling by the end of the two weeks?

2. Describe any changes in your level of in-class attention and focus as a result of asking questions.

3. Will you continue to ask questions in your classes? Why or why not?

paper has such a line already printed on it). You will record your notes to the right of that line and use the space on the left (which we will call the *recall column*) for summarizing the main points of the lecture notes (Figure 6.1).

Recording Your Notes

The third key factor in Step 2, Taking Organized Notes, is to have a systematic way to record the lecture material. Although there are many approaches for recording information on paper, ranging from paragraph form to concept maps, we introduce one approach that is straightforward

Name of course

Name
Date
Page No.

Record notes here...

Recall
column

Figure 6.1   Example Page for Taking Organized Notes

and provides an organized, easy-to-review summary of the lecture material. This approach, the outline format, is sequential and hierarchical. When a main point is presented in a lecture, it is listed to the left and is generally preceded by a Roman numeral (I., II., and so on). Next, as the instructor provides supporting material for the main point, you record the information by indenting it under the main point and then labeling it with a capital letter (A., B., and so on). Subpoints of the supporting information or examples that illustrate the material are further indented and labeled with an Arabic number (1., 2., and so on). It seems simple enough, yet this approach can be challenging at first because it may be hard to distinguish main points from supporting material. Thus, some students have a difficult time determining the levels at which information should be written ("Is this C. under I., or is it II.?"). As you practice taking notes, though, the natural order of most instructors' lectures will become more obvious. (Many of them work from outlines themselves!) When it does, the process of taking notes using this format will become much easier. Also, many more instructors are using PowerPoint slides to illustrate their lectures, and these may form the basis of your outline format. To illustrate this note-taking approach, we provide you with a page of notes taken on the topic of goal setting (Figure 6.2). We also have filled in the recall column (which we discuss under Step 3) so that you have an example of what that might look like when it is completed.

However you record your notes, whether it is the outline format we have introduced or a more visually illustrative approach, such as concept maps, which many visual learners like, it is important that you always take notes during the lecture, even during discussions, because supporting material, such as examples/illustrations, may be presented. Although it might seem that your instructors are just "telling a story" when they give examples, in fact, these stories provide context for making the material personally meaningful, which aids in learning. Also, make sure to record sufficient detail to support the main points of the lesson. Main points serve an important organizational function (and may be what is listed in an instructor's PowerPoint slide), yet they are insufficient when it comes to learning the material and performing successfully on exams. The devil, and the learning, is in the details.

Step 3: Review Your Notes

The final step in this note-taking system is reviewing your notes. Remember, notes represent the permanent storage area for the information you have obtained in your classes. Without reviewing, the effort you have put into actively listening to and thinking about the lecture material would be wasted. After a few days, you would remember only snippets of a class lecture if you did not review it. Reviewing is the process through which you come to understand and learn the material from your classes.

Reviewing involves three time frames— daily, weekly, and pre-exam. Because we cover

Achieving Academic and Athletic Success   *Jane Student*
                                                             Date — Page 1

What Is Goal?
—is what I want
—like map, gives
   direction

I. What is a goal?
   A. Goal is something I want to attain or place/position I want to reach
      1. its like a map I follow
      2. gives me direction for what I am doing
   B. There are key areas in which I can set goals

Set goals in diff. areas of life:
   —athlet.
   —acad.

      1. athletics — ex: may try to play 25 minutes a
         game this season
      2. academics — make the Dean's List this semester
      3. comm. service — ex: volunteer at an adult
         literacy program each week
      4. personal — ex: call my family once a week
      5. career — ex: decide on a major by next semester
      6. financial — ex: pay off credit card bill during next 3 months

Why set goals?
will help me
   —stay focused
   —be motivated
   —be confident

II. Benefits of setting goals
   A. I pay attention to what I'm doing and less likely to be distracted.
   B. More motivated and put forth more effort
      1. goals help me determine my progress
   C. Increase my confidence and lower anxiety when I make progress toward
      my goals.
      1. Ex: want to increase strength in leg squats by 100 lbs,
         set that as goal for end of the semester with monthly goals
         to measure progress, if my step is to improve 40 lbs and I do,
         then I will be more confident and motivated to continue.

System for setting goals
—make them the:
   S
   M
   A
   R
   T
   E
   S
   T
—Goals

III. How to set effective goals
   A. Use the "SMARTEST" system:
      1. S — Short- and Long-Term Goals
      2. M — Measurable Goals
      3. A — Achievement Strategies
      4. R — Realistic Goals
      5. T — Time-Bound Goals
      6. E — Exhibit Your Goals
      7. S — Seek Support for Your Goals
      8. T — Target Obstacles to Achieving Your
   B. Once you decide on a goal, make sure they confo
      be successful!

Figure 6.2   Example of Notes Taken Using an Outline Format for a Lecture on Goal Setting

weekly and pre-exam reviews in Chapters 5 and 7, we will only discuss daily reviews here.

Daily Reviews. Within the first 24 hours of taking notes, find time to review them. As discussed in Chapter 5, people generally forget the most during the first 24 hours after an experience. Reviewing within this time frame thus reinforces your learning and helps you retain the information.

Do the daily review as soon after the end of the class as possible. If you have a break after the class, then use this time to spend about 10 minutes reviewing your notes. If your schedule does not allow for

Watch for Instructor Cues!

Believe it or not, instructors knowingly and unknowingly give you cues as to which information they consider important. When you notice these cues during a lecture, make sure you accurately record the information being presented at that time. You may even want to highlight the information to make sure you review it thoroughly for your exams. Here are cues you can watch for:

1. *Repetition.* If an instructor repeats a point, then it's probably important. For example, if we wanted to emphasize the importance of this point, we would reiterate that students should pay attention to information that is repeated by the instructor.

2. *Introductory or concluding phrases.* As in your books, pay attention to phrases (e.g., "I want to introduce . . ." or "In summary . . .") that signify the beginning or end of a topical area, because they often signal that a main point of the lecture is about to be given.

3. *Information that is listed or qualified.* If material is presented as part of a list (if your instructor says, "First . . .," "Second . . .," and so on) or is introduced by phrases that include qualifiers, such as "most," "best," and "always," then it is likely to be important and should be recorded in your notes.

4. *Information that is written on the board or projected on a screen.* Information written on the board, projected on a screen, or part of notes on the instructor's Web site is likely to be important information.

5. *Material that the instructor reads directly from his/her notes or from a Power-Point slide.* Instructors vary in the degree to which they stick with a "scripted" lecture. Some will talk in a seemingly extemporaneous manner, whereas others will rely more on their notes. In either case, pay particular attention when instructors read directly from prepared notes or slides because it signals that the information to follow is important.

6. *Anything the instructor indicates is important or will be on the test.* Don't miss the obvious! If your instructor tells you directly that certain material is important or will be covered on the exam, then make a note of it during the lecture and study it sufficiently later. Do not make the mistake of being overconfident in your ability to simply remember it.

7. *Personal examples or illustrations.* Personal examples or illustrations are crucial information, particularly for kinesthetic learners. Examples and illustrations provide essential details for understanding the concepts of the class and help you make the information personally meaningful, which is a deep-level learning strategy.

> " A good hockey player plays where the puck is. A great hockey player plays where the puck is going to be. "
>
> WAYNE GRETZKY
> *National Hockey League MVP and Future Hall of Famer*

that, then make sure you spend about 10 minutes going over your notes within the first 24 hours after you take them. Investing this small amount of time now will provide huge savings when the time comes to study for your exams because you will not have to learn all the class material from scratch.

As you do your review, if you find any points that are unclear or incomplete, mark them and ask the instructor for clarification during the next class. In addition, select keywords or phrases from the notes or generate new questions that summarize what you recorded from the lecture. Write these words, phrases, or questions in the re-call column next to the corresponding material from the main body of your notes. (See Figure 6.2 for an illustration of a completed recall column.) By summarizing your notes in the recall column, you create a study system that you can use to quiz yourself at any time (almost like making flash cards out of your notes). Spend time testing yourself to see how well you know the material in the body of your notes. To do this, cover up this section and then try to answer the questions and define the key terms you have in the recall column.

To give you the opportunity to practice the three-step process for taking notes that we have introduced in this chapter, you may want to complete Exercise 6.4.

Performance: Learning Aids

In this section, we discuss two learning aids that are key for increasing your comprehension of class material—personal examples, which are particularly helpful for kinesthetic learners, and graphic organizers, which are particularly helpful for visual learners.

The Use of Examples

College-level material is complex, often seeming abstract and unfamil-iar to students. As a result, you may view the material as irrelevant or having no practical value. One of the most effective ways to avoid this problem and make seemingly complex and abstract information meaningful is to put definitions of new concepts into your own words and to create examples from your own life to illustrate the new ideas. Making information personally meaningful is a deep-level processing strategy that facilitates learning and understanding (not to mention simply making the material more interesting). Personal examples are another excellent way to facilitate generative learning, particularly making connections with what you already know.

Exercise 6.4   Practicing Your Note Taking

1. In this chapter, we introduced you to a three-step pro-cess for taking notes. Over a two-week period, choose at least one class in which you will take notes using the ideas presented in this chapter. In doing so, make sure that you set the stage for taking good notes, use an organized system for taking notes, ask questions in class, and review your notes within 24 hours. Re-member, too, to summarize the main points and write them in the recall column. Although taking notes in this way initially may be challenging, make sure you follow through on all steps for the entire two weeks.

2. After you have taken notes for the two-week period, answer the following questions:

   a. What are the strengths or positive characteristics of taking notes using the process presented in this chapter?

   b. What are the limitations of taking notes using the process presented in this chapter?

   c. Compare and contrast the note-taking process sug-gested in this chapter with the way you previously took notes.

   d. What system(s) will work best for you when taking notes in your classes? In other words, describe your ideal note-taking system.

Consider these two examples. First, suppose you are given the following formal definition:

Irony. Irony is an event or situation that is the opposite of what is promised or expected and which, therefore, seems to mock one's expectations.

Isabella created this personal example: "After lunch one day, I decided to take a short nap before practice. I was so tired that I knew I would have a bad practice if I did not get some rest. I set my alarm for an hour before practice so I would not be late. Unfortunately, the electricity went off and so my alarm did not. I overslept and showed up one hour late for practice. Coach was so angry with me that she kept me after practice for over an hour. I ran stairs, did push ups, sprints, you name it—I was so tired when she finally let me go that I thought I wouldn't make it home. My idea, to get some rest so I could have a better practice, ended up a nightmare."

Isabella's definition: You try to do something or expect something to happen, but whatever it is, it turns out to be the opposite of what you thought it would be. You feel a little ridiculous.

Or take another example:

Self-efficacy. Self-efficacy is people's belief in their abilities to organize and execute courses of action required to attain a specific, desired outcome.

Hector created this personal example: "I have a big gymnastic meet in the next two weeks, and I had to learn a new, difficult move on the high bar. At first, it was really hard, but I kept working on it because I knew that I could learn it and perform it well. After about a week, everything fell into place. My coach said that I had the move down, but I should keep practicing over the next week to really integrate it into my routine. My performance at the meet was nearly perfect."

Hector's definition: You feel confident in yourself and your abilities to do something specific, such as fix a car or read a textbook, and you keep working until you perfect it.

And a third example:

Lobbyist. A person or group of people who try to bring pressure to bear on legislators to pursue policies favorable to the lobbyist's interests.

Jennifer found an example from an article on the tobacco companies constantly having people talk about how tobacco is not so bad for you and giving money to legislators to vote their way.

Jennifer's definition: People who buy votes.

When you encounter new and difficult material, put the technical definitions into your own words and then find examples from your life, from books, movies, and newspapers to relate the material to your experience. The material will seem more relevant and will be more memorable if you have actively made it your own.

To help you see the power of constructing personal examples, you may want to complete Exercise 6.5.

Graphic Organizers

Although graphic organizers are especially useful for visual learners, almost all students can increase their learning by representing class and

> "It's not the will to win that matters—everyone has that. It's the will to prepare to win that matters."
>
> BEAR BRYANT
> *College Football Coaching Legend*

Exercise 6.5   Creating Personal Examples

1. Think of two concepts you have recently learned in your courses. Write the concepts' formal definitions.

_____

_____

_____

_____

2. Now, give an example for each one from your own experience.

_____

_____

_____

_____

_____

3. Finally, define the concepts in your own words.

_____

_____

_____

_____

_____

_____

text material graphically. In this section, we examine three such visual learning aids: pro-con T's, concept maps, and information matrices.

Pro-Con T. A pro-con T provides a visual mechanism for summarizing the reasons for and the reasons against some particular decision or course of action. In other words, it compares two sides of an issue. To create a pro-con T, take a piece of paper, draw a big T on it and then list reasons for the decision or action on one side and reasons against on the other. For example, consider deciding whether or not to ask someone out on a date (Figure 6.3).

The pro-con T can be used in a variety of situations. You might use it to think critically about a position being discussed in your political science class, or the negative and positive aspects of a theory in your sociology class. The pro-con T can also be a good way to start organizing a persuasive or a compare/contrast paper you have to write. It automatically suggests the paragraphs you might want to include, one for each reason. Finally, as illustrated in Figure 6.3, the pro-con T can help you deal with personal issues and make thoughtful decisions. To practice using pro-con T's, you may want to complete Exercise 6.6.

Concept maps. A concept map depicts a variety of relationships other than simple class inclusion. You sometimes see them in entertainment magazines to sort out complicated plot and story lines of movies or television shows. A concept map of some of the relationships among learning styles and different ways to take notes is shown in Figure 6.4. As you might surmise, concept maps are particularly useful for visual learners.

Pro	Con
I like this person a lot	I'm shy and have a hard time talking
We would have fun	I might make a fool of myself
I haven't been out for a while	I don't have much money now, so I don't know where we would go
They might say "yes"	They might say "no"

Figure 6.3   The Pro-Con T

Exercise 6.6   The Pro-Con T

1. In the space provided, construct a pro-con T to list the advantages and disadvantages of asking your professor questions in your classes. After you have compared both sides of the question, indicate whether you will continue to do so.

Pro	Con

2. Now, think of a personal issue or problem like whether to work during the summer months as opposed to train full time or take the next step in a relationship. Construct a pro-con T to help you make a decision.

Pro	Con

Information matrix. An information matrix provides a structure for integrating course material. It allows you to illustrate material that lends itself to comparison by common dimensions. Information matrices use units or groups about which similar questions may be asked, such as comparing different universities' athletic programs, wars, religions, theories of development, or models of psychoanalysis. Again, a common example involves the many comparison matrices used in magazines like *Consumer Reports,* where different brands of, say, computers are compared in terms of cost, memory storage, speed, ease of operation, and so on. *Entertainment Weekly* also periodically publishes information matrices of current movies and compares the movies with respect to such things as appropriate audience, who to see the movie with, what to wear, where to go afterwards, and so on. Finally, *Sports Illustrated* uses an information matrix-like system in its "The Pop Culture Grid." In this grid, different athletes answer five different questions.

Constructing an information matrix involves putting the material in a rectangular array with the items to be compared across the top of the array. Note that the comparison items must be logically comparable. If you are trying to decide what Division II university you are going to attend,

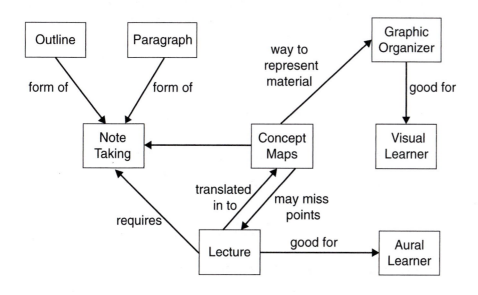

Figure 6.4 Concept Maps

then you shouldn't list the University of Michigan or UCLA (Division I universities) in the comparison group. List the questions on which the items will be compared down the side of the matrix. Questions should be specific enough to provide useful information and must apply to all of the comparison items. A general summary question that indicates what the information map tells you should be put in at the top.

Once you have set up the matrix, fill each individual cell with key-words or short statements that are abbreviations for answers to the questions. (You can obtain the answers from lecture notes, textbooks, or other research.) Once the matrix is complete, you can obtain either in-depth information or a broad comparison. For example, if you looked down a column, then you would find a fairly complete picture of the features of one of the items being compared. If you looked across a row, then you would get a rather complete picture of how the comparison items vary on that specific question. Empty cells in the matrix identify gaps in your knowledge and are indicators of what to fill in when studying for a test.

Figure 6.5 is an example of a partially completed information matrix on infant development from an introductory psychology course. Looking across the first row, you get a picture of physical growth and sensorimotor development in infants up to five months. Look down a column for a fairly complete picture of what an infant of that age

What are the norms for infant psychological and motor development?

	1 Month	2 Months	3 Months	4 Months	5 Months
What are the characteristics of physical growth and sensory-motor development?	Follows movement w/eyes; retains large objects	Blinks at object; lifts head; holds it erect	Sits w/support; head steady	Picks up cube w/palm grasp; sits with slight support	Effort to sit independently; turns from back to side; partial use of thumb
How does the baby interact socially?		Smiles socially	Reacts to disappearance of adult's faces		
What signs of acquiring language appear?	Responds to sound; vocalizes occasionally		Vocalizes to adult smiles/talk; searches for sound		Makes distinctive vocalizations
What are the signs of cognitive development?	Quiet when picked up	Anticipatory excitement; recognizes mother; inspects surroundings	Anticipatory adjustments to lifting	Head follows moving objects; inspects own fingers/hand; awareness of strange situations	Discriminates between strange and familiar objects

Figure 6.5 Information Matrix

Exercise 6.7   Using Information Matrices

Construct an information matrix of some area in one of your courses. Use the matrix to study and anticipate test questions in that course.

---

looks like in terms of several kinds of development. Empty cells need to be filled in to study the material adequately.

An information matrix is one of the most useful ways of summarizing and making connections among course topics. Matrices also provide you the information you need to construct practice exams for a course. In the information matrix example we provide, each row and column become obvious test questions. Looking at the first row, a possible examination question might be "Trace the characteristics of physical growth over the first five months of the infant's life." Looking at the first column, an obvious question would be "At one month old the infant has what social, linguistic, physical, and cognitive characteristics?" To help you learn to develop information matrices, you may want to complete Exercise 6.7.

Post-Game Review

In this chapter, we discussed the importance of making a record of the material covered in your classes and introduced you to a three-step note-taking system. Although note taking may be a skill you have not fully developed, it is important that you be self-responsible in this area. As you attend class and practice your note taking, you will likely notice improvements in the way you organize and record the material presented by the instructor. In addition, you will likely notice an increase in your self-efficacy, making you more confident about your ability to take notes in all your classes. Remember, because lectures are one of the two primary channels through which course material will be communicated to you, if you cannot take adequate notes in your classes, you decrease your chances of academic success.

Thinking Critically about Taking Notes and In-Class Behaviors

1. Summarize what you now know about note taking based on the information presented in this chapter.

_____

_____

_____

2. What additional questions do you have about these topics and how to use the skills introduced in this chapter?

_____

_____

_____

3. What conclusions can you draw about this topic and how it might help you be a more effective and successful student and athlete?

_____

_____

_____

Achieve IT! Setting a Note-Taking Goal

1. Based on your self-assessment and your responses to Thinking Critically, select a goal in relation to taking more effective notes or being more successful in the classroom that you would like to achieve this term.

2. Now identify three short-term goals that will help you reach your goal this term.

3. For the short-term goals, identify the attainment strategies you will need to reach them.

4. List any obstacles you might face in trying to reach these goals and identify your plan for overcoming each one.

Don't forget to make your goal visible and tell others about them, so they can keep you accountable regarding what you want to achieve.

Chapter 6 Review Questions

1. Taking notes in your classes is not that important as long as you actively listen to lectures. (True or False)

2. Note taking serves two primary functions, including

    a. Encoding and retrieval.
    b. Storage and memory.
    c. Encoding and perception.
    d. Encoding and storage.

3. Maria has heard that generative approaches will help her more effectively learn her class material. She does not, however, know what generative learning entails. You explain to her that it involves

    a. Reviewing her notes within 24 hours of taking them.
    b. Making connections between current class material and information she has previously learned.
    c. Asking questions in class.
    d. Watching for instructor cues.

4. To "set the stage" to take good notes, you should

    a. Eat well and be rested.
    b. Review your notes from the last class.
    c. Read the textbook assignments.
    d. B and C.
    e. All of the above.

5. By sitting in the front and center of your classes, you

   a. Increase your chances of getting to know your instructors.
   b. Increase your chances of staying awake.
   c. Increase your chances of staying focused and taking more complete notes.
   d. A and B.
   e. All of the above.

6. When you are listening to lectures, you should think about what the instructor is saying and then record your notes in your own words. (True or False)

7. When instructors lecture, they often give cues as to what material is important. Such cues might include

   a. Repetition.
   b. Sending you an e-mail.
   c. Telling you something is important.
   d. A and C.
   e. All of the above.

8. You should first review your class notes within _____ hours of taking them.

   a. 24
   b. 48
   c. 72
   d. 168

9. _____ help(s) you make complex and abstract class material more meaningful.

   a. Personal examples
   b. Taking notes
   c. Reading your textbook
   d. Self-efficacy

10. Information matrices allow you to visually map out linkages amongst common elements in the material you are studying. (True or False)

Chapter **7** | Succeeding
in the Classroom
Reading and Studying Textbooks

Game Plan:

In this chapter, you will learn:

- How to study your textbooks effectively and efficiently

- How to minimize distractions while you read and study

- About three basic principles for successfully studying textbooks in college

- How to make reading for pleasure and knowledge a part of the rest of your life

© Vladimir Wrangel, 2009 / Used under license from Shutterstock.com

"If you want to be good, you have to practice, practice, practice."

ALEX ENGLISH
Former NBA All Star

Self-Assessment—Perceive It!

Read the following statements and place a checkmark next to each one you generally do. For you to change and develop new and effective academic, athletic, and personal strategies, you must be accurate in your self-perception. So, be honest in how you answer each question.

1. When I read my textbooks, I am rarely distracted. _____

2. Before I begin studying a textbook, I take a few minutes to look over what I am about to read. _____

3. I finish all my assigned readings before they are due. _____

4. I read all the assigned materials in all of my classes. _____

5. When I read my textbooks, I can successfully determine the main points and identify the supporting details. _____

6. I do a short review of my reading immediately after completing it. _____

7. Before a test, I review my textbook readings over the course of several days, usually studying for a few hours each day. _____

8. Whenever I read my textbooks, my goal is to understand what I am reading as opposed to just trying to get it done. _____

9. When I review my textbook assignments, I make connections among related material and try to understand the material in my own words. _____

10. When I read my textbook assignments, I am actively involved—I take notes, highlight sections in the book, look for answers to my questions, and so on. _____

11. I study and read at times when I am most alert and attentive. _____

12. Before I read a textbook assignment, I develop questions that I use to focus my reading and help keep me focused. _____

13. As I read, I monitor how well I am learning the material and, if I do not understand, then I go back and review. _____

14. I read other materials, such as books, newspapers, magazines, or Web sites, on a regular basis. _____

15. When I read and do not understand a word, I determine its meaning before proceeding. _____

Take a moment to review your responses. How many items did you check? Each one you checked represents a current strength. Now consider the items you did not check. These represent areas where focus and growth are needed. Now, to summarize your self-perception, complete the following statements:

1. My areas of strength are:

_____

2. The areas I need to improve are:

_____

As you read this chapter and participate in your classes, keep your strengths and areas of improvement in mind. At the end of the chapter, you will have the chance to set a goal related to these areas. Achieving these goals will help you become a more effective student and athlete.

Introduction

Ciara was a freshman on the women's swimming and diving team. She had been heavily recruited to compete for the school, but was intimidated by the institution's academic reputation. Even so, she got off on the right foot during her first few weeks on campus. She attended all her classes, read her textbook chapters as assigned, went to study hall five days a week, and sought tutoring as needed. After a month of carrying out this schedule, though, she was growing tired of the routine of going to classes and studying. She continued to attend all her classes (she had to, because the athletic department advisors kept track of her attendance!) and to take notes on the lectures. In study hall, she would review her notes, but she now tended only to skim her reading. She had discovered that her instructors' lectures were quite similar to the textbook chapters they assigned. Given the overlap, she decided not to waste her time. Besides, swimming training was getting more intense and she needed to be as efficient in her studying as possible.

Through her next set of exams, she continued to attend class but neglect her readings. On her first set of exams she had done okay, earning mostly Bs. This time, though, her performance was much worse. (Her highest grade was a C.) She did not know what the problem was. She went to class, listened to the lectures, and reviewed her notes before each test. Even so, she just didn't seem to know the material as well as the instructor expected. Now she was in trouble. The semester was two-thirds over, swimming was in full swing, and she only had one more set of exams on which to improve her performance before finals. In addition, she found that there was more and more reading in her classes and more material that the instructor was not covering in class. She knew she had to do her readings, but it was hard to concentrate because she was so tired when she studied at night. Although she tried to study more, she never was able to get through all her readings. Most of the time, she did not do them until a few days before her exam. Needless to say, her academic performance did not improve. She was able to maintain her eligibility (barely), but the first semester had been a wake-up call. If she did not find a more effective and efficient way to study her readings, then she would never make it at this school.

Ciara's experience is not unique among college students. For many student-athletes, one of the biggest academic challenges is adjusting to the amount of reading assigned in each course. In college, most classes require at least one textbook, if not several, and you are responsible for learning the material in these and in the class lectures. In addition, your instructors expect you to read your textbook assignments outside of class, in preparation for the next lecture. Like Ciara, though, many college students do not keep up with their readings or have difficulty understanding and learning what they have read.

There are, however, several strategies that "effective" readers use to enhance their learning (Dole, Duffy, Roehler, & Person, 1991):

1. *Determine the importance of the material.* Effective readers learn to identify the important, main ideas in the textbook, highlighting only what is essential to learn. Less successful readers get themselves bogged down in too much information and feel overwhelmed. (They highlight too much.)

2. *Create summaries when they have finished reading.* At the end of sections and the entire chapter, in their own words, effective readers write an integrative summary of the main points of what they have read. In this summary, they organize the information in personally meaningful ways and elaborate on its presented meaning, making connections to previously learned material.

3. *Draw inferences.* Effective readers use inferences to fill in the blanks of what they have read and to elaborate on the meaning of the material. To do this, they ask themselves higher-level questions about the material. For example, in a developmental psychology class, they might ask: "What does the author really mean when she discusses the importance of understanding the influences of nature vs. nurture?" or "How does what the author has presented compare and contrast with other points of view on the influences of genetics vs. environmental factors in

determining personality?" To answer these questions, the reader must think beyond the printed words on the page.

4. *Generate questions.* Prior to and during reading, effective readers generate questions about the material in the textbook. (See Chapter 6 for information on the different types of questions you create for yourself.) They then use these questions to focus their attention and, by trying to find the answers as they go, make reading an active and deep-level learning experience. Simply reading and highlighting, as many students do, is an ineffective, passive, and surface-level approach—one that is not conducive to learning.

5. *Self-monitor their comprehension.* As they read, effective readers determine how well they understand the material by continually asking and honestly answering questions such as "How well do I understand what I just read?" They also use the questions they have created as a tool for monitoring their level of understanding. If they can answer their questions without referring back to the textbook, then they know their comprehension is good. If they cannot, then they have feedback indicating that they need to study that section more.

In this chapter, we discuss several strategies that will help you become proficient at doing what effective readers do each time they read a textbook. Although we will introduce a specific system for effectively reading your textbooks, we begin by focusing on two important issues: your motivation and the place where you study, both of which can interfere with students being effective readers.

Preparation: Setting the Stage to Study

Often, being successful in your studying requires two simple things. The first is just getting started, even if you do not feel motivated. If you wait until you feel motivated before you begin your studying, then you will often be waiting until the last minute; this is not a good plan. Instead, get started; it may be tough at first, but the longer you stay focused and make progress, the stronger your motivation is likely to become. Yes, motivation sometimes follows action. Sometimes you just have to fight every urge you have to put things off and to NOT get started and just begin. You can use goal setting as a tool to help you when you are not feeling motivated. Set a realistic, measurable, short-term goal, such as reading 10 pages in your history book. Make your goal part of your daily to-do list or daily schedule and then get started. Remember, success (finishing the 10 pages) breeds higher self-efficacy, which raises motivation! It's a positive cycle you want to start for yourself. So, follow the classic Nike ad and "Just do it!"

Second, being successful requires intense focus and as few distractions as possible. If you study in an environment where you are constantly interrupted or unable to concentrate, then you decrease your chances of learning. To help you examine the environments in which you study and the possible distractions you face, you may want to complete Exercise 7.1.

> "It takes education to be successful in the game of life."
>
> BOB LANIER
> *NBA Hall of Famer*

Exercise 7.1   What Distracts You?

1. Describe in detail the place where you usually study, including whether you study by yourself or with other people around.

_____

_____

2. Within your study environment, what distracts you?

_____

_____

3. Of these distractions, which are under your control or can be changed?

_____

_____

If you have been honest with yourself, then you will probably find that many of your distractions are under your control—that is, you can do something about them.

As a college student, you will have the freedom to choose where you study (except if you are mandated to study in your athletic academic center). Finding a place that is conducive to focused reading and studying is like creating an ideal training environment. Think about your practices. Is that environment basically free from distractions? Does it help you focus and be ready to practice? In other words, when you walk into the gym, onto the field, or onto the pool deck, does the environment help your mind and body get ready to practice? If you are like most student-athletes with whom we have worked, then the practice environment brings about an almost automatic response or readiness to perform (somewhat like your bed brings about the response of going to sleep!). Your coaches create ideal practice environments so the time you spend there can be devoted to one thing: improving in your sport. The place where you study is no different. In fact, that environment may be more important than where you practice because your academic self-efficacy may be lower than your efficacy as an athlete. Because your coach will not be determining where you study (unless you study at your athletic academic center), you need to take the responsibility to create an environment that is free from distractions and helps you focus on the task at hand: effectively reading and studying your textbooks. To help you create an ideal study environment, you may want to complete Exercise 7.2.

In thinking about your study environment and routine, here are some common distractions you may experience and some suggestions for coping with each.

1. *Teammates and friends.* Studying with other people has pluses and minuses. On the positive side, working with others can facilitate understanding material, particularly for aural learners. They can help you learn material by assisting you in making connections, developing personally meaningful examples, and in quizzing you on what you have read so you can determine your level of comprehension. On the negative side, they can be a source of distraction—talking with you, texting, or passing notes. Although all of these may seem more interesting than 50 pages of reading, they interfere with reaching your academic goals.

   If people distract you (you are naturally drawn to them and want to talk), then study in an environment, such as the library, where you are by yourself or are not allowed to talk. If

---

Exercise 7.2   An Ideal Study Environment

For this exercise, you will need to identify a student-athlete (on your team or not) who is academically successful. If you are not sure who that might be, ask your athletic academic advisor/coach to identify someone who fits the description. After identifying this student-athlete, you will ask them the following questions:

1. Where do you study? Why do you study in this location?

_____

_____

2. What are the components of your study environment (e.g., a desk, good lighting, by yourself)? Of these, how does each one help you stay focused on your studying?

_____

_____

3. What do you do to minimize distractions and maximize your focus and attention when studying/reading?

_____

_____

Now, answer the following questions:

4. Compare and contrast this "ideal environment" (as described to you by the student-athlete you interviewed) with your current study environment (see Exercise 7.1 if you need a reminder of your study environment).

_____

_____

5. Now, describe your ideal study environment. In doing so, state specifically what needs to be in the environment, when you would study during each day (and during each week), with whom you would study, etc.

_____

_____

---

you are required to attend study hall, then sit by yourself away from your friends in a spot where you can concentrate on your work. If your friends are offended by this action, then they will just have to deal with it. Remember, you are in college to get an education.

2. *Studying in your room, apartment, or house.* For many students, these places are ideal for studying because they are convenient, comfortable, and safe. For others, though, these environments present too many distractions: TVs, iPods, computers, roommates, cell phones, magazines, refrigerators, beds, friends stopping by, etc. If studying in your room is distracting, then make a change. Certainly one choice is to go somewhere else, such as the library. If you choose to, or must, stay at home, then consider doing the following:

   a. Turn off the TV, iPod, computer, cell phone, and so on. TiVo any TV shows you like so you can watch them after your homework is done.

   b. Close the door to your room and put an "I'm studying" sign on your door.

   c. Study at a desk or table, in a comfortable chair, with good lighting. If you study in bed or on a couch, then you increase your chances of becoming distracted and falling asleep.

   d. Reward yourself when you finish your studying. For example, you might go next door and talk with your friends after you finish your reading assignments.

3. *Physical and mental fatigue.* As a student-athlete, you will expend considerable physical and mental energy each day in practices and competitions. Here are some things you can do to help minimize your level of fatigue:

a. Sleep a consistent and sufficient number of hours each night. If you need seven hours each night to be rested, then make sure you get them. Don't stay up until 3:00 A.M., wake up at 7:30 A.M. for an 8:00 class, and then wonder why you are tired. For more information on this topic, see Chapter 10, "Health and Performance."

b. Study your most difficult material, such as reading your biology text, when you are most alert and energized. If you practice in the afternoon and are exhausted by the time you get home at 7:00 P.M., then consider doing your homework earlier in the day, when you are not so tired. Although many student-athletes' mornings and early afternoons are filled with classes, there is often some time (though perhaps not every day) that can be used for studying. Take advantage of those "open" times, whether 10 minutes or two hours, to get your studying done. During other times when you are tired, do studying and tasks that require less focus and mental energy, such as retyping a paper or making note cards.

Credit Cards—Easy Money or Future Peril?

If you do not already have a credit card by the time you enter college, then you are likely to get one over the next five years. On most college campuses, credit card companies use all sorts of promotional tools to entice you to join and use one of their cards. You will be offered 0 percent interest for a certain number of months, a $20.00 iTunes card, T-shirts, baseball caps, etc., if you will just sign up for their card. These promotions (and pressured sales) are so successful that 84 percent of college student have credit cards, and over half have more than four cards (Source: Sallie Mae, April 2009, *How Undergraduate Students Use Credit Cards*). Unfortunately, what these salespeople do not tell you in their pitch is that the average college student carries $2,169 in credit card debt (Source: Nellie Mae, May 2005, *Undergraduate Students and Credit Cards in 2004: An Analysis of Usage Rates and Trends*), and we can guarantee they are not getting it for 0 percent interest!

As we discussed in Chapter 1, most credit cards offer you a "free" short-term loan (though some do not offer this grace period and start charging you interest immediately upon making a purchase, so be aware of the conditions associated with your credit cards). If your card does have a grace period, the process works like this. When you purchase an item (and we recommend that you keep *all* your receipts), the cost of that item is transferred to your account; all your purchases during your billing cycle, which generally lasts 30 days (for example, your cycle may end the 18th of each month) will end up in your account. Within a few days of your cycle ending, you will be sent a bill (or, if you do your banking and financial transactions on-line, you can view what you owe and make payments in real time). The bill will include a list of all your transactions, the date on which they occurred, the merchants, and the amount spent. To prevent credit card fraud or theft, you should immediately review the transactions to make sure that you made each one (you can compare them against your receipts; if you notice a discrepancy, immediately call your credit card company to alert them so they can investigate). If your transactions are correct, then you have one of two options. First, you can pay the entire balance by the due date, which is what we encourage you do every month. If you take this option, then you truly are receiving a "free" short-term loan from the credit card company. Second, you can pay at least the minimum amount (you can pay this minimum up to the full amount you owe) by the due date. If you take this option, then you will be paying interest on the balance and that these interest rates can be 9 percent, 12 percent, 18 percent, or higher. Also, if you do not pay your bill by the due date, you may be charged a late fee of $25.00, $50.00, or higher. All of these charges, interest, and late fees can add up quickly and only make it more difficult for you to pay off your balance in the future. Credit card companies hope you carry a balance with them because this is one way they make money.

Although you may have a large credit limit with your card (e.g., $5,000.00), only spend each month what you can pay off when your bill is due. Certainly, there are financial emergencies where you will need to pay a bill or cover an expense and your credit card is the only option. But for situations over which you have more control, such as voluntary purchases (e.g., iTunes, movies, coffee, drinks, clothes, shoes), stay within your budget. If you consistently spend more than you have, and you put those purchases on your credit card, then you will leave college with a potentially large debt that may take years to pay off (and remember, as you make these payments, much of the money is going toward the interest you owe the credit card company, not to pay down your balance). Debt such as this also can affect your credit score, which will be important should you want to rent an apartment, lease a car, buy anything on store credit, or take out a mortgage to buy a house. Credit cards may seem like easy money, but they come with definite costs if you are not able to be self-responsible with your spending. To avoid these pitfalls, you should:

1. Carry only one, maybe two credit cards.

2. Carry credit cards that have no annual fees and low interest rates. Shop around to find the best card for you.

3. Every credit card company uses a different way to calculate interest rate. It's required by law for your credit card company to provide you with a notice about changes to and information regarding your interest rate, along with a statement telling you which method they will use to calculate the interest on your account. Read these statements carefully when making your decision about what credit card to choose.

4. Know your monthly budget and make sure you stay within it. Remember, it may seem like free money at the time, but you have to pay off your credit card purchases at some point in time.

5. Pay off your balance each month. If you cannot, then pay as much as you can so you can get it paid off as soon as possible.

6. Always make a payment by the due date to avoid late charges/fees.

4. *Injury.* Even minor ones can be a source of distraction and require a significant amount of energy and time each day, and thus may interfere with your ability to be an effective student. Injuries also can cause severe emotional distress, such as depression and anxiety, which may disrupt your concentration. If an injury is making it difficult to follow through on your responsibilities, then talk with someone in the athletic department, such as your athletic trainer or academic advisor, to find out what assistance might be available on your campus. Most schools have counseling centers with trained professionals, and some athletic departments have support groups for injured athletes. Services such as these can help you learn to cope more effectively with the demands and the stress of being injured. If you do choose to talk with someone, then be honest about the problems your injury is causing so you can get the assistance you need.

5. *Hunger.* Being hungry is a major distraction, so make sure that you eat nutritiously, taking into account the energy demands of your sport. Try to eat smaller meals and snacks throughout the day so you can maintain a high level of physical energy and mental focus. Too many times, student-athletes will skip meals or just eat non-nutritious foods. Then later, after practice, they will binge to make up for what they have missed during the day. Such an approach makes it harder to be a high-level performer, whether in athletics or in academics. Treat yourself as you would a prized car. You too need the proper type and amount of fuel if your "engine" is to function at its highest level. (See Chapter 10, "Health and Performance," for more information.) If you are hungry while you are studying, then take a short break to eat a snack. Of course, don't let getting food become a distraction in itself.

6. *Unresolved problems or other things on your mind.* If you are distressed by a recent breakup with your boyfriend/girlfriend, worried about where you are going to get the money to pay your rent, or anxious about how you will manage three exams and an out-of-town competition, then you may be so preoccupied with your problems that you cannot concentrate on your studying. With more serious problems, it may be useful to talk with a professional counselor to help you solve your problems by offering support and a different perspective. For less serious problems, you might talk with a friend or write about the problem in a journal. Sometimes just getting the problem out of your mind and onto paper can help free you from thinking about it for a while.

Finding a time and a place that help you concentrate on your reading and studying is crucial for academic success. If, after completing Exercise 7.2, you determine that you need to find a new place to study, such as the library, be sure you give yourself sufficient time to adjust. Don't give up after one or two tries. Instead, plan to stick with this new behavior for at least a month before you determine

whether it will work. We have known many student-athletes who initially balked at the idea of studying during the day or at the library ("The library is too quiet," or "I want to take a nap during that time") but later decided that these options were best. Trying something new can be uncomfortable at first, so give it time.

Preparation: The Fundamentals of Reading in College

In most sports, there are certain basic skills, or fundamentals, that you simply need to master if you are going to excel. Without doing so, an athlete's chances for success are seriously diminished. The same is true when it comes to reading your textbooks. There are three fundamentals with respect to college reading that, if followed, will increase your chances of being successful in school (Petrie, Petrie, Landry & Edwards, 2002):

1. *Read ALL the assigned material in ALL your classes.* Basic, straightforward, but rarely followed. If instructors assign textbook chapters or other written materials, then they expect you to read them. Textbooks are independent sources of information that you are responsible for learning, and you can be tested on anything from them. Treat your class readings like your sport's playbook: read and learn everything!

2. *Read ahead in all your classes.* In most if not all college classes, you will receive course syllabi that provide a schedule of topics to be covered along with the assigned textbook readings. Instructors expect you to read the material before you come to class. If Chapter 5 is assigned for the fifth week of school, then you should have completed the reading prior to the instructor's lecture. Reading ahead also gives you a context in which to understand your lectures. If you have already read about the day's topic, then you are in a better position to learn, remember, and ask questions to clarify the material that is being presented.

3. *Read to understand the material.* Whenever you sit down to study, make sure you are ready to understand the material. Don't just let your eyes drift across the words on the page. Be active in your reading. Don't try to memorize the assignment, either; instead, try to determine what the material really means and what the author of the text is trying to communicate. Taking this approach while you read your assignments will increase your chances of being prepared for your exams and other classroom assignments.

Performance: A Method for Effectively Studying Textbooks

To learn college material, you have to be able to read actively for comprehension. In this section, we discuss a method for studying your textbooks that will help you do so. Based on the SQ4R system

Study Time: Quality vs. Quantity

Whether in athletics or academics, to be successful, you have to spend a lot of time practicing and preparing (in fact, some sport psychologists suggest that it takes upwards of 10 years of practice [about 10,000 hours of deliberate practice] to become an expert in anything). If you don't put in enough hours studying, then you decrease the likelihood that you will be adequately prepared for your exams and other assignments. But is the amount of time you spend studying always the only indicator of your level of preparation? No! What also matters is how focused and attentive you are during your practice and preparation; that is, *what was the quality of the work you did?* For example, consider two equally intelligent student-athletes, Gretchen and Jessie, who had to prepare for the same college algebra exam. If you knew only that Gretchen had studied 10 hours and Jessie 6, then you might assume that Gretchen would do better on the exam. To more accurately determine who would perform better, you would need to know the quality of their study time. In this case, Jessie studied in the library, averaging two hours a day on each of the three days before the exam. She was undistracted and able to focus completely on her work. She took the time to review her notes and textbook readings, applying deep-level learning strategies, such as elaboration and association. Gretchen, on the other hand, studied in her room. Friends were always there, and the TV was on. In addition, most of the time she studied was spent the night before the exam, when she was tired from a physically demanding day of practice. Needless to say, the quality of Gretchen's studying was quite poor. In this case, quality trumped quantity. So, when scheduling your study time and location, always keep in mind the idea of quality vs. quantity.

(Robinson, 1946), and other recent work in psychology, this method provides you with strategies that help you prepare yourself to read effectively (like practicing your sport), read actively and for comprehension (like performing your sport), and review what you read to facilitate learning (like the post-game review).

Before introducing this method, though, we want to remind you that being actively involved in reading and studying takes time, energy, and effort, as well as self-responsibility. You cannot hope to learn anything from your textbooks if you simply let your eyes drift across each page. You have to be an active, involved, interested participant in your reading. Although this method can help you to increase your focus and become more actively involved, its value will be limited unless you implement the fundamentals of reading we introduced earlier in the chapter.

Step 1: Preparing to Read

Being successful in your sport requires that you understand your opponent, whether that be an individual, team, or even a physical environment, such as a golf course. You learn about your opponent so you will be better prepared when the competition actually begins. A similar idea applies in reading and studying. Before you actually begin reading your textbook, you want to find out what you are up against and then formulate questions that will help focus your attention while you read.

So, before you start, take some time to learn about what you are going to read by doing the following:

1. *Read the title of the book and the table of contents to determine what topics will be covered.*

2. *Read the preface of the book (if, again, you are at the beginning).* The preface is a statement by the author or editor that describes the overall purpose of the book: the perfect place to get an overview of what you will be learning during the semester.

3. *Review the chapter objectives or purpose.* What specific learning goals has the author identified? For example, at the beginning of this chapter, you would find that one of our objectives is for you to learn the fundamentals of college reading.

4. *Review the introduction to the chapter.* What is the main idea or point of the chapter? What topics will be covered in the chapter?

5. *Review the section headings and subheadings.* What subject areas do the authors consider important and include in the text? How have the authors organized the material?

6. *Review the summary, review questions, and the glossary at the end of the chapter.* What content areas or terms did the author think important enough to present again at the end?

7. *Pay attention to any visual aids, such as figures, charts, or tables.* What information has the author made prominent in this way?

8. *Examine any boldfaced or italicized terms.* What terms does the author think are important and want you to learn?

By taking the time to survey your text, you provide yourself with an overview of the topic(s) to be covered in the reading assignment. Having a broad understanding of the material before you begin reading provides you with a framework within which to better learn and remember what you read. In addition, if you have a basic idea of what is to be covered, then you may feel more confident and comfortable when you actually begin reading.

How long should you spend surveying? Initially, it will take a little longer to do, just as any new skill takes longer when you are learning it. In fact, you may feel a little awkward at first and may not be convinced that this is a good use of your time. Don't skip over this step! After you practice and become more proficient at previewing your reading, you will likely spend no more than five minutes doing so. This initial investment of a few minutes may, in the end, help you save time because it helps you become more actively involved in the reading process.

While previewing, you also want to take a few minutes to create questions that can focus your attention and help you become more actively involved when reading. To develop these questions, take the headings/subheadings, introductory sentences, chapter learning objectives, or other items that you have previewed and turn them into queries. (Always make sure that your questions include all types, ranging from

Improving Your Vocabulary While You Read

As you progress through college and take classes in different disciplines, you will be exposed to words and terms that may, at times, seem quite foreign (the terminology of a discipline can be like a foreign language that must be learned and put into words you do understand). Part of being an active and involved reader is recognizing when you do not understand the meaning of a word or term, and then doing something about it. If you do not know how to pronounce a word or do not understand what it means, then do NOT just skip over it. Instead, follow these strategies to help you learn new words and terms and, in the process, improve your vocabulary:

1. Mark the word in some way, such as highlighting it, so you can easily identify it in the future.

2. Try to determine its meaning based on the context of the sentence in which it is used. Oftentimes you will be able to discern the meaning based on what is being communicated.

3. If you cannot figure out the word's meaning based on context, then see if the word is in the book's glossary (basically, a dictionary placed at the end of textbooks in which terms that are important in that discipline are defined). If so, write the definition on the page of the book where the word is located.

4. If there is no glossary or the term is not presented there, then look up the word in a dictionary. Always have a dictionary with you when you study and read. It can be a small paper copy or you can use one of the many online dictionaries, such as the Free Dictionary, by FarFlex (http://www.thefreedictionary.com/).

5. Once you have found the word in a dictionary, pay attention to how it is pronounced, how the word is used (e.g., noun, adverb), the definition of the word, synonyms, and how it can be used in a sentence. It is not enough just to know the definition.

6. To make this word part of your lexicon (you might want to look up "lexicon"), you can use note cards to help. Write the word on one side (with how it is pronounced) and then on the other side, write how it is used, the meaning, and then a new sentence in which you use it properly.

7. With your note cards from your reading, make a commitment to use these new words over the next few days. That is, use them when talking with your instructors, in conversations with your friends, in your writing, post it on your Facebook wall. . . . What are you doing right now? ("Learning a new word, chimera."), etc. Just like in sports when a new skill or play is introduced, you practice it live to facilitate learning. The same strategy applies here.

Having an extensive vocabulary will serve you well in your life, be it in relationships or your career. Although you live in an age where "usg slng is OK, u wil nd 2 rite prprly in ur jb or evn 2 get one in the 1st place." So, take the extra time when you read and are exposed to new words to expand your vocabulary and your ability to communicate extensively and effectively.

Exercise 7.3 Developing Questions

Review the headings/subheadings, learning objectives, and introductory sentences of this chapter with the intent of developing questions. In the margins of your text, list at least five different questions, making sure that the questions include both factual and conceptual types. If you can, compare these with the questions a classmate has developed to give you even more ideas. Next, develop questions in a textbook for another class and use those to improve your understanding and retention.

---

factual to "what if." See Chapter 6 for more information.) For example, in this chapter, you could develop questions using the chapter learning objectives ("What are the three basic guidelines for reading successfully in college?"), the section headings ("How do the steps of the reading method build on each other?"), or the special boxes ("Why is the quality of your study time so important for learning?"). Next, write the questions in your book beside the relevant sections. As you read, you can look at each question before you begin that section. This method will help you focus on the material because you now are reading with a purpose: to find the answer to your questions. Instead of just letting your eyes drift across the page, you are searching for specific information. When you read in this way, you are bound to be more interested, focused, and alert. To help you practice developing questions, you may want to complete Exercise 7.3.

Step 2: Reading Actively for Comprehension

Sounds simple enough, but reading is an active process that requires energy, effort, and focus if you want to truly understand and learn the material. However, if you have prepared yourself well, just like if you have practiced sufficiently in your sport, then you have set the stage for a great performance.

Read with the intention of finding the answers to the questions you developed during your preparation. Taking this approach will help you to be more interested in and focused on your task. As you read, reflect on the material and try to understand it in your own words. Thinking about and then creating answers to your questions requires a deeper level of understanding than simply memorizing what is on the page, and it increases the likelihood that you are learning the material. When you have formulated your answer, write it in the margin beneath the question. If you are highlighting your book, then mark the sentences that contain the answers to your questions. Identifying the answers, in some form, provides you with a permanent record of what you have read and makes future reviewing and studying easier to do.

Students often take one of two approaches when highlighting information in their texts. First, they don't highlight anything because they want to sell their books back at the end of the term. Like a car, however, once purchased, a book loses much of its resale value. Thus, don't worry about what you might get back financially at the end of the term. Instead, think about how you can use your book to its fullest advantage now—to learn about the material being taught in the class.

> "There are worse crimes than burning books. One of them is not reading them."
>
> JOSEPH BRODSKY
> *Poet*

Second, students fail to discriminate between important and not so important information, and thus highlight far too much. When you read, you must determine what is so important it should be marked in some way. Part of becoming a skilled reader is learning how to discern what is important, such as main points and supporting details, and what is not. After you read a section, think about the material before you make any marks on the page. What parts of the section help you to understand the topic better? What is a given passage telling you? What information answers your question? After you have thought about the material, highlight the important text or write your answer in the column. Being deliberate will give you the time to identify the most important points. In the long run, this approach will save you time because you do not have to reread the chapter when you study for an exam. Instead, you can focus on the questions and answers you wrote in the margins or the text you highlighted. For an example of how a section of text might be highlighted, see Figure 7.1.

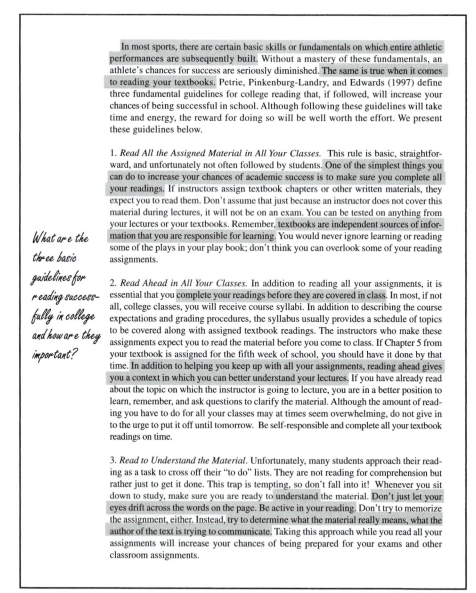

What are the three basic guidelines for reading successfully in college and how are they important?

In most sports, there are certain basic skills or fundamentals on which entire athletic performances are subsequently built. Without a mastery of these fundamentals, an athlete's chances for success are seriously diminished. The same is true when it comes to reading your textbooks. Petrie, Pinkenburg-Landry, and Edwards (1997) define three fundamental guidelines for college reading that, if followed, will increase your chances of being successful in school. Although following these guidelines will take time and energy, the reward for doing so will be well worth the effort. We present these guidelines below.

1. *Read All the Assigned Material in All Your Classes.* This rule is basic, straightforward, and unfortunately not often followed by students. One of the simplest things you can do to increase your chances of academic success is to make sure you complete all your readings. If instructors assign textbook chapters or other written materials, they expect you to read them. Don't assume that just because an instructor does not cover this material during lectures, it will not be on an exam. You can be tested on anything from your lectures or your textbooks. Remember, textbooks are independent sources of information that you are responsible for learning. You would never ignore learning or reading some of the plays in your play book; don't think you can overlook some of your reading assignments.

2. *Read Ahead in All Your Classes.* In addition to reading all your assignments, it is essential that you complete your readings before they are covered in class. In most, if not all, college classes, you will receive course syllabi. In addition to describing the course expectations and grading procedures, the syllabus usually provides a schedule of topics to be covered along with assigned textbook readings. The instructors who make these assignments expect you to read the material before you come to class. If Chapter 5 from your textbook is assigned for the fifth week of school, you should have it done by that time. In addition to helping you keep up with all your assignments, reading ahead gives you a context in which you can better understand your lectures. If you have already read about the topic on which the instructor is going to lecture, you are in a better position to learn, remember, and ask questions to clarify the material. Although the amount of reading you have to do for all your classes may at times seem overwhelming, do not give in to the urge to put it off until tomorrow. Be self-responsible and complete all your textbook readings on time.

3. *Read to Understand the Material.* Unfortunately, many students approach their reading as a task to cross off their "to do" lists. They are not reading for comprehension but rather just to get it done. This trap is tempting, so don't fall into it! Whenever you sit down to study, make sure you are ready to understand the material. Don't just let your eyes drift across the words on the page. Be active in your reading. Don't try to memorize the assignment, either. Instead, try to determine what the material really means, what the author of the text is trying to communicate. Taking this approach while you read all your assignments will increase your chances of being prepared for your exams and other classroom assignments.

Figure 7.1 Highlighting
Your Text

Step 3: Post-Reading Review

To learn anything, you must practice. Think about when you are trying to learn a new skill or play in your sport. How do you do it? In most cases, the skill or play is presented, and then you practice it many, many times. The same idea applies to your reading. If you want to learn what you have read, then you will need to think about it (with the book closed); don't just look at the book over and over again. Whenever you finish a major section in a chapter, take a minute or two to go over its main points. If you have answered your questions in the columns or highlighted your text, then simply review the important information. This type of practice can enhance your understanding and, in the end, decrease your study time, because you will be learning the material more thoroughly the first time around.

When you finish your reading—for instance, when you complete a chapter—follow these strategies:

1. *Review your reading immediately upon finishing.* You are not finished when you reach that last page of the chapter. This end of the chapter review will be more thorough than the section reviews you have been doing throughout your reading and will act as a comprehension and memory check. For this review, close the book and think about what you have just read. If you want, you can write down the information in a notebook (but again, do so with your book closed). You also could use your questions to "quiz" yourself (e.g., cover up the material in the book, ask yourself the question, and then determine if you can answer it; again, do not look at the material in the book). You also can use the words in the glossary or the chapter review questions to test yourself. If there are any questions that you have difficulty answering, then make a note of them so you can spend additional time on them during future study sessions. Again, a key to this review is that you *think* about the material and you do so without looking at the material in the book (keep it closed!).

2. *Review within one day after you finish your reading assignment.* Just as you spend several days in a row practicing the same skill, such as learning a new dismount off of the balance beam, you will need to do the same with your studying if you are truly going to master the material. For this review, spend about 10 to 15 minutes going over the reading, again thinking about what you have read and considering your questions. Don't just reread the material in your book. Just like in your sport, you have to move from a controlled practice/scrimmage (which is what rereading your text is like) to playing live (which is what thinking about and discussing what was in your reading, with the book closed, is like). Also, make sure you are organizing the information (e.g., creating an information matrix), creating associations with other related material, and developing personal examples to make it more meaningful.

> "A competitor will find a way to win. Competitors take bad breaks and use them to drive themselves that much harder. Quitters take bad breaks and use them as reasons to give up."
>
> NANCY LOPEZ
> *LPGA Hall of Fame Golfer*

© Christopher Halloran, 2009/ Used under license from Shutterstock.com

Identifying the Main Ideas

When you read, an important step is to identify the main ideas that the author is trying to communicate. By understanding the big picture, you provide yourself with a context in which to learn and remember the important details. To assist you in locating and recognizing main points, consider the following suggestions:

1. Pay attention to introductory and concluding remarks. Generally, these sentences concisely present or summarize the main idea(s) of the paragraph. For example, the first sentence of this section introduces the idea that we are trying to communicate: the importance of being able to identify main points.

2. Pay attention to text that has been boldfaced, italicized, indented, or otherwise made prominent. In many textbooks, particularly introductory ones, authors make important terms or points easily identifiable and accessible by varying the **typeface** they use, often by **bolding** or *italicizing* a word or sentence.

3. Pay attention to information presented in list form, such as a series of numbered or bulleted items.

4. Look for phrases or words such as *in summary, in conclusion, the most important/essential, the following, thus,* and so on. Generally, these phrases or words signal that the information that follows is important. For example, in introducing this list of suggestions for identifying main points, we use the phrase "consider the following suggestions."

5. Pay attention to visual aids, such as charts, diagrams, graphs, illustrations, and photographs, particularly if you are a visual learner. For example, in Chapter 1, we provide an illustration that shows how goals, self-efficacy, and self-responsibility are related to one another.

Although being able to identify main points is important, you must also learn the details of the subject. If you don't, then (a) your understanding of what you are studying will probably not extend beyond a very basic level, and (b) your performance on exams (which generally focus on the details) will likely be mediocre.

---

3. *Review at the end of each week.* Similar to the daily review, yet this one should integrate all the readings from that week. Because you will be covering more material, the review may take longer, about 45 to 60 minutes. Again, create information matrices to help you organize and integrate the material.

Consistently conducting these reviews will save you time in the long run. As in sports, practice leads to mastery. Insufficient practice generally leads to subpar performances, whether on the playing field or in the classroom. However, the amount of time you practice will not in itself guarantee successful learning. To efficiently master a new skill or learn new ideas, you also have to spread your practicing out over time. Think about your sport, for example. Would you spend six to eight hours the night before a big competition practicing and trying to learn new plays or skills? Never! In fact, for most sports, the day before a competition is a light workout day; the necessary training has already been accomplished during the days preceding it. As one Olympic coach

---

Reading for Fun

Many students spend very little time on books or other written materials, such as Internet news sites, other than their assigned texts. In fact, college students often spend more than twice as much time watching TV as they do reading for pleasure. There is a time and a place for watching TV or playing video or computer games, but doing so will not help you become a better reader. In fact, the passive approach that is often sufficient for watching TV is just the opposite of what you need when you are reading—active involvement with the words on the page.

To practice your reading, you need not limit yourself to your textbooks. In fact, we encourage you to spend time reading for pleasure (not that reading your texts isn't fun). Do you receive the local newspaper? Popular magazines? Do you read news stories via websites, such as ESPN.com or msn.com? Are there fiction or nonfiction writers you like whose books you could check out from the library? In addition to helping you become a more effective reader, reading such materials can help you relax, keep you up to date on world events, and improve your vocabulary, especially if you keep a dictionary handy while you read. Don't let reading become a lost art in your life. Find materials that you enjoy, find time in your day, and read!

---

we work closely with likes to say, "The hay is in the barn." So why not take this approach when you prepare for a big exam?

Post-Game Review

Reading is one of the primary means through which you will learn information in your college classes. In this chapter, we provided you with the fundamentals for college reading as well as a method for reading your textbooks that can help you improve your attention, focus, and comprehension. If you adopt them, then these strategies can make your reading more productive. We encourage you to give these ideas a try to find out whether they will work for you.

To be successful in your reading, you have to commit to and follow through with the strategies and fundamentals we discussed in this chapter. Although trying some of these practices may be uncomfortable at first, we encourage you to stick with them. If you do, then you are likely to experience some new successes in your reading of textbooks and studying for exams, and develop a higher level of self-efficacy in this area.

Thinking Critically about Reading and Studying

1. Summarize what you now know about reading and studying based on the information presented in this chapter.

_____

_____

_____

2. What additional questions do you have about these topics and how to use the skills introduced in this chapter?

_____

_____

_____

3. What conclusions can you draw about this topic and how it might help you be a more effective and successful student and athlete?

_____

_____

_____

Achieve IT! Setting a Learning Style Goal

1. Based on your self-assessment and your responses to Thinking Critically, select a goal in relationship to improving your reading and studying that you would like to achieve this term.

2. Now identify three short-term goals that will help you reach your goal this term.

3. For the short-term goals, identify the attainment strategies you will need to reach them.

4. List any obstacles you might face in trying to reach these goals and identify your plan for overcoming each one.

Don't forget to make your goal visible and tell others about them, so they can keep you accountable regarding what you want to achieve.

Chapter 7 Review Questions

1. As an effective reader, Jerome is likely to do which of the following:

   a. When he is done with his reading, he will make a short summary of what he just read.
   b. He will develop questions before he starts and then look for the answers as he reads.
   c. As he reads, he will monitor how well he understands the material.
   d. A and B.
   e. All of the above.

2. List the three fundamentals for reading in college and discuss the importance of each.

3. When studying, student-athletes may be distracted by which of the following:

   a. Physical fatigue.   **b.** Teammates.
   c. Internet.   **d.** A and C.
   e. All of the above.

4. When preparing to read, student-athletes should do which of the following:

   a. Answer questions they have asked.
   b. Preview the chapter, including objectives and headings.
   c. Write a summary integrating material from several sections.
   d. A and B.
   e. None of the above.

5. When you have finished reading an assigned chapter, you do not need to review the material until the next day. (True or False)

6. Doing the majority of your studying the night before exam is an efficient and effective way to prepare. (True or False)

7. When you are reading for main points, it is important to pay attention to

   a. Introductory sentences.   **b.** Graphs or diagrams.
   c. Boldfaced or italicized words.   **d.** A and C.
   e. All of the above.

8. When in college, it is best to not waste your time reading other things, such as magazines, blogs, and nonrequired books. (True or False)

9. If you do not understand a word or term in your reading, you should:

   a. Skip it and come back to it later.
   b. Try to determine its meaning from the context of the sentence.
   c. Look it up in a dictionary.
   d. B and C.
   e. All of the above.

8 | Succeeding in the Classroom

Preparing for and Taking Exams

Game Plan:

In this chapter, you will learn:

- About the different test formats used in college

- Specific study skills and strategies for taking tests

- Mental and physical approaches to prepare for and take tests

- How to manage test anxiety and use arousal to your advantage

- How to analyze your test results for your future benefit

© Dmitry Argunov, 2009 / Used under license from Shutterstock.com

"A true champion is someone who wants to make a difference, who never gives up, and who gives everything she has no matter what the circumstances are."

DOT RICHARDSON, M.D.
Gold Medalist, 1996 Olympics, Softball

Self-Assessment—Perceive It!

Read the following statements and place a checkmark next to each one you generally do. For you to change and develop new and effective academic, athletic, and personal strategies, you must be accurate in your self-perception. So, be honest in how you answer each question.

1. When I take tests, I feel prepared mentally and physically. _____

2. I understand the differences between subjective- and objective-type tests. _____

3. My test preparation is flexible, and I apply the study strategies that best fit the format of the test. _____

4. I review what I am learning in my classes for at least 15 minutes each day and for at least 30 minutes each weekend. _____

5. I am well rested on the day of my exams. _____

6. I rarely experience high levels of anxiety before an exam. _____

7. As I prepare for an exam, I try to learn more than I need to for the test. _____

8. I know how to adjust to special testing situations, such as having multiple exams on the same day or needing to arrange a makeup exam. _____

9. I rarely cram the night before an exam. _____

10. I am usually pleased with my test grades. _____

11. If I have trouble answering a test question when I first read it, I make a note and work on it later. _____

12. When taking exams, I answer the easiest questions first and then the more challenging ones. _____

13. Before I answer any questions, I budget my time so I know how much to spend on each section of the test. _____

14. When my exams are returned, I try to learn from my mistakes by looking for patterns in the questions I missed. _____

15. After I get the results of an exam, I seek feedback from my instructor on how to improve my performance for next time. _____

Take a moment to review your responses. How many items did you check? Each one you checked represents a current strength. Now consider the items you did not check. These represent areas where focus and growth are needed. Now, to summarize your self-perception, complete the following statements:

1. My areas of strength are:

_____

2. The areas I need to improve are:

_____

As you read this chapter and participate in your classes, keep your strengths and areas of improvement in mind. At the end of the chapter, you will have the chance to set a goal related to these areas. Achieving these goals will help you become a more effective student and athlete.

Introduction

*S*weaty hands, a racing heart, scattered thoughts, and feelings of helplessness are what Vick experienced whenever he took an exam. Regardless of the type of exam or the class in which it was given, he never felt ready, and he never expected to do well. He never seemed to have enough time to take the test and always felt rushed. Vick rarely performed well and began to doubt that he would be able to graduate from junior college and accept a scholarship offer he had from a four-year school, because taking tests was so difficult and unpleasant for him.

An outstanding quarterback, Vick never had these symptoms or feelings when he took the field in big games. In fact, he relished the challenge of facing a tough opponent in a must-win situation. He felt calm, confident, and prepared in such situations because he had been successful in the past and always came into the game in great physical shape and with a thorough knowledge of the strengths and weaknesses of the opposing defenses. He took *pride in his mental and physical preparation for competition and took advantage of all the tools he could use to improve his performance.*

Carefully going over game films paid big dividends for him. After watching the films, he visualized himself facing the various defenses played by the opposing team. After each game, he watched films of his performance so he could quickly identify and correct any mechanical flaws in his delivery and make adjustments in his play selection. He even requested additional time with his position coach to go over every detail. Vick desperately wanted to achieve the same success taking tests that he had when playing football.

One of the hallmarks of our society is its emphasis on merit and objective outcomes, such as whether you win or lose a game and whether you pass or fail a test. Although this focus on winning or losing and passing or failing allows us to assess performance for large numbers of people, it does create certain problems. For example, one of the steps in getting your degree is earning enough credits. To earn credits, you must pass classes, and for most classes, tests are the major tool for evaluating students. This reality can create additional pressure to perform well on exams and cause students to adopt negative attitudes toward tests. Students cannot avoid tests, so finding effective ways to prepare for and take them, and manage the anxiety that many of you experience, is critical for academic success.

In this chapter, we introduce a number of ideas that may help you prepare for and succeed when taking exams. We begin by discussing how to most effectively review for exams, and then discuss the types of tests you are likely to encounter in college. As you will see, different test formats call for different preparation strategies. Later, we address the importance of being mentally and physically ready to take exams. You have a choice as to how you view the testing experience, and your test-taking attitude plays a major role in determining your success. Finally, we discuss how you can examine your exam results, just like you do previous competitions, to increase your chances of future success.

Preparation: Getting Ready for Success

The most important aspect of taking any test, regardless of its format, is being prepared, and the first step in preparation is making a commitment to the process. It is no different from what is necessary to achieve success in your sport. Preparation involves more than just sitting down and passively reading over your notes and textbooks two or three times, a day or two before the exam. It means being self-responsible, such as finding out what kinds of questions are likely to be on the test and what topics will be emphasized. Often, information concerning the types of questions can be found in your syllabus, but if not, ask your instructor. As for what will be emphasized, some instructors will provide study guides or specific ideas, but many others will not. Most professors will expect you to figure out what topics are most important. In fact, many instructors view your ability to make that determination as a critical part of the learning and evaluation process. Perhaps the most significant difference between high school and college academics is who is responsible for learning. In college, the responsibility falls squarely on you. By being a self-responsible learner, though, someone who is able to discern main points and supporting details, organize course material in personally meaningful ways, and create associations and connections among course topics, you set the stage for being successful.

Once you have made the commitment to be actively involved in your learning and preparing for your exams, the next most important thing to do is study. There is no substitute for frequent, thorough reviews of the material you want to learn. In the following sections, we discuss the different time frames during which you should study.

Daily Reviews

The principle behind daily reviews is quite similar to daily practice in your sport. In your sport, you are introduced to new plays, formations, and techniques in small chunks, and you practice them every day in order to master them. This approach is a much more effective way of learning new skills and plays and improving your performance than waiting until the night before a big competition to practice everything you need to know to be successful. Coaches would never hold their toughest and longest practices the day before the game. In fact, most coaches use practice time the day before to review and stay fresh. Cramming the night before an exam is the same as holding a "killer" practice the day before the game. You would never do it in your sport, so don't do it when you study. Think of your daily reviews as academic practice sessions.

You can complete a daily review by devoting about 15 minutes after each lecture to going over your class notes from that day. Although that is not a lot of time, it is important to do it within the same day as when the notes were taken. As we discussed in Chapter 5, most of what you forget is lost in the first 24 hours after it is presented. We understand that your days are busy and full of activities that demand your attention. However, if you spend 15 minutes a day reviewing the material in each of your classes, you will save yourself considerable time and aggravation in the long run. In addition, you will actually be learning the material (not just memorizing it), and you won't have to cram the night before. Cramming usually results in more confusion than comprehension. As you do these daily practices, your ability to retain information increases, and you become more likely to perform well on an exam that requires recall or recognition, concepts we discuss later in this chapter. By studying every day, you increase your chances of success.

Daily reviews have other benefits:

- You become more involved in the material you are learning,
- You can identify the material you don't know well, so you can spend more time studying it prior to exams, and
- Review provides you with a context in which to understand upcoming lecture material and readings.

Most students—student-athletes included—have several 10- to 15-minute blocks of time throughout the day; be sure you use them. We know that the best students use these small blocks of time consistently. Daily reviews, although not glamorous, are effective and similar to the work you do each day in your sport practices.

> "It's not necessarily the amount of time you spend at practice that counts, it's what you put into practice."
>
> ERIC LINDROS
> *Former NHL All Star and MVP*

Weekly Reviews

Weekly reviews represent the next level of the review process, and provide a time during which you can integrate the information covered that week. They create an overall framework for what you are studying. Seeing the "big picture" is like understanding the game plan for your next competition. It helps you grasp the material better. If you see the big picture, or overall plan, then the little things you do each day make much more sense. Weekly reviews help you make connections within the material covered during the past week and begin the process of elaborating on and organizing the information in meaningful ways. They can also be used to develop practice test questions, allowing you to monitor your level of comprehension. For this review, set aside about one hour per class, preferably on the weekend. The exact amount of time will depend on the class and on the amount of material. If you have kept up with your daily reviews, then your weekly review should be relatively straightforward. Despite the effectiveness of these reviews, we have heard many student-athletes say that there are more exciting things to do on the weekend than review their class materials! There are, but you have to remember what your goals are for being in college. Besides, making the relatively small sacrifice of reviewing on the weekend will allow you to enjoy your other activities even more.

Final Review

The final review is the last part of your study process. Many students assume that the final review is what you do the night before the exam. Wrong! This review is your final push and occurs in the week before the exam, not the night before. By the time you reach this stage, you should be familiar with all the major concepts from the text and lectures that will be covered on the exam. This review is the time to clarify questions you have either about the material or the format of the test. In this review, apply the principles of the daily review; that is, use several smaller blocks of time, spread over the week, to study. The exact length will depend on the amount and nature of the material you need to know, as well as on your own ability to focus and concentrate. Therefore, it is crucial that you be aware of your limits. If you can't sit still for several hours at a time, then break your review into blocks of time that match your attention span (see Chapter 5). One hour of focused study will be much more useful than six hours of staring at the same page. Emphasize the *quality* of time you put in, not just the *quantity*.

Before starting your final review, take a step back to get a perspective on what you'll need to know for the exam. Start by getting organized. Make a list of text readings and lecture notes that will be on the test to ensure that you cover all the material in your review. If, for example, you have five chapters to cover and you've allowed yourself a week to prepare, then you can set a goal of reviewing at least one chapter per night for the first five nights. But when you review, don't just passively reread the chapters. Instead, keep your book closed and think about what you know, integrating material from across what you have covered. You can use the last two nights to go over clusters of chapters to solidify your understanding of the material. Similarly, if you have 10 lectures to cover, then you might review at least two per night for the first five nights. On the last two nights, you can review them in clusters of five per night. This may sound like a lot of work, but remember, you are doing this in conjunction with daily and weekly reviews, so it won't be as difficult or time consuming as you might think. An extra benefit of adopting this approach is that you'll have established clearly defined study goals against which you can measure your progress; then you can reward yourself for your accomplishments.

Summary of Review Process

Each of the three types of reviews is important in its own way. In the daily review, you regularly rehearse small chunks of information, whereas in the weekly review you integrate smaller chunks of information into larger units. The final review solidifies your understanding and provides a chance to fill in any gaps in your knowledge. As your final preparation for the exam, it deserves serious attention and thoughtful planning. Don't fall into the trap of waiting until the night before to begin studying! Even if you have not kept up on your weekly reviews, you still may be able to learn the material well enough to earn a good grade, if you give yourself sufficient time during the final review session. Beware of relying on cramming to pull you through. Concentrated practice of this type is ineffective for learning! You wouldn't pull an "all-nighter" to prepare for an athletic competition, so don't do it with your classes. Approach preparing for a test in the same way you would athletic competitions: Distribute your practice (i.e., studying) over the week before the test to give yourself the greatest chance of success. In addition, make sure you use deep-level processing strategies, such as elaboration, creating associations, organizing information, and making information personally meaningful, to ensure that you actually learn the material. It's not overstating it to say that taking a test should be a celebration of your hard work and preparation, just like game day.

Performance: Test-Taking Strategies and Types of Exams

Once you have established a review schedule, focus on study strategies tailored to the type of exam you will be taking. Knowing the format or type of exam you will be taking can be most helpful in structuring the way you prepare for it. Although there are many formats for tests, most fall into one of two basic categories: objective and subjective. As you read about these exam formats, think about the types of tests you are taking in your own classes. Do most of your exams follow a particular format? If so, you will want to pay particular attention to the studying and test-taking strategies that best fit that format. We begin by discussing some general test-taking strategies that apply regardless of the type of test.

General Test-Taking Strategies

1. *Arrive early*—the time before an exam is like the time before a sport competition; you want to use it to get yourself physically and psychologically ready to perform. Develop a routine that works for you and then implement it right before each test.
2. *Accept you might be anxious*—some anxiety is normal, and if you are prepared for it to occur, then it will not take you by surprise or particularly disrupt your performance.
3. *Carefully read the directions and scan the entire exam*—be sure to pay attention to any instructions, information, or corrections that your instructor points out at the beginning, and see how the point totals break down for each section.
4. *Budget your time*—it's an awful feeling to realize that the last item on the test is an essay question worth fifty percent of the point total, and you only left yourself 5 minutes to answer it. So, make sure you plan your time so you devote enough to each section/question. You may also want to wear a watch or locate a clock in the classroom to help you keep track of time.
5. *Take a deep breath*—before beginning, close your eyes for a moment and repeat your best self-statement (or prayer) that creates confidence or puts the exam in perspective for you.
6. *Write down key information*—when you get the test, at the top, write down information, such as equations, formula, lists,

definitions, or other material that you want to make sure you don't forget as the exam progresses.

7. *Answer easiest questions first*—this approach should boost your self-confidence, jog your memory so you can complete the other questions, and ensure that you don't lose points by failing to answer questions that you know.

8. *Answer all the questions*—if there is no penalty associated with incorrect answers, then make sure you do not leave anything blank. There is an art to intelligent guessing, and we will provide you with an exercise later in the chapter that will help you to master it. Of course, the student who has prepared and mastered the course content will not have to resort to this type of Statue of Liberty trick play (see Boise State vs. Oklahoma 2007 Fiesta Bowl)!

Taking Objective Tests

Objective tests include multiple-choice, true-false, matching, and fill-in-the-blank formats. If you have completed the review questions in this book, then you have seen a number of questions that are objective and follow these formats. Although these formats are quite different from one another, they are similar in that there is only one correct or best answer; either you get the answer right or you don't. There is no middle ground and no partially correct answer.

Because the answers are already provided, some students see multiple-choice tests as being easier than other kinds of tests. This belief often leads to studying simply for recognition, using surface-level approaches to learning, such as repetition and skimming notes. As you have learned, surface-level approaches do not facilitate learning. Because multiple-choice tests are often as difficult as essay exams, requiring thought, analysis, integration, and practical application, to best prepare you need to use deep-level processing strategies. Such an approach allows you to understand how the information is related and to be able to discriminate between answers that are similar. Knowing the information only well enough to recognize it, which is what you achieve with surface-level strategies, does you little good if all the choices on a multiple-choice exam look good, if they are all familiar, or if they are worded somewhat differently from the way you have them written in your notes. So, study using deep-level processing strategies and avoid this problem.

Multiple-Choice Tests

Read multiple-choice questions carefully and then try to answer them in your head before looking at the provided answers. If the answer is not obvious to you, then eliminate options that you are certain are not the answer. Other questions on the exam may provide you with information or prompt you to remember material to answer earlier questions.

Pay close attention to words in questions that are "qualifiers," such as *always, never, all, none,* and *every* (Chickering & Schlossberg, 2001). Options with absolute qualifiers in the answer are rarely correct. For example, the multiple-choice option "*All* successful professional golfers specialized in their sport early in childhood" is a false statement. Although most professional golfers do begin playing as children, there are examples of those who have taken up the sport later in life. Conversely, options with conservative qualifiers, such as *generally, often, some, most, rarely, tend to,* or *may sometimes be,* are more likely to be correct. When you spot a qualifier, circle it to ensure that you pay attention to it when determining your answer. Consider another example, and compare the following two statements: "The only way to master college material is to read the textbook" vs. "In general, a good way to master college material is to begin by reading the textbook." Obviously the first statement, with the qualifier "only," is false. (There are many different effective ways to master new information.) The second statement, though, is likely true because it does not contain the absolute term *only,* but instead, uses the more conservative qualifier *in general.*

In multiple-choice answers, longer ones are more frequently correct. Choices that are more general than the other options also are likely to be correct. If there are two choices with similar meanings, then one of those is likely to be the correct answer. Choices that are in the middle value range (the range can be low to high or most recent to the past) are likely to be right. Finally, with multiple-choice questions (as well as all objective questions in general), make sure that you eliminate any options that do not result in grammatically correct sentences. Most instructors will not "trick" you in this manner, but it's better to be safe than sorry. Look for cue words, such as *an, as, that, the,* and *these.* For example, if there is a statement "An _____ is the mascot for the University of California, Irvine." The word *an* would indicate that the correct choice of the type of mascot would need to begin with a vowel. Of course, you might be able to answer that question without that cue since it's commonly known that UC-Irvine's mascot is an Anteater!

True-False and Other Objective Tests

Many of the techniques suggested for multiple-choice questions also apply to the other objective test questions (true-false, fill-in-the-blank, matching). For example, qualifiers should be carefully considered when answering true-false questions. Fill-in-the-blank answers should be logical and grammatically correct when chosen. Be sure to note the length of the blank(s) that the instructor has given you. It may give you a clue as to the length of the word(s) for which she is looking. If you can think of more than one correct response, then you may want to write them both in the space. Your instructor may reward you for your initiative and creativity.

Matching questions ask the student to select a word or term in one list that matches or "fits" with another word, term, or definition in another list. Carefully read the directions for matching questions, and be especially aware of whether or not an option can be used more than once. Matching questions can be made even more complicated if the professor has multiple answers for matches and wants them all noted. In general, it's best to do all of the match-ups you are sure of first, crossing out both parts (word and term) if the exam format permits.

When you are left with matches about which you are not certain, think outside the proverbial box. Are there clues, associations, or connections you might not have thought of the first time through the lists?

We have two caveats concerning all of these strategies. First, they do not work all of the time. In volleyball, for example, certain plays work well against perimeter defenses, but those same plays may be ineffective against rotation coverage. Similarly, no single test-taking strategy will always be successful, because not all objective exams are the same. Second, most of these strategies are only *guessing* strategies that will help you to increase your chances of choosing the right answer. However, if you use deep-level processing strategies when studying, then you increase your chances of learning the material and thus decrease your need to guess.

To practice using these objective test-taking strategies, you may want to complete Exercise 8.1.

Exercise 8.1   Testing Your Test Taking When You Don't Know the Answer

For each question that follows, place an "X" beside each one that is false and an "O" next to each one that is true.

_____ **1.** Smarmikins always live under the sea bottom.

_____ **2.** Smarmikins vishnuch when their body temperature drops below 89 degrees Fahrenheit.

_____ **3.** Scientists know that smarmikins live longer than sumpkinists because there are 24 hours in a day and 170 hours in a week.

_____ **4.** Smarmikin and sumpkinist are organismic classification labels. The labels smarmikin and sumpkinist are not devoid of the letters S, N, K, I, and M.

_____ **5.** Smarmikins and sumpkinists are labels seldom applied to the genre pulpamnuck.

For each of the following questions, circle the option that best answers the question.

_____ **6.** When smarmikins and sumpkinists fight:
A. smarmikins camouflage themselves effectively and usually outwit their less intelligent sumpkinist opponent
B. sumpkinists always win
C. smarmikins bleed white
D. sumpkinists retreat

_____ **7.** Sumpkinists often repel smarmikins with an _____.
A. shrill sound
B. violent gesture
C. gustatory expectoration
D. obnoxious odor

_____ **8.** Smarmikins give birth to smarmikits and hatch smarmeggs. How many young are in each litter?
A. 1–2   C. 9–10
B. 8–9   D. 14–15

_____ **9.** The length of sumpkinists at birth is:
A. 12–18 inches.   C. 1–2 feet.
B. 12–24 inches.   D. 125–150 feet.

_____ **10.** When a smarmikin's body temperature drops below 89 degrees, it will always vishnuch. Vishnuching means:
A. shivering.   C. shrinking.
B. turning blue or green.   D. all of the above.

Answers (and reasons):

1. X Did you remember to follow directions and use an X or O? "Always" is an absolute qualifier and thus this would be FALSE.
2. O Answer can be found question 10, so it is TRUE. Remember, if you do not know the answer, you might find it in another question later in the test.
3. X If any part of a true-false question is false, then the question is false. There are 168 hours in a week, not 170, so the answer is FALSE.
4. O "Not devoid" is a double negative which makes it positive. The letters are all in the label, so the answer is TRUE.
5. O "Seldom" is a conservative qualifier, so the answer is TRUE.
6. Did you remember to circle your answer? A. Longer answers are frequently correct.
7. D. Only answer that is grammatically correct.
8. B. or C. Mid-range and choices that are similar are frequently correct.
9. A., B., and C. are the same, and you cannot have two "correct" answers in an MC test unless you have the option of "B and C." A. is more similar in range to other choices.
10. D. If more than one option is correct, then "All of the above" becomes the correct response.

Taking Subjective Tests

Subjective tests make up the second broad category of exams, and include short-answer and essay formats. They require you to recall and organize what you have learned and communicate that to the instructor in either a few sentences or several paragraphs. Deep-level processing strategies will probably lead to greater success on all types of exams, but it is essential for success on subjective exams because of the need to integrate information from different sources. As you study, try to learn the material well enough that you could explain it to someone else (that is the basis of this type of exam).

Key Essay Words

To successfully answer essay questions, you must understand what you are being asked to do. As you review these terms, recognize that some require only a factual understanding of the material whereas others require that you engage in higher-level thinking skills, such as conceptualization, evaluation, and synthesis.

Enumerate. List several events, reasons, characteristics, and so on one by one.

State. Explain precisely.

Define. Provide the exact meaning with sufficient supporting detail.

Trace. Provide a chronology of the development of events or ideas.

Outline. Provide an organized overview of the main ideas, characteristics, or events.

Analyze. Break into parts and discuss each part separately.

Interpret. Explain your personal view of facts and ideas and how they relate to one another.

Illustrate. Give concrete examples to clarify a point or idea.

Summarize. Provide a condensed account of the major points, ideas, or events under consideration.

Describe. Give a detailed account of something, including who, what, where, when, why, and how that paints a complete picture.

Discuss. Consider the pros and cons of an issue.

Compare. Demonstrate how items or events are similar to one another.

Contrast. Demonstrate how two or more items or events are different from one another.

Evaluate. Critically consider a position or idea from different perspectives, discussing its strengths and weaknesses in depth.

Prove. Support or validate a position or idea with facts.

Criticize. Express judgments as to the correctness or merits of a situation, topic, or position.

Justify. Provide a detailed rationale for a course of action, position taken, or event.

Clearly, these words overlap in terms of their focus. To help you better understand them, take a moment to group the words according to their purpose. For example, *define, state, outline,* and *enumerate* are similar in that they all require the presentation of basic facts and knowledge.

Subjective exams require a somewhat different set of strategies. Chickering and Schlossberg (2001) suggest that you begin by making sure you understand the question. Students often cause problems for themselves by failing to read and understand the questions thoroughly. No matter how well written your answer, you will not get credit if it doesn't address the question! When you take essay exams, pay special attention to the keywords that are often used in constructing the questions. For example, if you are asked to compare and contrast ideas in an essay exam, then be sure you do both. Don't just list or describe the ideas. Before you begin writing, take a few minutes to write down all the ideas that come to mind as possible responses to the question. Brainstorming in this way can also jog your memory for other connected concepts and relevant points.

Outlining your answer will help you cover the key points in a logical, coherent fashion and provide an overall structure. Be brief and to the point in your answers, but not at the expense of eliminating supporting evidence for your main points. Begin each paragraph with a focused sentence that communicates the main point you will address in that paragraph (each paragraph should correspond to a main point in the outline). Also, make sure that the transitions from one paragraph to the next make sense. Your introductory paragraph should directly present the purpose of your answer and should include a thesis sentence—the single statement that presents the main focus of the answer. Lengthy introductions and restatements of the same point will not impress your instructors. Be concise.

You may want to leave blank spaces in your answer if you are unsure what to write. Remember, you may remember relevant details later (as you answer other questions), and it is helpful if you are able to go back to an answer and fill in important missing information. Unless specifically requested (e.g., *interpret*), leave out your personal opinions. Always make sure the verb tense is consistent and your sentences grammatically correct. Always write something. If you run out of time but have written an outline, you might receive partial credit. If you are unable to remember information, then use strategies that are consistent with your learning style and how you encoded and stored the information to promote retrieval (see Chapter 5). Finally, if you have time, then reread your answer for clarity and make additions/deletions as needed.

Take-Home and Open-Book/Note Exams

Take-home and open-book/note exams are typically subjective, rather than objective, and require you to solve problems, think, discover, and integrate a variety of concepts as opposed to just recall or recognize information. These exam formats create higher performance expectations than in-class exams because of the extended time given and access to reference materials you have.

Although you have access to reference materials during an open-book/note exam, you still need to study! Being able to look at your notes or your book does not help if you don't know what information is relevant and important, and where to find it quickly. Moreover, you will still have to organize and integrate the relevant information.

> "Failure to prepare is preparing to fail."
>
> JOHN WOODEN
> *Basketball Coaching Legend*

Exercise 8.2　Your Testing Profile

1. Identify the format or type of test on which you usually perform your best. Why?

As you read through the remainder of this chapter, pay particular attention to material about the type of tests that give you the most difficulty.

2. Which types of tests give you the most difficulty? Why?

Planning and organizing your answers is crucial for take-home and open-book/note exams. To help you learn more about how you can handle the different types of exams we have discussed, you may want to complete Exercise 8.2.

Performance: Using Study Techniques While You Review

Within the context of daily, weekly, and final reviews, you can use a variety of methods and techniques to study for your exams. Many students use a combination of techniques, depending on the nature of the course and their individual learning styles. We suggest that you try several techniques and identify the ones that best fit the way you learn (see Chapter 2 for more information). No matter which approach you prefer, you will be successful only if you take the responsibility to put the necessary time and effort into your studying and test preparation.

Flash Cards

Flash cards are a method often used by students to help them study for an exam. Flash cards work particularly well in courses where you are required to know formulas, vocabulary, or scientific or technical terms and when the test format involves short answers. Making flash cards is quick and relatively simple. Write the question or the term to be learned on one side of the card, and the answer or definition on the other side. For example, on one card, you might write "Objective Tests." On the other side of the card, you would write "Tests where there is only one correct answer. Formats include multiple-choice, true-false, and matching." Flash cards are convenient to study and give you the opportunity to think about the material when you create them. Flash cards can be used during those small pockets of free time you have throughout the day. If you use flash cards, *think* about the material as you go over it. Do not simply memorize terms and concepts without understanding them. Be an active learner at all times!

Audio Taping

Pinkney (1996) has suggested that studying audio recordings can be very effective, especially for student-athletes who are aural learners. With this technique, you *record* your notes and write them down. You can also make brief summaries, define concepts, and record other

Special Circumstances with Tests

Despite your best efforts to prepare, life sometimes gets in the way and makes it hard to do your best. Here are some solutions to problems you may have in connection with tests.

- *Cutting Your Losses.* If you are ever in the position of possibly not being able to pass a course, then you need to talk with your instructor to carefully and honestly assess the situation and determine your chances. If your chances are slim, then you may wish to focus your studying on your other classes. By doing so, you increase your chances of doing well in them. Although we want you to pass all of your classes, we don't want you to spend so much time and effort trying to salvage one class that you risk not passing the others. Before you drop a class under these circumstances, consult with your athletic academic counselor to make sure that you are not jeopardizing your eligibility.
- *Makeup Exams.* As a student-athlete, you will most likely need to take makeup exams because of scheduling conflicts caused by travel for competitions. This issue is sensitive for some instructors, and you need to be diplomatic when you bring it up. Many colleges have a policy dealing with absences for reasons, such as representing the school in off-campus activities like athletics. In general, this means that you will be granted some type of opportunity to make up the missed exam. The *way* you will be permitted to make it up, however, is usually left up to the instructor. Common options are to take the exam early, take a proctored (supervised) exam on the road, take an alternate form of the test when you return, skip the exam and have another one weighted more heavily, or complete an alternative assignment. To avoid last-minute problems in this area, look over your syllabus and your travel and competition schedule at the beginning of each term and talk with your instructor about any potential conflicts early in the term.
- *Multiple Tests.* Sometimes you may have to take more than one exam during the same week, or possibly even during the same day (a common occurrence during finals week!). If you have completed a long-range plan as suggested in Chapter 3, then you should be able to spot the times when multiple tests will occur. What should you do if this happens? First, check your school's policy (via the student handbook or on the school's website) for multiple exams because there may be guidelines for handling this situation during finals week. Second, under certain circumstances, you may be able to request that one of the exams be rescheduled; just ask. Most of the time, however, you will need to figure out how to manage taking multiple exams.
- *Learning Disabilities.* If you have a diagnosed and documented learning disability, then you may be eligible for special accommodations, such as extended time to take tests. Consult with your school's athletic academic advisor and office for disability services as soon as you arrive on campus. These individuals will help you receive the appropriate accommodations and make sure your instructors know what they need to do.

important information using this method. Taped studying can be particularly effective in classes that use subjective test formats, because by verbally recording your notes, you are putting the important information into your own words.

Your school may participate in Apple's iTune U or another resource that provides podcasts of lectures. Tapes or podcasts are like flash cards in that you can listen to them in a variety of locations while you do other things. Students who downloaded podcast lectures may achieve substantially higher exam results than those who attend the lecture in person (McKinney, Dyck, and Luber, 2008). You can listen to tapes or podcasts on your way to campus or in between classes. Listening to tapes or podcasts before or after studying can reinforce the material you're learning. It also allows you to replay difficult parts of a lecture. Recording class lectures also provides a backup to your written notes and allows you to fill in any gaps, which can reduce the anxiety some students feel when they aren't able to get everything written down the first time it is presented. In order to get this benefit, however, you must be an *active* listener. Listening to tapes or podcasts is *not* a substitute for taking and reviewing your notes and reading the text.

Previous Exams

Studying previous exams can help you predict the types of questions you might see on the exam. Looking at old exams also can alert you to patterns in the instructor's test construction style. Like most people, your instructors have their preferred ways of doing things; these may become apparent if you review their old exams. You might determine, for example, that your instructor emphasizes lecture material, rather than the text readings. You can use old exams to help identify any of these tendencies, much as you use game films to review the tendencies of your opponents. If your instructor makes old exams available, then take advantage of that opportunity and look at them. A word of caution is in order here: Just as you would never substitute watching game films for practice, do not substitute reviewing old exams for studying. Old tests are subject to change and should be treated as a supplementary tool in addition to your other sources of information. Finally, make sure your instructor does not forbid the use of old exams before you review one.

Study Groups

Using study groups is another technique you might find useful, particularly if you are an aural learner. This format is well suited for dealing with highly complex material, a high volume of material, or assignments where it is important to provide a variety of perspectives. Studying with others can give you different views and help you think of possible test questions. A few cautions about study groups, though. First, they are not for everyone. Some students find it distracting or anxiety-producing to study in a group. Second, if your pace is significantly different from the group's, then you may be frustrated. Third, study groups can become social events if members don't take the work seriously or stay focused. Fourth, you cannot rely on the group to "carry" you. You must have a handle on the material yourself if you are going to actively participate and benefit.

Exercise 8.3 Choosing Study Techniques

Based on what you just read about study techniques and other ones you might currently use, list two that you think would be most helpful to you in preparing for exams. For each one, indicate how it fits with your learning style and why it would help you prepare.

1. _____
_____

2. _____
_____

Consult with Your Instructor

Although your instructor is unlikely to tell you exactly what is to be covered, she may provide suggestions about what will be emphasized on the exam and ideas on the best way to prepare. It never hurts to ask, and in doing so, you communicate your interest in doing well in the class. Use your instructor's office hours if you wish to consult in this manner.

We have introduced you to several techniques you can use to study for your exams. It is important to find the strategies that work best for you. Don't assume that because a technique is widely used, it will fit your learning style. To help you determine the strategies that would be most useful in your test preparation, you may want to complete Exercise 8.3.

Preparation: Being Mentally and Physically Ready

Studying is the primary factor that will determine your success on exams, but how you think about your exams also will play a major role, as will your ability to harness your *arousal*, our term for mental alertness, and use it to your advantage. To learn more about your general attitude toward taking exams, you may want to complete Exercise 8.4.

Mental Preparation

Unfortunately, many student-athletes have a negative attitude toward taking exams (What did you identify in Exercise 8.4?). Tests require a lot of extra work and preparation and represent the primary way students are evaluated in classes. As a result, tests are often a source of considerable anxiety and influence your academic self-confidence. However, the attitude you take when approaching a task—especially one that you

"**Pressure is something you feel when you don't know what the hell you're doing.**"

PEYTON MANNING
NFL All-Pro and MVP Quarterback

Exercise 8.4 Your Test-Taking Attitude

1. Summarize your *feelings* about taking tests. Are you very anxious when you have to take a test? Are you relaxed and calm? Excited? Sad? Angry?

_____

_____

2. Discuss what taking a test means to you. Is it an obstacle to overcome? An opportunity to show what you know?

_____

_____

3. Students have many different thoughts about tests, themselves in relation to tests, etc. What things do you say to yourself as you get ready to take a test? Of these, identify which statements are positive/helpful and which ones are negative/problematic.

_____

_____

© Jason Stitt, 2009 / Used under license from Shutterstock.com

dread—is a major factor in determining the quality of your performance. Therefore, one of the keys to being successful on exams is to make sure your attitude towards tests is positive and confident. If those descriptors seem unrealistic, then perhaps you can at least aim for a neutral attitude or approach exams with a sense of curiosity.

Games and competition are, of course, a significant part of a student-athlete's life. Part of what makes you successful in your sport is your willingness to take on the challenge of competing against other athletes, and your ability to perform your best even under adverse conditions, such as poor weather or a hostile arena. You probably take great pride in being able to turn difficult circumstances to your advantage. For example, one university's football team struggled when they played at home, losing to several teams that were obviously less talented. Strangely, though, they performed extremely well on the road. Somehow this team was able to band together and become more focused under adverse conditions than they could at home, where they were supposedly more comfortable. How did they do this? Part of the answer can be found in their ability to shift their attitude. Rather than looking at playing on the road as a burden, or an obstacle, they chose to look at it as a challenge—an opportunity to put their game on display and have fun in the process.

Believe it or not, you can take a similar approach with your exams. Charlotte, a senior basketball player, did just that in preparing for the law school entrance exam. Her initial attitude toward taking tests may have been much like yours: She didn't want to do it, it was a lot of work, and the test had nothing to do with how good an attorney she would be. As she soon discovered, this attitude was not helping her get through the three months of studying she faced. Charlotte then decided a different approach was in order, and she chose to turn the process into a competition of sorts, something with which she could have fun. So instead of becoming frustrated and angry over having to go through the exam process, she turned it into a game against an opponent she wanted to beat. Setting measurable short-term goals and "keeping score" of how she did on practice exams were important steps in this process. She felt much better, and in the end, was able to pass the exam with a score much higher than she had expected.

Physical Preparation

In addition to preparing yourself mentally by adopting an effective attitude, you also want to make sure that you are physically ready. Proper rest before an exam is as important as it is when you compete. Getting a good night's sleep before your exam is one of the keys to being successful. If you are tired, then you will have difficulty staying alert and focused. Fatigue also tends to magnify the symptoms of test anxiety. A primary reason most students don't get adequate rest is cramming the night before the exam. Distributing your review across the week before an exam is most effective. If you use that strategy, then you won't need to cram, and there should be nothing that prevents you from being well rested.

Eating nutritiously can be an important part of your test-day preparation. If you are hungry while taking the exam, then you will likely have a difficult time concentrating. Your body needs sufficient nutrients for maximum functioning. Some student-athletes may become so anxious before an exam that they lose their appetite or become nauseous around food. If that happens to you, then turn to foods that are easy on your stomach, such as bananas, bagels, or sport nutrition bars, staples used by athletes before competitions. Caffeine intake can also be an issue as too much will increase anxiety and jittery feelings. Stick to your typical amount. In general, make a balanced meal part of your test-day game plan!

Being physically comfortable is also important for optimal performance. Relaxation tapes, deep breathing, and progressive muscle

---

Pre-Competition Plans

Pre-competition plans or routines help relax and focus athletes. Routines are comforting, which is why many athletes choose to use them. These routines can be flexible (stuff happens at competition sites that can't be predicted), but remain mostly the same regardless of the importance of the performance. Well-prepared athletes utilize the same pre-competition plan whether it's the Olympics or an early season dual meet against another conference team.

Here's a brief example of a pre-competition plan for a fencer:

1. The night before competition, she reviews the focus and strategy plan that she discussed with her coach. She makes sure she is in bed early enough to allow time to go through a brief relaxation routine and spend 15 minutes visualizing how she expects to perform tomorrow, from her en garde position to the end of the bout.

2. During the morning of the competition, she does a quick body scan for any muscular tension and does progressive muscle relaxation if tension is present. She does a final imagery session and reminds herself of the positive self-talk cues she chose earlier in the week for this performance. She also listens to the upbeat iPod mix that she created for this competition.

3. At the competition site and an hour or more before the bout, she talks casually with teammates who will be a positive distraction. She reminds herself to have fun and focus on the process of the bout, not the outcome.

4. As she approaches the en garde line and gets ready to engage her opponent, she takes several deep, cleansing breaths; sees a final positive image; and says "Seize the Day."

Then it is time to compete, and she is ready to go!

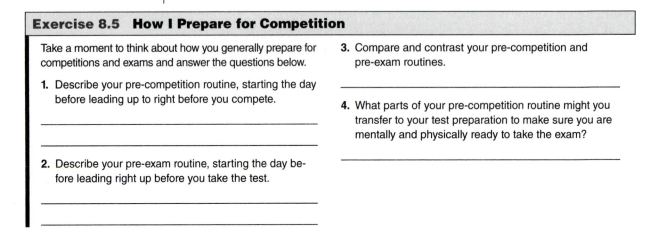

> "To give anything less than your best is to sacrifice the gift."
>
> STEVE PREFONTAINE
> *Running Icon*

relaxation exercises can all be used to help you achieve a comfortable balance between arousal and relaxation. You can also enhance your physical preparedness by wearing comfortable clothing. It may seem like a minor item to focus on in preparing for an exam, but you want to do everything you can to minimize potential distractions and maximize your comfort level going into the exam.

Another way to prepare yourself is to develop a consistent preperformance routine, whether in your sport or for exams. To learn more about how you prepare for exams, you may want to complete Exercise 8.5.

Preparation: Test Anxiety

Some students experience test anxiety; that is, they become especially nervous and worried immediately before or during an exam. If you have mastered (and we mean knowing the material inside and out) what you have studied, yet your mind goes blank, or you make silly mistakes or misread questions, then you may be experiencing test anxiety. Anxiousness due to lack of preparation is not test anxiety. You should be anxious if you're not prepared. Common symptoms of test anxiety include shaking, trembling, increased heart rate, muscle tension, nausea, headaches, difficulty concentrating, becoming easily distracted, lack of confidence, and negative self-statements (King, 1997). Before we discuss coping strategies, though, let's first look at the relationship between arousal and anxiety, as well as some of the causes of test anxiety.

Arousal and Anxiety

Although test *anxiety* is not a good thing to experience, you should understand that having some level of *arousal* is helpful. People generally perform their best when they have a moderate level, which you may have experienced as an athlete. Being underaroused, or "flat," leaves you without the energy or the sense of urgency you need to perform well in competition. On the other hand, being overly aroused, or too "pumped up," also prevents you from performing your best, because you can easily become distracted. Generally, you want to be somewhere in between when you compete, which also is true when you are taking tests. Good athletes and good students realize that a moderate amount of arousal/anxiety is something to be expected and embraced as part of the process of achieving excellence. It's your mind and body's way of telling you that you're about to engage in an activity that is important. You need a certain level of arousal to care about what you're doing, to stay awake, and to be alert. You also want to avoid being too aroused or anxious, because that would impair your ability to focus and concentrate in a relaxed fashion. Sometimes, your arousal can be an important cue. It might alert you that you need to prepare more than you have, but it can also just let you know that you are ready and energized for the task ahead. How you interpret your own arousal is important. Appropriate levels of arousal can sharpen your reflexes, alertness, and mental processing ability. Thus, when preparing for an exam, just as when preparing for an athletic competition, you want to find the level of arousal (which is generally moderate) that is optimal for you. To help you identify your level of arousal when taking exams, you may want to complete Exercise 8.6.

Causes of Test Anxiety

There are several common causes of test anxiety:

- Overstating the importance of exams.
- Fear of disappointing others.
- Focusing excessively on the outcome, rather than on effort, improvement, and learning.
- Having unrealistic performance expectations.
- Poor preparation.
- Lack of skills necessary for success.

We will discuss these reasons next and make suggestions as to how to cope.

Overemphasized importance. Self-inflicted pressure is a major reason behind students' test anxiety. One source of such pressure is the negative self-talk students engage in about exams and about their ability to perform well. Some students overstate the importance of a given exam by telling themselves that they are worthless if they don't do well, that performing poorly is "the end of the world," that if they don't pass, they'll flunk out of school, and so on. These types of statements are self-defeating

---

Exercise 8.6　My Test Arousal Level

1. Think about how you generally feel when you take exams. What is your general level of arousal? Are you too relaxed (apathetic)? Are you too pumped up (anxious)? Describe how you generally feel, both physically and emotionally.

_____

_____

and don't contribute to helping you feel confident and relaxed going into an exam. Thus, put your exams in the proper perspective—yes, they are important but they are not matters of life and death. To identify your negative thinking about exams, you may want to complete Exercise 8.7.

Disappointing others. Sometimes the self-inflicted pressure comes from students' perceptions of how *others* will respond to a poor performance. They worry that they'll disappoint their families, their coaches, or perhaps their instructors if they don't do well. Although it is always nice to be able to please those who are important to you, focusing most of your attention on that usually spells trouble. It detracts from what helps you be academically successful. Instead, focus on what you can control, which is the amount of effort you expend in preparing for the exam.

Focus on outcome. Focusing on the outcome, rather than on your effort, improvement, and learning is another common source of pressure.

Calculating Grade Point Averages

Your grade point average (GPA) provides you with an objective measure of how well you are doing academically. At the end of each term, you will have access to your grades (generally via the school's Internet reporting system), your academic term GPA (the one you earned that term), and your cumulative GPA (what your GPA is across all the terms you have been at school). Thus, it is important for you to understand what your GPA is and how it is determined.

   GPA = (Total Number of Grade Points)/(Total Number of Credit Hours)

For example, Sandra was taking four classes during her first semester. Two of her classes were worth 3 credit hours each, one was worth 2, and one was worth 4, so her total course load for the term was 12 hours. At Sandra's school, grades were assigned the following point values: A = 4 points; B = 3; C = 2; D = 1; F = 0. Thus, the number of grade points she might earn in each class would be equal to the point value multiplied by the number of credit hours for that class. If Sandra earned an A in one of her 3-credit-hour classes, then she would have 12 grade points for that course (4 [point value for earning an A] × [number of credit hours for that particular course] = 12).

   For her first semester, Sandra earned the following grades: A in a 3-hour course, B in a 3-hour course, C in the 2-hour course, and B in the 4-hour course. To determine her total number of grade points for that term, you would multiply each grade by the number of credit hours for that specific course:

   A (4 points) × 3-credit course = 12 grade points
   B (3 points) × 3-credit course = 9 grade points
   B (3 points) × 4-credit course = 12 grade points
   C (2 points) × 2-credit course = 4 grade points

   Total grade points = 12 + 9 + 12 + 4 = 37

   GPA = 37 (total grade points)/13 (total credit hours) = 2.84
   Sandra's GPA for her first term was 2.84

One important thing about GPAs is that they are very hard to increase in your later semesters. So, make sure you get off to a good start during your first semester.

Exercise 8.7 Negative Thinking

1. List three negative self-statements that you commonly make when preparing for an exam.

_____

_____

_____

2. List three negative self-statements that you commonly make when actually taking an exam.

_____

_____

_____

3. In general, how do the things you tell yourself about the meaning of tests and your performance on them affect how you feel about yourself and the pressure you experience while in the exam?

_____

_____

We have stressed throughout this book how important it is to concentrate on giving the best you can. If you focus exclusively on outcomes, then you're bound to be disappointed, because outcomes are based on many factors not directly under your control. Effort, on the other hand, is one thing you do control. As an athlete, you've probably experienced a defeat (outcome), but were still proud of your performance (process).

Unrealistic expectations. Having unrealistic expectations is another source of pressure. Some students place enormous pressure on themselves with the expectation that they should perform perfectly all the time. Setting perfection as a goal will guarantee dissatisfaction and possible failure. However, this should not be confused with setting high but attainable goals, which we do encourage.

Poor preparation. If you failed to practice well, commit to off-season conditioning, or to develop a thorough game plan before competing, then you would probably be fairly anxious about your performance during a competition. Your coaches would certainly be nervous! The best way to avoid this, of course, is to prepare thoroughly. In other words, *the best way to reduce test anxiety is to be prepared*. Make sure you take the time to know the material upon which you'll be tested. Mastery of the material is the goal rather than knowing enough to just get by. If you follow the suggestions made earlier in this chapter on daily, weekly, and final reviews, then you will increase the likelihood of being prepared.

Lack of skills. Some students lack the skills needed to be confident in their ability to succeed. Some students arrive on campus knowing they are deficient in areas such as reading comprehension, writing, information processing, note taking, and so on. Knowing that you have a weakness in one or more of these areas usually produces anxiety, especially if you know that you will be evaluated on a task that requires those skills. If you have weaknesses in any of these areas, then working through this text should help. You may also want to consult with your tutors, your athletic department advisor, or other university academic support services (e.g., Student Success Center) to get additional assistance on your campus. To evaluate your current skill sets, you may want to complete Exercise 8.8.

Exercise 8.8   Identifying Your Skill Deficiencies

1. Identify two skill deficiencies you have when taking exams—areas where you know you need to improve your skills. Do not focus on specific course content areas; instead, consider broad areas, such as reading or writing skills.

_____

_____

2. With respect to these two areas, what steps can you take to improve (be specific)?

_____

_____

Performance: Managing Test Anxiety

Fortunately, there are a number of strategies you can use to turn test anxiety into test confidence.

Prepare, Prepare, Prepare!

Without a doubt, preparation is the single best strategy you can use to counteract test anxiety. It is no secret that the better prepared you are, the more confident you'll feel on test day because you know the material. It's the same when you prepare for sport competitions. The more you have practiced and trained, the more likely it is that you will feel confident about the upcoming event. To maximize preparation, be sure to begin your final review considerably before the date the exam will be given. Consider reviewing for exams as an ongoing process. You may find it beneficial to treat the entire interval between exams in a class as your review period. This approach will help you to learn and _understand_, rather than just to memorize, the material.

Spacing your review over a longer period of time is a more effective way of learning than cramming at the last minute. Believe it or not, cramming can actually _raise_, rather than lower, your level of test anxiety, and it certainly interferes with your ability to get enough rest the night before the exam. There is no substitute for the hard work and effort that are needed to prepare for exams. Approach test taking as a challenge, just as you would an athletic competition—be prepared, confident, and relaxed. We frequently see students walking to class during final exams week still studying material, or studying notes until moments before the professor is handing out the exam. If you have not reached a stopping point in your studying, then you are communicating to yourself that you are not prepared for the exam. As part of your preparation, determine an appropriate stopping point for studying before exams. You'll feel better for it.

Visualize Success

Mental imagery is another technique that can help reduce exam anxiety and improve test performance. When using this technique, you imagine yourself performing a specific activity without actual physical movements. Visualization is helpful because it provides you with a simulation of the actual experience while preparing your mind and body to carry out the task at the appropriate time. You may have had experience with visualization, or mental rehearsal, while training in your sport. For example, a basketball player might visualize herself picking up the basketball, spinning it, dribbling it three times, assuming the stance and grip she uses, and then shooting a free throw. Applying this to exam situations, you might visualize yourself being confident and in control. You sit down at your desk and look calmly around the room. You take a deep breath as the exam is handed out and remind yourself that this is just another type of performance or competition; you are prepared and ready to excel. You write your name on the exam and carefully read the directions before answering the questions correctly. If you use visualization, then you will probably find that your levels of stress and physical tension are reduced, while your confidence and performance levels increase. When using visualization, practice it along with relaxation exercises and visualize positive outcomes. Remember, visualization is not a substitute for solid, thorough preparation. It is a supplement to studying, not a replacement for it. We cover visualization in greater depth in Chapter 11.

Establish Your Comfort Zone

Another strategy to lower test anxiety is to be familiar with the testing environment. Charlotte, our aspiring law school student, always made sure she arrived early at the room where the test was to be given, so she could get comfortable with the environment. She found this especially helpful if the room was unfamiliar. Arriving early made it possible for her to sit in a seat she preferred, which helped her to feel physically comfortable and allowed her to focus on the test, not on her body. She was able to use this strategy successfully when she took her entrance exam. If possible, try to study in an environment that is physically similar to the one in which you will be tested, which is like practicing your sport under conditions similar to the ones you will experience during competition. For example, if your cross-country races are always in the morning, then you should run some of your harder workouts (e.g., intervals, tempo runs) at a similar time instead of the afternoon. Although you cannot duplicate the conditions of the actual competition or exam, the more similarity there is when you practice or study, the more likely you will be to perform well when you compete or take your exam.

Relaxation

Muscle relaxation can also help reduce anxiety because, physiologically, you cannot be tense and relaxed at the same time. Alternately tensing and relaxing your foot, leg, arm, neck, and torso muscles is an excellent way to reduce physical symptoms of anxiety. Like muscle relaxation, deep breathing can help and be used before or during the exam. As you breathe, make sure your breaths are even and slow, but steady. Do not hold your breath too long, or you may increase your level of tension. For more information on relaxation techniques, see Chapter 11.

> "The successes I had didn't surprise me because I'd already experienced them in my mind."
>
> MICHAEL JORDAN
> *Former NBA All-Star and MVP*

Accentuate the Positive: Be Optimistic

Learn to manage your thoughts and counter negative self-talk about yourself and your performance. Negative self-talk does not help you reach your goal of a successful performance. Instead of focusing on self-statements that Vick used, such as "I'm so stupid that I'll never pass this test" or "If I don't pass the test, I'll flunk out of school and lose my scholarship," use positive statements. In doing so, you might say to yourself, "It's okay, I'll work on another question for a while and then come back to this one." This type of positive approach will help you to concentrate and focus on the remaining questions. Speaking to yourself in a positive, nonthreatening manner will help you to feel calm and confident when faced with difficult situations. Remind yourself that you are prepared and that exams are just opportunities to show what you know. As you take the exam, focus your thoughts on the test, not on other students or even on how you are doing on the test. Remain positive. Your performance on one exam is not a measure of your worth as a person, nor is one imperfect performance the end of the world. It may even be useful to expect that there will be items that you won't be able to answer (King, 1997). This is not to suggest that you should not prepare yourself for the exam or give less than your best effort; it just means that you should not allow yourself to be distracted and upset by a difficult question. Remember that most tests are constructed with the intent of measuring a fairly wide range of content mastery, so there will be items with varying degrees of difficulty. On a well-constructed test, answering every question right is the exception, not the rule. To help you begin to change your negative thinking, you may want to complete Exercise 8.9.

Test Anxiety: Some Final Thoughts

If you believe excessive anxiety is a problem when taking tests, then you may wish to consider looking for help at your campus counseling or health center. These centers have professionals who are trained to assist students with such concerns in a supportive and confidential environment. If you are experiencing test anxiety or related problems, then it is your responsibility to seek help. Don't become an academic casualty! Be proactive and take advantage of the skills and strategies offered in this book and the services available on your campus.

Post-Game Review: After the Exam

You've read the book, you've studied your notes, you've created flash cards, you've created acronyms, you've visualized success, and you've taken the exam. Now that the test is behind you, your work is done, right? No! In reality, the process of becoming a successful student-athlete

---

Exercise 8.9   Changing Your Negative Thinking

Think about the negative self-statements you identified in Exercise 8.7. What positive self-statements could you substitute regarding tests and your performance?

continues. One aspect of taking tests that students consistently overlook is what happens *after* the exam. As a student-athlete, you are well aware of the importance of making a post-competition evaluation of your performance in order to make the necessary adjustments for the next competition. In football, for example, a considerable amount of time is spent studying the films from yesterday's practice in preparation for today's. Sunday afternoons are often spent looking at film from Saturday's game. Even though the game is history and the outcome can't be changed, evaluating the performance is crucial for the next game. As you might imagine, the same is true with your exams. Analyzing your test results is essential if you wish to do better on the next exam.

How can going over your test results be helpful? There are several ways. To illustrate, let's look at Marcus. Marcus practically lived in his coach's office, constantly watching films of his performance on the field to improve his chances of getting to the pros. He clearly saw the relationship between analyzing his performance and getting better at his sport. When it came to school, however, Marcus rarely bothered to analyze the results of his exams. As a result, he never knew whether the score he received was accurate or what kinds of mistakes he made, so it was almost impossible for his tutors and his academic advisor to help him. Not surprisingly, school was a constant struggle for Marcus. Because he didn't look at his exams after they were graded, he never saw the patterns in the types of mistakes he made, and of course, he couldn't take the steps necessary to correct those mistakes. He also never knew if his test was graded correctly because he never went over the answers that were marked incorrect on his exam with his instructor to understand why he missed them and, if in fact, they were wrong.

What else can you gain by taking time to go over the results of your tests? If you performed poorly, then you can learn about the types of errors you made. For example, perhaps you tend to miss questions in one specific content area or maybe your errors were distributed across multiple areas. Perhaps you missed certain types of questions, such as those that required application of knowledge as opposed to those that were definitional or factual. With a multiple-choice exam, understanding why you chose the wrong answer and missed the correct one can be very useful for future exams. Some students, for example, tend to consistently misread questions and thus answer them incorrectly. Failing to read the question as it is written is a common mistake. It can lead to choosing alternatives such as "all of the above" when only one or two answers are true. Sometimes students choose items that include the terms *all, always,* or *every,* though in reality it is rare for a statement like this to be true. Choosing the first *good* answer, and not the *best* answer, is another common mistake students make on multiple-choice exams.

If you don't go over the results of your exam, then you may miss seeing patterns of errors. On essay exams, for example, you may find a pattern of failing to provide supporting evidence for the assertions you make, and you may be losing points for that. Failing to answer all parts of the question is another common error. If you only "compare" when you are supposed to "compare *and* contrast," then your grade may suffer. Again, if you don't take the time to look at your test, then you may never become aware of these patterns.

Another pattern you might identify from reviewing your exams is studying the wrong material, or placing too little or too much emphasis on different class material. You may study the textbook, but the instructor leaned heavily on lecture material for the exam. You will also find that it is much easier for tutors, academic advisors, and instructors to help you if you've carefully gone over your results. They can provide another perspective on your test-taking style if you have trouble identifying your own patterns of mistakes, not unlike the feedback your coaches give you on your athletic performance. Analyzing your performance even after tests on which you did well will help reinforce the positive patterns in your test-taking style. If your final exam is cumulative—that is, if it addresses material covered during the entire term—then it is quite possible that it will include questions from previous exams, especially if many students missed those questions the first time around. If you learn to focus on the material the instructor emphasizes, then you will be better off the second time you're tested on it. Retesting on previously missed items is a way for your instructor to find out whether the material has been learned.

Finally, as Chickering and Schlossberg (2001) have suggested, the most important basis for interpreting your test results is your own frame of reference. Although knowing how you did in comparison to others is useful and knowing how well you met specific knowledge requirements is more useful, neither tells you much about your own progress. As a student-athlete, you know that improvement from day to day, week to week, and year to year is a primary goal. It is also the reason you feel the pride of achievement when you go from being unable to execute necessary skills in your sport to mastering the fundamentals. A focus on improving in the classroom is similar. Improvement is also something that instructors often reward. They are interested in what you know, but they also want to see you improve over time. Using the feedback from your exams is an important way of measuring your progress over the course of the term. If your performance wasn't what you wanted on the first exam, then look at your mistakes and focus on improving. You never truly fail as long as you take steps to improve.

Post-Game Review

Self-responsibility is a key factor when it comes to successfully preparing for and taking college exams. If you have weaknesses in your test-preparation skills or in your test-taking skills or if you become excessively anxious about taking exams, then establish specific goals for improvement in these areas. Identify smaller, measurable steps you can take, rather than simply saying "I have to get better at taking tests." Committing yourself to using the review strategies presented in this chapter is an example of the kind of steps you can take to reach your goal of doing better on tests. Be self-responsible and accept the challenge of taking steps to improve your performance, rather than waiting for someone else to force you to do so. Analyzing your performance after exams and taking the initiative to deal with unusual test circumstances, such as resolving exam-travel conflicts, are other areas where you have

---

> **Exercise 8.10   Learning More about Taking Exams**
>
> Many university learning or career resource centers and even some for-profit businesses provide extensive information on how to prepare for and take exams. Using an Internet search engine, such as Yahoo!, Google, or Bing, type in the words "College Exams" or "Exam Preparation" or "Test Preparation" or "Test Taking Strategies" and visit some of the websites that you locate. When you do, read through the suggestions made for improving exam performance. Identify three strategies/techniques that were not covered in this chapter that help you better prepare for and perform on your exams.

---

an opportunity to be self-responsible. To learn more about preparing for and taking tests, you may want to complete Exercise 8.10.

Thinking Critically about Test Preparation and Performance

1. Summarize what you now know about preparing for and successfully taking exams based on the information presented in this chapter.

_____

_____

_____

2. What additional questions do you have about these topics and how to use the skills introduced in this chapter?

_____

_____

_____

3. What conclusions can you draw about this topic and how it might help you be a more effective and successful student and athlete?

_____

_____

_____

Achieve IT! Setting a Test-Taking Goal

1. Based on your self-assessment and your responses to Thinking Critically, select a goal in relationship to improving your preparation for and performance on exams that you would like to achieve this term.

2. Now identify three short-term goals that will help you reach your goal this term.

3. For the short-term goals, identify the attainment strategies you will need to reach them.

4. List any obstacles you might face in trying to reach these goals and identify your plan for overcoming each one.

Don't forget to make your goal visible and tell others about them, so they can keep you accountable regarding what you want to achieve.

Chapter 8 Review Questions

1. In general, subjective tests are based on the assumption that there is one correct (or best) answer. (True or False)

2. Which of the following is not an objective test?

   a. Multiple choice.
   b. True-false.
   c. Matching.
   d. Fill-in-the-blank.
   e. None of the above.

3. Cramming leads to better retention of information than spreading your studying out over several days. (True or False)

4. As a student-athlete, when you miss an exam and have to take a makeup you should

   a. Not worry about it because it's not your responsibility.
   b. Tell the professor what kind of test you want to take.
   c. Immediately contact the instructor to find out what you have to do for the makeup.
   d. Have your coach or academic advisor call your instructor to arrange the makeup.

5. According to the text, which of the following techniques is *not* useful in studying for an exam?

   a. Flash cards.
   b. Tape-recording lectures.
   c. Reviewing old exams.
   d. Hypnosis.

6. Nutrition and rest are irrelevant to test performance. (True or False)

7. Which of the following strategies should be used when you are taking an objective test?

   a. Look over the entire exam before answering any questions.
   b. Answer the questions you're sure of first.
   c. Try to answer a multiple-choice question in your mind first, before looking at the options provided.
   d. Be careful when you see absolute terms such as *always* or *never* in the questions or the multiple-choice answers.
   e. All of the above.

8. Name two techniques you can use to generate high-quality answers for essay exams.

9. Identify three common symptoms of test anxiety.

10. Visualization can help you cope with test anxiety by

    a. Helping you feel more confident.
    b. Giving you the chance to practice taking the test before you actually do.
    c. Helping you feel more relaxed.
    d. A and C.
    e. All of the above.

11. When you receive your graded exam from your instructor, you should review your results to determine

  a. If the exam was scored correctly.
  b. The areas in which you made mistakes and how you can improve them on future exams.
  c. If you scored higher than your friend.
  d. A and B.
  e. All of the above.

Chapter 9 | Communication and Diversity

Succeeding in Life and Relationships

Game Plan:

In this chapter, you will learn:

- The benefits of cultural diversity

- The characteristics of satisfying multicultural communication

- Communicating effectively with people from different cultural backgrounds

© Jeff Thrower (WebThrower), 2009 / Used under license from Shutterstock.com

"The secret of winning football games is working more as a team, less as individuals. I play not my 11 best, but my best 11."

KNUTE ROCKNE
College Football Coaching Legend

Self-Assessment—Perceive It!

Read the following statements and place a checkmark next to each one you generally do. For you to change and develop new and effective academic, athletic, and personal strategies, you must be accurate in your self-perception. So, be honest in how you answer each question.

1. I am able to communicate effectively with people whose ethnic and cultural backgrounds or sexual orientation are different from mine. _____

2. I feel comfortable with people whose sexual orientation is different from mine. _____

3. I recognize that people from any single racial or ethnic group share comon characteristics but are also unique and different from one another. _____

4. I have friendships with people from a variety of racial, ethnic, and cultural backgrounds. _____

5. It is important to learn about people whose racial, ethnic, and cultural backgrounds are different from mine. _____

6. I can recognize cultural, racial, ethnic, and gender stereotypes when I see them in the media, such as in movies, TV, and newspapers. _____

7. I try to understand things from another person's point of view. _____

8. I am willing to speak out against racist, sexist, or other prejudiced or stereotypical views expressed by others. _____

9. I attend or participate in events or other activities that reflect a culture or lifestyle different from mine. _____

10. I understand that people from racial, ethnic, or cultural groups different from my own may have different values, beliefs, and ways of communicating. _____

11. I am aware of the values and beliefs of my racial, ethnic, or cultural group. _____

12. When I interact in a multicultural context, I look for similarities between myself and the other person, yet I also respect the differences that may exist. _____

Take a moment to review your responses. How many items did you check? Each one you checked represents a current strength. Now consider the items you did not check. These represent areas where focus and growth are needed. Now, to summarize your self-perception, complete the following statements:

1. My areas of strength are:

_____

2. The areas I need to improve are:

_____

As you read this chapter and participate in your classes, keep your strengths and areas of improvement in mind. At the end of the chapter, you will have the chance to set a goal related to these areas. Achieving these goals will help you become a more effective student and athlete.

Nora was a heavily recruited basketball player from a poor neighborhood in a large city. She was in her first year at college, on a large, predominantly white campus in a rural setting, far from her hometown. She was the first person in her family to go to a four-year school, so naturally she was a bit apprehensive and unsure what to expect.

Nora's first term in college was especially difficult. She felt out of place on campus and was quite homesick. She missed her girlfriend at home, and the early part of the season wasn't going well. A late-summer knee injury made it difficult for Nora to get into shape, so her coach was planning to redshirt her. In addition to these concerns, Nora was sinking fast in her classes. She had never been a strong student, so she lacked the academic preparation and habits to be immediately successful; thus it was no surprise that she quickly fell behind in her work and soon began skipping classes and failing exams. Not surprisingly, her coaches became concerned and started coming down on her hard.

Introduction

Nora's academic advisor, whose ethnic background was similar to hers, also became concerned about her progress. Working with Nora's coach, she arranged to meet regularly with Nora in the hope of getting things straightened out before Nora flunked out of school. Nora and her advisor met each week for several weeks. Each time, Nora reported that everything was fine, but the evidence suggested otherwise. Despite the well-intended efforts of her advisor, Nora was uncomfortable, could not connect with her, and decided to discontinue their meetings. She told her advisor, "We just come from two different worlds."

Although they shared a common racial/ethnic background, they did have differences. Nora was the product of a tough inner-city neighborhood, with few positive academic role models. Although her family and girlfriend tried to support Nora's academic pursuits, they didn't understand what she was facing. Her advisor, on the other hand, came from an upper-middle-class home where education had been stressed from the beginning. Nora and her advisor spoke differently and dressed differently; they lived differently. One thing they did share was the desire for Nora to be successful at school. Unfortunately, all Nora could see was the differences. Had she been able to focus more on the similarities, they might have connected, and the advisor could have offered her some assistance. As it was, Nora continued to struggle and finished her freshman year uncertain about returning to school. Neither Nora nor her advisor was sure what had gone wrong.

Diversity and multicultural communication are complex, and for some, controversial. It often takes unexpected turns, as illustrated in the above story. Athletics mirror our larger society in many ways, so it is not surprising that societal challenges regarding diversity are also present in sport. In college athletics, though, ethnically and socioeconomically diverse groups of people are brought together and, for the most part, are judged not so much by the color of their skin or the accent of their voice, but by their performance and contribution to a common goal. Such coming together, though, does not occur in all areas of diversity (Wolf-Wendel, Toma, and Morphew, 2001). For example, with sexual orientation, there often still is a lack of acceptance that results in feelings of isolation, depression, and fear—and in the worst cases culminating in suicide—and poor athletic performance.

More than any other chapter in this book, this one explores issues on which it is hard to stay neutral. Diversity and multicultural communication require you to take a serious look at your personal values and beliefs about other people—especially the ones you see as different. Our goal in writing this chapter is to encourage you to examine your experiences with and views about cultural diversity and to provide you with some strategies for improving your multicultural communication. And, because of the interconnected world in which we live, diversity is not just related to racial/ethnic groups in the United States (e.g., African American, Asian American), but addresses differences across nationalities, religious groups, sexual orientation, etc. Basically, it is about the values and beliefs that you hold and how they are similar to and different from those of others. To help you begin to consider diversity in your own life, you may want to complete Exercise 9.1.

Exercise 9.1   Diversity in Your Life

1. How do you define diversity? What are some of the characteristics/dimensions that you consider when determining if a person is similar or different from you?

2. Think about your friendships for a moment. How diverse are they in terms of the characteristics that you mentioned in question 1? Along what dimensions do your friendships seem to vary? In what ways are your friends most similar to you?

3. Thinking more broadly, what diverse groups of people (based on race/ethnicity, religion, nationality, sexual orientation, etc.) do you accept the most? Why? Accept the least? Why?

4. What specific experiences in your life have influenced your feelings about different groups of people (as you indicated in question 3)?

5. Have national and international events, such as the election of the first African American president in the United States or the wars in the Middle East, affected your views and acceptance of diversity?

6. What are your family's views about diversity and, in particular, different groups of people (which ones do they accept the most and accept the least)?

In the next section, we define some of the key concepts of the chapter—culture, diversity, and multicultural communication—and discuss the value of diversity. We also look at what can happen when communication breaks down between cultures. Later, we address the related issues of stereotyping and discrimination. Finally, we offer some strategies to help you communicate effectively with people from different backgrounds.

Preparation: Defining Culture, Diversity, and Communication

Brislin and Yoshida (1994) suggest that culture contains three central features:

1. Concepts, values, and assumptions about life and the world that guide behavior and are widely shared.
2. Ideas that are transmitted implicitly and explicitly across generations. Culture is passed on through clear statements of the ways things should be done and through modeling of the way life should be lived.
3. Culture becomes most clear when people interact with others from different backgrounds.

Culture is so deeply ingrained that we often fail to think about it or become aware of its impact unless we see others whose culture contrasts or conflicts with ours.

Cultural diversity can be defined as the presence of persons from a variety of cultural and/or ethnic groups within a single setting, such as a college or an athletic team. The individuals involved must see themselves as belonging to distinct cultural groups formed on the basis of one or more prominent and meaningful distinguishing features. The individuals who belong to these groups must be present in the same setting at the same time for diversity to occur. Thus, our definition of diversity includes race/ethnicity, religion, sexual orientation, nationality, and physical or mental disability, as well as nearly any characteristic an individual uses to define herself or himself as different from the groups in that setting.

The term *multicultural communication* refers to interactions between two or more parties who come from different cultural backgrounds. Communication can take many forms; however, in this chapter our primary focus will be on direct, face-to-face interactions. Nora's story illustrates an important point about multicultural communication. Despite Nora and her advisor sharing a common ethnic background, there were other cultural elements at work between them, such as socioeconomic status and educational background, in which they were quite different. All of these contributed to their multicultural communication.

Before you can communicate effectively across cultures, it is important to be aware of the cultural factors that have influenced your own development. What are the important cultural characteristics that help to define who you are as a person? Do you consider yourself to be a member of more than one cultural group? If so, are there conflicting values among those cultures? What characteristics do you consider when you are interacting with someone from a different cultural group? To help you think about your own culture, you may want to complete Exercise 9.2.

Why Diversity?

Why is a discussion about diversity important? Chickering and Schlossberg (2001) point out that most people grow up in small communities of people like themselves. As a result, you learned early on the social norms for your community: what was good and bad, right and wrong, acceptable and unacceptable. You were taught community standards of dress, manners, and language. You learned norms for interpersonal behaviors, such as appropriate boundaries and personal space when talking to strangers, friends, and relatives. You also took on, as part of your personality, a set of expectations, attitudes, and behaviors that you think of as normal. All these things emerge as you observe and interact with others in the world. People who do not behave as you expect are, in a sense, not "normal" to you, and that can be puzzling, upsetting, or threatening.

Encountering cultural diversity can be simultaneously exciting and threatening for majority and minority student-athletes. For majority students, it can be exciting to encounter people whose backgrounds and lifestyles are unfamiliar. This opportunity can lead to personal growth and be a primary reason many students attend college and where they choose to go. Athletics and college provide common meeting grounds for people from different backgrounds in ways that are not common in other settings. At the same time, encountering cultural diversity can be threatening to majority students because of the challenge of getting

---

Exercise 9.2   Examining Your Own Culture

1. With what cultural group(s) do you identify?

2. What are some of the characteristics or features, such as behaviors, speech patterns, or styles of dress, which define these cultural groups?

3. What are the values and beliefs that you associate with these cultural groups? How do these values guide the current way that you live?

used to entirely new groups of students whose skin color, religious values, sexual orientation, and national origin may be quite different from theirs. Cultural diversity may challenge your values, beliefs, and long-held assumptions about the world. It may cause you considerable discomfort; it may rock your world.

Minority student-athletes can have similar experiences, but they also face the potential issue of *marginalization,* which occurs when a group is perceived as existing outside of the mainstream and is treated as if it were unimportant or marginal. Often, minority student-athletes come from settings where they were used to being in the majority. When they enter predominantly white colleges and universities, however, they may be isolated by their status as athletes *and* as members of minority groups. At times, their presence on campus may even be resented by those who assume these students were admitted only because of their athletic abilities. These students must adjust to a different culture while maintaining ties to the ones from which they came. This can be a difficult juggling act, but it can be made a bit easier by connecting with mentors on campus or in the community and by participating in student organizations.

In college, you will have the opportunity to interact with a variety of people who have diverse interests and views of the world. Among them will be faculty, staff, and students from various parts of the United States, as well as individuals from other countries. Even if you do not choose to build close relationships with a diverse group of people, you still have the opportunity to learn about them and about yourself in the process. Remember, the more you know about people from various backgrounds, the more likely you are to be able to communicate with them.

The realm of athletics illustrates some of the difficulties that can arise when people of different cultures come together. For example, consider a situation involving a Caucasian coach and an African American athlete. The coach, who is a generation older, came from a relatively well-to-do background, one in which authority wasn't questioned. It was acceptable for an authority figure to yell at someone in order to make a point. The athlete's circumstances were quite different. He was younger and came from a tough background in which screaming was a sign of disrespect and was not to be accepted. This kind of situation is fairly common in athletics.

What can happen when people from such diverse backgrounds come together? One possible outcome is conflict, leading to threats and physical violence, which is what happened in this situation. The coach may simply have yelled at the athlete to help him become a better player, meaning no disrespect. After all, that was how things had been done when he was a player. On the other hand, the athlete saw the situation quite differently, through the lens of his own cultural background. For him, the yelling was an unacceptable insult. It was a personal attack that went past mere "coaching." For the athlete, in his world, people who treated him that way were not tolerated. This unfortunate situation shows how important it is to be able to communicate effectively and be able to recognize the role of culture in interpersonal interactions. With more sensitivity to cultural differences, the coach might have found a better way to get his points across to

> "Travel is fatal to prejudice, bigotry, and narrow-mindedness, and many of our people need it solely on these accounts."
>
> MARK TWAIN
> *Author*

© Christopher Futcher, 2009 / Used under license from Shutterstock.com

the athlete. Similarly, the athlete might have recognized that the coach meant nothing personal, thus not feeling disrespected and avoiding a negative reaction.

Many of you may find yourself in circumstances similar to that of the athlete described previously. Your coach may be considerably older and have a cultural and social background different from yours, as may teammates and fellow students. The skill with which you learn to handle such differences will be vital to your success as a college student-athlete. To help you begin thinking about this issue in your own life, you may want to complete Exercise 9.3.

Whether or not you personally believe in the importance of appreciating and embracing cultures different from yours is a question of your personal values. From our perspective, however, much can be gained by being able to function in a world where you interact with people from a variety of backgrounds. Many universities require that students participate in a study abroad experience before graduation in recognition of the world's globalization. Whether it is in the classroom, in athletics, or in the world of work, your success will be influenced by your ability to interact with people whose backgrounds and values are different from your own. The remainder of this chapter will focus on general principles you can use to improve your ability to communicate with people from different cultural backgrounds.

Exercise 9.3   Understanding Multicultural Conflicts

1. Take a moment to think about your own experiences as a student-athlete. Have you had any interactions with coaches, teammates, or other students that were difficult because of cultural differences? Describe the situation and the cultural factors that contributed to the difficulties you experienced.

2. Could this situation have been avoided or handled more effectively? If so, how?

Performance: Communicating Effectively Across Cultures

Because individuals from different cultural groups have different life experiences, their verbal and nonverbal behaviors will vary and thus may be interpreted differently than they intended. In these situations, misunderstandings may be hard to avoid. Increasing your familiarity with other cultures will reduce the likelihood of such problems but will not eliminate them entirely. Also, as we mentioned earlier, even when you become familiar with other cultures, you are still dealing with *individuals* who have their own interpretation of their culture. Despite the lack of absolute rules, it is still beneficial to get some understanding of the cultures we encounter. You should also remember that most people appreciate efforts to understand their lives and backgrounds, so whether or not you grasp all the norms and behaviors of a given culture is less important to others than your willingness to learn. To help you begin to learn about the similarities and differences between groups of people, you may want to complete Exercise 9.4.

Exercise 9.4 Multicultural Interview

For this exercise, find two people from different cultural, racial, or ethnic backgrounds, sexual orientation, or nationality—other than your own, of course—who are willing to talk about their culture and its influence on communication. In addition to the questions provided here, prepare at least three of your own to learn more about communication within the racial or ethnic group of each person you are interviewing.

Name of Interviewee Number 1: _____
Diversity Factor (how this person is different from you—be specific):

1. What similarities and differences do you notice in the nonverbal behavior of your cultural group as compared to others, such as differences in eye contact, body language, words used, and so on?

_____

_____

_____

2. Can you remember any situations in which you have felt misunderstood because of cultural differences? If so, what happened and how did you respond?

_____

_____

_____

3. In terms of verbal and nonverbal communication, what similarities and differences do you notice among men and women from your cultural group?

_____

_____

_____

4. How would you describe your culture, such as your beliefs, values, characteristics, and symbols, to someone who knows nothing about it?

_____

_____

_____

5. What else would you want someone to know about you to help them better understand you?

_____

_____

_____

Name of Interviewee Number 2: _____

Race/Ethnicity: _____

1. What similarities and differences do you notice in the nonverbal behavior of your cultural group as compared to others, such as differences in eye contact, body language, words used, and so on?

_____

_____

(continued)

2. Can you remember any situations in which you have felt misunderstood because of cultural differences? If so, what happened and how did you respond?

_____

_____

_____

3. In terms of verbal and nonverbal communication, what similarities and differences do you notice among men and women from your cultural group?

_____

_____

_____

4. How would you describe your culture, such as your beliefs, values, characteristics, and symbols, to someone who knows nothing about it?

_____

_____

_____

5. What else would you want someone to know about you to help them better understand you?

_____

_____

_____

Preparation: Stereotypes and Discrimination

Stereotyping

Understanding culture is an important part of understanding individuals, yet not everyone from any one cultural group is the same (Ford, 1994). If you think about people only in terms of their cultural group membership, then you are stereotyping. For example, people often view members of ethnic groups as part of a single culture, making references to a "black culture," a "Hispanic culture," or a "white culture." Although African Americans share a common ethnic heritage and history in the United States, you would need much more information about a person than the simple fact that she is African American before you could say you "know" her. You would need to know about her socioeconomic background: Is she wealthy, middle class, or poor? You would also need to know where she's from: Is she from the South, the Midwest, the Northeast, or perhaps the West Coast? Even armed with all that information, you would still need to know how her culture and ethnicity affect her. Cultural background and ethnicity are factors that could be important to her, or perhaps they matter less to her than to others. In reality, there are many African American, Hispanic, and white cultures. African Americans from Los Angeles and the rural South have about as much in common as do whites from New England and Appalachia. A similar phenomenon can be seen with other minority groups, such as religious minorities or gay, lesbian, bisexual, or transgendered groups.

The world of athletics is not immune from stereotyping. Positional stereotyping has been common in football and baseball. For many years, there were almost no African American quarterbacks in major college or professional football. It was believed that these athletes did not possess the intelligence to play such a key position. In contrast, the "speed" positions—defensive back, wide receiver, and running back—have been dominated by African Americans, particularly in recent years. There are relatively few African American baseball pitchers, but a high proportion of outfielders are African American. Several years ago, a longtime baseball executive lost his job after expressing

Exercise 9.5 Stereotypes in Your Sport

1. Think for a moment about your sport. What are some of the stereotypes that exist?

2. What factors contribute to these stereotypes? Do they vary along racial/ethnic lines? Position played? Sexual orientation? Being in the sport versus not?

doubts that African Americans had the intellectual capabilities required to manage a baseball team. In basketball, the terms *heady, gritty, an overachiever*, and *a coach on the floor* have often been used to describe successful Caucasian athletes, whereas successful African Americans are labeled *talented, gifted,* and *athletic*. The implied stereotype suggests that Caucasian basketball players don't have physical tools and African Americans don't have the intellect. These stereotypes hurt all involved. To help you think about the stereotypes that exist in your sport, you may want to complete Exercise 9.5.

Stereotyping takes other forms as well. Ordinarily, people tend to make a number of assumptions about other people. For example, when you see someone who is like you racially, religiously, sexually, etc., it is common to assume that person is like you in other ways (e.g., beliefs, values, behaviors); that is, they see the world as you do. It is also fairly common for us to see members of our own group as being quite different from each other, while seeing members of other groups as having much more in common with each other than they actually do. Any of these assumptions can make us fail to understand others adequately. For example, you may have heard someone say something to the effect that "all African Americans (or Hispanics, or Caucasians) are…" Not only are such statements inaccurate, but they are also hurtful. Such comments rob individuals of their uniqueness because they are seen solely through the lens of group membership.

When we expect others to be just like us and they aren't, we can get caught in a cultural gap (Ford, 1994). When something is said that offends us or someone acts in a way that shocks or angers or horrifies us, one reaction is to pull back and withdraw into what we find familiar and acceptable and to reject anything or anyone that is different. Recent tragic events in our country have caused some to respond this way, which can give rise to racist, sexist, and homophobic attitudes, behaviors, and feelings. Discovering that others are not exactly like us can create a boundary, across which real communication and honest human interchange often cease to exist. Instead, these are replaced by stereotypical labeling based on misunderstanding, anger, fear, and unresolved emotions. To address this boundary, take time to examine your own stereotypes of cultural or ethnic groups other than your own. Contrast your stereotypes of other groups with those you have about your own cultural group. As you do so, consider how these stereotypes were transmitted, what evidence supports or contradicts the stereotypes, and the possible impact of the stereotypes upon communication.

Anger is one of the most powerful and most often misunderstood human emotions. Learning how to manage emotions, including anger, is one of the primary developmental challenges that college students face (Chickering & Reisser, 1993). Because almost no one goes through life without experiencing adversity and frustration, self-regulation of anger is critical for your success as a student, an athlete, a worker, and

> "Visions are never the sole property of one man or one woman. Before a vision can become a reality, it must be owned by every single member of the group."
>
> PHIL JACKSON
> *NBA Champion Head Coach*

a friend. Teachers, coaches, and other authority figures are sometimes the impetus behind feelings of frustration and anger that you might experience, though you also might react to the actions of friends, partners, and family members. Regardless of the factors or persons giving rise to your anger, you must develop effective ways of dealing with it. It's essential to your physical, psychological, and spiritual health.

When confronted by a situation that leaves one feeling angry, there are two generally maladaptive approaches that may be taken: stuffing and escalation (Judd, 2000). Stuffing is an internalizing process of simply convincing yourself (and perhaps those around you) that you are not angry. Stuffing is just another word for denial. "Stuffers" are guided by the (often-unrecognized and mistaken) belief that anger is necessarily an unhealthy, dangerous, and abnormal human emotion. Like most strategies, stuffing can be useful in the short term or with problems or people you are completely unable to confront or won't ever have to deal with again. In the long-term, stuffing tends to build resentments and an explosive response. Paying attention to the language that you or someone else uses when angry can help you to identify stuffing. "I'm not angry or upset," "I messed everything up; I must be stupid," and "I really don't have any right to be angry," are all examples of stuffing.

Escalating, on the other hand, externalizes the anger and turns it into verbal abuse, threats, and physical violence, none of which are satisfactory responses in the long run. In fact, such responses simply increase the probability of more anger. Name-calling is one example of an escalating response. Others include: "Why did YOU do that?" or "You made me angry." or "It's all your fault." Misdirecting anger—directing anger to someone other than the person you are angry with—is another maladaptive and often destructive response style.

Fortunately, you are not limited to dealing with anger by stuffing or escalating; other options exist. First, however, you need to be able to recognize your anger cues. This may seem obvious, but many people have difficulty distinguishing anger from other feelings. Anger cues are the physical and behavioral signals that let you know when you are starting to become angry. As you know from experience in your sport, anticipation is critical to executing skills and strategies for success. Likewise, recognizing and understanding your anger cues puts you in an excellent position to choose other ways of responding. To help you identify your own anger cues, you may want to complete Exercise 9.6.

Judd (2000) has identified several adaptive responses to anger including the following:

- *Direct anger.* Openly acknowledge and state that you are angry and why.
- *Time out.* If you are unable to appropriately express your anger, then sometimes it is best to step away, calm down, and then return to deal with the situation.
- *Forgive.* Similar to being direct, forgiveness is often effective but difficult to implement.
- *Harness anger.* Sometimes, it is possible to channel the adrenaline that comes with anger into positive pursuits; properly harnessed it can be motivation.

Exercise 9.6   Identifying Your Anger Cues

1. Think about a recent situation (perhaps in a class, in practice or a competition, or involving a friend) in which you became angry. How did your body feel at that time? List four body signals that you get when feeling angry. What were you thinking about? List four thoughts you had that contributed to or maintained your anger.

_____

_____

_____

_____

2. Thinking about the same situation, how did you respond to the other person? Did you blame them, call them names, or ignore them? List four things you did.

_____

_____

_____

_____

From your answers, you now have internal physical and cognitive and external behavioral cues to help alert yourself to when you are becoming angry.

- *Seek other opinions.* Sometimes confusion is at the root of anger. Your anger may be fueled by unrealistic expectations for the situation, so check with someone you trust to see if your position is reasonable.
- *Accept.* Sometimes it's best to simply accept the situation as one that can't be changed. Acceptance is not the same as stuffing; it means acknowledging our anger and moving on. Playing through a bad call by an official is a great example of acceptance.

At the heart of all of the adaptive responses to anger is the idea that your ultimate goal is not to "win," save face, or get in the last word. It is to achieve a satisfactory resolution to the situation that stirred your anger.

Discrimination

An outcome of stereotyping is discrimination, which occurs when a person is denied access to opportunities generally available to others because of a personal characteristic that is irrelevant to the issue or task in question. For example, denying a qualified prospective buyer the opportunity to purchase a house in a certain neighborhood simply because she is Asian American is discrimination. Discrimination can be a painful experience for its victim and may also prevent the perpetrator from increasing his or her understanding of the world. Discrimination is common and can take many forms, both subtle and obvious. To help you begin thinking about discrimination in your life, you may want to complete Exercise 9.7.

Among the factors that make discrimination a sticky issue are the difficulties that can arise when people try to identify it. Some individuals are quick to see discrimination in every multicultural exchange that does not go their way. Certainly, many times discrimination is there, but sometimes it is not. Take a moment to reflect on your responses to Exercise 9.7, paying particular attention to questions 1 through 5. Are there alternative explanations for what happened in this situation, aside from discrimination? If so, what might they be? Claiming discrimination is serious—one that has significant implications for all the parties involved. Therefore, it should not be made without careful consideration of alternative explanations.

Exercise 9.7   Discrimination

Identify a situation in which you felt discriminated against by another person, group, or institution.

1. Describe the situation in which you were discriminated.

_____

_____

2. What was the basis for the discrimination? Race/ ethnicity? Gender? Religion? Sexual orientation? Economic status? Other?

_____

_____

3. How did you feel when this situation occurred?

_____

_____

4. What was your response? Did your response help or hinder the situation?

_____

_____

5. Could you have responded in a way that educated the other person? If so, how?

_____

_____

Next, consider a situation in which you may have discriminated against someone else.

6. Describe the situation and answer the following questions.

_____

_____

7. What was the basis of the discrimination? Race/ ethnicity? Gender? Religion? Sexual orientation? Economic status? Other?

_____

_____

8. How did you feel when this situation occurred?

_____

_____

9. How did the other person respond to your discrimination?

_____

_____

10. Would you respond the same way in a similar situation in the future? Why or why not?

_____

_____

Performance: Positive Multicultural Communication

There are several characteristics associated with satisfying multicultural communication, including (Hecht, Ribeau, & Alberts, 1989):

Minimal stereotyping—satisfying multicultural communication involves a minimum of indirect (e.g., talking only about topics thought to be of special interest to African Americans, such as sports or music) and direct stereotyping in conversation. It also is not assuming that the attitudes, beliefs, perceptions, and actions of a particular minority group member represent those of all members of that group.

Acceptance—allowing others to express their feelings and thoughts and conveying respect for them is vital. Acceptance is not simply allowing others to share feelings and opinions, it is also about listening and not judging.

Emotional expressiveness—sharing what you are feeling about a situation or person suggests a greater level of investment in the interaction. Emotion, however, should not overwhelm the content of the conversation.

Being authentic—simply put, "being authentic" means "being yourself" when you're around others, which is important for both parties and helps everyone feel more comfortable and satisfied with the interaction.

> "You must be the change you wish to see in the world."
>
> MAHATMA GANDHI
> *Former Leader of India*

One of the quickest ways to short-circuit any interaction, but especially a multicultural one, is for the party viewed as the majority or authority figure to behave in ways that are not genuine, thus raising suspicions and lowering trust.

Feeling understood—individuals who feel understood generally have more positive experiences with multicultural communication. So, take the time to understand the other person's perspective.

Goal attainment—situations in which both individuals solve problems, exchange information that is mutually important, or complete projects together are related strongly to satisfactory communication. Finding common ground and then working together is a key factor.

Reduce feelings of powerlessness—poor communication often occurs when one person feels controlled, trapped, or manipulated in some way. For members of minority groups, such feelings are especially strong and will likely result in unsatisfying interchanges with members of majority groups. Therefore, interactions in which the conversation is balanced, interruptions are minimal, and there is no coercion will likely be the most satisfying.

Performance: Fostering Understanding

Ford (1994) has identified a number of steps that you can use to enhance your multicultural communication skills. These steps are based on several of the characteristics of positive multicultural communication we have described in the previous section.

Observe Your Reactions

Awareness of your behavior and feelings is, of course, the first step in making any changes, and is an important part of accepting others, minimizing stereotypes, being authentic, and promoting mutual understanding. You can become aware of whatever your reaction is, be it fear, anger, frustration, being offended, or something else. Without withdrawing, you can observe your reaction and its source—your preconditioned expectations and beliefs. Like so many concepts in this book, awareness requires work and commitment. Because it may conflict with what you have been taught, you have to practice being aware while you are communicating with others. Through awareness, you can adjust how you interact with others.

Be Open-Minded

You can help foster multicultural communication by accepting your set of views as one of many possible perspectives on reality. In the same way, you can accept someone else's views as just as viable as your own. We are not saying you should not hold strong opinions and beliefs. You are certainly entitled and encouraged to do so; however, we do suggest that you look at the possibility that other viewpoints have their own merits for the people who hold them. If you do, then you might find that these other perspectives offer something useful to you. Take a moment to consider the way you respond to disagreement.

Do you become angry and defensive? Do you consider the perspective of the other person and look for a middle ground? Do you simply say nothing and hope the problem will go away? Developing the ability to consider others' opinions will be a key to success throughout life.

Focus on the Relationship

A relationship is a triad consisting of you, the other person, and what is created by the two of you. Rather than being concerned with what you said and what was said to you, invest your energy in being aware of the quality of the exchange that is taking place. Shifting your focus from each individual side to the relationship can help reduce feelings of powerlessness. Move beyond focusing on yourself and the other person, and direct your attention to the relationship that is being created when you are communicating with that person. Focusing on this relationship will help to create the climate of authenticity and emotional expressiveness that promotes positive communication.

In addition to the steps suggested by Ford (1994), we suggest the following ways of enhancing multicultural communication.

Enhancing Interpersonal Communication Skills

McKay, Davis, and Fanning (2009) have identified the following four general guidelines you can use to improve your ability to communicate.

- *Speak directly.* It is crucial to know when something needs to be said, and when it does, say it directly to the person. You can see the importance of this approach in your sport. For example, when you are performing poorly, it is most helpful when your coach immediately tells you how to improve. It would not be useful for your coach (or for you) if he or she only told one of your teammates what *you* needed to do. You might get the message, but then again, you might not, and your performance probably would not improve. Your coach probably does not want to take that chance. Speaking indirectly, or hinting at what needs to be said, usually leads to confusion and frustration.
- *Be immediate.* In general, messages should be immediate because that increases the likelihood that others will find out what you need and adjust their behavior accordingly. It also increases your connection to the person with whom you are communicating; however, you should treat this suggestion with some caution. Balancing immediacy and good judgment is important; you do not want to rush to say something if the situation is highly emotional because your communication could be counterproductive. Here again, your interactions with your coach illustrate this suggestion and the balancing act that must be performed. Most of the time, your coaches give you immediate feedback on what you are doing well and what you need to improve. Sometimes, however, if they are too upset to convey the message they want to communicate, then they may wait before talking to you.
- *Be clear.* Make your messages clear and congruent—that is, make the verbal content and the nonverbal behaviors consistent. The content of clear messages

is also internally consistent, avoiding double or mixed messages. Double messages are communicated when we say contradictory things at the same time. Inviting your boyfriend to a party, but then spending most of your time with other people is an example of a double message. Clear messages also focus on one issue at a time.

- *Be supportive.* Make messages supportive whenever possible. This does not mean you should sugarcoat the message; it means you should use positive (rather than negative) language. It also means you should communicate what you would like to see someone do, rather than focusing on what you *don't* want him or her to do, or simply criticizing. Criticizing is likely to leave people feeling defensive, and focusing on what they are doing wrong does not tell them what you want them to do. For example, most coaches understand the importance of delivering messages in a supportive fashion. Although they point out what they don't like or what needs to be corrected, they combine that information with encouragement and positive instruction. If your coach stops criticizing you, then it may be time to worry about your position on the team!

- *Use "self" statements.* Using "self" or "I" statements means taking responsibility for your wishes, feelings, goals, and expectations. Statements such as "you should" or "you made me" are not only inaccurate most but they are provocative and likely to cause the other person to become defensive. Instead, use statements like "I want…" or "I feel…" Not only are such statements impossible to dispute, they also indicate your willingness to assume self-responsibility.

By following these suggestions—delivering direct, immediate, clear, and supportive messages—you increase your chances of being an effective communicator and of having positive relationships.

Seek Similarities, Respect Differences

One helpful step you can take is to look for ways in which you are similar to the person with whom you are interacting. Often you can find common elements you share with people, even when you come from different backgrounds. As a student-athlete, you certainly share a love of your sport with other student-athletes, no matter what part of the country or the world they come from. Similarly, as a student-athlete, you share common experiences of balancing academic, athletic, and personal obligations. You might share common interests, perhaps in music or various hobbies and activities. Perhaps you are linked to someone through mutual friends and acquaintances. You might even share common beliefs and perspectives about the world or have similar goals. Unfortunately, people often focus on superficial characteristics, overemphasizing the way others look, dress, or speak, while ignoring what they have in common.

As you seek similarities with others, it is also important that you respect the real differences that exist. For you to get the most from your college experience, you must learn to accept differences and respect the beliefs, values, and norms of other cultures. Respect means recognizing that other cultures have a right to their norms, regardless of whether or not you agree with those norms. Failure to respect other cultures ultimately puts the survival of your own culture at risk.

> ❝**You can observe a lot by watching.**❞
>
> YOGI BERRA
> *Major League Baseball Hall of Fame Player*

Talking with the Media

Dealing with the media is an opportunity for growth, but it can also be challenging and potentially damaging to you if not handled properly. Here are some general guidelines to follow, though you also should consult with your sports information director:

- *Avoid criticizing.* Provide an honest assessment of your own performance, but don't criticize your teammates and coaches; it will only make you look bad and undermine their respect for and confidence in you. If their performance was poor, then commend their effort.
- *Always assume you are "on the record."* Know that whatever you say may be published or broadcast in some form, be it on TV, radio, the newspaper, or the Internet.
- *Technology is sensitive.* Cameras have zoom lenses and microphones are extremely sensitive, so you may never be out of reach. Be careful about what you say, the language you use, and, of course, your gestures and body language.
- *Don't give out personal information.* Anything you say may go on the record, so be careful; you can't take back what you have said.
- *Beware of strangers.* Only provide interviews to people who have been cleared by your sports information director (SID) or media relations director. If you receive a phone call from a "reporter," then have them contact your athletic department to arrange the interview.
- *Set limits.* Don't be pressured into giving interviews you don't have time for. If you are pressed for time, then let your SID know and arrange for a more convenient time. Also, don't answer any questions with which you are uncomfortable. If you don't like the tone of the interview, then stop it and seek help from your SID.
- *Think first.* Always think before you say anything to the media. Remember, you live in a fishbowl where everything you do may be viewed by someone else. So, don't be caught somewhere you shouldn't be, or say something you shouldn't say.
- *Be personable.* Be friendly and cooperative with the media whenever possible. Most media are just trying to do their jobs professionally and, like you, are under pressure, so they can use your help. Offer them "snapshots"—short but interesting comments about you, your athletic performance, and your academic achievements.

> "Go to the people. Live with them, learn from them, love them. Start with what they know. Build with what they have."
>
> CHINESE PROVERB

Let Others Teach You

One of the smartest things you can do is to allow others to teach you things you don't understand but need to know. You cannot know everything about any single culture, let alone a broad range of cultures, but you can certainly allow others to teach you about their cultures. One of the most beneficial and enjoyable experiences you can have in college is finding out what it's like to live in a different culture. There are a number of ways to learn about other cultures. If you are interested in learning from an academic perspective, then you can enroll in anthropology, sociology, or ethnic/cultural studies classes. Not only will such classes provide you with information about various cultural groups, they are also likely to present opportunities for you to interact with instructors and other students from those different cultural groups. Some athletic departments are even arranging study abroad opportunities for their student-athletes that also factor in the need to continue training while traveling.

Another way of learning from others is participating in multicultural activities. For example, you can check out activities sponsored by various ethnic student associations on your campus. Listen to new music you wouldn't normally listen to or try a new cuisine that you wouldn't normally eat. You might also consider attending the religious services of a different faith or ethnic group.

© kristian sekulic, 2009 / Used under license from Shutterstock.com

Be Patient

You must be patient when you are communicating across cultures. Because multicultural communication involves built-in differences in behavioral norms, ways of seeing the world, values, and perhaps even languages, you have to process a great deal of information in a short period of time. In a way, this is similar to learning new plays, formations, or terminology in your sport. It doesn't always come right away, and it takes practice. You can help yourself by being patient with yourself and with the other person. Don't expect to understand everything right away, and try not to become frustrated with the other person as you learn from and about each other.

Social Networking Sites

Although there are many different social networking sites, Facebook is the one used most frequently by college students. The ubiquity (check the dictionary) of Facebook is such that it's used as both a verb and noun, "I'm going to pull up my Facebook (noun) page and Facebook (verb) Keke right now." There are over 25 million Facebook users under the age of 25, although there was a 276% increase in users aged 35–54 in 2008. So, don't be surprised to have your mom or dad posting something on your wall! Of course, you'll have to decide for yourself whether or not to accept them as a friend.

For most college students, it's not whether you will have a Facebook account (you likely will), it's that you use it appropriately. In 2006, the Northwestern University women's soccer team posted photos of them hazing their freshmen, which ended up on Bad.Jocks.com and was an embarrassment to everyone involved. Most athletic departments require student-athletes to surrender their user names and passwords, so department personnel can monitor Facebook accounts (written material and photographs). Other athletic departments hire social network monitoring services, such as YouDiligence, which track hundreds of keywords and phrases that could be seen as damaging to the image of the student-athlete or the institution.

(continued)

Here are a few of the pros and cons to consider when using Facebook:

Pros

- Allows you to develop new relationships
- Exposes you to different perspectives
- Keeps you connected to friends and family, especially for freshmen
- Allows you to creatively express yourself
- Medium for organizing and sharing photos
- Interact with classmates on assignments without having to meet face-to-face

Cons

- The quality and depth of your Facebook relationships may be superficial
- May decrease your direct social contact with others and encourage isolation especially in your early transition to college
- May hinder your personal development and growth toward adulthood if your decisions are being monitored by all of your Facebook friends and family
- Being tagged in photos on others' pages, poked by friends, or wall postings can be embarrassing or a source of jealousy with your partner
- Can be a significant time waster and source of procrastination
- Personal information will likely be available to future employers and others who might be influential later in your life
- Information posted on Facebook lacks context, so others can easily misinterpret what is posted

Social networking sites are now part of our cultural fabric. Researchers are only beginning to consider what the long-term impact of social networks will be. Although we are sure you will see the pros of Facebook outweighing the cons, just make sure you use this tool carefully. To help you do so, we offer a few commonsensical guidelines:

1. Under Settings look for the Privacy section and click Profile to control who can see your pages. You should limit it to friends and also be selective who you include as a friend.

2. Never post addresses, e-mail addresses, birthdates, cell numbers, class schedules, or basically, anything you wouldn't want a stranger to know about you.

3. Take great care in the photos that you (or your friends) post (drunken party pictures, not a good idea), as well as avoid crude or vulgar messages.

When in Doubt, Listen

You can never go wrong by allowing the other person time to say what he or she wants to say. Most people enjoy talking about themselves, so asking questions facilitates the conversation. There is no single skill that will help you more than the ability to listen intently to others. Listening serves at least three important functions.

1. It gives you the opportunity to learn.
2. It prevents you from saying something that could get you into trouble.
3. It communicates your interest in others.

Listening is crucial for any interpersonal interaction, but it is especially important in multicultural interactions, because you may not necessarily share common norms, perspectives, or ways of understanding things, and you need to hear the other person out before you can understand him or her.

We have described in some detail the conditions that have been found to promote better multicultural communication, and we have identified some practical steps you can take to improve your skills in this area. Fortunately, you probably already possess many of these skills, although you may never have realized it. The skills you don't have now can be developed with practice and commitment, just as you develop the skills you need in your sport. To help you become more involved in diversity, you may want to complete Exercise 9.8.

Exercise 9.8 Encountering Diversity

1. Identify three ways on your campus (aside from your involvement in athletics) or in the surrounding community that you can learn about persons whose cultural or ethnic backgrounds are different from your own.

_____

_____

_____

2. From the three ways you identified, choose one to try out. As you participate in that activity, pay particular attention to your own feelings and reactions during the

experience. Did you feel anxious? Excited? Threatened? What did you learn about the other culture? What did you learn about yourself in the process? After you have completed the activity, record your thoughts, reactions, and feelings.

_____

_____

_____

_____

Post-Game Review: Conclusion

In this chapter, we have discussed the complex and often confusing issues of cultural diversity and multicultural communication. If these issues cause you discomfort, then work on dealing with your discomfort and with the issues themselves. If you find yourself falling short of where you would like to be, then consider using some of the strategies we have presented in this chapter to improve your multicultural communication skills and increase your exposure to diverse cultures. By doing so, you will enhance your prospects for success in what is a global, interconnected world.

Because cultural diversity is a controversial topic for many people, it is especially important that you practice self-responsibility in determining your own views. Some people will try to persuade you to adopt a particular perspective either for or against cultural diversity. Although our position is that diversity, on the whole, is beneficial for all parties, you need to make up your own mind. We hope you will at least explore cultures other than your own before you make judgments about their merits. Recognize your position, whatever it may be, and take responsibility for making changes as needed.

Thinking Critically about Communication and Diversity

1. Summarize what you now know about communication and diversity based on the information presented in this chapter.

_____

_____

_____

2. What additional questions do you have about these topics and how to use the skills introduced in this chapter?

_____

_____

_____

3. What conclusions can you draw about this topic and how it might help you be a more effective and successful student and athlete?

_____

_____

_____

Achieve IT! Setting a Communication Goal

1. Based on your self-assessment and your responses to Thinking Critically, select a goal in relationship to improving your communication and/or appreciation of diversity that you would like to achieve this term.

2. Now identify three short-term goals that will help you reach your goal this term.

3. For the short-term goals, identify the attainment strategies you will need to reach them.

4. List any obstacles you might face in trying to reach these goals and identify your plan for overcoming each one.

Don't forget to make your goal visible and tell others about them, so they can keep you accountable regarding what you want to achieve.

Chapter 9 Review Questions

1. Culture involves:

    a. A specific racial/ethnic group.
    b. Ideas that are transmitted across cultures.
    c. Religion.
    d. A person who is from a country outside the United States.

2. Cultural diversity is an issue that only nonminority students have to face. (True or False)

3. Post-9/11 events have made concepts of diversity and multicultural communication less important. (True or False)

4. Why are diversity and multicultural communication skills important for career development?

5. Knowing a person's ethnic or racial background is sufficient for you to really understand that person. (True or False)

6. Fred was denied a job in the library because he is gay. This is

    a. Stereotyping.   **b.** Discrimination.
    c. Prejudice.   **d.** Racism.
    e. None of the above.

7. Which of the following are characteristics of satisfying multicultural communication?

    a. Acceptance; minimal stereotyping.
    b. High levels of emotional expressiveness; high authenticity.
    c. Feeling understood; mutual goal attainment.
    d. All of the above.

8. Identify three steps you can take to increase multicultural understanding and communication.

9. Listening is important because:

    a. It provides an opportunity to learn.
    b. It prevents you from saying something that could get you in trouble.
    c. It's a way of communicating your interest.
    d. All of the above.
    e. A and B only.

10. Athletic departments are strong proponents of student-athletes' First Amendment (freedom of speech) rights and will not monitor your Facebook account. (True or False)

Chapter **10** | Succeeding in Life and Relationships
Health and Performance: Success Through Healthy Living

Game Plan:

In this chapter, you will learn:

- The importance of healthy and nutritious eating in relation to success in school, sports, and life

- About the need for getting sufficient sleep on a consistent basis

- How to make safe and satisfying decisions about sexual relationships

- How alcohol and drug use can interfere with athletic and academic performance, and undermine healthy interpersonal relationships

© Shawn Pecor, 2009 / Used under license from Shutterstock.com

"If you don't do what's best for your body, you're the one who comes up on the short end."

JULIUS ERVING (DR. J)
Former NBA All Star, Hall of Fame

Self-Assessment—Perceive It!

Read the following statements and place a checkmark next to each one you generally do. For you to change and develop new and effective academic, athletic, and personal strategies, you must be accurate in your self-perception. So, be honest in how you answer each question.

1. I can identify the main food groups. _____

2. Taking into account the physical demands and nutritional needs of my sport, I eat the necessary amount of carbohydrates, proteins, and fats to perform my best. _____

3. I eat meals throughout the day as opposed to fasting and then binging at one meal. _____

4. Each day, I drink the necessary amount of liquid to remain adequately hydrated (e.g., I have to urinate every hour or so and my urine is clear). _____

5. I sleep seven to nine hours every night so that I am well rested the next day and do not have to take a nap. _____

6. I am aware of the risks involved in using alcohol and other drugs. _____

7. I do not drink alcohol or use drugs during my competitive season. _____

8. When I do drink alcohol, I do so in moderation and never to excess. _____

9. I know what I want from intimate relationships and clearly communicate my sexual needs and limits to my partner(s). _____

10. I am aware of the various sexually transmitted diseases and know how to protect myself if I am sexually active. _____

Take a moment to review your responses. How many items did you check? Each one you checked represents a current strength. Now consider the items you did not check. These represent areas where focus and growth are needed. Now, to summarize your self-perception, complete the following statements:

1. My areas of strength are:

_____

2. The areas I need to improve are:

_____

As you read this chapter and participate in your classes, keep your strengths and areas of improvement in mind. At the end of the chapter, you will have the chance to set a goal related to these areas. Achieving these goals will help you become a more effective student and athlete.

Introduction

*L*isa's life was fairly structured. During the week, her high school classes lasted until midafternoon, and then she had gymnastics practice until about 6:00 P.M. After practice, she would have dinner with her parents and her brother and then do her homework. She generally went to bed early (about 9:00 P.M.) because of her exhausting schedule. On the weekends, she often had meets that required a considerable amount of time for travel and competition. Because of her time demands, she did not work, except for what she did at home, and her social life was limited to a few friends with whom she'd occasionally go to the movies or a school event.

Her life at college was quite different. She attended an out-of-state school and lived in the residence halls with other freshmen. Her roommate was another student-athlete, though not a member of the gymnastics team. During the first few weeks of college, Lisa went out more than she had during her entire senior year of high school. She stayed up late talking with her friends, going to parties (and drinking), and just enjoying her new freedom.

Seduced by this lifestyle, Lisa continued in this way for the next few weeks. She did cut back a bit on the weeknight socializing, but she still stayed up late and went out on the weekends. As a result, she was often tired and sometimes *had a hangover. To compensate, she tried to sleep late whenever possible or take naps in the afternoons. This plan did not work very well, because the dorms were noisy and she had to be in the training room early for treatment.*

In addition, Lisa was not eating well. She did not like the food that was served in the cafeteria, so she and her friends would grab a bite at one of the local fast-food places or snack on foods they bought at the grocery. Although Lisa tried to eat "low-fat" foods, her diet did not have much variety, nor did it contain adequate amounts of carbohydrates or fruits and vegetables.

Because of her late-night habits, weekend partying, poor sleep schedule, and bad diet, Lisa generally felt tired and lacked energy; this affected both her academics and her athletics. In classes, she had a hard time concentrating on what the instructor was saying; she even occasionally fell asleep in her larger lecture classes. In practices, her performances were not as sharp or consistent as she knew they could be. Her coaches had helped her develop new routines, but she was not making as much progress with them as the coaches had expected. By the end of her first semester, she was physically and psychologically exhausted and far behind where she wanted to be athletically and academically.

Although student-athletes' physical appearance would suggest they are the model of health, in reality, many abuse themselves and their bodies. Like Lisa, they may be tired, improperly nourished, or even under the influence of drugs and/or alcohol. Although being young and in good physical shape may allow you to avoid some of the more serious consequences of such behaviors, if you do not take care of yourself you increase the chances of performing below your academic and athletic potential. In fact, being in good physical health is essential for coping effectively with stress.

In this chapter, we identify four primary health-related behaviors and discuss them in relation to your performance as a student and as an athlete. We begin by examining the basic issue of eating and proper nutrition, and then discuss eating disorders and provide information for identifying them and for obtaining help. Second, we consider sleep and being fatigued. Sleep deprivation is common among adults and only you can control if you get sufficient rest each night. Third, we address drug and alcohol use among student-athletes and identify the effects of these substances. Fourth, we discuss sex and relationships. Because most student-athletes will be sexually active at some point during their college careers, we address this topic in some detail so you can make informed, satisfying, and safe decisions.

> "The right diet directs sexual energy into the parts that matter."
>
> BARBARA CARTLAND
> *Author*

Preparation and Performance: Eating

Maintaining a Healthy Diet

Proper nutrition is vital for people involved in high-intensity and high-endurance physical activities, such as college athletics. At its simplest level, eating is the way you provide energy to your body. The foods you eat are the fuel your body uses. Poorly fueled, your body will function below its potential. If you eat nutritiously, though, your body will work more efficiently, and you will have the energy to meet your physical demands.

What constitutes nutritious eating? The U.S. Department of Agriculture (USDA) has developed the food pyramid (Figure 10.1), which

Figure 10.1 Food Pyramid
Source: U.S. Department of
Agriculture, Center for Nutrition
Policy and Promotion.

provides good basic nutritional guidelines for healthy eating (see www.
mypyramid.gov for more information). The pyramid is comprised of
five major components, each one associated with a major food group:

Grains—represented by pasta, rice, bread, cereal, crackers, etc.
They are a primary source of carbohydrates and the USDA recommends that you choose whole-grain products for at least half your intake because they are more nutritious and contain dietary fiber.

Vegetables—the USDA recommends varying your intake of vegetables to include dark green (e.g., spinach, broccoli), orange (e.g.,
carrots, sweet potatoes), legumes (e.g., dry beans, tofu), starchy (e.g.,
potatoes, corn), and other (e.g., tomatoes, celery, green beans).

Fruit—the USDA recommends that you eat a variety of types, particularly fresh (though frozen, canned, and dried are good), and drink
minimal amounts of fruit juice.

Milk—and other milk products (e.g., yogurt) are excellent sources
of calcium. The USDA recommends using low- or no-fat varieties whenever possible.

Meat and Beans—choose low-fat, lean cuts of meat and poultry.
The USDA recommends including fish, beans, nuts, and seeds to add
to the variety of your diet.

The pyramid also recognizes that fats and oils are a part of your diet,
but should be eaten in the smallest quantity, in particular saturated and

trans-fats, of all the food groups. Grains, vegetables, and fruits should be eaten in the highest quantity. These foods are important because they are nutrient dense (contain essential vitamins and minerals) and are high in carbohydrates (particularly complex carbohydrates), which help replenish the body's stores of liver glycogen (which is a primary source of blood glucose) and muscle glycogen. In fact, carbohydrates are the body's main source of fuel and are crucial for high-intensity training and for competing in prolonged athletic events (Coleman, 1998). Thus, athletes must eat adequate levels of carbohydrates to maximize their performance potential. Milk products, meats, and legumes are important sources of protein and other nutrients, but should represent a smaller percentage of your overall caloric intake than grains, vegetables and fruits.

How many calories to ingest and the specific sources of those calories, such as the percentage of carbohydrates vs. proteins, depend on several factors, including age, gender, metabolic rate, body mass, and physical activity level, to name just a few. Thus, we only offer some general comments about caloric intake (for individual planning, consult with a sport nutritionist/dietitian at your school to develop a healthy meal schedule that will meet your energy needs):

1. Athletes who are involved in high-intensity physical activity each day will need greater numbers of calories per day than sedentary individuals.
2. Athletes, on average, will train and perform better on a high vs. moderate or low-carbohydrate diets (Coyle, 2004). Inadequate carbohydrate intake will lead to depletion of muscle glycogen.
3. Percentages of carbohydrate, protein, and fat intake should vary based on training and competition needs. During high-intensity training of long duration, a greater amount of carbohydrates will need to be ingested.
4. Ingested carbohydrates should be of the complex variety, as opposed to simply sugars.
5. Ideally, begin eating carbohydrates within two hours of finishing training because the highest rate of glycogen storage occurs at this time (Riewald and Barnes, 2002).

Remember, when you are determining overall caloric intake, (a) 1 gram of fat is equal to 9 calories, (b) 1 gram of protein is equal to 4 calories, and (c) 1 gram of carbohydrate is equal to 4 calories. Thanks to labeling on food packaging, determining caloric intake as well as percentages of carbohydrates, proteins, and fats consumed is much easier than it was in the past.

> **"I can accept failure. Everyone fails at something. But I can't accept not trying."**
>
> MICHAEL JORDAN
> *Former NBA*
> *All-Star and MVP*

There are many excellent nutritional sources that are developed specifically for athletes. For example, the Gatorade Sport Science Institute has a library of information on nutrition and hydration that you can use to help determine what you should be eating to maximize your performance (see www.gssiweb.org). The NCAA also offers information about nutrition and performance on its website (see http://www.ncaa.org/wps/ncaa?key=/ncaa/NCAA/AcademicsandAthletes/PersonalWelfare/Nutrition-performance/).

Many athletes do not eat nutritiously, nor do they consume adequate levels of carbohydrates to support their training loads (Steen, 1998)—is

Eating on the Road

When traveling for competitions, you will face many challenges to eating nutri-tiously, including being away from normal food sources, hectic schedules, and eating at fast-food restaurants. As a result, you may not make good food choices, depriving yourself of needed energy stores and essential nutrients. To help you eat more nutritiously on the road, consider the following suggestions (Berning, 1988; Sherman, 1989; Steen, 1998):

1. Avoid fast-food restaurants because their food choices are often high in fat and low in important nutrients. If you have no choice, then select foods that are leaner (e.g., chicken), not fried (e.g., baked potatoes), and made from whole grains (e.g., whole wheat buns, brown rice). In addition, order fruits and vegetables, such as an apple or a side salad, instead of a fried fruit pie or cookies.

2. Prior to the trip, discuss with your coach or athletic trainer where you will eat to make sure the restaurant will be able to serve the high-carbohydrate, nutri-tious meals that you need.

3. Eat needed amounts of carbohydrates (e.g., grains) to replenish muscle and liver glycogen stores following training/competitions, ideally within two hours of finishing.

4. Eat one to four hours before competing, particularly if your sport is a high-endurance activity. Extended time between eating and competing allows more complete emptying of your stomach and thus minimizes the chances of gastric distress. Eat adequate levels of carbohydrates at this meal (up to 80 percent of the calories should be carbohydrates), though don't eat so much that you are uncomfortable during competition.

5. Don't fast prior to competition because it can lower levels of glycogen and negatively affect your performance. In addition, fasting increases the likeli-hood of binge eating on less nutritious food at a later meal. Make sure you eat throughout each day to keep your body adequately fueled.

6. Bring along nutritious snacks, such as fresh fruits and vegetables, bagels, raisins (and other dried fruits), pretzels (low salt), crackers, fig bars, breakfast bars, and high-carbohydrate beverages. Try to avoid typical travel foods, such as candy and soda, which offer almost no nutritional benefits.

7. Stay adequately hydrated by drinking water and sport drinks. Avoid drinking beverages that are high in sugar, such as sodas.

Keep in mind that these are general suggestions and that what you do will vary based on your body mass, gender, age, activity level, and metabolic rate, and the nutritional demands of your sport. Before you undertake any major dietary changes, talk with a sport nutritionist/dietitian or exercise physiologist on your campus to develop an individualized meal plan that will help you meet the spe-cific energy demands of your sport.

that you? Eating nutritiously so you are well fueled to practice and compete each day requires self-responsibility. If you do not make the commitment to eat nutritiously every day, then you will likely follow the route of most Americans and eat a diet that is too high in fat and too low in essential nutrients. International student-athletes may gain weight (without trying) when they begin their college careers due to the switch to a typical American diet. Do you want to take that risk with your health and your athletic performances? To help you become more aware of the nutritional value of your current food intake, we encourage you to complete Exercise 10.1.

Exercise 10.1 Tracking Your Food Intake

There are many different programs for helping you track your food intake and learn more about the nutritional content of what you are eating, but one of the best is the "My Pyramid Tracker" program that was developed in association with the new dietary guidelines. This program allows you to track not only your food intake, but also your physical activity as well. This site is not designed to help you "diet," but rather to help you become more aware of what you are eating and learn more about those foods' nutritional content. To start the process, follow these directions:

- Go to www.mypyramid.gov/.
- On the left side, click on "My Pyramid Plan."
- Enter your age, sex, height, weight, and physical activity level, then click the "submit" button.
- Your pyramid results will be shown.
- Next, on the bottom right side of the screen, click on the location where it states "for a more detailed assessment of your diet quality and physical activity go to My Pyramid Tracker."
- On the next screen, you will see two sub-divisions ("Assessment" and "Access"). Under the "Access" portion, click on "New User Registration."
- You should now be at the page titled "Login." Enter a user ID, password, password hint, e-mail address, and zip code, and then click "save today's changes." Once you have saved your information, click on "proceed to food intake" (you can take the other option "proceed to physical activity" later).
- You should arrive at the home page, where you can enter in food and physical activity information (*** if you need to enter your food or physical activity information for a previous day or need to fill in missing information, then you can change the date [to the date you would like to enter information for] under your "personal profile" page after you log in***).

Food Intake Assessment:
For this part of the assessment, each day for the next 3, 5, or 7 days (we recommend monitoring for a week), you will visit the site and go to the food intake section where you will enter the food you ate during the previous day. Follow these instructions to do so:

- In "Enter Food Item" section, enter a food item you have eaten during the day in the blank box and click on the "Search" button. For example, if you ate pizza, you would type that word into the box.
- A list of foods specified by your search criteria should appear.
- Click on the food that best describes what you ate and it should then appear on the right side of the page.
- Click on the "Select Quantity" button, where you will select the serving size information and number of servings you ate of that food.
- After you enter this information, you should click on the "Enter Foods" to add more food items into your daily intake record. Once you have entered all the foods you ate on that day (and specified the quantities for each), then you will click the "Save and Analyze" icon.
- Once the "Save and Analyze" icon is clicked on, you will arrive at the "Analyze your Food Intake" page. On this page you will see many different options for analyzing your food intake and learning more about your nutritional status.
- The "Calculate DG Comparison" lets you see your recommended food groups and nutrient intakes within your energy needs, and your intakes of basic food groups, compared with the Dietary Guidelines for Americans (2005) recommendations.
- The "Calculate Nutrient Intakes from Foods" allows you to see your nutrient intake scores and recommended intake information.
- The "Calculate My Pyramid Stats" lets you see your recommendation based on your energy level and a comparison between your intake and the My Pyramid recommendation.

You can use this information to learn more about how well your current food intake is measuring up to dietary guidelines and recommendations based on your height, weight, gender, age, and activity level. This information also would be very useful if you were going to work with a sport nutritionist, who would want to know what you have eaten in the last week.

Once you have completed your week of monitoring your food intake, review your results. Are there areas where you are not meeting nutritional guidelines? If so, what might you change in your food intake to improve your nutritional status and better fuel yourself as an athlete?

Prevalence and Symptoms of Eating Disorders

For many young people, "eating healthy" often translates into achieving a certain body build/type. For women, that societal body ideal is thin and lean, but with ample breasts, and represented by *Sports Illustrated* swimsuit models. For men, the ideal is defined by leanness and muscularity—wide shoulders; narrow waist; and defined muscles in the chest, arms, and abdomen. In addition to these general societal pressures about body size and shape, the sport environment may present additional demands that contribute to the development of disordered eating for some athletes, including (1) limitations on the weight an athlete can be (e.g., wrestling), (2) judging criteria that emphasize thin and stereotypically attractive body builds (e.g., gymnastics, diving), (3) sports that encourage a very low percentage of body fat for successful performances (e.g., cross-country), (4) coach pressures about weight and body size (e.g., holding public weigh-ins, mistaken belief that lower weight always leads to better performances), and (5) pressure from teammates to use pathogenic weight loss strategies (e.g., exercising after practice, vomiting). Indeed, these pressures may encourage an unhealthy focus on weight and body shape that is often associated with dietary restraint, increased exercise, and other eating pathology.

Eating disorders are psychiatric disorders that affect people's psychological, physical, nutritional, interpersonal, and emotional functioning. These disorders are characterized by dysfunctional eating patterns and disturbances/distortions in perception of body size and shape. For women, approximately 0.5 to 1.0% and 1.0 to 3.0%, respectively, suffer from anorexia nervosa (a psychiatric disorder characterized by refusal to maintain a minimal body weight, fear of gaining weight, and disturbances in the way one's body size/shape is perceived) or bulimia nervosa (a psychiatric disorder characterized by binge eating and purging to prevent weight gain, and self-worth that is strongly tied to body shape and weight). Rates for men are estimated to be one-tenth or less of these percentages (American Psychiatric Association, 2000). For both genders, the prevalence of subclinical disorders, such as binging, dieting, and excessive exercising, is much higher (Cohen and Petrie, 2005). For college student-athletes, no men and 2% of women reported clinical symptoms, and 20 to 26% were classified as subclinical (Greenleaf, Petrie, Reel, and Carter, 2009; Petrie, Greenleaf, Reel, and Carter, 2009). In terms of the methods used to control their weight, most student-athletes used exercise and dieting, as opposed to vomiting, diuretics, or laxatives.

Individuals with clinical and subclinical eating disorders often report body dissatisfaction, depression, low self-esteem, concerns about weight and appearance, lack of assertiveness, perfectionism, dietary restraint, anxiety, and feeling out of control. Further, disruptions of physiological and physical functioning are not uncommon, including electrolyte imbalances and mineral deficiencies, reductions in metabolic rate, increased food efficiency, amenorrhea (absence of menstruation in women), decreases in serum testosterone (in men), dehydration, loss of dental enamel, and cardiac arrhythmias.

Fluid Replacement: Staying Hydrated for Optimum Performance

The harmful effects of dehydration on physical health and sport performance are well known, yet many athletes perform in a dehydrated state, lowering their performance potential, increasing the strain on their cardiovascular systems, and raising their core temperatures. When dehydrated athletes train in hot and humid environments, their risk of suffering heat-related illnesses, such as heat cramps, increases substantially. There are two basic ways to monitor hydration: color of your urine (clear urine is an indication of hydration) and loss of body weight during exercise (if you lose weight during exercise, you have lost fluid, which needs to be replaced). Thirst is a poor indicator of hydration and you should not rely on it to determine if you need to take in more fluids.

To help you avoid the many problems caused by dehydration, consider the following recommendations (Burns et al., 2001; Clark, 1989; Maughan, Leiper, and Shirreffs, 1996; Murray, Stofan, and Eichner, 2003):

1. During the 24 hours before competition, which includes the pre-event meal, eat a balanced diet and to drink sufficient liquid.

2. About two hours before exercising/training, drink a sufficient amount of cool fluid, such as water, to hydrate yourself (e.g., 16–20 ounces); though more may be required if you have been dehydrated. Doing so this far in advance will improve hydration and give you time to expel excess fluid. If you are adequately hydrated, then you have to urinate every hour or so and the color of your urine is clear.

3. In the 15 minutes before exercing/training, you may want to drink another 6–12 ounces of cool fluid, especially if you were dehydrated from the previous training session.

4. When exercising/training, begin drinking fluids as early as you can, and then continue at regular intervals throughout (about 6–8 ounces every 15–20 minutes).

5. For exercise/training lasting longer than one hour, fluids consumed should contain proper amounts of carbohydrates and electrolytes, such as those found in commercially available sport drinks. For exercise lasting a shorter time, water is likely an adequate source of fluid replacement. However, be careful not to overdrink water as it can lead to hyponatremia (i.e., low levels of blood sodium).

6. After physical exercise, it is important to continue drinking liquids to recover and adequately rehydrate for subsequent competitions or training. It is recommended that athletes drink about 24 ounces for every pound of weight loss that occurs during physical training. Indeed, it may be necessary for athletes to consume fluids in the amount of 150% or more of weight loss to rehydrate within six hours of physical training.

7. Soft drinks are generally *not* good sources of fluid replacement, when rehydrating is important, because they contain very little or no sodium. Instead use sport drinks.

8. It is best to avoid drinking alcohol in the 24 hours before and after a competition, because it interferes with proper hydration. Alcohol inhibits the release

of antidiuretic hormones and thus encourages urination, even among already dehydrated individuals. It also is a poor source of nutrients and carbohydrates and thus has no benefits for athletic performance.

9. Make sure that fluids are readily and immediately available during exercise, and the beverage is cold and tastes good to you.

As you read through these recommendations, remember that most athletes, when left to their own devices, do not adequately replace the fluids lost during training. Thus, you must train yourself to be a better drinker with respect to fluid replacement. Always work with your school's athletic training staff and exercise physiologist to ensure that what you are doing meets your physical specifications and your sport's specific training demands.

Some of the symptoms associated with clinical and subclinical eating disorders, such as extreme weight loss or binge eating in the presence of friends and family, are noticeable, but many others are not or may be deliberately hidden by the athlete. For example, various purging behaviors, such as vomiting, will likely be carried out in private to

Warning Signs and Behaviors Associated with Eating Disorders

1. Excessive concern with or self-deprecating comments about body size and shape.

2. Noticeable fluctuations in weight.

3. Changes in the person's usual eating behaviors, such as eating less; becoming preoccupied with caloric content; fasting; eating more or binge eating; eating secretively; not eating with friends or teammates during planned meals; stealing or hoarding food; creating lists of foods to be avoided, such as those containing sugar.

4. Exercising far beyond the requirements of the sport, such as working out for an hour or two on one's own in addition to required practices and training.

5. Changes in mood—feeling depressed and/or having low self-esteem.

6. Evidence that the individual is using diet pills, laxatives, diuretics, or syrup of ipecac.

7. Frequent trips to the bathroom after meals.

8. Fear about gaining weight or becoming fat even when weight is normal or below normal.

9. Bloodshot eyes, smell of vomit, nicks or cuts on knuckles or fingers after visiting the bathroom.

Although none of these signs automatically indicates the presence of an eating disorder, don't ignore a sign because early identification and treatment is critical. If you notice any of these signs in yourself or a friend, then consult with a counselor at your school's counseling center or with your athletic trainer, who may be able to help you find assistance on your campus.

avoid detection. Still other behaviors, such as exercising and fasting/dieting, may go undetected because within the sport environment they are seen as "normal" or rewarded as signs of the athlete's dedication. If you or anyone you know is experiencing such problems or if you would like to learn more about preventing and treating eating disorders, then contact your school's counseling center or health center to talk with a trained eating disorder specialist. You also might talk with your athletic trainer, who may be able to refer you to a specialist on your campus.

Preparation and Performance: Sleep

Insomnia is a common problem for adults, with approximately 15% reporting chronic symptoms in a given year (National Center for Sleep Disorders Research, National Institutes of Health). According to the National Sleep Foundation's 2005 *Sleep in America Poll*, 75% of adults have at least one symptom of a sleep problem (e.g., difficulty falling asleep, waking a lot during the night, waking up too early and not being able to get back to sleep) for a few nights a week or more. Similarly, about 75% of student-athletes indicate that they get insufficient sleep on a daily basis, regardless of whether or not they are "in season." In fact, the majority of student-athletes get adequate sleep on only one to two nights each week (Selby, Weinstein, and Bird, 1990).

So, why do student-athletes get adequate rest on so few nights in a given week? One reason may be academic and athletic responsibilities. In order to meet those time demands, student-athletes may sacrifice important hours of sleep. A second reason may be socializing—remember Lisa from our introductory story? Some college student-athletes, particularly those in their first year of school, spend far too much time in social activities that often take place late at night and/or involve drinking and partying. As a result, their sleep schedules are poor. Sleeping a sufficient amount each night requires a high level of self-responsibility in the face of great social temptations.

Sleep is necessary for optimal functioning. Although moderate sleep deprivation, such as not sleeping for 24 hours, does not seem to have severe effects on high-intensity physical activity (Hill, Borden, Darnaby, and Hendricks, 1994), such as an athlete participating in practice, it does affect mental functioning. Sleep deprivation contributes to general fatigue, irritability, inattention, poor decision making, and impairments in concentration and short-term memory, all of which can negatively affect academic performance, coping with stress, and managing interpersonal relationships. Thus, although being young and healthy may help you handle moderate sleep deprivation, we encourage you to maintain a consistent sleep schedule so you maximize your chances of being at your best every day.

Just how much sleep is enough? According to the Centers for Disease Control (CDC), adults need between seven and nine hours a night, though the exact amount will vary from person to person. To determine your specific schedule, pay attention to your own natural rhythm, or "internal clock" (also known as the circadian rhythm), that

© Nicholas Moore, 2009 / Used under license from Shutterstock.com

tells your body when to sleep and when to be awake. Although this cycle can be varied to suit specific situations, such as staying up late one night to study or watch a movie, generally people have set times when they would naturally fall asleep and when they would naturally awaken. Thus, when you plan your sleep schedule, keep in mind what your body would naturally do. If you are a "night person" and are most alert at that time, then use the night for important tasks, such as studying, and sleep in later in the morning. If you are a "morning person," make sure you go to bed when you are tired and then get up early to do your work. Also, try to schedule your classes to fit the times when you will be most alert and best able to function. Again, if you are not at your best at 8:00 A.M., you may want to avoid early-morning classes (if possible) and schedule later ones.

Coping with an Injury

During the second half of the conference championship soccer game, Walter was making a cut move with the ball when his cleats caught in the turf and his knee twisted. He immediately collapsed. At first, Walter was overwhelmed by the physical pain—he had never been injured like this before. As he was being carried off the field to the training room, the pain lessened and he became numb. He knew that he was hurt badly, and he just could not believe that something like this had happened to him.

Like Walter, you may experience a serious injury (or have to deal with a chronic problem) during your college sport career. If so, consider the following ideas because they can help you cope more effectively and return to play with confidence:

1. Upon injury, in addition to physical pain, you are likely to experience emotional distress. Athletes often experience a range of emotions—anger, guilt, frustration, anxiety, sadness—when injured. How you respond will depend on how you interpret the injury (how you make sense of it in your life), but emotional responses are normal. Do not be surprised, too, if your emotions vary a great deal across your recovery.

2. Gather information about your injury from your athletic trainer, physician, physical therapist, websites, etc. The more informed you are about your injury, the recommended treatment, and the course of rehabilitation, the more comfortable, confident, and invested you are likely to be.

3. As much as possible, stay involved with your team throughout the time you are "out" due to injury. Although it can be emotionally challenging to sit on the sideline watching your teammates practice, avoid the temptation to isolate yourself, which can contribute to your emotional distress and slow your recovery.

4. Be actively involved in your treatment and rehabilitation. Don't just passively accept recommendations from athletic trainers and physicians; ask questions about your condition and be involved in your rehabilitation.

5. Talk with teammates, friends, athletic trainers, family members, etc., about what you are feeling in relation to your injury and the assistance you need from them to recover. As noted in point 1, you likely will feel distress over the course of your recovery, and the more you talk about your feelings, the better you are likely to cope.

6. If talking with teammates, friends, family, etc., is not sufficient, then seek help from professional counselors and sport psychologists who are trained in working with injured athletes. These individuals also can help you address the mental side of being injured, such as fear and loss of confidence. Some athletic departments also sponsor injury-recovery support groups. If yours has one, then consider joining it to obtain the social support you need.

7. Adhere to the rehabilitation program designed for you by your physical therapist and/or sports medicine physician. If you have any questions, ask. Maintaining open communication with these individuals about your progress will be an essential part of a successful rehabilitation.

8. Although no one plans to be injured, it can be a benefit, giving you time to focus your attention on other important life areas. For instance, you may have

more time to concentrate on school and significantly improve your grades or spend more time building your relationship with your partner. Use this "extra" time wisely to help you achieve all your goals.

We understand that not all athletes who have been injured want to return to their sport. Some athletes view their injury as an acceptable reason for leaving their sport. If you are in this position, then talk with a professional counselor or sport psychologist about your thoughts and feelings. They can help you determine what you truly want to do and then help you communicate what you need to with your coaches, family, teammates, and others.

There are several things you can do to improve your chances of falling asleep easily and resting soundly throughout the night (Source: National Sleep Foundation):

1. Be consistent in terms of when you go to bed and when you wake up, even on weekends. Do not sleep only 4–5 hours a night during the week (with naps during the day) and then 12+ hours on the weekends. It's a myth that you can catch up on sleep in this manner.

2. Follow a regular, relaxing bedtime routine each evening, which might include casual reading or listening to music. Such routines are particularly important to follow when you are on the road at competitions.

3. Sleep in an environment that helps you fall and stay asleep. Bedrooms that are dark, quiet, comfortable, and cool are ideal.

4. Have a comfortable mattress and pillow. And, when you travel, do not hesitate to take your pillow if you think it will help you be more comfortable and sleep more soundly.

5. Use your bed for only two things—sleep and sex. You want to create a strong association between your bedroom and falling asleep.

6. Do not eat or drink within a couple of hours of your regular bedtime. Eating too closely to bedtime can make you feel uncomfortable and drinking too many fluids can cause you to waken during the night to go to the bathroom.

7. Regular exercise can enhance sleeping, but make sure you complete any physical activity a few hours before you plan to fall asleep.

8. Do not ingest caffeine (e.g., coffee, tea, soft drinks, chocolate) near your bedtime. If you're especially sensitive to caffeine, then you may have to cut off your intake early in the afternoon.

9. Do not drink alcohol near the time you are planning to fall asleep.

It's all right to deviate from your regular sleep schedule from time to time, but in general, listen to your body's natural rhythms and get the consistent sleep you need to be an effective student, athlete, and person. If you follow these guidelines, then you should be able to sleep more consistently and soundly. If, however, you still are having problems sleeping, talk with your athletic trainer and/or sports medicine

---

Exercise 10.2 Your Current Sleep Patterns

1. How many hours a night do you need to feel sufficiently rested—that is, to wake up rested and refreshed and not need to take a nap during the day?

_____

2. In an average week, on how many nights do you get sufficient rest (as defined in question 1)?

_____

3. On the nights when you get inadequate sleep, what interferes with your getting the rest you need?

_____

_____

4. Of the reasons or activities you listed in question 3, which are under your control and which are not? Keep

in mind that you have more control over what happens in your life than you might imagine. For example, you might think of "had to study for midterm" as something you could not change, but you probably spent your time in a way that made it necessary to study at the last minute. Be self-responsible and honest with yourself when you make your lists.

_____

_____

_____

5. Looking at the items you listed as being under your control, discuss how you could change your environment, sleep schedule, or anything else so that you can achieve your desired amount of sleep each night.

---

physician. Your problems with sleep will likely have a negative effect on your athletic and academic performances, so take the time to find a solution. To help you become more aware of your current sleep needs and what might be contributing to poor sleep, you may want to complete Exercise 10.2.

Preparation and Performance: Alcohol and Other Drugs

To begin this section, we encourage you to complete Exercise 10.3 to determine how much you know about alcohol.

The use of alcohol is a major problem on college campuses, even for those students who are under the legal drinking age. Amongst college students in general, 31% met diagnostic criteria for alcohol abuse, whereas another 6% were classified as alcohol dependent (Knight, Wechsler, Kou, Seibering, Weitzman, & Schuckit, 2002). About 44% of college students binge drink (defined as consuming five or more drinks in a row for men and four or more drinks in a row for women). Of these binge drinkers, 48% indicate that they do so for the purpose of getting drunk, and almost one-quarter (23%) report drinking 10 or more times per month (Wechsler et al., 2002). Like college students in general, student-athletes drink a great deal of alcohol. For example, 61% of men and 50% of women who were involved in athletics reported binge drinking at least once during a two-week time frame (Wechsler, Davenport, Dowdall, Grossman, and Zanakos, 1997), which is significantly higher than found among nonathletes (Toben and Wechsler, 2001).

Drinking, but binge drinking in particular, can have negative effects on the academic, athletic, social, physical, and occupational functioning of student-athletes. Binge drinkers, more so than nonbinge drinkers, are much more likely to experience a variety of alcohol-related problems, including:

- Having a hangover
- Doing something they regret

> "The taste of defeat has a richness of experience all its own."
>
> BILL BRADLEY
> *Former NBA All Star and U.S. Senator*

- Missing a class
- Forgetting where they were or what they did while drinking
- Getting behind in their schoolwork
- Arguing with friends
- Engaging in unplanned sexual activity
- Getting hurt or injured
- Damaging property and getting into trouble with the police
- Having unprotected sex
- Driving after having five or more drinks
- Riding with an intoxicated driver
- Earning Lower grade point averages (Wechsler et al., 1994, 2002).

Even if you do not use alcohol frequently, binge drinking increases your risk of behaving in ways that have severe, if not life-threatening, consequences. Just one episode of drunken driving or unprotected sex can change your life forever.

Although the initial effects of alcohol, such as lessened inhibition, may make you think it is a stimulant, it is not. Alcohol is a depressant that affects all areas of your brain and impairs your coordination; increases your reaction time; disrupts your voluntary muscle control; and interferes with your reasoning, decision making, and judgment. When used in excess, alcohol causes death by putting to sleep the core areas of your brain that regulate breathing and heart rate. Your body, specifically your liver, can process only a certain amount of alcohol each hour (about one ounce, or the equivalent of one beer), so the more you drink, the longer you will be under its influence. Also, if you

---

Exercise 10.3   Alcohol Knowledge Test

Listed below are several questions about alcohol. Use them to test your knowledge.

1. Alcoholism runs in families. (True or False)

2. What is the number one killer among youths?
   a. In-home accidents
   b. Guns
   c. Alcohol-related deaths

3. A 12-ounce beer, a 5-ounce glass of wine, and a 1-ounce shot of liquor all have the same alcohol content. (True or False)

4. What is the most abused drug in the United States?
   a. Marijuana
   b. Alcohol
   c. Methamphetamines
   d. Cigarettes

5. The best way to sober up after drinking is to
   a. Take a cold shower.
   b. Drink lots of coffee.
   c. Wait for the body to process the alcohol out of your system.

6. Drinking a beer after an athletic competition is a good way to rehydrate and get needed carbohydrates. (True or False)

7. Sweet-tasting, fruit-flavored drinks, such as margaritas, generally have
   a. A lower alcohol content than beer.
   b. The same alcohol content as beer.
   c. A greater alcohol content than beer.

8. To help stay sober during an evening of drinking, it is best to
   a. Drink only one type of beverage (e.g., beer), no matter how much you consume.
   b. Start the evening with hard liquor, but switch to something "lighter" toward the end.
   c. Moderate the amount of alcohol you consume, no matter what kind you drink.

9. Eating before and during drinking can help slow the absorption of alcohol into your system. (True or False)

10. In most states, if a person's blood alcohol content (BAC) exceeded _____ percent, he or she would be considered to be driving while intoxicated (DWI) if found operating a motor vehicle.
   a. 0.10
   b. 0.15
   c. 0.20

drink too much too quickly, then you may overwhelm your body's processing capacities and cause serious alcohol-related problems, such as alcohol poisoning or even death. If you are of legal age and are going to drink, then avoid the tendency to binge. Instead, drink moderately (no more than one or two drinks over the course of several hours) and always make sure you have a nondrinking designated driver or friend who can help you get home safely. In the long run, if you take a more moderate approach, then you may save yourself from social embarrassment or much more serious problems.

Concerning other drugs, such as marijuana, there has been increased use among college students (Kuo, Lee, and Wechsler, 2003); about 17% of students indicated using it during the past 30 days and 30% over the past year. Concerning other illicit drugs, such as amphetamines, tranquilizers, heroin, ecstasy, and cocaine, college student use ranged from 7% (during the last 30 days) to almost 16% (during the past year). Further, almost all of the students (98%) who reported using either marijuana or another illicit drug also used another substance (i.e., used another drug, smoked, or binge drank). Athletes appear to use drugs other than alcohol, such as marijuana, amphetamines, and cocaine/ crack, as well, but at rates lower than those of nonathletes (Anderson et al., 1991). One reason for these differences may be that random drug testing by their schools and by national governing bodies, such as the National Collegiate Athletic Association, deters student-athletes from using illegal drugs (Anderson et al., 1991; Spence and Gauvin, 1996). To learn more about drug testing at your school, talk with your coaches and athletic trainers, or you can visit the NCAA website (http:// www.ncaa.org/wps/ncaa?key=/ncaa/ncaa/legislation+and+governance/ eligibility+and+recruiting/drug+testing/drug_testing.html). Even some over-the-counter medications contain substances that are banned and would produce a positive test result if you were taking them. Remember, it is your responsibility to avoid potential drug-testing problems. Be proactive and talk with your sports medicine staff about any medications you might take (whether over-the-counter or not).

Even given the deterrent of random drug testing, some athletes still use drugs. They may experience some of the same negative consequences, including poor academic and athletic performances, unsatisfying relationships, financial problems, and even arrest, that binge drinkers do. If you or anyone else you know has a drug or alcohol problem, then please get help. Talk with a counselor at your school's counseling center who is trained in working with alcohol/drug use problems. If you are not comfortable with going to the counseling center, then talk with your academic advisor or athletic trainer, who can help you get assistance.

Preparation and Performance: Sex and Relationships

Sexual Decisions

College means freedom, and with that, many students will date and be sexually active (if they were not already). You will make decisions about whether to be romantically involved—heterosexual and/or

Is Your Alcohol (Or Drug) Use a Problem?

Although the questions below are written specifically in relation to alcohol use, you could substitute "drugs," "use," "using," or "user" and answer them a second time to determine the extent to which you might have a problem with prescription or illegal drugs.

Answer the questions below honestly as they apply to your current drinking behaviors (or your current drug use). If other people, such as teammates, have commented about your alcohol (or drug) use or if you have been concerned about it, then these questions may be particularly important for you.

1. Have you tried to stop or quit drinking but been unable to do so? YES NO

2. Have you ever experienced "blackouts," periods of time when you were drinking that you could not remember? YES NO

3. Do you drink while alone or hide the fact that you have been drinking from others? YES NO

4. Do you drink as a way of coping with your problems, for instance to forget about a bad athletic performance or troubles in a relationship? YES NO

5. Have you ever done something while drinking, such as being violent or sexually intimate, that you later regretted? YES NO

6. Do you find that you need to drink to enjoy social situations? YES NO

7. Do you tend to be the "biggest" or "fastest" drinker whenever you go to a party? YES NO

8. Have you ever failed to fulfill obligations, such as going to class or practice, because of drinking? YES NO

9. Has anyone—for instance, family members, teammates, or athletic trainers—expressed concern about the amount you drink and/or the way you behave when drinking? YES NO

10. Have you ever had financial problems because of your drinking? YES NO

11. Have you ever been in trouble with the police or other authorities because of your drinking (for instance, being cited for public intoxication)? YES NO

12. Have you ever operated a car or motorcycle when you were under the influence of alcohol? YES NO

13. Do you plan your daily schedule so you can drink? YES NO

14. Do you need to drink more now than you did in the past to get the same effect? YES NO

If you answered "Yes" to any of these questions, then you may have a problem with alcohol (or drugs). For more information or to get help, contact your school's counseling center or talk with one of your academic advisors so you can find assistance on your campus.

homosexual—and whether to be sexually intimate in those relationships. Deciding whether or not to be sexually intimate is a personal choice. For some, the decision will be easy. For others, deciding whether to be sexually active, and if so, with whom, will be more challenging. Whatever your decision, think through what you want in

Exercise 10.4 Making Informed Sexual Decisions

To help you make an informed choice, we provide a series of questions to consider (you may have others), either by yourself or with your partner, before you decide whether to be sexually intimate.

1. How do sex and physical intimacy fit into my view of relationships and love?

_____

_____

_____

2. If I choose to be sexually intimate, with what types of behaviors (such as masturbation, oral sex, and/or intercourse) will I be comfortable? Why or why not?

_____

_____

_____

3. If I choose to become sexually intimate, (a) what type of protection and birth control will I want to use, and (b) how will my partner and I decide on a method of protection?

_____

_____

_____

4. If applicable, how do my or my partner's past sexual relationships influence the way we view one another?

_____

_____

_____

5. What are my and my partner's statuses with regard to HIV and other sexually transmitted infections (STIs)?

How can I know whether my partner is telling me the truth? Should we be tested for HIV and other STIs?

_____

_____

_____

6. Whose responsibility is it to initiate sex? Why?

_____

_____

_____

7. How will I let my partner know when I want to be sexually intimate?

_____

_____

_____

8. How will I respond if I feel my partner is pressuring me to be sexually intimate, and I either am not ready to make that commitment or just do not want to be intimate at the moment?

_____

_____

_____

If you have questions or need additional information about sexual issues, then visit the resources that are available on most college campuses, such as the student health center or counseling center. These centers have current information and trained professionals who can help. You also may want to talk with your family, with trusted friends, or with a religious/spiritual advisor.

a relationship, whether you want to be sexually active, and if so, in what ways. Although college is a time of "experimentation" for many, it is important that your choices about being sexually active (or not) be made wisely and be consistent with your values and beliefs. To help you get started thinking about this topic, you may want to complete Exercise 10.4.

Sexually Transmitted Diseases

In addition to making value-consistent decisions regarding sex and intimate relationships, all students should be knowledgeable about STIs, especially those who choose to be sexually active. Although an "it can't happen to me" attitude is pervasive, increasing numbers of college students are being treated for STIs, and we have worked with many student-athletes whose lives have been changed forever because they did not protect themselves. Don't let ignorance or an unfounded feeling of invincibility put you at unneeded risk. You can protect yourself and still enjoy being sexually active. To help you

© Sergios, 2009 / Used under license from Shutterstock.com

learn about the different types of STIs, you may want to complete Exercise 10.5. Doing so may help you avoid becoming just another sexual statistic.

So how do you lower your risk of contracting STIs? Certainly the most reliable way to prevent STIs is to not be sexually active, and many students, whether for personal or religious reasons, will choose this option. Even with abstinence, though, you must make choices and be responsible. Does abstinence mean simply not engaging in sexual intercourse (but allowing for other forms of sexual activity, such as touching or oral sex), or does it mean no genital contact of any kind? If you have completed Exercise 10.4, then you probably have some idea of where you stand on this issue. If you choose to have genital contact, then you increase your risk of exposure to STIs (and pregnancy in heterosexual relationships) and thus should be aware of and use other forms of protection.

If you choose to be sexually active, then you will have to decide if you are going to do so in the context of a monogamous relationship (i.e., being sexually active with only one partner), or if you are going to have multiple partners at any one time. Certainly not if you have multiple partners, but even if you choose to be monogamous, there is no guarantee that you will have no risk of exposure. As you learned in Exercise 10.5, many STIs are asymptomatic (show no symptoms) and thus can go untreated in a person. If either you or your partner has had any previous sexual relationships, then you may unknowingly have been exposed to and infected with an STI. If that is the case, even though you are currently in a monogamous relationship, you are at risk. Although being tested for STIs before entering into a new sexual relationship may seem unnecessary to many students, it is the only way to know whether or not you or your partner have an STI. Obviously, you will have to make your own decision about testing. But realize that from an STI perspective, when you are sexually active with your current partner, you are active with every partner he or she has

Exercise 10.5   STI Knowledge Test

Listed below are some of the more common STIs, along with descriptions of each. Test your knowledge by matching each STI to its correct description.

_____ **1.** Chlamydia

A. Also called "crabs," they live between the roots of the hairs and cause intense itching. Passed through sexual contact with an infected person, they must be treated with special shampoos.

_____ **2.** Genital Herpes

B. Causes the body's immune system to become defenseless against diseases. Passed through exchange of bodily fluids, such as blood, semen, or vaginal secretions, though a person may be unaware of being infected for many years. Can affect men, women, and children of all racial, ethnic, sexual orientation, and socioeconomic status groups. Currently there is no cure, though there are treatments to delay onset of opportunistic infections.

_____ **3.** Gonorrhea

C. Transmitted during intercourse when blisters or lesions are active in the infected partner. Symptoms, which are small blisters that develop into painful sores, generally develop within three days to three weeks after infection. There is no cure and some people will suffer from repeated outbreaks, which are often influenced by stress.

_____ **4.** Human Papillomavirus (HPV)

D. One of the most common STIs. Women often do not show any symptoms and thus may not seek treatment, leaving themselves vulnerable to developing pelvic inflammatory disease (PID). Men generally experience symptoms, particularly pain and burning during urination. If symptoms are present in women, these include vaginal discharge, mild abdominal pain, and difficulty urinating. This STI is treatable with antibiotics.

_____ **5.** Pubic Lice

E. A virus that causes venereal warts (small pink growths or larger cauliflower-like growths) on the genitals of men and women. There is no cure, but treatments exist for removing the warts. There are long-term health risks for women, because this STI can infect the cervix and cause cancer.

_____ **6.** HIV or AIDS

F. Also called "the clap," it is caused by bacteria and can be treated with antibiotics. Men, more than women, will show symptoms, including yellow discharge from the penis, sores on the penis, and pain during urination. Untreated, this STI can lead to health problems in men (such as sterility) and in women (such as infertility).

If you believe you have one of these STIs, or have had unprotected sex and are just concerned, then do not put off getting tested at your school's health center or by a team or private physician. Left untreated, these STIs can cause serious health problems that may last you a lifetime, as well as harm others with whom you are sexually intimate.

> **"The rewards are going to come, but my happiness is just loving the sport and having fun performing."**
>
> JACKIE JOYNER KERSEE
> *Olympic Gold Medalist, Track and Field*

had. If you have not done so already, then you may want to complete Exercise 10.4 to help you think further about this issue.

A final option, where appropriate, is to use a condom. Condoms, particularly latex ones with a spermicide, offer the best protection because they act as a barrier between the two individuals' genital areas and prevent the transmission of bodily fluids. Lambskin and other natural condoms are generally more porous and thus are not as safe because fluids can cross the barrier. If you use a condom, then it can be helpful to use a lubricant as well (if they are not already lubricated). If you do, then make sure the lubricant is a water-based one such as K-Y jelly, because petroleum-based products, such as Vaseline, can damage the condom and cause it to break. Although condoms do offer the best protection against STIs for sexually active individuals, they are not foolproof. Condoms can break and, if not used properly, can come off the penis during or just following intercourse. If you use a

Anabolic Steroids and Other Muscle-Building Supplements

Anabolic steroids, which are synthetic derivatives of testosterone, are a problem in sports, as evidenced by the ever-widening scandal in Major League Baseball. At one time thought to be solely the province of weightlifters, body builders, and football players, steroids and steroid-derivatives are now used in most sports, among men and women (though prevalence rates are higher for men) and among high school athletes. For college student-athletes, despite testing by organizations such as the NCAA, use is higher than among their nonathlete peers (McCabe, Brower, West, Nelson, and Wechsler, 2007). Although these drugs are taken for their performance-enhancing effects, such as increasing muscle mass and strength, decreasing body fat, and increasing one's ability to train for longer amounts of time, they have serious physical and psychological side effects that outweigh any supposed benefits (Middleman and DuRant, 1996; Potteiger and Stilger, 1994). On the physical side, steroid use has been associated with testicular atrophy and gynecomastia (breast enlargement) in men, masculinization in women (such as facial hair, reduced breast size, and deepening of the voice), hypertension, acne, liver dysfunction, and unhealthy changes in cholesterol levels. On the psychological side, side effects often associated with steroid use include increased aggressiveness ("roid rage"), depression, irritability, anxiety, euphoria, and dependency. Because many steroids are injected, users also run the risk of contracting HIV if they share needles with infected people.

Other nonsteroid muscle-building supplements, such as creatine, protein powders, and "andro" compounds, also are popular among athletes. Although the physical and psychological risks associated with taking these products is lower than with anabolic steroids, some of these are banned and do not always deliver the results expected (Eichner et al., 1999). The reality is that, for most athletes, improvements in strength, stamina, and performance are likely to occur in conjunction with years of hard work and training.

Given these facts, we suggest the following for improving your performances (Eichner et al., 1999):

1. Complete regular strength-training workouts under the supervision of a qualified strength and conditioning coach

2. Develop your mental toughness by working with a sport psychologist

3. Hone your physical and sport-specific technical skills by working extra time with your coaches

4. Eat a nutritious, performance-enhancing diet developed specifically to meet the demands of your sport by a sports nutritionist.

When making these changes, give yourself time to develop increasing strength, stamina, and speed, and improving your performances does not occur overnight.

condom, to avoid problems, pay attention to what you are doing. Also, remember that your health and possibly your life are at risk when you become sexually active. If you believe a condom should be used, then stick with your decision even if your partner pressures you to have sex without one. For many, "No glove, no love" is an adage to live by.

Birth Control and Pregnancy

When two people engage in heterosexual intercourse, the woman can become pregnant. If you are a woman, then you need to decide whether you want that to occur at this point in your life. If you do not, then you must consider how you will prevent pregnancy while remaining sexually active. If you have completed Exercise 10.4, then you and your partner may have some ideas as to the birth control methods you might choose. If you have not completed Exercise 10.4, then please do so now and discuss your thoughts with your partner. A wide range of birth control options are available, ranging from hormone-based products (such as the implant, patch, or pill) to barrier methods (such as condoms or diaphragms), so you and your partner should decide together what method will be right for the two of you. For more information about the types of birth control available as well as their rates of effectiveness, consult a medical specialist at your school's student health center or a family planning clinic in your local community, such as Planned Parenthood (www.plannedparenthood.org), or your private physician. Before you make any decisions, get the information you need and discuss the options with your partner. Birth control is a shared responsibility; one to be thought through in advance and then used consistently.

There also is an emergency form of birth control, generally referred to as the morning after pill. This hormone-based birth control can be used in situations where the female partner has been exposed to the possibility of becoming pregnant due to (1) having unprotected sex, or (2) having used protection, but having that form of protection not work, such as when a condom breaks or the woman has not been consistent with taking her birth control pills. This form of birth control can be taken up to five days after intercourse to prevent pregnancy (for more information, you can visit Planned Parenthood at www.plannedparenthood.org/health-topics/emergency-contraception-morning-after-pill-4363.htm). Remember, though, that this form of birth control is for emergencies and should not be considered a regular or consistent way to prevent pregnancy.

Even when birth control is used, unplanned pregnancies can occur. If you and your partner find yourselves in such a situation, then you will need to decide whether you want to continue the pregnancy. Obviously, a decision of this nature needs to be thoroughly discussed and thought through, though it is important for your health (and possibly the health of your baby) that you decide as soon as possible. If you and your partner are having difficulty deciding what to do, then you may want to talk with a supportive and nonjudgmental friend, family member, or religious advisor or with a counselor at your school's counseling center. These individuals may help you make sense of your thoughts and feelings and provide you with a supportive and unbiased perspective that can shed new light on your decision making.

If you choose not to continue with the pregnancy, then you and your partner will need to consult the local community resources, which we have mentioned previously, to find out your options. If you choose to continue with the pregnancy, then it is critical that you seek medical attention as soon as possible. You need to be responsible in taking care of yourself and your child as early in the pregnancy as possible, even if you plan to have the baby adopted when it is born. Good prenatal care and support can go a long way toward ensuring a healthy life for yourself and your child.

Although we have discussed being sexually intimate primarily with respect to intercourse, there are many risks associated with oral sex as well. STIs can be transmitted orally as well as during intercourse. So, remember, any unprotected contact with your partner's genitals and related fluids (whether with your mouth or with your genitals) can increase your risk of contracting an STI. Again, one episode of unprotected sex can change your life forever. So think ahead about what forms of sexual activity are comfortable for you and how you want to protect yourself—abstinence, monogamy, and/or condoms—and then make sure you stick to your decisions.

Sexual Assault

College students, particularly women, often have to deal with unwanted sexual advances and behaviors. Almost 5% of college women report being raped since the beginning of any given school year (Kuo, Dowdall, Koss, and Wechsler, 2004), and 60% of college women have experienced some type of unwanted sexual behavior, ranging from rape to sexual intimidation (such as having their breasts grabbed; Tripp and Petrie, 2001). Over 80% of sexual assaults are perpetrated by someone the victim knew, such as a classmate, a date, or a nonromantic friend (Frintner and Rubinson, 1993). Student-athletes are not immune to such experiences. Female student-athletes are subjected to similar types of unwanted sexual experiences, including being fondled against their will, coerced or pressured into having sex, and sexually assaulted (Jackson, 1991).

Men are the perpetrators in almost all sexual assaults against women, and male student-athletes commit a disproportionately high number of such acts (e.g., Frintner and Rubinson, 1993). For this to change, men need to change the ways they think about and behave toward women. Only men can eradicate the threat and reality of sexual assaults. Until they do, though, women will need to take action to protect themselves and lower their risk of being assaulted. We offer some suggestions as to how men can behave in more respectful ways toward women and how women can protect themselves.

1. *No means no.* This is true for both parties in any sexual encounter. The person who does not want to be sexually active should take the responsibility to clearly communicate that fact, both verbally and nonverbally, and the recipient of the message should respect and follow it. No means no!

2. *Alcohol.* Alcohol is the number one contributing factor in college sexual assaults (Kuo et al., 2004). Thus, men and women, if they are going to drink, must do so in moderation and not engage in inappropriate acts or put themselves in dangerous situations.

   For women who go out and drink, limit the amount you drink (or not drink at all) so that you remain in control of yourself and can exercise good judgment. You can have a great time without being intoxicated. Second, establish a "buddy" system with your friends before you go. Look out for one another to make sure no one is drinking too much, no one is taken away (for instance to a room upstairs), and no one leaves with a person who is not part of the original group. Remember, most assaults are perpetrated by acquaintances, so don't abandon your responsibility if you see your friend leaving with someone she knows or you know.

If you are a man, then you need to understand that intoxication does not excuse your behaviors. If you tend to "get out of control" when drinking, then you may need to limit your intake (or not drink at all) or make sure you have a friend who will watch out for you. If you don't, you may commit an act that can change another person's life and your own forever. In most states, if either party has been drinking, then consensual sex cannot occur. You must be sober to communicate consent for sexual intimacy.

3. *Sexual Assault Self-Defense Training*. If you are a woman, then consider taking a sexual assault self-defense training class. These classes are generally offered either by your school's counseling center, through the police department, or as a physical activity course in the kinesiology department. They can give you basic information on how to best avoid and, if necessary, defend yourself from a sexual assault. Be proactive and get this type of training during your first term.

4. *Sexual Assault Awareness Training*. Also referred to as rape education, these classes are generally designed to help men and women better understand their responsibilities in relationships and the ways their behaviors affect members of the opposite sex. We believe it is essential for all college students, men in particular, to attend such classes as a step toward eliminating sexual assaults.

Even though many students get training and take precautions, sexual assaults still happen. If you are sexually assaulted, then know that you are not alone, that you are not to blame, and that there are resources on your campus to assist you. These things are true even if you know your assailant. Acquaintance rape is no less traumatic—nor is it any less of a crime—than rape by a stranger.

If you are attacked, then one of the first decisions will be whether you will report the assault to the police. We encourage you to file a report (just to have it in place in case you decide to take action later on), though we recognize that not all women will be able to do so following the trauma of a sexual assault. If you are going to report the crime, then the sooner you do so after its occurrence the better. In fact, the best way to maintain evidence of the crime is to call the police immediately or have someone take you to a hospital. If you are scared, you may want to have someone—a friend, a family member, or a rape crisis center counselor—accompany you when you make the report. Although you may want to shower and clean up, it is important that you don't. By showering, douching, or cleaning up in any way, you may destroy key evidence that could convict the perpetrator. Although you may feel frightened and out of control after the assault, know that the police who take the report and the medical personnel who examine you are trained professionals whose job it is to assist you in a supportive and caring manner.

Drugs and Sexual Assault

Unfortunately, alcohol is not the only drug women have to worry about in connection with sexual assaults. Drugs, such as Rohypnol (also known as roofies, rib, rope, roachies, and R-2), GHB (also known as G, cherry meth, liquid ecstasy), and Ketamine (also known as bump, kit-kat, special K) are potent sedative/hypnotics that have been used in sexual assaults in the United States, particularly among high school and college-age individuals who attend night clubs and parties. These drugs are generally colorless, odorless, and tasteless and thus can be placed in an intended victim's drink without detection. Within 5 to 30 minutes of consuming these drugs, the person may feel dizzy, faint, and nauseated. The person also may experience impairments in judgment, speech, and motor control. Passing out is often the end result, a state that may last for many hours. In addition, the victim has few, if any, memories of what occurred while drugged. Further, these drugs are generally cleared from the body quickly so detection is difficult.

   Given this very real threat, you need to be extremely cautious when you go out, whether or not you are with friends. Here are some strategies for protecting yourself from becoming a victim:

- Don't accept drinks from other people, even if the person is a friend or acquaintance.
- Open all containers yourself.
- Never leave your drink unattended by you; even take it to the bathroom with you.
- Don't share your drink with someone else and definitely don't take sips from someone else's drink.
- Punch bowls or other common, open containers can easily be drugged, so do NOT drink from them.
- If a person offers to get you a drink from a bar or at a party, then go with them and order your own drink. Watch it being poured or opened and then carry it yourself.
- If you are drinking something and it tastes strange, smells funny, or has an odd color, then stop immediately! Sometimes, these drugs can cause these effects.
- Always go out with a "buddy" and have that friend make sure nothing happens to you and you do not leave with anyone else (even if the person is an acquaintance or friend). Get on the same page with your buddy before you go out. Once intoxicated, your friend may try to convince you to change the plans. Be persistent.
- If you may have left your drink unattended, even if for only a short period of time, then do not drink any of it; instead pour it out and get a new drink for yourself.
- If you start to feel lightheaded, confused, nauseous, dizzy, or just generally "drunk" (and you have not had much or anything to drink), then tell a friend and then get help right away.

Although these suggestions may seem to take the fun and spontaneity out of partying, they can increase your chances of having a safe evening out and not being the victim of a sexual assault (Source: National Women's Health Information Center, U.S. Department of Health and Human Services).

A second decision you will have to make is how you will cope with the trauma you have experienced. Certainly, one way is to help the police prosecute the person who attacked you. Working with them can help you regain a sense of control and power in your life. Another important way is to talk to supportive people about whatever feelings and thoughts you may have about the attack. For some women, talking with family and friends may be sufficient. Others, though, may need a kind of objective and professional assistance that family and friends cannot provide. If you are in this position, then seek support from the resources that are available on campus and in your community, such as your school's counseling center, student health center, a community or campus women's center or shelter, or a local rape counseling center. Regardless of where you go, the important thing is that you talk with someone about what has happened. Know that there are many caring, supportive, and skilled individuals who can help you get through it.

Post-Game Review

Throughout this chapter, we have discussed the importance of learning to take responsibility for your health-related behaviors. "Doing the right thing," particularly in the face of strong social temptations and peer pressures, is not always easy. Even so, it is important that you think through your decisions about eating, sleeping, drinking, and being sexually active so that your subsequent behaviors are consistent with your values and the life goals you have set for yourself. By making good choices when your health is involved, you set the stage for maximizing your current performance potential, in both athletics and academics. You also develop a habit of healthy living that will serve you well throughout your life.

Thinking Critically about Your Health

1. Summarize what you now know about healthy behaviors based on the information presented in this chapter.

_____

_____

_____

2. What additional questions do you have about these topics and how to use the skills introduced in this chapter?

_____

_____

_____

3. What conclusions can you draw about this topic and how it might help you be a more effective and successful student and athlete?

_____

_____

_____

Achieve IT! Setting a Healthy Behavior Goal

1. Based on your self-assessment and your responses to Thinking Critically, select a goal in relationship to changing a behavior to be healthier that you would like to achieve this term.

2. Now identify three short-term goals that will help you reach your goal this term.

3. For the short-term goals, identify the attainment strategies you will need to reach them.

4. List any obstacles you might face in trying to reach these goals and identify your plan for overcoming each one.

Don't forget to make your goal visible and tell others about them, so they can keep you accountable regarding what you want to achieve.

Chapter 10 Review Questions

1. The primary source of fuel for your body is found in

    a. Fats.
    b. Proteins.
    c. Carbohydrates.
    d. Minerals and vitamins.

2. Fasting before a competition is likely to _____ your athletic performance.

    a. Improve
    b. Negatively affect
    c. Not change

3. Most athletes adequately replace fluids lost during training. (True or False)

4. Having a beer or two after a competition is a good way to rehydrate and replenish your carbohydrates. (True or False)

5. Eating disorders affect _____ more than _____.

    a. children; adults
    b. women; men
    c. athletes; nonathletes
    d. B and C
    e. None of the above

6. To create a situation that helps you fall asleep you should:

    a. Exercise just prior to bedtime to tire yourself out.
    b. Have your lights on until just before you are going to go to sleep.
    c. Only sleep in your bed and have a comfortable pillow.
    d. All of the above.

7. List three behavioral problems associated with binge drinking.

8. The use of steroids is a problem only for football players and weight lifters. (True or False)

9. _____ condoms offer the best protection against STIs.

    a. Natural
    b. Latex
    c. Ribbed
    d. Silicone

10. Alcohol plays a prominent role in sexual assaults. (True or False)

Chapter **11** | Succeeding in Life and Relationships
Coping with Stress and Improving Performances

Game Plan:

- What stress is and how it might affect you

- About common stressors that college student-athletes face

- About the process of coping with stressors and identifying positive ways you might cope

- That most competitive athletic careers end by college graduation and that you must begin preparing for that reality now

© Galina Barskaya, 2009 / Used under license from Shutterstock.com

"All of us do well when things are going well, but the thing that distinguishes athletes is the ability to do well in times of great stress, urgency, and pressure."

ROGER STAUBACH
NFL Hall-of-Fame Quarterback

Self-Assessment—Perceive It!

Read the following statements and place a checkmark next to each one you generally do. For you to change and develop new and effective academic, athletic, and personal strategies, you must be accurate in your self-perception. So, be honest in how you answer each question.

1. I know how I tend to react when I am stressed. _____

2. When I am stressed, I talk with others, such as family members or friends, about how I am feeling so that I do not become overwhelmed _____

3. When I am stressed, I try to determine what the problem is and then come up with a solution. _____

4. I keep up with my schoolwork so that I don't become overwhelmed by having too much to do at one time. _____

5. I use all the available services and resources at my school, such as the counseling center and tutors, to help me cope with the demands of being a student-athlete. _____

6. When little things happen, such as being late for class, I keep a positive perspective so that I don't become overly stressed. _____

7. When I have problems and need help, I am able to admit it. _____

8. Before I compete in my sport or on tests, I visualize myself handling the situation and performing well. _____

9. I can distinguish between situations that are stressful and those that are simply challenging. _____

10. When I am deciding how to cope with a stressful situation, I first think about whether I can eliminate the stressor from my life. _____

11. By doing things such as choosing a career path and taking the necessary classes, I am preparing now for the reality that my competitive athletic career is likely to end within the next four years. _____

12. I know how to use proper deep-breathing techniques to relax. _____

13. I understand the physiological effects of chronic high levels of stress. _____

Take a moment to review your responses. How many items did you check? Each one you checked represents a current strength. Now consider the items you did not check; these represent areas where focus and growth are needed. Now, to summarize your self-perception, complete the following statements:

1. My areas of strength are:

_____

2. The areas I need to improve are:

_____

As you read this chapter and participate in your classes, keep your strengths and areas of improvement in mind. At the end of the chapter, you will have the chance to set a goal related to these areas. Achieving these goals will help you become a more effective student and athlete.

Introduction

Although Alonzo was a sophomore academically, this was his first year playing football full time because he had been redshirted as a freshman. Because of the change in his playing status, Alonzo purposely took a lighter academic load. Even so, he underestimated the time football and school was going to take. After practices and training table, which generally lasted until 7:00 P.M., he would go to study hall for two hours and then to his room where he would study more if he had extra homework to do. He also had an instructor who was not fond of student-athletes and thought that the time spent on football was a waste. By the middle of the semester, Alonzo was feeling very stressed.

In football, he had earned a starting spot on special teams, and hoped to play more as the season unfolded so he could improve for the following year. During the sixth game of the season, two of the starting defensive backs sustained serious injuries. Alonzo was now a starting cornerback on defense! Although Alonzo had always dreamed about being a starter, the reality was tougher than he had expected. The coaches worked him even harder in practice to help him prepare for his new role. In addition, the remaining teams on the schedule primarily played a spread offense and would challenge him at corner with their passing attack. Much of the team's success was riding on how well he and the other defensive backs performed.

Alonzo's first game was positive. He was beaten only once, on a pass play, and made a couple of tackles that contributed to the team's win. Although he had hoped his performance would lessen the pressure, Alonzo felt even more now. He had to do well during the remaining games so the team would receive a bowl game invitation, which meant spending more time reviewing game films and working out. But the academic demands from his classes also were increasing and his girlfriend wanted to see him more; he did not know where he would find the time. Alonzo tried cutting back on his sleep, which seemed to work at first. After a few days, though, he fell asleep in class and the instructor asked him to leave. At that point, Alonzo did not think he could handle the pressure any more. He just wanted a break from all the demands he was facing!

Being a student-athlete can be very stressful. As a student, you have to handle being away from home for the first time, performing well in your classes, developing new friendships, and establishing romantic relationships. As an athlete, you also have unique stressors, such as sport performance demands, practices and travel, physical injury, public visibility, and fatigue. Combined, all these stressors can leave some student-athletes feeling overwhelmed.

In this chapter, we discuss how you can reduce the stressors in your life and cope more effectively with what remains. To begin, we introduce the idea that stress is not inherently bad or negative. We then identify general responses to stressors. Finally, we discuss coping and present a variety of ways to handle common stress reactions. As an athlete, you may have some well-developed coping skills, so our goal is to help you transfer what you already have and introduce you to some new ones that may assist you further.

> "They say good things come to those who wait. I believe good things come to those who work."
>
> WILT CHAMBERLAIN
> *Former NBA All-Star, Basketball Hall of Fame*

Preparation: Stress

Stress is a psychological state in which an individual perceives an event as threatening or endangering his or her well-being and as exceeding his or her resources or ability to cope (Folkman, 1984). This definition makes several important points:

1. Stress is not universal—it is individually determined through your perception of the event.
2. Stress is not constant—it can vary over time based on how you appraise the situation.
3. There is a reciprocal relationship between you and the environment—you can influence your environment (and what may be causing you stress) as much as it affects you.
4. You only experience stress if you feel threatened or you lack the resources to cope.

You can see these concepts at work in the following example:

Valerie and Kerri were teammates on their school's gymnastics team. During the spring term, a hectic travel schedule required them to miss many classes. Valerie, a sophomore, had gone through this last year so wasn't bothered by the absences. She saw being away as an opportunity to escape the daily grind of school and catch up on her readings. She knew she could balance the time demands of away competitions with her academic responsibilities. Kerri, who was a freshman, had never faced this kind of situation. Traveling and keeping up with her studies was new to her, and she worried a lot about whether she could keep up with her class work and perform well on her exams. Because Valerie viewed traveling with the team as an opportunity, she felt positive and excited about the upcoming competitions. Kerri, on the other hand, saw traveling as a burden; something with which she could not cope. As a result, Kerri felt anxious about having to be away from her classes and had a hard time focusing on her athletic performance.

According to Folkman (1984), we understand the events in our lives based on the meaning we assign to them, which occurs through two appraisal processes:

Primary appraisal is the process of deciding how stressful a situation or event is. How you think about the situation or event determines whether something is considered a positive challenge or stressful problem. Your primary appraisals are influenced by your *self-efficacy* in the situation (i.e., do you feel confident about your abilities in this situation?), your *optimism* (i.e., is the situation viewed as temporary or permanent, and does the situation seem to affect a specific area of your life or all of it?), and *what is important* in your life (i.e., your goals and values). For example, Les viewed earning an "F" on his English paper as a challenge because his self-efficacy with respect to writing was generally high, and he knew that his performance on this exam had been affected by the fact that his mom was ill and in the hospital, a situation that was not permanent. He also had set the goal of earning an "A" in this English class so he was motivated to do well.

Secondary appraisal involves evaluating your resources for coping with the demands of the current situation. In other words: "What can I do in this situation to make it better?" As with primary appraisals, secondary appraisals are influenced by your efficacy beliefs and your level of optimism, and are likely to change as you attempt to cope with the situation. For example, if your initial coping efforts are successful, then your subsequent appraisals may be more positive, since you now are more confident you can handle what is going on.

So, in every situation, you first determine if it is stressful or not. If not, the appraisal process stops. If so, then you determine how well you believe you can cope. If you think your coping will be successful (and your initial attempts are), then your stress response will be reduced. If you are not successful in your coping efforts, then your stress response is likely to increase. We will discuss specific coping strategies later in this chapter, but now turn our attention to the events that may cause stress in your life.

> "If you had to define stress, you would not be far off if you said it was the process of living."
>
> STANLEY SARNOFF, M.D.
> *Physician*

Preparation: Stressors

Stressors are the life circumstances, events, or internal perspectives that cause stress and make you adjust or adapt. In general, stressors are external events that occur in your life, such as being away from school because of team travel or failing a class. Some of these events can be major; that is, they happen infrequently and are generally of considerable magnitude (e.g., earning an athletic scholarship or a death in the family). Other events may be relatively minor, such as losing five dollars or having a bad practice. We generally associate stress with negative events, but in reality, positive events can also disrupt your life and require change or adaptation. Most people would view earning a starting spot on an athletic team or getting a job promotion as positive events, but because they pose new challenges and require adaptation, they may be perceived as stressful by some individuals. What is stressful is determined by the way you think about the events you experience. As a result, you can lower your stress just by changing the way you think about the events in your life. We will discuss various ways to do this later in the chapter.

Even though what is stressful varies with the individual, there are some common challenging life events experienced by most student-athletes:

1. Not attaining goals in sport,
2. Being apart from your boyfriend/girlfriend because of your sport,
3. Being absent from school because of your sport,
4. Failing an important exam,
5. Feeling pressure to gain/lose weight because of your sport,
6. Financial pressures connected with school,
7. The daily grind of practices and competitions,
8. Expectations from teammates, coaches, alumni, the university, the surrounding community, and yourself to perform well and win,
9. Not receiving sufficient playing time, and
10. Being injured and unable to play.

In addition to these specific events, there are some general categories of stressors that all students are likely to face:

1. *Academic*—finding sufficient time to study, learning how to take college-level exams, choosing a major, and meeting the expectations of your instructors are just some of the stressors you will face. Such stressors can seem even more overwhelming when you are attending a highly competitive institution whose academic standards are quite rigorous.

2. *Financial*—even with scholarships and other aid, students still may experience financial pressures. Becoming responsible for your own money and having to budget for expenses, such as food, travel, clothes, and entertainment, can be challenging. It can be especially so if you have few family resources or limited income beyond what financial aid provides.

3. *Relationships*—whether with teammates, coaches, roommates, or classmates, relationships can be a major source of stress. They require time to develop and maintain, as well as compromise, understanding, and the ability to communicate clearly. As a result, many students do not have a large circle of close friendships. Romantic relationships pose the same challenges of compromise, understanding, and communication found in other relationships, with the added component of physical intimacy and the choices and decisions to be made around it. The stress can be even higher when your romantic partner is a teammate or another student-athlete. So, be careful when choosing a romantic partner and understand that the relationship may end and there will be fallout with which you will have to attend.

4. *Family*—although families generally are supportive, they can also be stressors. For example, parents may have and communicate (either directly or indirectly) unrealistic expectations regarding achievement in school and athletics. They may also exert undue pressure in matters of major and career choice. Often, the desire to please parents and other family members can be a stressor, especially if your choices and behaviors are at odds with their preferences or you are unable to live up to their standards and expectations.

To help you identify your specific stressors, you may want to complete Exercise 11.1. We will return to these stressors later in this chapter, when we discuss coping.

Exercise 11.1   What Are Your Stressors?

List the events in your life that you currently consider to be stressful in each of the following areas:

Athletics

_____

Academics

_____

Relationships (friends and romantic)

_____

Family

_____

Finances

_____

Other

_____

Preparation: Stress Reactions

Like stress, our responses can vary from individual to individual. In general, though, stress reactions fall into four major categories (Bernstein, Clarke-Stewart, Roy, Srull, and Wickens, 1994):

1. *Physical/physiological*—in stressful situations, such as being in a car accident, taking an exam when you have not studied, or being on the line to shoot the game-winning free throw, you may have strong and immediate physical reactions, such as: elevated heart rate, rapid breathing, increased sweating, shakiness, and dry mouth. These changes generally are brought about by the release of chemicals in your body, specifically adrenaline and noradrenaline. This type of physical reaction is often referred to as the "fight-or-flight" response, because the body is preparing itself either to fight off the stressor or run from it. Although this immediate physical response is adaptive, if the stressor remains unresolved for a long period of time, then your body can lose its ability to fight off illness as your immune system is suppressed by the release of other chemicals, such as cortisol. For example, it was the weekend right before final's week and Paulette had two exams on Monday and one on Tuesday. She also had her final English paper due by noon on Wednesday. Further, she was upset by the recent breakup with her boyfriend. She was behind, and she was stressed. That weekend, when she wasn't playing in the conference softball championship, she was studying. She got very little sleep but was able to get through her exams and turn her paper in on time. Wednesday night she went out to celebrate with teammates, but when she awoke on Thursday, she had a sore throat and a terrible cough.

   Many individuals experience other stress-related physical complaints, such as tension headaches, stomach ailments (e.g., nausea, excess acid), muscle tension, and jaw pain from grinding teeth. For example, Cody, a golfer, had not been playing very well during practice rounds and had not been chosen to compete in any tournaments this season. He was a senior and was worried that he would not get to play during his last year of eligibility. In fact, the more he thought about his performance, the more distressed he became. At first, he experienced only a little tension in his shoulders. But over time, this tension worsened to the point that he would get headaches and become nauseated before practices. Of course, Cody's physical condition did not help his play or his chances of being chosen to travel with the team. Although not everyone experiences these physical symptoms, such symptoms do occur at varying levels of intensity and duration for many people. As you can see from Cody's situation, it is important to manage the stressors and pressures in your life to reduce your chances of experiencing such potentially harmful physical reactions.

Termination of Your Sport Career

Although there will be many transitions in your life, few may be as important or challenging as ending your competitive playing career. At some point, every athlete does end his or her career. For many, this event will coincide with the completion of college eligibility and could be called a planned or expected transition. For others, though, termination of their sports careers may be unexpected, caused by events such as career-ending injuries or being cut from the team.

Whether or not your termination is stressful will depend on many factors:

1. Your perception of the transition. Do you see it as a new beginning, or a significant loss that makes you question the direction and meaning in your life?

2. The strength and exclusivity of your role as an athlete. Student-athletes who identify strongly with multiple roles, such as athlete, student, family member, and romantic partner, are more likely to cope effectively with the transition than those who see themselves solely as athletes.

3. Personal and institutional support that is available to you at the time of transition. Student athletes who receive support, whether it is emotional, such as talking with friends and family about the change, or strategic, such as working with career counselors to plan out an after-college job search, may more successfully weather the transition than those who receive the wrong types of support or inadequate support.

Although you may be at the beginning of your college athletic career, it is never too soon to begin planning for your transition out of sports. Begin thinking now about what you want to do after your sport career has ended, and then take action to move toward that goal. Some student-athletes mistakenly believe that if they actively plan for the end of their athletic careers and life after sport that this will somehow detract from their goal of playing at the "next level." Pursuing a career in professional sports and planning for athletic retirement are not mutually exclusive goals. Also, consider becoming involved in other activities and roles outside of being an athlete. Finally, if your sport termination, be it expected or unexpected, is stressful, then make sure you seek assistance. This help can come from your family or friends or from professionals on your campus. Counseling center staff can be a tremendous emotional and problem-solving resource during this difficult time. Remember, every student-athlete will one day face termination of his or her sports involvement, so plan in advance to make this transition a positive one.

2. *Emotional*—have you ever felt overwhelmed, depressed, irritable, angry, apathetic, or helpless or found yourself easily upset? These are some emotional reactions that may result from facing the various stressors in your life. For example, Jana was a diver who had transferred from a junior college to compete at a Division I school. This was the first time she had been away from home for any extended period of time, and she was having

a hard time adjusting and making new friends. She also was struggling academically and athletically because nothing she did seemed to satisfy her teachers or her coaches. As a result, she started to become easily upset and frustrated by the smallest things, such as not being able to fix her hair or not being able to find what she wanted to eat in the cafeteria. One evening, her roommate found Jana sitting on her bed crying because Jana could not find her economics notebook to study for an exam. Jana was overwhelmed by the stressors in her life. Although not all student-athletes respond as strongly as Jana did, many experience some level of emotional distress in response to life stressors.

3. *Behavioral*—during times of stress, some people eat more or less, some cry or curse, some drink alcohol to excess, some isolate themselves from others, and some engage in risky behavior, like driving too fast or having unprotected sex. Others become physically violent. These are just a few of the behavioral changes that may occur in response to life stressors. For example, Darnelle was a gifted athlete who was expected to start on the basketball team her freshman year. Although she began the practice season with a good attitude, her behaviors changed for the worse toward the end of the academic term. She was thrown out of practice once for getting into a fight with a teammate. She also stopped attending her classes. When confronted by her coach, Darnelle admitted that she was overwhelmed by her own and others' academic and athletic expectations. She knew she was not "behaving like herself," but she did not know what else to do. Similar to the other responses, your behaviors may vary in frequency, duration, and intensity. As in Darnelle's case, behavioral reactions to stress are often maladaptive and actually result in more problems and stress!

4. *Cognitive*—these reactions concern disruptions in the ways people think about situations and process information. Student-athletes who experience this type of response may have difficulty concentrating, focusing attention, thinking clearly, and remembering information. Other reactions include increases in self-doubt and a tendency to worry more. For some, the presence of stressors can worsen problematic ways of thinking that already exist, such as:

   • *Catastrophizing*—is the tendency to focus on the negative and make every situation much worse than it is. In doing so, you generally avoid believing or paying attention to anything positive. For example, Nicolette, a student-athlete, earned a "C" on her first midterm exam. She reacted by thinking that she was going to fail the class, would not be able to pass her other classes, would go on academic probation, would have to stop participating in her sport, and would have to drop out of school. You can see how this kind of thinking can get out of hand quickly and be distressing.

- *Personalizing*—is the tendency to negatively relate social interchanges and situations to your worth as a person, whether or not these events are even related to you. For example, Sam's roommate, Don, had been in a bad mood for a couple of weeks but wouldn't say why. Sam, a student-athlete, began to think maybe he had done something to upset his roommate. Sam felt guilty and responsible for Don's bad mood, even though in reality Don was upset because he had just found out that his scholarship would not be renewed for the next year, something that had nothing to do with Sam.

- *Either-Or Thinking*—is the tendency to view people and situations in absolute terms; either totally good or entirely bad. If you are not a winner who performs perfectly every time, then you are a loser. For example, Ben did not win the 100-meter finals. Instead, he took third place and just missed setting a PR by 0.02 second. When talking with his coach afterwards, Ben called himself a loser and told the coach he should give up because he obviously would never be any good.

As with the other stress reactions, some individuals will experience more severe reactions that disrupt their daily functioning or will fall prey to these distorted ways of thinking. Other individuals, however, may have only minor problems, such as slight difficulties concentrating, which really do not interfere with what they want to accomplish each day.

Although we have discussed the stress reactions separately, it is important to realize that (1) they often occur simultaneously, and (2) one may precipitate reactions in other areas. For example, the physical reactions you have before an important competition, such as a racing heart or "butterflies in the stomach," may increase your worry about whether you are prepared to play (a cognitive reaction) and then actually cause you to play poorly during the game (a behavioral reaction). Because stress reactions are often circular and self-perpetuating, you must learn how to interrupt the stress cycle. To help you become more aware of the different ways you react to stressors in your life, you may want to complete Exercise 11.2.

Exercise 11.2 Understanding Your Stress Response

Review the stressors that you listed in Exercise 11.1. Think about these different stressors and how you tend to respond. Indicate your typical responses in each area.

Physical Responses:

_____

_____

Cognitive Responses:

_____

_____

Emotional Responses:

_____

_____

Behavioral Responses:

_____

_____

Post-Game Review: Stress, Stressors, and Stress Reactions

Everyone experiences stress. Without it, your life would be boring, and you would be fairly unmotivated to improve or change in positive ways. Think about your athletic practices from a stress perspective: Often you are pushed, physically and mentally, beyond what you think are your capacities; in other words, you are stressed. This stressful situation, though, is often perceived as positive and challenging as opposed to negative and threatening. When you work through such challenges, you learn and grow, such as developing new skills; learning new plays; gaining strength, speed, and stamina; or becoming more focused and disciplined. Other situations, though, may overwhelm your current resources and be truly stressful.

Your goal should not be to remove all stress from your life; that would be impossible and unrealistic. Stress is important and can be functional, motivating you to change and adapt so that you develop and grow. Thus, you need to learn to distinguish between the situations that are truly overwhelming and stressful and those that are simply going to challenge you. Because you will likely experience many overwhelming situations in your life, it is important to be able to (a) identify those events that truly are stressful, (b) know how you generally react to them, and (c) learn effective ways to cope with the various stressors and reactions you have.

Preparation: Coping

Coping is the cognitive and behavioral efforts, regardless of outcome, that you use to handle the demands of and responses from the stress process (Lazarus and Folkman, 1984). There are two primary directions for individuals' coping efforts (Folkman, 1984):

1. *Emotion-focused coping*—you use cognitive and behavioral strategies to manage your thoughts and emotional responses to the stressor (over which you may have limited control) and perhaps change what the situation means to you.
2. *Problem-focused coping*—you use cognitive and behavioral strategies to actually change the situation (over which you have some control) that is causing the distress, by modifying the environment and your own behaviors. Often this approach involves problem solving and taking direct action.

Both emotion- and problem-focused coping are likely to be used during times of stress. If you perceive a stressor as unchangeable (or out of your control), then an emotion-focused approach may be best. If the situation can be changed, then a problem-focused approach becomes appropriate and likely to give you the most relief. As we discuss specific coping strategies later, keep in mind the importance of matching them to your perceptions of stressful situations.

Let's revisit our introductory story to illustrate emotion-focused and problem-focused coping. As you may remember, Alonzo was feeling overwhelmed by the many stressors in his life. At first, his coping response (a problem-focused strategy) was to stay up more hours to meet all his athletic and academic responsibilities; this approach did not work. After being kicked out of class, Alonzo sought help from a counselor at the school's counseling center. During their first meeting, the counselor and Alonzo talked about his frustrations and feelings of being overwhelmed (an emotion-focused approach). Alonzo was relieved to have someone listen to his concerns and support him. At their next meeting, the counselor discussed the different things Alonzo could do to change his current situation (a problem-focused approach). They determined that Alonzo was putting a lot of pressure on himself in relation to his athletic performances, and the counselor suggested that Alonzo might actually play better if he were less concerned about having to win the game and more focused on just playing and giving his all. Wisely, Alonzo took an active approach to coping with his problems. He sought assistance from outside sources and then dealt with the emotional distress and the specific problems he was facing. Other students, though, use avoidance as a way of coping. Instead of actively and directly addressing their stressors and their reactions, these students either try to completely avoid their problems or try to diminish their emotional distress through indirect means, such as eating, partying, or playing computer/video games. Although avoiding problems provides initial relief, it is not an effective long-term solution. Instead, take a more active approach to solving your problems and handling your emotional reactions. To help you become more aware of how you typically cope with stressors and stress reactions, we encourage you to complete Exercise 11.3.

Exercise 11.3   Your Coping Tendencies

Take a moment to review the stressors and stress responses you listed in Exercises 11.1 and 11.2. As you answer the following questions, keep them in mind.

1a. I tend to cope with academic or school-related stressors by:

_____

b. How effective are these approaches in dealing with academic stressors and your subsequent responses?

_____

_____

2a. I tend to cope with stressful relationships or interpersonal situations by:

_____

b. How effective are these approaches in dealing with interpersonal stressors and your subsequent responses?

_____

_____

3a. I tend to cope with financial stressors by:

_____

b. How effective are these approaches in dealing with financial stressors and your subsequent responses?

_____

_____

4a. I tend to cope with sport stressors by:

_____

b. How effective are these approaches in dealing with work stressors and your subsequent responses?

_____

_____

Performance: Coping Strategies

In this section, we discuss two major categories of coping strategies: behavioral approaches and cognitive approaches. With behavioral approaches, you are changing your behaviors in some way such that you receive some direct relief from the stressor or from your responses to it. For example, learning how to relax is one behavioral strategy. Cognitive approaches, however, emphasize changing the way you think about yourself, the event itself, or your environment. As you read over these, remember that you have to determine which ones will work for your specific stressors and stress reactions. In addition, always match your coping responses to the stress of the specific situation. A certain coping strategy that works in one situation may not work in another. Although presented separately, these strategies can be used concurrently.

Behavioral Strategies

Eliminating Stressors

One of the first things you should do when evaluating a stressful situation is determine if you can eliminate any of the stressors in your life. For example, Jacqui, a member of the golf team, came to her university's counseling center because of high levels of stress. She had not been eating or sleeping enough and looked haggard. She was behind in most of her coursework and had begun to notice declines in her athletic performance—mostly, she thought, because of a lack of focus in practice. When talking with a counselor, she admitted that the major stressor in her life was her current romantic relationship. Jacqui felt a lot of pressure from her partner, Chris (who was not a college student), to behave in ways that were not comfortable, such as drinking and partying. Their relationship was very intense—they experienced extreme feelings of love and anger almost every day. Although Jacqui knew she "loved" Chris, she was finding the emotional ups and downs to be too much. In addition, their arguments seemed to be getting more extreme and lasting later into each night. As a result, Jacqui was tense, irritable, and had little time to sleep or do her homework.

What could Jacqui do to cope with her stressor? Clearly, she had many options. She could learn relaxation strategies to help her sleep better at night, she could change her attitude toward the situation so she would be less upset by Chris's demands, or she could try to get Chris to come for counseling so they could discuss their problems together and jointly work toward a solution. Although Jacqui initially wanted Chris to join her in counseling, Chris' refusal was a turning point. As Jacqui continued in counseling by herself, she came to realize that another possibility was to end the relationship because it was the stressor; the negatives outweighed the benefits. Leaving the relationship would help her feel better about herself, get back on track academically, and improve her athletic performances. Although the breakup initially was draining, Jacqui soon felt happier, less stressed, and better able to focus on school and on her sport.

Why Athletes Don't Seek Help

Despite a wide range of student resources, such as counseling centers and academic advising, on most campuses, student-athletes may actually underuse these potentially beneficial services (Pinkerton, Hinz, and Barrow, 1989). There are many reasons why, including (Ferrante, Etzel, and Lantz, 1996):

1. Athletes are "high-visibility" students, which may make it difficult to blend in and privately receive services like nonathlete students.

2. Because of student-athletes' busy schedules, their free time to use services that are generally only open 8 A.M. to 5 P.M. is limited.

3. Many student-athletes believe, oftentimes incorrectly, that the athletic department will meet all their needs. Thus, student-athletes may not see the benefit of using general student services even though these services are not available in the athletic department.

4. Personal characteristics, such as being highly self-reliant, that are associated with athletic success may stop them from seeking help. Some student-athletes also believe that a good sport performance can solve all their problems and thus don't look for more direct and effective solutions.

5. Many student-athletes share the stereotype that anyone who sees a counselor or asks someone else for help is either "crazy" or weak. Perhaps because of this stereotype, student-athletes are reluctant to seek counseling. In fact, seeking help is an assertive (and brave) way of addressing a difficult situation.

If any of these barriers exist for you, then work through them and take advantage of the services on your campus. We have spoken with too many junior and senior student-athletes who have needlessly struggled for years because they did not know help was available or because they were reluctant to seek assistance out of the fear of looking "bad" to others. Your academic, athletic, and personal well-being is far too important to jeopardize by not getting help. The demands of being a student-athlete can be overwhelming, so you must be self-responsible to take advantage of the campus services. There is no shame in getting help to cope more effectively. Besides, in the end, seeking assistance can make you a more successful student *and* athlete.

Sometimes eliminating the stressor—whether dropping a class, ending a personal relationship, or even quitting your sport—is your best choice. If you do, first think through the potential ramifications of following through on your decision. Would the results of taking such an action be worse than the stressor? Better? How would you handle the fallout that resulted? Then, decide on a time frame and put your plan into action. If eliminating the stressor is not viable, then explore other strategies for coping. To give you an opportunity to practice the idea of eliminating stressors, you may want to complete Exercise 11.4.

Relaxation

Relaxation techniques can be another effective way to cope with a variety of stress reactions. For example, student-athletes who experience

Exercise 11.4   Eliminating Stressors from Your Life

Review your stressors in Exercise 11.1 (or any other you may be currently experiencing).

1. Which of your life stressor(s) might you eliminate? If you did not list one in Exercise 11.1, think of one now.

_____

2. For each stressor you listed in question 1, what are the potential ramifications associated with eliminating it and how you would feel as a result?

_____

3. For each stressor you listed in question 1, what are the benefits you might accrue from eliminating it?

_____

4. Based on your evaluation of the costs and benefits, what stressors will you actually plan to eliminate and, for each one, when will you implement your plan?

_____

headaches, muscle tension, insomnia, or concentration difficulties may benefit from learning to relax. Although there are a variety of relaxation techniques, we will introduce two: *deep breathing* and *progressive muscle relaxation*. First, by breathing slowly and deeply, you can calm yourself and reduce your muscle tension. This approach is easy and straightforward to implement (Davis, Eshelman, and McKay, 1995); it involves lying down, closing your eyes, and then putting one hand on your abdomen, right at the waistline, and the other hand on the center of your chest. As you inhale, notice which hand goes the highest. If the hand on your chest rises the most, then you are breathing from your chest, which may actually be associated with an increase in your level of tension. Try to breathe deeply so that your abdomen rises more than your chest. To practice deep breathing, try the following:

1. Find a quiet location and assume a comfortable position where your spine is straight (lay down on the floor with your knees bent and feet several inches apart may work).
2. Position your hands—one on your abdomen, the other in the center of your chest.
3. Inhale slowly and deeply through your nose and into your abdomen, with your chest rising less than your abdomen.
4. Exhale slowly through your mouth.
5. Practice these steps at least once a day for 5 to 10 minutes at a time.

Once you have mastered this technique, which may take a few weeks, you will no longer need to be lying down when doing it. Instead, you can breathe deeply wherever you are (e.g., on the foul line just about to shoot a game-winning free throw) to help yourself feel less tense.

Second, through progressive muscle relaxation (PMR), which involves systematically tensing and then releasing different muscle groups, you can achieve a deep state of physical relaxation. This approach is more involved than deep breathing, and we cannot adequately teach it to you in this chapter. However, if your stress reactions, particularly the physical ones, are strong and interfere with your athletic, academic, or personal performance, then you may want to pursue this form of relaxation training through your university's counseling center or with a sport psychologist through your athletic department. Professionals in these centers can help you to determine whether PMR or some other relaxation approach is appropriate and, if so, help you to learn it. They

can also help you to obtain or create relaxation CDs or podcasts to use at home.

To illustrate the use of relaxation, let's consider Hector (a tennis player) whose academic and athletic performances were negatively affected by his strong physical reactions. Since entering college, he had come to view classes and tournaments where he had to "perform" as being very stressful. When stressed, he experienced an increased tightness in his shoulders and arms that interfered with his swing, affected the way he struck the ball, and lost him points. In addition, he became nauseated before exams and had a hard time concentrating. Hector was concerned, so he consulted with his school's sport psychologist. Over the next two months, Hector worked with the sport psychologist to learn how to relax using PMR. As a result, Hector was able to reduce his muscle tension and better control his physical reactions, and thus improve his academic and athletic performances.

Before leaving this section, we want to differentiate between the active, solution-focused approaches to relaxation that we have described and activities that some may find relaxing. Sitting around doing nothing or spending time in sedentary activities, such as watching TV, is not an active approach to relaxation. Although these may be enjoyable ways to take a break, they generally don't solve your problems and may simply be a form of avoidance. The more active approaches we have discussed are skills you can use in situations across your life. When you apply these approaches, you are likely to notice decreases in physical tension and improved performances in the areas that are troublesome to you.

> "One way to break up any kind of tension is good deep breathing."
>
> BYRON NELSON
> *Professional Golfing Legend*

Develop and Use Support Networks

An important task for all students is developing new support networks while in college. Often, college marks a transition away from existing support network. Without social support, which can come from friends, family, teammates, coaches, etc., problems can be that much more difficult to handle. Here are some of the types of support the important people in our lives can provide:

- Emotional—they listen to and care about you when you are feeling distressed.
- Financial—they provide monetary resources when you are in need.
- Tangible—they offer their time and efforts to concretely help you accomplish tasks.
- Problem solving—they help you determine the best solutions for your problems.
- Technical—they help you learn new skills or information that may allow you to cope more effectively in the future.

Coping with Grief and Loss

All of us, at some point in time, will experience a significant loss and the feelings of grief that accompany it. Some of you already may have had such an experience. Loss is typically associated with the death of a loved one; however, we may grieve similarly with other types of losses, such as ending a relationship, the death of a pet, or even a career-ending injury. Loss is a universal experience; however, grieving is complex and unique for each one of us. Katz (2000) has summarized some of the factors that influence the focus, intensity, duration, and form of our grief:

- relationship to the deceased,
- the nature of the attachment to the lost one,
- the manner in which the loss occurred (e.g., expected vs. unexpected, natural vs. violent),
- social and cultural expectations for how loss is to be handled,
- the presence of other stressors in our lives, and
- how previous losses have been handled.

Thus, if you experience a loss, know that there is not a correct or right way to grieve. All of these factors will influence how you appraise (think about) the loss and that will affect how you respond emotionally, behaviorally, physically, and cognitively. Some people will experience strong feelings, such as sadness and anger, whereas others' emotional reactions may be more subdued or internal. Also, there is no set time in which a person should have finished grieving; some people will "get over" losses quickly, whereas others will take a long time to work through the experience. Because there is no "one-size-fits-all" prescription for dealing with grief and loss, individuals must cope in ways that are best for them. In many cases, the passage of time itself will be the best healer, although there is no specific point by which we should be "back to normal." However, if you have suffered a loss and are having difficulty coping, then your college or university's counseling center can be an excellent resource, and we encourage you to take advantage of this assistance, particularly if you are not getting what you need from your current support system.

So, whenever you are stressed, reach out to your support network. Ask friends, family, teammates, etc., for the assistance you need. Doing so can help you resolve or lessen the impact of your stressors. However, even with well-established and helpful support networks, there may be problems that require professional help, such as from a counselor at your school. These individuals can offer support and assistance when your family and friends cannot or will not. At times, a perspective from someone outside your usual support system can be useful, especially if family or friends might be part of the problem.

Cognitive Strategies

Changing Cognitions and Perceptions

As we discussed previously in the chapter, the way you think about a situation in relation to your current resources will determine whether or not you view it as stressful. Thus, an important thing you can do to cope is to reevaluate your perception of the situation and change it in a way that is more positive, or at least neutral. For example, you might initially consider a situation stressful when it could actually be viewed more positively, perhaps as a challenge for you to mature or improve. Or, you may have underestimated your ability to cope. By reevaluating, you can change your perception and thus reduce your experience of stress.

The cognitive approaches to coping involve two primary strategies: learning how to change your ways of thinking and mental visualization. We will describe these strategies in detail later, but first let's look at how the way you think about and perceive situations influence your ability to cope. Consider Marcy, a sophomore who had just transferred to her current university. On the tennis team, she played number 2 singles and number 3 doubles. About halfway through the season, though, her coach made some changes in the lineup. The changes meant that Marcy moved to number 5 singles and dropped completely out of doubles play. At first, she was upset by the change. She viewed it as unfair and shortsighted, and felt angry and resentful toward her coach. Marcy had not transferred to her new school to play at number 5! As a result, her effort in practices decreased, and she developed a bad attitude toward tennis. Later that week, Marcy was talking to a friend about what had happened. Her friend asked Marcy why she thought the coach had changed the playing order and what she was doing to earn back her spot. At first, Marcy had a hard time answering the question. What was *she* doing? It wasn't her fault! After some thought, though, she realized that the coach had made the change because the team had been playing inconsistently and had been only moderately successful in their matches. Marcy also realized that what she was doing was not going to help her regain her former position. By talking with her friend, Marcy took a new perspective about what had happened. She no longer viewed the event as unfair, arbitrary, and stressful. Instead, she recognized her role and how she could make things different if she wanted. She made a commitment to improve her play so she could move up to playing number 2 by the season's end.

Your cognitions (thoughts) and perceptions about yourself, other people, and situations are tremendously important. As illustrated by Marcy, you, through your perceptions of events and people, determine your reactions. For example, if you approach your athletic practices with thoughts such as "It's going to be a drag again today, we never do anything fun" or "I can't wait to get through practice so I can go home and chill," then you are likely to have negative behavioral reactions (e.g., decreased effort) and negative emotional reactions (e.g., anger, resentment) that interfere with your performance. If you approach practice with more positive thoughts, such as "I can't wait to get started, I want to keep working on some of my skills" or "For the next two hours, I'm focused and ready to go," then your reactions are likely to be more positive and performance-enhancing.

So, thinking negatively or irrationally can lead to distressing, even destructive consequences, such as missing a key shot on goal during a shoot-out or failing an exam. To cope better, you have to become aware of and then improve your less effective ways of thinking. Although this process of change sounds simple, learning to think more positively,

> "In a real sense, through our own self-talk, we are either in the construction business or wrecking business."
>
> DOROTHY CORKILLE BRIGGS
> *Author*

rationally, and optimistically about yourself, other people, and the events in your life takes time, effort, and focus. To help you begin the process of examining how you think about yourself and the world, you may want to complete Exercise 11.5.

Exercise 11.5 Changing Irrational/Negative Thinking

The way you think about yourself, others, and the events in your life determines your emotional and behavioral reactions. To cope more effectively and to be happier, you need to become aware of negative cognitive patterns and to learn how to think more positively. Here we have listed several commonly experienced student-athlete stressors. For each one, identify any negative thoughts you might have and then generate more positive, self-enhancing statements that you could substitute. To help you get started, we offer examples of negative and positive thinking for each event.

1. An important upcoming athletic competition that your team critically needs to win.

Negative, ineffective thinking

a. They've always beaten us in the past.

b. _____

c. _____

Positive, effective thinking

a. We've worked hard this year and are ready to play our best.

b. _____

c. _____

2. Failing an important academic assignment.

Negative, ineffective thinking

a. I'm so stupid; I should have done better.

b. _____

c. _____

Positive, effective thinking

a. I'm disappointed that I didn't do better. I'll work even harder now.

b. _____

c. _____

3. Breakup of a romantic relationship that was not wanted.

Negative, ineffective thinking

a. He/she was my whole life. I'll never be able to get over it or find someone else.

b. _____

c. _____

Positive, effective thinking

a. This hurts, but I can use the breakup to learn more about myself so my future relationships will be better.

b. _____

c. _____

In the space provided, list other recent stressors you have had to cope with. As you did for the previous items, identify your negative thoughts and then develop more positive, self-enhancing ones.

4. Stressor: _____

Negative, ineffective thinking

a. _____

b. _____

c. _____

Positive, effective thinking

a. _____

b. _____

c. _____

5. Stressor: _____

Negative, ineffective thinking

a. _____

b. _____

c. _____

Positive, effective thinking

a. _____

b. _____

c. _____

Visualization

Just like your thinking, your mental images should be positive and success-oriented. Mental visualization is the processing of seeing, in your mind's eye, yourself performing some behavior or engaging in some activity, and is a strategy athletes use to improve their performances. Mental visualization also can help you cope with your stressors and stress reactions.

First, visualization can help you relax. By seeing yourself in relaxing scenes, you may be able to reduce the tension, worry, and/or distress you are experiencing. For example, Juanita experienced strong physical stress reactions. She often experienced tension in her neck and shoulders that left her feeling tired and irritable. Although she tried relaxation strategies, she could not stop worrying about all the things she had to do. When she used visualization, though, she was able to achieve the level of relaxation she desired. Instead of worrying about what she had to do, she occupied her mind with images of relaxing scenes.

Second, visualization is a way to learn and mentally practice behaviors, such as different coping responses, before you implement them. Visualization allows you to simulate an experience, and thus prepares your mind and body for the actual situation. In visualization, you can try out a variety of behaviors without the risks you would face if you were actually implementing them. For example, Ben experienced stress in two important areas of his life—athletics and academics. He had the tendency to become quite stressed when he took tests and when he had to shoot free throws. As a result, his performances in both areas were far below his potential. To cope with this problem, Ben began to use visualization. For the test situations, he imagined himself being calm and relaxed as he entered the classroom. When he received the exam, he saw himself answering the questions confidently and correctly. For basketball, he saw himself at the free-throw line feeling relaxed, confident, and ready to shoot. He was focused only on the ball and basket, not the fans or other players. He saw himself bounce the ball three times, get set, and then release his shot toward the basket. He also practiced the way he would respond if he missed the first free throw and had to make the second one to tie the game. Basically, he visualized situations in which he struggled but then managed to succeed. This approach helped to ensure that he would be able to persevere and overcome momentary problems.

For many student-athletes, mental visualization is an excellent way to lower stress levels, reduce physical tension, learn new skills, and improve levels of physical and mental performance. For others, though, visualization is not as helpful because they have a hard time producing clear and compelling mental images. Thus, you should only use visualization if it is comfortable and effective for you. If you

© Ken Inness, 2009 / Used under license from Shutterstock.com

do decide to use it, then there are a few important points to remember:

- Do your visualization while in a relaxed state.
- Always try to visualize positive outcomes and, whenever possible, practice overcoming setbacks or obstacles as well.
- Use both internal (first-person, like you were performing the task) and external (third-person, like watching yourself on film) perspectives as needed to promote learning and confidence.
- Incorporate as many of your senses, such as hearing or touch, as possible into your images to make them vivid and real.
- Do not use visualization as a substitute for real-life practice; it's only one of your preparatory routines.

Post-Game Review

As a student-athlete, you face the general stressors that all college students experience as well as the unique demands of being a high-level sport performer. Thus, it is crucial to develop effective coping strategies to help you handle overwhelming situations and strong stress reactions. It is not enough, though, just to have knowledge about the different ways to cope. You have to be self-responsible and actually implement your strategies. Take an active approach to coping with the events in your life. Don't shy away from or avoid life stressors. We do not believe in the old adage that what does not kill you only makes you stronger, but stressful situations, if managed appropriately, can make you a better student and athlete. Although your past attempts to manage life stressors and stress reactions may have been only moderately successful, practice can bring higher levels of confidence in your ability to cope. To help you begin to implement more effective ways to cope with your life stressors and stress reactions, you may want to complete Exercise 11.6. In doing so, keep in mind your responses to Exercise 11.3, where you evaluated your current ways of coping with different life situations. From that exercise, you may have found that you cope better with certain circumstances than with others. Now that you have been introduced to new strategies and skills, consider how you might now cope more effectively with stressors in the various areas of your life.

Thinking Critically about Stress and Coping

1. Summarize what you now know about stress and coping based on the information presented in this chapter.

_____

_____

_____

Exercise 11.6   New Coping Strategies

For the stressor "Flunking a Course" we have provided examples of ways to cope. In the space below that, list some of your current stressors and different ways you might cope with each one.

Stressors

1. Flunking a course

Ways to Cope

Take a study skills course
Tutoring
Form a study group or study with a friend
Talk with the instructor
Start studying a week in advance
Make a budget for yourself
Work study program

2. _____

3. _____

4. _____

5. _____

2. What additional questions do you have about these topics and how to use the skills introduced in this chapter?

_____
_____
_____

3. What conclusions can you draw about this topic and how it might help you be a more effective and successful student and athlete?

_____
_____
_____

Achieve IT! Setting a Coping-with-Stress Goal

1. Based on your self-assessment and your responses to Thinking Critically, select a goal in relationship to improving how you cope with the stressors in your life that you would like to achieve this term.

2. Now identify three short-term goals that will help you reach your goal this term.

3. For the short-term goals, identify the attainment strategies you will need to reach them.

4. List any obstacles you might face in trying to reach these goals and identify your plan for overcoming each one.

Don't forget to make your goal visible and tell others about them, so they can keep you accountable regarding what you want to achieve.

Chapter 11 Review Questions

1. _____ are the life events that cause you to adapt or change.

   a. Stress reactions
   b. Stress processes
   c. Stressors
   d. None of the above

2. How you think about or perceive a life event has a minimal effect on your experience of stress. (True or False)

3. Athletes may not seek help for the stress in their lives because:

   a. They often think they can handle things on their own.
   b. They often are visible on college campuses and thus would not have as much privacy in seeking help.
   c. The counselors at most counseling centers would not understand the problems of student-athletes.
   d. A and B.
   e. All of the above.

4. Your reactions (emotional and behavioral consequences) are caused primarily by

   a. The stressors in your life.
   b. How you think about or appraise the stressors in your life.
   c. Adrenaline and noradrenaline.
   d. All of the above.

5. When using mental visualization, you should

   a. Use relaxation in conjunction.
   b. Incorporate as many senses as possible.
   c. Practice overcoming obstacles.
   d. A and B.
   e. All of the above.

6. Trying to eliminate stressors in your life may be a useful approach to coping. (True or False)

7. Emotion-focused coping would be most appropriate for which of the following situations?

   a. Your boyfriend/girlfriend has just broken up with you.
   b. Your schedule was just scrapped and you now have to register again for classes.
   c. You have a flat tire on the side of the highway.
   d. Your parents are coming for the weekend and you have two parties to attend.

8. There is a set of stages that all people will go through when they grieve a loss of some type. (True or False)

9. Friends and family can provide which of the following types of social support?

   a. Emotional.
   b. Physical.
   c. Tangible.
   d. A and C.
   e. All of the above.

10. Bill was stressed by losing his starting position on the team. That night, he went out driving his car and was pulled over for doing 100 in a 60 mph zone. Bill's response to stress might be categorized as:

    a. Crazy.
    b. Physical.
    c. Behavioral.
    d. Problem-focused.

Chapter 12 | Choosing a Major and a Career
Succeeding in Life and Relationships

Game Plan:

In this chapter, you will learn:

- How to schedule classes effectively and efficiently

- About balancing the demands of academics, athletics, and other life responsibilities

- What your interests, abilities, values, and personality style are and how they relate to choosing a major and a career

- The location of career resources on college and university campuses and the services they offer

- The basics of writing cover letters and interviewing

© John Lumb, 2009 / Used under license from Shutterstock.com

"Sport is the only profession I know that when you retire, you have to go to work."

EARL "THE PEARL" MONROE
Former NBA All-Star

Self-Assessment—Perceive It!

Read the following statements and place a checkmark next to each one you generally do. For you to change and develop new and effective academic, athletic, and personal strategies, you must be accurate in your self-perception. So, be honest in how you answer each question.

1. I have spoken with at least one person who currently works in a career related to my major about his/her job. _____

2. I know the educational requirements of my major. _____

3. I am pursuing a major that will allow me to work in the career area I want. _____

4. I have met with my academic advisor at least once this term to discuss my progress and my academic and career plans. _____

5. I have investigated the educational requirements, employment opportunities, and work conditions for people with my career interests. _____

6. I have a clear time frame for completing my bachelor's degree. _____

7. I take part in extracurricular activities (community service, campus clubs and organizations, residence hall leadership) that will enhance my future job prospects. _____

8. I am aware of what interests me in school and in life. _____

9. I know what my best skills are and can identify ways to apply them in my career. _____

10. I know what is important to me in a career, for instance, working with people or making a lot of money. _____

11. I know how to write an organized and literate cover letter for my resume. _____

12. I have completed a job interview. _____

Take a moment to review your responses. How many items did you check? Each one you checked represents a current strength. Now consider the items you did not check. These represent areas where focus and growth are needed. Now, to summarize your self-perception, complete the following statements:

1. My areas of strength are:

_____

2. The areas I need to improve are:

_____

As you read this chapter and participate in your classes, keep your strengths and areas of improvement in mind. At the end of the chapter, you will have the chance to set a goal related to these areas. Achieving these goals will help you become a more effective student and athlete.

Introduction

*O*ne day in the spring term of his senior year, Miguel, a senior baseball player, dropped in to chat with his academic advisor. During their conversation, Miguel's advisor asked him what his future plans were. After all, he was graduating in a few weeks, and his career search should have been well under way, especially since he was not drafted and had no current plans to play professionally. When Miguel's advisor asked if he wanted some help with his resume, Miguel replied that he hadn't given much thought about a resume. He said he didn't have anything to put on one, adding that he had never had a job, so there wasn't anything for him to describe on a resume.

His advisor was somewhat disappointed that Miguel, who had spent the past five years in school playing major college baseball and going to class, believed that he had gained no marketable experience during that time. After all, Miguel had been a starter and had played a lot during his career. There was no question that he possessed great persistence, dedication, mental preparation, and physical toughness, which was shown by his overcoming a severe injury as a sophomore. He was elected team captain as a junior and a senior, so he also had *strong communication and leadership skills, among other outstanding charac-teristics. His biggest challenge was figuring out how to apply these skills and abil-ities. Fortunately, after speaking with his advisor, Miguel realized that he had a lot to offer prospective employers and started taking steps to demonstrate it.*

The issue for Miguel, like many student-athletes, was not that he lacked experience and skills, but rather that he *thought* he had none that would be relevant in a future job/career. As we discussed in Chapter 1, recognizing the *transferability* of your skills is one of the most important tasks you face in college. It is important to understand how the skills you acquire in one area of your life, such as athletics, can be applied to other areas, such as your career. In this chapter, we discuss the processes of choosing a major and a career and the relationship be-tween them. We explore the influence of your interests, values, skills, and personality in choosing among majors and careers and outline the stages of the career development process. We also discuss the concept of transferable skills and provide sources of career information. We begin, however, by discussing the importance of identifying your aca-demic and career goals and choosing a major and a career.

Preparation: Selecting a Major and a Career

The reasons students enter college are quite varied. Some attend because of parental expectations or because they need a degree to pursue their career of choice. Others enroll because of friendships or because they aren't sure what else to do. Although these reasons apply to student-athletes as well, they also are recruited, or choose to go to college as a means of entering the professional ranks and playing at the "next level." For example, Miguel chose to attend college because he was recruited to play baseball. If he had not been recruited, then he might not have gone to college at all. No matter why you entered college, at some point you will need to choose a major. As a student-athlete, you must do so not only to satisfy the requirements of your col-lege but to be eligible to compete in your sport. Choosing a major is also important because your major provides the structure for your academic program and determines what classes you may take.

> "What I put into my basketball is what I get out of it."
>
> GRANT HILL
> *NBA All-Star*

Before discussing how to select a major, we first need to clarify the relationship between majors and careers. Many students believe that choosing a major is the same as choosing a career. Although this may *seem* perfectly sensible, it is not always true. In some instances, you *do* need to major in a specific area in order to work in that field, such as nursing and engineering. Without the specific training provided within these majors, it would be difficult to pursue and obtain one of these careers. In contrast, if you are interested in a career in business or law, then you can pursue a number of different undergraduate majors, such as political science, history, psychology, and communication.

Before you decide on a major, give some serious thought to what you want to be doing 5 to 10 years from now. For example, T.J. was an outstanding football player in college and was drafted by a professional team. He had never been a serious student, but he had a promising career ahead doing what he had always planned to do: play football. Unfortunately, T.J., who was recently married and expecting a child, suffered a career-ending knee injury shortly after he signed his contract and never played in a game as a pro. Suddenly, he had to think about what he wanted to do with his life and how he could support his family. If you have certain career goals in mind, then you can begin to participate in activities that will increase the chances of your reaching those goals. Having career goals in mind does not mean that you have to make a firm commitment at this point. Many students enter college not knowing what they want to do careerwise; others think they know, and later change their minds. In fact, there are many career counselors who recommend taking your freshman year to get your bearings in college before declaring a major. It is also quite common for students to change their majors more than once in college; student-athletes are no exception (although eligibility and satisfactory progress requirements are more stringent, so you have to work closely with your athletic academic advisor to ensure that you are not putting yourself at risk in terms of eligibility).

If you enter college knowing what you want in a major and career, then start taking actions that will help you achieve your goals. You can, for example, pursue extracurricular activities that help you develop the skills, knowledge, and abilities necessary for your chosen career. Many skills are valuable in any career: managing time effectively, following through on tasks and assignments, communicating effectively orally and in writing, and being accountable for your actions. Let your long-term career goals guide your current actions, such as choosing a major that will allow you to enter the career of your choice. Be an active participant in the career decision-making process; it's your life, so be involved in the planning of it. In contrast to T.J., Juliana, a field hockey player who wanted to be a youth counselor, participated in a number of paid and volunteer activities throughout her time in college: speaking to children in elementary schools, working as a day camp counselor in the summer, and tutoring high school students. As a student-athlete, she had multiple opportunities for community service and participated whenever it did not conflict with her school and sport schedule. All these experiences helped to prepare her for the career she wanted and gave her a competitive advantage in finding the job she wanted. To begin identifying your career goals, you may want to complete Exercise 12.1.

Preparation: Why Is Choosing a Major Important?

A career goal can guide the selection of a major, which in turn can be a long-term goal in and of itself. As we discussed in Chapter 7 on goal setting, long-term goals are important during any extended activity, such as attending college or competing in athletics. A major can help you in the following areas:

Exercise 12.1 Identifying Your Career Goals

A. Find a place where you will not be distracted, and then take a moment to think about what you want to be doing in your career five years from now, and what your typical work day will be like. Use the following questions to guide you through this process.

1. On a typical day, what do you do in the morning before going to work?

2. Describe the place where you work.

3. Describe what you do at your work. How do you spend a typical day?

4. In what area of the country do you live? Why?

5. Describe where you live (apartment, house)?

6. Who is living with you?

7. What type of education/training did you need to get this job?

8. How do you dress for your job?

9. How much do you get paid for your job?

10. Can you imagine doing this job for 10 more years?

B. From this exercise, the job/career I believe I will have in five years is:

_____

_____

This "looking ahead five years" exercise is a basic goal-setting tool used by career counselors and can help you clarify some of your major life goals.

Focus. A major provides a focus for your studies and can make your classes more meaningful, relevant, and coherent. When you have a major, you essentially have an academic game plan, a sense of how all your classes fit together. Your major provides the structure for your degree program by identifying the classes you are required to take for graduation and the classes you can select from for your degree program. A major can also provide a unifying theme for classes that might appear at first glance to be a confusing mix of unrelated areas. Student-athletes who have declared a major usually have clear goals and are ready to move forward.

Connection. A major provides you with a sense of identity (e.g., "I'm a biology major") and a connection to other students and faculty specifically and to your college or university in general. Many campus activities and clubs are organized according to major (e.g., Psi Chi for Psychology). Your major is your ticket to engage in these valuable experiences.

Motivation. Four or five years is a long time to spend taking classes, and almost certainly there will be times when you wonder whether it is worth it. Trust us, it is! But when those times occur, having a major that is meaningful and enjoyable will remind you why you are in college and help you remain motivated and continue to put forth the necessary effort in your classes so you can be successful.

Eligibility. As a student-athlete you need a major in order to maintain your athletic eligibility after a certain period of time in school. In most cases, you will need to declare a major by the beginning of your fifth semester (or seventh quarter). Regardless of your year in school when you declare a major, always talk with your athletic department academic advisor so they can guide you in this process. The NCAA (and most athletic conferences) has very strict rules about making normal and steady progress toward a degree, so you do not want to have any problems in this area and jeopardize your eligibility.

Four-Year Career Plan

Here we offer a basic plan for how you can get the most out of your four years (and summers!) in college. There may be some variability depending on your major and school, but this plan may serve you well in providing a framework for what you want to accomplish each year you are in school.

I. **Freshman Year—"Self-Inquiry and Career Awareness"**
- Enroll in core courses
- Even if you choose a major, take courses that would satisfy general college/university electives
- Become involved in clubs, organizations, and other activities as time allows
- Get to know faculty, counselors, and administrators outside of the athletic department
- Meet new people and get feedback on your interpersonal style
- Consider enrolling in a career planning course or seminar/workshop
- Take interest and personality inventories through your school's career or counseling center
- If you have not already chosen a major, then begin exploring possible career choices (and majors) with a career counselor
- Look at examples of resumes so you can prepare for a summer job search

Summer
- Get a job or internship in a career area that interests you or doing something that might be fun and adventurous (e.g., be a white water raft guide, work as a counselor at a residential wilderness camp, tutor children in economically disadvantaged areas)
- Based on your work experiences, assess your interpersonal skills and get feedback from your employer
- If you have to stay on-campus and take classes during the summer, then consider taking a career planning course

II. **Sophomore Year—"Assessment and Exploration"**
- Enroll in a career planning course/seminar/workshop if you haven't already done so
- Complete self-assessment: values, skills, interests, and goals
- Research specific careers and required qualifications
- Investigate the employment outlook for your options
- Continue to be active in extracurricular activities and to develop interpersonal skills
- Attend career days and career seminars
- Check into internships for summer and your junior year
- Discuss career questions with an academic advisor or career counselor

Summer
- Get a job or internship in an area related to your career interests
- Continue to develop interpersonal skills and get feedback
- Develop good work ethic, on and off the field

III. Junior Year—"Evaluating Career Options"
- Review your academic plan as it relates to career options with an academic advisor
- Take elective courses that will make you more competitive for the world of work
- Get a part-time job or internship in a related field, if possible
- If you still are undecided, research career options in relation to your interests, skills, values, and goals
- Job shadow or conduct interviews with professionals in careers that interest you to gain information and network
- Make decisions about getting a job after graduation or going to graduate or professional school
- Begin studying for the Graduate Record Examination (GRE) or other graduate or professional school examinations (e.g., GMAT, MCAT, LSAT) and researching potential schools
- Complete a resume if you have not already done so and put it on file in your career center
- Attend career fairs and job search seminars
- Continue to seek advice from faculty, advisors, counselors, and significant others about your progress, your preparation, your career choice, etc.
- Begin building a professional wardrobe

Summer
- Compile self-evaluations from previous jobs and make a list of your qualifications
- Get a job/internship in chosen field to test interests
- Take GRE or other exams

IV. Senior Year—"Realization: Making Decisions"
- Complete course requirements for major
- Discuss career choice with advisor or career counselor as needed
- Maintain contact with faculty and administrators for future letters of recommendation
- Continue relevant work experience
- Join professional organizations in your field
- Schedule a mock interview in your career center to practice your interviewing skills
- Research specific information about employers prior to actual interviews
- Take the GRE, GMAT, MCAT, LSAT, or other standardized exam (if you have not already) as part of the admission requirements for graduate or professional school
- Continue researching and/or apply to graduate or professional schools
- Attend career fairs and job search seminars
- Update resume; have a career counselor review resume; load resume into career services database if available
- Continue contact with your network so they can give you leads on jobs
- Participate in on- and off-campus interviews
- Follow up on job vacancy announcements
- Send resumes and inquiry letters to target employers
- Evaluate career employment options and make final decisions

Summer
- Begin your full-time employment! Good luck and have fun!

Students in Flux: Undecided Majors

Some students are undecided about their majors when they enter school and do not select one until their sophomore or junior year. Others will come in with a major but change it several times while in school. For student-athletes, this approach can cause difficulties because of regulations, such as the "40–60–80 percent" rule that requires a certain percentages of courses be completed toward a major for eligibility purposes. The rules are too complex to discuss here—see your academic advisor in athletics for details—but they do have a bearing on the issue of selecting a major, making it even more important to find something you will enjoy.

So what can you do if you are undecided? One common strategy is to take general academic courses, which has two benefits:

Exposure. Taking general academic courses exposes you to a variety of academic disciplines, such as psychology, geography, sociology, and anthropology. Typically, introductory classes provide an overview of the discipline and acquaint you with research that faculty on your campus may be doing. In addition, getting to know your instructors can give you a greater understanding of the field and provide you with valuable references for future employment or for graduate school.

Progress. Most universities have course requirements that all students must complete regardless of their major. One purpose of these requirements is to broaden the scope of your education. Another purpose is to allow you to make satisfactory academic progress as you explore different academic disciplines. For example, you might be required to take a class in the arts, even though you plan to major in biology. Those student-athletes who begin their academic and athletic careers at a junior college, in essence, get to complete these same general education requirements or core courses prior to transferring to a four-year university.

No two students will approach choosing a major and a career in exactly the same way, because no two students are identical. For some, the choice is relatively simple and clear. Sherry, a field hockey player, had always been interested in medicine. Her mother was a physician and her father a biomedical researcher, so she had a good sense of what was involved in a career in medicine. For her, the decision to major in biology was sensible and necessary to achieve her goal of entering medical school and becoming a physician. For other students, the process is more difficult. Kaylie, for example, was a student-athlete who entered college knowing that she wanted to be a counselor and thinking she had to major in psychology to become one. After taking a couple of psychology classes, she quickly saw that psychology was not the major for her, although she still wanted to work with adolescents. Kaylie's task was one of identifying an alternative path toward the same goal. Kaylie's advisor helped her to find a much better match. Majoring in human development and family studies gave her the academic preparation she was looking for so she could become a counselor.

The first two years of college are a time of transition, exploration, and discovery for nearly all students, especially student-athletes. Use this time to figure out what you want to do with your life and try to remain open to the diverse people, classes, and experiences you will encounter.

> **"In order to excel, you must be completely dedicated to your chosen sport."**
>
> WILLIE MAYS
> *Major League Baseball Hall of Famer*

Problems in Choosing a Major

So why do so many students remain undecided or later change their majors? There are a number of reasons, but some of the more common ones are internal and external pressures; difficulty organizing and applying self-knowledge; and lack of career-specific information, world-of-work information, and long-term career goals.

Pressure. Pressure to choose a certain major can lead to poor decisions. Parents, friends, coaches, and advisors are all potential sources of such pressure. Colleges, by virtue of their academic requirements, may reduce the number of major options available to students. Students may even pressure themselves to choose a particular major. Kaylie, our aspiring counselor, entered college believing that she had to major in psychology in order to fulfill her career goal. However, if she had remained in psychology, she would have had a difficult time. Fortunately, she was able to overcome her internal pressure and make a better choice for herself.

Lack of Self-Knowledge. Students often lack self-knowledge or have a difficult time organizing it to help them identify and choose a suitable major or career path. For example, what are your interests, values, transferable skills, and personality style, and how do they fit with different careers or work environments? How do these personal characteristics relate to being successful in different careers? Unfortunately, there is often a disconnect between who the student is (e.g., their abilities, values, interests) and careers that would be a good match for them.

Lack of Career Information. Students' inability to choose a major also is influenced by a lack of sufficient information about what it is like to be a member of the working world, the breadth of career options that exist, and what people actually do in specific careers. These deficits exist because student-athletes may not have worked in a job (instead spending the majority of their free time practicing and competing in their sport), may have been exposed to only a few different careers (e.g., those held by their parents or other adults in their lives), and may have obtained much of their career information from distorted sources (e.g., from watching TV, or seeing different careers displayed in movies).

In the sections that follow, we will provide you with the opportunity to increase your self-knowledge and then learn more about the world of work and different careers that might fit with your personality and ability.

Performance: A Model of Career Development

Career development includes four different stages (Sharf, 2005):

1. Self-Assessment,
2. Career Research,
3. Experiential Learning,
4. Career Implementation.

Although we will focus on the first two steps in this chapter, we also will provide information on the last two stages—experiential learning and self-marketing/career implementation—that will help you to make your decision and act on it (Figure 12.1).

Self-Assessment: What Do You Need from Work?

In this stage, you explore your interests, transferable skills and abilities, values, and personality style to learn more about them as they relate to selecting a major and a career. The purpose of career counseling is to help you make the best match between your attributes, such as skills and values, and those of the work environment. In your sport, it is important to find the position or event that best suits your talents. In work, it is no different. You want to find the occupation and work setting that fit you best so you can maximize your chances of career success and satisfaction. The better the fit, the more satisfied you will be, and the longer and better you are likely to work in your chosen career. A poor fit creates unhappy workers and employers. The best way to optimize the fit is to identify and articulate what you *do* well (transferable skills

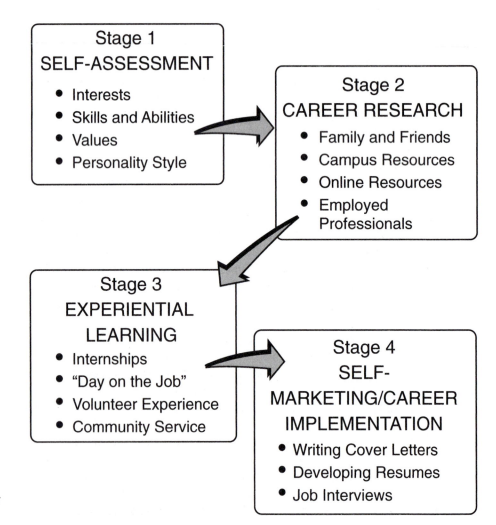

Figure 12.1 The Path to Success: A Four-Stage Model of Career Development

and abilities), what you *like* to do (interests), what is *important* to you (values), and how you typically *interact* with others and with the environment (personality style). Optimizing the fit between you and your career does not mean you need to—nor can you, in all likelihood—use all your important skills and abilities, express all your values, or fulfill all your interests in your work. You also can do so avocationally, that is, in your social and personal lives.

Psychological Types. One way to examine the issue of the fit between you and the work environment is through a system of psychological types developed by psychologist John Holland (Holland, 1994). He used this system to describe individuals' and work environments personalities to determine how well they matched. Consider his six types, which differ largely in their relative emphases on people, data, and things.

- **Realistic.** The Realistic type places the greatest emphasis on working with objects. Keywords describing this type are *athletic, physical, independent, stable, honest,* and *practical,* so it is not surprising that athletes often have this type as part of their personality. Realistic types like to work with their hands and with machinery, tools, and equipment. They are active in life and in problem solving. Examples of Realistic occupations include *engineer, airplane pilot, mechanic, forester,* and *construction worker.*
- **Investigative.** The Investigative type places the greatest emphasis on working with data and ideas. Keywords describing this type are *inquisitive, cautious, focused, observant,* and *logical.* Investigative types may appear reserved or introverted. They are typically strong in mathematics and the sciences and enjoy intellectual pursuits and solving problems by thinking them through. Investigative occupations include *chemist, pharmacist, physician,* and *sociologist.*
- **Artistic.** The Artistic type may emphasize working with ideas or objects, depending on the person's preferred mode of expression. Keywords describing this type are *expressive, imaginative, nonconforming, original,* and *inventive.* Artistic types focus on beauty, form, sound, color, and aesthetics and may at times seem to be unorganized or unfocused. They often have artistic abilities and enjoy solving problems through creating and viewing situations in novel ways. Examples of Artistic occupations are *architect, clothing designer, writer, musician, actor, painter,* and *photographer.*
- **Social.** Not surprisingly, the Social type places the greatest emphasis on working with people. Many athletes are primarily Social types. Keywords describing this type are *cooperative, friendly, responsible, understanding, supportive,* and *tactful.* They enjoy relationships, like to work with people individually or in groups, and often assume roles involving teaching and leadership. They typically have good social skills but may lack scientific or mechanical interests and abilities. They approach solving problems by involving others. Among the Social occupations, examples include *athletic trainer, coach, professional athlete, clinical psychologist, teacher, physical therapist,* and *social worker.*

- **Enterprising.** The Enterprising type also places the greatest emphasis on working with people, although differently than Social types. Keywords describing this type are *persuasive, engaging, outgoing, self-confident, ambitious, adventurous,* and *enthusiastic.* Enterprising types like to work with people by managing, selling, directing, and achieving. They enjoy status, power, and money, and solve problems by taking risks and trying new things. Enterprising occupations include *manager, business owner, lawyer, sales representative,* and *broadcaster.*
- **Conventional.** The Conventional type blends emphasis on working with objects, data, and people. Keywords describing Conventional types are *precise, practical, careful, reliable, persistent,* and *efficient.* Conventional types like to work in environments where order and control are valued, and they generally possess clerical, arithmetic, and organizational skills. They excel with details and solve problems by following rules and established procedures. Examples of this type include *accountant, building inspector, financial analyst, clerical worker,* and *bookkeeper.*

Although presented independently, the six types are related to one another. The six types share common features, but have them to different degrees. In fact, most people are not purely one type, such as Social or Artistic, but are best described by a combination of two or three of these types. Social and Enterprising qualities are often found in the same person, as are Realistic and Investigative features. It's much less likely that you would see a person with both Conventional and Artistic features. It is difficult to be creative and original (artistic), and at the same time, cautious and guided by standard rules and procedures (conventional).

Areas of Self-Assessment

We now focus on the primary areas where self-assessment occurs—interests, skills, values, and personality style—and offer some assessments that you can use to increase your self-knowledge and make a better career choice.

Interests. The first assessment area concerns what you like and dislike in activities, work situations, academics, and people, and is the foundation upon which the other assessment areas are built. The *Self-Directed Search* (SDS; Holland, 1994) is a popular, easy-to-use questionnaire (available on the Internet and as a paper-and-pencil booklet) that many students find helpful in identifying their interests. The SDS categorizes interests and personality in terms of the six types that we discussed earlier. You can complete the SDS as part of the course you are taking now or on your own at your school's counseling or career center. The next step is to compare your code type (e.g., Social-Enterprising; Realistic-Investigative) to work environments that have been categorized using the same system. *The Occupations Finder* (Holland, 1994) provides this list of work environments and can be used to help you generate a list of career options that could work well for you. If you complete the SDS, then you may wish to compare these results with your results from Exercise 12.3.

"Nobody can make you feel inferior without your consent."

ELEANOR ROOSEVELT
Former First Lady

Another approach to self-assessment is to take a more formal test, such as the *Strong Interest Inventory* (SII, 2005). The SII provides you with information about your level of interest across a wide variety of occupations. Using the Holland types we discussed earlier, the SII is usually completed on a computer and is available at most college counseling or career centers. The SII assesses your interest in broad psychological types as well as in specific jobs, and provides information about the importance to you of participating in general categories of life activities, such as helping others through teaching, playing music, or participating in religious activities. You will need to complete one or both of these inventories for the Career Search project (Exercise 12.7) that is discussed later in this chapter. If you take a career exploration class, and we recommend that you do if you have the opportunity, then you will likely take the SII as part of the course requirements.

Transferable Skills and Abilities. The second assessment concerns what you do well and where you can apply your skills. As a student-athlete, you probably already have some knowledge about the skills you use to succeed athletically, but it may be harder to see how those skills can be applied in other areas. Here your task has two components: (1) identifying your transferable life skills and (2) identifying your work-specific abilities. To identify your transferable, or depend-

Exercise 12.2   Identifying Your Transferable Skills

Identify three significant positive experiences or successes you have had within the past three years that have been from different areas of your life. The experiences you choose should be ones in which you played a significant role in making the positive outcome occur. For example, you may have earned an "A" in a difficult class, which involved reading and writing skills, time management, and persistence. Or, perhaps you helped your team win a championship using communication skills, physical strength, and leadership skills.

1. Briefly describe the experiences in the space below.

   Experience 1:

   _____

   Experience 2:

   _____

   Experience 3:

   _____

2. List the skills you used to make those experiences happen.

   Experience 1 Skills:

   _____

   Experience 2 Skills:

   _____

   Experience 3 Skills:

   _____

3. As you look at the various skills you listed, which ones are common to more than one experience?

   _____

4. How could these skills be applied to other areas, such as work?

   _____

   _____

   _____

able, life skills, you will want to consider information from a number of sources. Jerald Forster has developed a process to help you with this assessment (Haldane and Forster, 1988). Although we will not go through the entire process here, Exercise 12.2 will help you to identify some of your transferable skills by looking at your role in creating significant positive experiences you have had. You will also have an opportunity to consider how your skills could be applied to areas in which you might be interested in working. If your aspirations include pursuing your sport professionally, then this should be easy, but how can these same skills apply to other areas?

To illustrate the idea of transferable skills, let's return to Miguel, the senior baseball player in our opening story. What are some of the transferable skills he might have developed over the years and how might he apply them in the world of work? First, as a student-athlete, Miguel developed physical strength, coordination, agility, and stamina. Although not many occupations pursued by college-educated individuals emphasize these attributes, they are still assets in areas such as law enforcement, fire protection, and physical therapy. Miguel's experience as a student-athlete and team captain helped develop his skills as a communicator and leader. He also learned how to work with others as part of a team and how to persist through difficult times in rehabilitating his injury. Certainly these attributes are highly valued in virtually every career.

Although Miguel had never held a "real" job, he did have a lot of unpaid work experience and had performed a great deal of community service during his high school and college years. Growing up, Miguel had spent a lot of time helping with the remodeling of his family's house. He had learned how to read blueprints, was good at using his hands to build things, and even did some of the design work. He enjoyed these activities. Such skills could easily be transferable to an occupation such as building construction. In college, Miguel devoted much of his free time to volunteering at a community youth center, where he worked with disadvantaged children, teaching them various sports and life skills. As a volunteer, he used teaching and supervisory skills—skills that can be applied in a number of settings. As you can see, Miguel had a lot of skills and experience, despite never having held a formal job; his skills just needed to be uncovered and identified.

It is not always easy to identify your transferable skills. If you had difficulty identifying your transferable skills on your own, then you may wish to ask for help from a trusted friend, a parent, or someone else who knows you well. In Exercise 12.3, we extend the concept of transferable skills into the realm of work. In this exercise, you have an opportunity to identify your abilities specifically as they relate to work.

Values. As we suggested in Chapter 1, values refer to the principles or standards that are most important in determining how you choose to live your life, providing you with meaning and purpose in what you do. For example, an important value for some people would be "spending time with family." For someone to whom this is important, certain career choices would not be suitable. Careers requiring a lot of time away from family would likely cause dissatisfaction. "Flexibility" is another example of a value. A highly structured work environment would probably be uncomfortable for a person to whom this value is important. You can see that values are quite different from interests and abilities, but must be considered when you are making career choices.

In many cases, your interests, skills, and values will fit nicely together. For example, Holli, a goalkeeper on the soccer team, is interested in the sciences, especially biology. She has good mathematical skills and places

---

Exercise 12.3   Identifying Your Work Abilities

1. Look over the following six clusters of terms or phrases that describe various work abilities. Circle the ones that describe terms that describe what you do well.

Cluster 1:
Realistic Skills

Assemble things

Use tools
Repair things

Work with your hands

Strength/stamina

Cluster 3:
Artistic Skills

Create

Draw/paint

Enjoy music

Write

Work independently

Imagine

Cluster 2:
Investigative Skills

Analyze information

Synthesize/integrate information

Experiment

Observe

Study

Cluster 4:
Social Skills

Guide others

Listen to others

Support/help others

Be a teammate

Teach others

Cluster 5:
Enterprising Skills

Organize activities

Persuade others

Run a business

Sell/advertise

Supervise/manage others

Cluster 6:
Conventional Skills

Focus on details

Follow rules/instructions

Work with numbers

Organize data/records

Proofread

2. Count the total number of skills you have for each cluster. Which three clusters contained the majority of your work abilities?

3. How do your work abilities compare to the transferable skills you identified in Exercise 12.2?

4. If you completed the SDS or SII, how do your abilities compare with your interests?

The skills represented in this exercise are just a few of the skills that you may have. However, the results can provide you with valuable information you can use to better understand your abilities as they relate to work.

a lot of importance on working independently and making a contribution to society. For Holli, choosing a career as a research chemist makes a lot of sense. For other students, however, interests, skills, and values do not fit together as well. If this is the case for you, then finding a good career match will probably be more challenging. To assess your values, you may want to complete Exercise 12.4.

Exercise 12.4 Identifying Your Work Values

Part One. Listed below are several different reasons why people work. On the scale provided (1, *Definitely No* to 7, *Definitely Yes*), rate the degree to which each value is true for you. Remember, in order to get the most out of this process, be honest!

1	2	3	4	5	6	7
Definitely No						Definitely Yes

1. I want to have my work recognized and valued by others. ____
2. I like to work on long-term, important projects. ____
3. I like to use my leadership abilities on the job. ____
4. I like the feeling of directly helping someone. ____
5. Salary and benefits are primary factors in any job I take. ____
6. I believe work builds character. ____
7. I like working in settings where creativity and artistic ability are valued. ____
8. Challenging, difficult work excites and motivates me. ____
9. I want to work with people with similar interests and values. ____
10. My job activities and responsibilities should vary from day to day. ____
11. My work environment should be physically pleasing. ____
12. My employer should be well known and established. ____
13. My work should lead to career advancement. ____
14. I enjoy planning and organizing programs and activities. ____
15. I would be happiest working in a service organization. ____
16. My job should provide frequent pay raises and promotions. ____
17. I feel satisfied after putting in a day of hard work. ____
18. I like to develop new ways of handling problems. ____
19. My job should give me the chance to work on complex problems. ____
20. I like being part of a group or working team. ____
21. My job should expose me to a wide variety of people. ____
22. A relaxed and friendly environment is important to me. ____
23. I want a career others consider prestigious. ____
24. I enjoy work that gives me the chance to learn from what I do. ____
25. I want to be in charge of large, vital projects. ____
26. The focus of my job should be helping others. ____

27. I want to make the highest possible income. _____

28. I want to work with colleagues who work as hard as I do. _____

29. I like to develop and use new solutions, rather than rely on established procedures. _____

30. I like assignments that require real learning and effort. _____

31. I want to work in a job where my coworkers are also my friends. _____

32. I want change and variety in my job. _____

33. It is important for me to work in a setting where people are happy to be there. _____

34. A professional or job title is important to me. _____

35. When I do something, it is important that I do it well. _____

36. I enjoy supervising or directing other people's work. _____

37. I want to use my energies and abilities to make the world a better place to live. _____

38. Having enough money to buy whatever I want is important. _____

39. Everyone should work to give back to society. _____

40. I like working in a job where having new thoughts and ideas is valued. _____

41. I enjoy work that is intellectually challenging. _____

42. I am at my best when I work with other people. _____

43. I would be bored at a job where I did the same thing every day. _____

44. Having a boss/supervisor who is fair, considerate, and concerned about the employees is important to me. _____

Part Two. To determine your scores from Part One, add your ratings across the items that comprise each value. Record your scores in the space provided.

- Recognition: obtaining respect, social approval, and prestige from your job/career.

    (Items 1, 12, 23, 34)   Total Score _____

- Achievement: attaining mastery of a field, self-advancement, growth.

    (Items 2, 13, 24, 35)   Total Score _____

- Leadership: exercising leadership, supervising, or having power and influence over others.

    (Items 3, 14, 25, 36)   Total Score _____

- Helping Others: doing something that is meaningful to someone else, working for society's or another person's benefit.

    (Items 4, 15, 26, 37)   Total Score _____

- Financial Status: attaining financial success, gaining in socioeconomic status, obtaining material wealth.

    (Items 5, 16, 27, 38)   Total Score _____

- Work Ethic: hard work is important and should be a part of the work environment.

    (Items 6, 17, 28, 39)   Total Score _____

- Creativity: contributing new ideas, being original and inventive.

    (Items 7, 18, 29, 40)   Total Score _____

- Challenge: handling difficult, complex work; being intellectually stimulated.

    (Items 8, 19, 30, 41)   Total Score _____

- Relationships: being with fellow employees, colleagues; getting along.

    (Items 9, 20, 31, 42)   Total Score _____

- Diversity: preferring a variety of activities on the job, not having to do the same thing every day.

    (Items 10, 21, 32, 43)   Total Score _____

- Environment: working in a setting that is pleasant, positive, and relaxing.

    (Items 11, 22, 33, 44)   Total Score _____

Circle your top five scores and list them in the space below.

_____

Were you surprised by your rankings? Were you disappointed? These are work values that you indicated were important, so you'll want to consider them in your decisions about majors and careers. Understanding your values will be helpful in choosing a career or work setting that is best for you.

Personality Style. The fourth assessment area concerns your personality; that is, the ways in which you interact with your environment and other people. Unfortunately, personality factors are often overlooked during the process of choosing a major and a career. This oversight is a problem because one of the main causes of dissatisfaction with a career choice is the poor fit between an individual's personality and the demands of the job and the work environment.

Although your interests, abilities, and values are all components of your personality, there is more than that to consider. You also need to think about whether you are primarily an active person, one who seeks to shape your environment, or a passive person, who is more comfortable responding to the world. Do you focus more on your own inner world of experiences or prefer to focus on the external world and other people? Do you like to have a lot of stimulation in your life, or do you like things to be calmer? Do you rely more on thoughts or on feelings to make decisions? There are many such personality factors you might consider.

One model of personality that has relevance for choosing majors and careers is *type theory,* developed by Katherine Briggs and Isabel Myers. Type theory (Myers, 1993) suggests four dimensions along which we can classify personality: *extraversion-introversion, sensing-intuition, thinking-feeling,* and *judging-perceiving.* We discuss these dimensions in the following sections.

Extraversion-Introversion. This dimension concerns the direction in which you prefer to focus your attention. You have probably noticed that some people direct their attention to the environment and toward external events. They tend to be interested and involved with other people and learn best by talking with others or doing things. It is often hard for them to be by themselves. These are *extraverts.* Extraverts tend to be active and have broad interests. In contrast, *introverts* prefer to focus on their own inner worlds of experiences and ideas. Although they interact with others, often quite well, it typically takes more energy and effort for them to do so. Introverts learn best by reflecting on experiences and they tend to think things through before acting. They tend to have narrow interests, but pursue them in great depth.

Sensing-Intuition. The second dimension concerns the way you prefer to take in information and learn about the world. *Sensing* types prefer to gather information through their senses: seeing, hearing, tasting, smelling, and touching. As a result of this preference, they tend to be practical and realistic, focused on the "here and now," and they like to rely on their direct experiences. *Intuitive* types, on the other hand, gather information by taking a broader view. They are "big picture" people, who are more interested in what is possible than in what is real. They value imagination and insight. These people look for patterns and rely more on theories than on facts. Intuitive types are good at seeing new and creative ways of doing things.

Thinking-Feeling. The third dimension concerns the way you tend to make decisions. *Thinking* types use detailed analysis and logic to solve problems. They try to be fair and objective at all times and focus mainly on determining the truth and applying their principles. They are less concerned with the emotional impact of their decisions. *Feeling* types are primarily concerned with the emotional impact of their decisions on themselves and on others. They are able to empathize with others, and they seek harmonious relationships with others whenever possible. These people are understanding and supportive of others.

Judging-Perceiving. The final dimension concerns the way you orient yourself to the outer world. *Judging* types tend to live well-planned, orderly, and structured lives. They tend to use a systematic approach when they make decisions. Once they make a decision, they don't look back, because they like to have things settled. Judging types work best when they have a schedule, and they don't like last-minute surprises. In contrast, *perceiving* types approach the world in a flexible, spontaneous way. They are more interested in experiencing and enjoying life, rather than controlling it. Because they are spontaneous, they enjoy last-minute pressures and frequent changes.

The *Myers-Briggs Type Indicator* (MBTI; Briggs & Myers, 1976) is a popular, easy-to-use questionnaire that many students find fun and helpful in exploring their personality styles and relating them to career choices. The MBTI categorizes personality styles along each of the four dimensions *(extraversion-introversion, sensing-intuition, thinking-feeling, judging-perceiving)* that we discussed earlier. Using the MBTI classification system, you are rated on each of the four dimensions, generating combinations of types such as INFP (introversion-intuition-feeling-perceiving), ESTJ (extraversion-sensing-thinking-judging), and so forth. In looking at the various types, it is important to understand that no one type is superior to another; each type has its own strengths and weaknesses.

Understand that most people are not exclusively one type or another. When we talk about the four dimensions, you should realize that these are *preferences*. Although we can use many terms to describe personality types, the dimensions of the MBTI seem especially relevant to choosing careers. You will want to have a clear sense of where you fit along these dimensions as you consider various career options. For example, if you know that you are generally quiet, reserved, and inclined to react to (rather than try to influence) the environment, then a career in sales is probably not ideal for you. At worst, you will be unhappy, and at best, you will have to expend a lot more energy than someone who enjoys the company of others and is aggressive. You might, however, be an excellent researcher.

You can complete the MBTI as part of your freshman seminar or on your own; the student counseling center or career services center on your campus should have it available for you. Once you have completed the MBTI or another personality inventory, the next step is to identify the work settings and tasks that fit well with your particular personality style.

After completing the MBTI, you should have a good understanding of your preferred ways of interacting with the world. You can combine this information with the information you gathered about your interests, transferable skills, and values to generate a fairly complete self-portrait. You will use the information from your self-assessments later in this chapter to complete Exercise 13.7, the Career Search. First, however, we discuss some of the ways you can learn more about specific careers of interest to you.

> "To find the unlimited scope of human possibility, look within yourself."
>
> JIM VALVANO
> *NCAA Champion Basketball Coach, Founder of the 'V' Foundation*

What Key Skills Are Employers Looking For?

Each year, the National Association of Colleges and Employers (NACE) conduct the Job Outlook Survey with its employer members. The JOS asks employers about their hiring plans and other employment-related issues to project what the job market will be for new college graduates. It also assesses a variety of conditions that may influence that market.

The 2009 JOS indicated that the vast majority of employers initially screen job candidates by grade point average, with a 3.0 being the cut-off. In other words, before any other skills and qualities are considered, you will have to clear the GPA hurdle before being considered for a job. After GPA, employers also consider other factors, including:

- type of major,
- college leadership positions,
- college extracurricular activities,
- university attended, and
- volunteer work.

With regard to preference for candidates' work experience, 76% of employers prefer to hire candidates with relevant work (related or specific to their company) experience, compared to 18% of employers who will to hire candidates with any type of work experience, relevant or not.

Once potential job candidates are evaluated on these hard and fast requirements (e.g., GPA, work experience), employers consider a range of "soft" or personal skills. Regardless of the job market (e.g., tight or sluggish versus growing or positive) or employment sector (e.g., manufacturing versus government/nonprofit), employers valued these "soft" skills or qualities:

- communication,
- strong work ethic,
- teamwork, and
- initiative.

Analytical skills, computer skills, flexibility/adaptability, interpersonal skills (relating well to others), problem-solving, and technical skills rounded out the top 10. You may be surprised to learn that self-confidence, leadership, and being friendly/outgoing did not make the top 10. Unfortunately, according to the JOS, many new college graduates lack communication skills, whether verbal or written. In particular, employers believed that students' poor writing skills were due to excessive use of texts and e-mails, and the abbreviations used in those methods of communication. Deficits in presentation, teamwork, and overall professionalism (e.g., lack of maturity, business etiquette, lack of understanding how to dress appropriately in a professional environment) also were noted by employers. In fact, employers often search social networking sites to see how job candidates present themselves, so take care in what you post on your site. Employers also reported that students, in general, lack a good work ethic. Specifically, recent college graduates have trouble with time management, are unable to multi-task in order to meet deadlines, and have unrealistic expectations of their new positions. They underestimate the work demands, are not committed or loyal to the organization, and lack patience. In other words, new hires have an enhanced sense of urgency to climb the career ladder quickly but don't want to put in the time or work.

So, as you progress through college, focus not only on developing the "hard" prerequisites for getting a job (e.g., GPA), but also on the "soft" skills that you will need to be successful. Through your coursework, interactions with your instructors, and devotion to your sport, you have the opportunity to develop these skills. So, don't let that pass you by.

Career Research: Finding What Is Out There for You

The second major phase of the career development process is career research. At this point, you will apply what you learned in the self-assessment phase to begin exploring specific careers and occupations. To start, we discuss three main sources of career information that you can use.

Sources of Career Information

Family and Friends. Your thinking about career options has probably been heavily influenced by what you saw your parents, older siblings, extended family, and friends doing. Often your first exposure to the world of work is through talking to or observing one or more of these people. In addition to these sources, you can speak with faculty members or other professionals in the fields you are considering to get more information about job responsibilities, educational requirements, and career opportunities. The more people you talk to, the more information you will get, and the better your chance of finding a good career match will be.

Campus Resources. Your school's career or counseling center is an excellent source of information. Often these centers will have counselors and career information libraries where you can find various printed materials about occupations that interest you. Your school's career information library carries general information books, such as the *Occupational Outlook Handbook* (OOH; Bureau of Labor Statistics, 2009), which provides a wealth of information about virtually every occupation imaginable.

The OOH provides descriptions of hundreds of occupations, including the necessary education and training, salaries, working conditions, employment prospects, and related occupations. The career information library should also have other books and pamphlets covering specific occupations in greater detail (and at most schools, this information is available online). Early in your tenure, familiarize yourself with the career resources your school has to offer.

Online Resources. The Internet is another source of valuable career information. In some cases, the Internet is the only way to access information. For example, many job listings are posted online, and a number of college career placement programs have you post your resume and cover letter electronically when you begin your job search. Again, a visit to your career services center will be worth your while in learning how to access career information online.

Researching Careers

In this step, gather information from one or more of the sources discussed in the preceding section and compare what you learned about yourself through the self-assessments—interests, abilities, values, and personality style. As we have pointed out, many students base their career decisions on limited information, perhaps considering only one or two factors, such as interests or abilities. They also fail to carefully and thoughtfully gather adequate information about the career possibilities they are considering, resulting in frustration, dissatisfaction, and wasted time. However, if you have taken the self-assessment task seriously, then you have demonstrated a commitment to avoiding these pitfalls. Remember, in the career decision-making process, you are meant to be an active, invested participant.

As you do your research, focus on the careers that match well with your assessment results. Understand, however, that no occupation or career is likely to be a perfect match for you, and you do not want to eliminate possibilities just because they do not fit perfectly with all your interests, values, abilities, and personality. Remember, if you are like most individuals, you will make several career changes in your lifetime. The goal is to make the *best* match at this point in your life, not necessarily the *perfect* match for the rest of your life. You will need to look to leisure and social activities, rather than your career, to meet some of your important needs. For example, you might have a strong desire to help others or to spend a lot of time enjoying outdoor activities. Your interests and abilities might point you toward a career—perhaps as a medical researcher—that does not allow these desires to be easily fulfilled in your work. Therefore, you will want to make sure that you use your leisure time to get involved in community service, or spend time outdoors. Take as much time to learn about the occupations you are considering as you did to assess your interests, values, skills, and personality style.

Through this search, you will be making decisions about your major and then implementing those decisions. Some majors will lead directly to the career you choose. If that is true for you, then your decision is fairly straightforward. In other cases, as we mentioned earlier, there will be a number of majors that could lead to your career goal. If so, you will want to choose the major that best matches your ability level and is of interest to you. The major you choose should be the one to which you can make the greatest commitment and feel the most passion. It won't matter what your major is if you aren't willing or able to do the necessary work to complete it. Never lose sight of the fact that employers hire *people,* not majors!

We have discussed several sources of information that you can use to get information about various occupations and careers. One approach that is especially useful is to talk with someone who is already doing what you would like to do. In Exercise 12.5, you have an opportunity to interview someone who is currently working in one of the occupations you are now considering.

Exercise 12.5 Career Interview

From your self-assessments and initial explorations, you should have identified careers of possible interest. To obtain more information about one of these careers, interview a person who is already working in the field. For example, if you are interested in becoming a physical therapist, then contact someone who is working in that field and ask if you could interview him or her to learn more about his or her job. Although some people will say "no," most will be thrilled to have the opportunity to share their experiences with someone who is interested in their field. Use the following questions to guide your interview and add your own questions if you like.

1. What is your name and where do you work?

2. What is your occupation and your current title?

3. How long have you worked in the field?

4. How did you become interested in this field?

5. What do you do in a typical workday?

6. How did you prepare yourself (e.g., education, work experiences, etc.) to get your current job?

7. Looking back, what other preparation or training would have been helpful to have before you started this job?

8. What are some of the skills necessary to be successful in this career?

9. What are the characteristics, expectations, or aspects of the job you like the most? The least?

10. What are the job prospects for new people entering this career field?

11. What are the opportunities for advancement once you have entered the field?

12. What skills, personal characteristics, and training experiences would you look for if you were hiring a new college graduate for a job in this field?

13. What are some of the challenges professionals in this field will face in the future and how can they best prepare to handle them?

14. If you were to do it again, would you pursue the same career?

When you have finished the interview, think about the individual's responses. Are you still interested in the field? If so, are you preparing yourself in the best possible manner to be a competitive job candidate? If not, what can you do differently to make sure that you have the skills, knowledge, and personal characteristics that will help you to be successful?

Experiential Learning and Career Implementation: Trying It On and Getting the Job

Your involvement in these stages will probably come later in your college career, but we want you to be familiar with them now. In the Experiential Learning stage, you will start to gather experiences related to the career(s) you are considering. Examples of the activities associated

© Dmitry Yashkin, 2009 / Used under license from Shutterstock.com

Exercise 12.6   Experiential Learning Options

1. List two or more ways *on your campus* in which you could obtain experience relevant to a future career while still in college. If you need help, then talk with your academic advisor. Be sure to take into account the demands of your schedule as you identify your options.

_____

_____

2. List two or more ways *off-campus* (in your community, for example) in which you could realistically obtain

experience relevant to a future career while still in college. Again, consider talking with an academic advisor or counselor first, as they likely will have information about connections to the local community.

_____

_____

Now consider pursuing these options to gain some experience in your field.

---

with this stage are internships, "days on the job," job shadowing, and volunteer work. As a student-athlete, you may find it a bit difficult to participate in a lot of these activities. Nonetheless, with careful planning, you should be able to create some opportunities for yourself, particularly during the summers. This stage is important because it often gives you the chance to learn marketable skills that you will need later. To explore some of the ways you can get practical work experience, related to careers of possible interest, while you are in college, you may want to complete Exercise 12.6.

The final stage, career implementation, is where you actually begin your job search. This stage consists of writing a resume and cover letter, registering with your school's career placement office, arranging job interviews, and so on. Although we will not go into detail here, we have provided some basic information in this chapter on cover letters and job interviews that may help you when you reach this stage in your career development.

Performance: Academic Advising

In many ways, your advisor is your academic coach. They are faculty and/or professional staff members who help students with various aspects of their academic planning, including selecting and scheduling courses; preparing degree completion plans; changing majors; understanding university policies, procedures, and general academic requirements; applying for transfer credit; and answering questions about choosing majors and careers. Academic advisors can be found in a number of locations, depending on the structure of your college or university. You may, for example, work with an advisor from the athletic department for all or part of your time in school, but also have an advisor in your academic department. At many schools, you will be required to use departmental advising, especially in your later years. Finally, some schools have undergraduate advising offices, staffed by professionals whose only responsibility is to advise students in a number of departments. Find out where you should start by checking with your athletic department.

Academic advisors also can serve as mentors and as general sources of support during your college years. Janie, for example, developed a

Writing Cover Letters

Like your resume, your cover letter is a statement of your individuality and the uniqueness of your experiences. Although you should be careful not to rely too much upon a standardized format for your letter, cover letters generally consist of three basic parts: the introduction, body, and closing.

- The introductory paragraph, which identifies the position you are seeking, how you found out about the position, and a clear statement of your interest in the position. Identify the specific job you are interested in and where you learned about it, such as the name of the person or the source of the advertisement.
- The body highlights your relevant experience and skills and demonstrates specifically how they address the responsibilities listed for the job. As a student-athlete, you may want to highlight the skills you have developed through athletics that may be important for the job. It is also a good idea to emphasize how balancing school and sports has been an asset for you. Leadership, communication, and time management are often skills student-athletes have developed.
- The closing paragraph, which restates your interest in the position, provides information about how to contact you, and thanks the evaluator for considering your materials. Give a current telephone number and an e-mail address where you can be reached. You may also choose to make a statement about when you will contact the employer to follow up. For example, you may state that you will follow up with the employer in 2 weeks to find out more about the position and the status of your application.
- Generally, your letter will be no longer than a page, unless you have significant work experience requiring more detailed explanation. If possible, be sure to find out specifically to whom the letter should be sent and then address it to that individual.
- Make sure, too, that your letter is thoughtful, grammatically correct, and has no misspellings. Also, use a formal writing style and avoid the use of slang, abbreviations, symbols, or other forms of communication you might use in e-mails or texting with friends. In this letter, you want to demonstrate your written communication skills (see Figure 12.2).

close relationship with her advisor while she was in college. She met with him regularly during her four years in school and learned a lot about the counseling profession by talking with him. She was also able to enlist him as a source of support when she had difficulties with classes, her sport, and with her personal life. Because of their close relationship, her advisor was able to provide Janie with an excellent letter of recommendation for graduate school and for her first job after college. Although not every advisor-student relationship will be quite as close as this, you can still benefit in a number of ways by taking advantage of what your advisor has to offer.

When working with your advisor, be patient and considerate. Most advisors are busy and see large numbers of students. Fortunately, the vast majority of advisors are committed to their work and dedicated to providing students with excellent service. Hopefully, your advisor is

214 Valley Drive
Medical Lake, WA 99900
April 15, 1999

Ms. Karren Darrow
Director, Human Resources
Memorial Medical Center
1 Hospital Drive
Medical Lake, WA 99900

Dear Ms. Darrow:

I am writing with regard to your recent advertisement in the Medical Lake Examiner for a physical therapy assistant. I am very interested in being considered for the position and believe that I have the experience and enthusiasm to be a valuable member of the medical center team.

I have enclosed my resume--which details my skills and experience--but I would like to highlight my qualifications here. I will be graduating this spring from State University with a degree in exercise science, with a 3.00 GPA. In addition, I have a minor in biology. My qualifications for the position also include having been a student athlete at State. I lettered in soccer all four years and was team captain as a senior. I gained firsthand knowledge of the value of physical therapy after undergoing knee surgery in my sophomore year. That experience really sparked my interest in becoming a physical therapist, and led me to volunteer in the training room at State and work summers in a rehabilitation clinic at the local hospital in my hometown. Those experiences (detailed in my resume) demonstrate my commitment to the profession and my willingness to work hard. I enjoy being part of a team and know how to balance and prioritize multiple demands and activities.

In closing, I would like to thank you for taking the time to consider my resume. I am very interested in the position and eager to speak with you about it at your earliest convenience. You can reach me at (509) 555-2222.

Thank you very much for your consideration.

Sincerely,

Lee Boyd

Lee Boyd

Figure 12.2 Sample Cover Letter

> "Every day is a new opportunity. You can build on yesterday's success or put its failures behind and start over again."
>
> BOB FELLER
> *Major League Baseball Hall of Fame Pitcher*

happy in their position after carefully going through their own career decision-making process, similar to the one you are about to engage upon. Providing high-quality service takes time, so be patient if you cannot see your advisor exactly when you want. Schedule your appointments in advance, especially during busy periods, such as preregistration, and be sure to keep them. Also, take advantage of the slow periods during the semester to meet with your advisor.

Second, make sure your advisor knows that you are a student-athlete. Advisors who do not work regularly with student-athletes may not always be aware of NCAA or other guidelines you must follow. Issues such as satisfactory progress requirements may be unfamiliar to them. In some cases, terms such as *satisfactory progress* may not have the same meaning for student-athletes that it has for the general student population. Advisors also may not fully understand the varying seasonal demands associated with your sport. Try to make them aware of these issues and concerns so they can give you the best possible guidance to help you meet your academic and athletic goals. Talk with your advisor before making changes in your schedule. You should always do this, but it is particularly important if your advisor works outside the athletic department.

Third, you should take an active role in your advising sessions. Come prepared with specific questions, ideas about courses you are considering taking, forms, transcripts, and other items you might need. Ultimately, your advisor cannot make decisions for you, nor will she have to live with the results of the advising sessions. Be sure to discuss your current term progress, your academic plans for the next term, and your long-range academic plans. Your advisor will help you make sure that your plans are feasible and that you stay on track for graduation. You can also get the most out of your academic advisor if you meet with her within the first few weeks of your arrival on campus

Job Interviews

When searching for a job, keep the following suggestions in mind. In addition, consult with a staff member from your college's career services center for more information about the job interview process.

- Know that you always are being evaluated in any contact with a prospective employer, even if the employer tells you that the interaction is informal. Speak clearly and avoid using slang. You can be less formal once you have the job.
- Because employers may call you to set up an interview or follow up once you have completed one, make sure your outgoing message is professional (e.g., don't have music or a clever message). The prospective employer may not share your taste in music or your sense of humor, and may see you as unprofessional.
- Dress professionally for an interview, even if the situation is described as informal and the people you are interviewing with are dressed casually. Failing to dress appropriately is often seen as a sign of disrespect for the employer and the situation. You may be viewed as someone who does not know the rules of the game. Your career services office can give you additional guidance about appropriate attire. Many career centers provide mock (practice) interviews which may include dressing the part of an interviewee and using video or webcams to critique your performance (just like reviewing game film from a competition!).
- Prepare yourself before you interview. Just as you wouldn't compete without reviewing a scouting report on your opponent, the same principle applies here as well. Take some time to learn about the organization for which you want to work. This communicates to the employer that you have a sincere interest in working for the organization. Also, generate a list of questions to ask if the opportunity to do so arises. Make sure some of your questions specifically address unique aspects of the organization or company. This approach will show that you've done your homework and are truly interested in the position.
- After you have completed the interview, send a follow-up letter expressing your appreciation for the opportunity to meet with the prospective employer (in some situations e-mails are appropriate, but in others this may be viewed as too informal). Be sure to emphasize your continued interest in the position (assuming you are still interested). Failure to follow up can be interpreted as a lack of self-responsibility and could take you out of the running for the job.

and regularly—at least once per academic term—thereafter. Unfortunately, many students wait until the last minute to make contact with their advisors, which doesn't allow advisors time to get to know them and their needs. Your advisor can be a valuable asset when the time comes to apply for graduate school or for a job; however, it will be difficult for your advisor to help you if she doesn't know you well. Meeting with your advisor regularly allows her to do the best job possible, and this helps you in the long run.

Performance: Scheduling Classes

Unfortunately, student-athletes often fail to think about what schedule makes the most sense for them when the time comes to select classes. Certainly, you need to consider the requirements of your major, as well as satisfactory progress rules, in developing your class schedule. Most student-athletes are aware of these things, but some overlook other important factors.

First, you should think about the long term before acting in the short term. Know what your overall academic plans and goals are, as we discussed earlier in this chapter. Having a long-range plan not only provides you with a structure, but it also allows you to tailor your class schedule to fit with the other areas in your life, such as athletics. For example, you know that you need to take certain challenging classes in order to complete your degree. Some of these classes are offered only every other year, so you can either take them during your first year, when you will be redshirting, or wait until your third year, when you will be getting a lot of playing time and taking other demanding classes. It is hard to make a good decision without a long-range academic plan. Meeting with your academic advisor before scheduling your classes can help here. Working closely with your advisor ensures that you meet all academic and satisfactory progress requirements for your degree and your athletic eligibility. Your advisor will also know about special circumstances, such as classes offered only once every year or two or prerequisites that could affect your ability to complete your degree as planned.

Second, think about what works best for you. Consider all your responsibilities. Know your practice and competition schedules when you are in season and your training schedule for the off season. If possible, avoid scheduling classes during times when you have athletic obligations or other important commitments. In some cases, it may be nearly impossible, for example, to schedule late afternoon labs around practice schedules. Balance your course load so that you have a blend of classes at different levels of difficulty. If writing does not come easily for you, then you might want to avoid taking too many classes at once that involve a lot of writing. This approach does not mean we advocate taking the easy way out; we simply urge you to be sensible in your approach. Knowing what works best for you also means looking at the rhythm of your year. If you play soccer or football, then the fall is probably not the time to take your heaviest academic load. If you play softball or tennis, however, fall term may be a better time to take more challenging courses.

Finally, find out about the instructors who teach the classes you are considering. Ask your teammates, roommates, and advisor about the instructor's teaching style and accessibility to students, especially student-athletes, or visit websites devoted to evaluating teachers and read other students' comments. Don't shy away from difficult classes or instructors. They may offer you a stimulating learning experience that challenges you to do your best.

As we bring this chapter to a close, we believe it is important for you to have the opportunity to integrate the stages of the career development model and to develop a framework for the exercises you have completed throughout the chapter. Exercise 12.7, the Career Search Project, is designed to give you an in-depth experience of choosing a career. In this project, you will integrate information from the assessments you completed in this chapter. Although you can complete this exercise on your own, we suggest that you do it with the guidance of your instructor or advisor. Because this project is extensive, you may wish to work on it over the course of the current academic term or the next one.

Exercise 12.7 Career Search Project

1. Using the results from the self-assessments of interests, abilities, work values, and personality, identify from 5 to 10 occupations in which you had a high interest and which seemed congruent with your abilities, values, and personality. The more you can identify, the better. If you completed the *Strong Interest Inventory* (SII) or the *Self-Directed Search* (SDS), you will have a list of occupations you can use as a starting point for this task. Next, go back to the counseling or career services center and obtain the following information about each career: (a) the basic activities involved in the job, (b) education/training required to obtain the job, (c) typical salary for the job, and (d) the current prospects for employment in the field. The *Occupational Outlook Handbook* is an excellent starting point for this information, but the career information library in the counseling center or career services center may have other books, pamphlets, and online resources as well. Be sure to make copies or printouts of the information you gather.

2. Read the information you obtained in step 1 and narrow your possible careers to one or two that you are most interested in. You may also wish to discuss the information you gathered with a friend, parent, or counselor before narrowing your choices. Exercise 13.5 (Career Interview) will also provide you with information you can use for this task.

3. After you have narrowed your career choices to one or two and conducted your career interview, use your college's catalog to identify *two majors offered by your college* that can help you to enter the career(s)

of your choosing. It is important to identify at least two majors because, for a variety of reasons, you might not be able to enter your first choice of majors. If you have trouble with this step, then talk to your advisor or a counselor. They can help you see connections that might not be obvious to you or tell you about majors you might not even know about.

4. List two or three ways you could obtain experience relevant to your career choices prior to seeking employment in them. For example, if you were a communications major, then you might complete an internship writing for your campus paper or broadcasting on your campus radio station.

Steps 5 and 6 are optional. If you are using this book in a class, or working through it under the guidance of your advisor, then you may wish to complete these steps.

5. Write a resume and cover letter for the occupation you would like to enter. Your instructor/advisor can help you with the basic elements you need to include if you are unfamiliar with the processes involved. As you develop these documents, you will want to give careful consideration to the skills you have developed through your various life experiences and activities.

6. To complete the career search project, turn in to your instructor/advisor the following items:
   a. The list of your 5 to 10 high-interest occupations.
   b. Your top one or two occupations, along with the information you obtained for them under step 2.
   c. The names of the two majors you identified.

Post-Game Review

As we have emphasized throughout this chapter, choosing majors and choosing careers are vitally important. It's a process that takes effort and time. Taking short-cuts during this process will only undermine you in the end. No matter how successful you are as an athlete, at some point your competitive days will come to an end. We want you to have a solid foundation for the next stages of your life. Making informed choices about your major and your career can help you build that foundation. Giving careful consideration to your interests, values, abilities, and personality style is a matter of self-responsibility, because no one else can truly make these assessments for you. Make the commitment now to identify your goals for your major and career and work toward completing them, even though they may seem far off in the future. Remember, this is a process that your generation will likely go through more than once in your lifetime. The world of work is changing exponentially faster than in the past, and you will have to adapt your skills to meet the speed of the changes. As you reach the goals you've set, you will feel the pride of accomplishing one of your life's major tasks.

Thinking Critically about Careers and Majors

1. Summarize what you now know about choosing a career and major based on the information presented in this chapter.

_____

_____

_____

2. What additional questions do you have about these topics and how to use the skills introduced in this chapter?

_____

_____

_____

3. What conclusions can you draw about this topic and how it might help you be a more effective and successful student and athlete?

_____

_____

_____

Achieve IT! Setting a Career Goal

1. Based on your self-assessment and your responses to Thinking Critically, select a goal in relationship to selecting a career or choosing a major that you would like to achieve this term.

2. Now identify three short-term goals that will help you reach your goal this term.

3. For the short-term goals, identify the attainment strategies you will need to reach them.

4. List any obstacles you might face in trying to reach these goals and identify your plan for overcoming each one.

Don't forget to make your goal visible and tell others about them, so they can keep you accountable regarding what you want to achieve.

Chapter 12 Review Questions

1. A major always leads directly to a career. (True or False)

2. Taking general academic courses can help you choose a major by exposing you to a variety of fields of study. (True or False)

3. The first step of the career cycle is

   a. Doing career research.
   b. Establishing your self-efficacy in a career area.
   c. Being involved in experiential learning.
   d. Meeting with your advisor.
   e. None of the above.

4. Holland's typology includes all of the following except

   a. Conventional.   **b.** Social.
   c. Structured.   **d.** Investigative.

5. To increase your self-knowledge and to make a better career choice, you should assess your

   a. Personality style.   **b.** Transferable skills/abilities.
   c. Values.   **d.** Interests.
   e. All of the above.

6. According to Holland's theory, people are most satisfied with their jobs when their interests align with the characteristics of the work environment. (True or False)

7. It is best to meet with your academic advisor before you schedule your classes. (True or False)

8. Name three things an academic advisor can help you do.

9. Name two career resources on your campus.

10. You should only select a career that can meet all of your important needs and values. (True or False)

11. Selection of a major and a career is a process that should be completed by the end of your freshman year. (True or False)

12. From the 2009 Job Outlook Survey, which of the following "soft" skills was not in the top 10 of what employers used to determine potential job candidates?

   a. Self-confidence.   **b.** Strong work ethic.
   c. Communication skills.   **d.** Teamwork skills.

Chapter 13 | Succeeding on the Field

Becoming a Mentally Tough Athlete

Game Plan:

In this chapter, you will learn:

- What defines a mentally tough athlete

- Skills for becoming a more committed, confident, consistent, controlled, and focused performer

- How to develop a pre-performance routine to implement whenever you practice and compete

© Josh Brown, 2009 / Used under license from Shutterstock.com

"I am the toughest golfer mentally."

TIGER WOODS
World Champion, Golf

Self-Assessment—Perceive It!

Read the following statements and place a checkmark next to each one you generally do. For you to change and develop new and effective academic, athletic, and personal strategies, you must be accurate in your self-perception. So, be honest in how you answer each question.

1. In practices and competitions, I am able to regulate my emotions so I play my best. _____

2. I am aware of my thoughts and behaviors during practices and competitions and don't worry about the things I can't control (e.g., opponent, weather, coach). _____

3. In practices and competitions, I focus only on those things that will help me perform my best. _____

4. When I become distracted, I am able to quickly refocus and get back into my performance. _____

5. When I compete and practice, I am fully present in the moment; not distracted by past performances, outside events, or a negative internal dialogue. _____

6. I have a pre-performance routine that I use consistently to help me get myself ready to perform my best in each competition. _____

7. I have fun playing my sport. _____

8. I try to learn from the mistakes and successes I have in practices and competitions. _____

9. I know why I am playing my sport and what I want to accomplish in it. _____

10. I understand my strengths and weaknesses as an athlete and take every opportunity to improve my performances. _____

11. I have confidence in myself as an athlete. _____

12. I know what I expect of myself as an athlete and set goals that are consistent with those expectations. _____

Take a moment to review your responses. How many items did you check? Each one you checked represents a current strength. Now consider the items you did not check. These represent areas where focus and growth are needed. Now, to summarize your self-perception, complete the following statements:

1. My areas of strength are:

_____

2. The areas I need to improve are:

_____

As you read this chapter and participate in your classes, keep your strengths and areas of improvement in mind. At the end of the chapter, you will have the chance to set a goal related to these areas. Achieving these goals will help you become a more effective student and athlete.

---

*T*wo *different athletes, two different sports . . . yet how they approached their performances and competed in their sports were strikingly similar. Morgan was the starting forward on her school's soccer team; Kiernan played defensive end and was a preseason all-conference selection. When each one stepped onto the field, they carried with them an aura of confidence that was palpable . . . they 'owned' their respective fields. When Morgan lined up against the defenders, she radiated intensity and focus . . . the message she conveyed was, "I am going to score today and you are going to have to bring your best game to stop me." Kiernan was playful and joking with his teammates, always talking on the line of scrimmage. But his play communicated a clear message, "I am here to play and I am going to stop you and everything you bring at me . . . are you ready for that?" From the first tick of the clock to the last second of the game, they played with intensity, focus, and confidence. They were committed to being their best in everything they did. They were not perfect, though. They knew that there was no such thing, so they focused on what they could control, such as how they prepared for each game or what they thought or*

Introduction

felt, and then went out and had fun. Whether they won or lost, they valued the competition because they knew that they could always learn something about themselves and their performances that would make them better players. Although they were intensely competitive and loved their respective sports, they each had other important things in their lives that kept them balanced and grounded. Morgan knew she was unlikely to play professionally, so she also was highly focused on her education and being involved in different academic societies that would help her reach her goal of going to law school. Kiernan was likely to get drafted and have a professional career, but he remained connected to his hometown through his church and volunteered time each summer to work with children through community sport camps. What defined these two athletes . . . mental toughness!

When you ask coaches and athletes what distinguishes good from great performers, one thing you hear consistently is "mental toughness." For decades, mental toughness has been viewed as an essential component of performance excellence. Coaches and teammates could point to athletes who "had it," and some could even define it. But, the essential question remained, how do athletes and teams develop it?

Maybe you have played with or against a mentally tough athlete or better yet, maybe you are one yourself. If so, then you have a real sense of what mental toughness is and what skills define it. You also then know that mental toughness is not innate, though it does seem to come more easily to certain athletes. In reality, mental toughness is a collection of characteristics that can be developed through purposeful training and the implementation of specific mental skills. In this chapter, we define mental toughness, introducing you to the key characteristics that underlie it. We also provide you with concrete mental skills that, if practiced and implemented, will help you become a mentally tougher competitor.

Preparation: Characteristics of Mental Toughness

Before reading any further, you may want to complete Exercise 13.1.

Although the idea of the "mentally tough" athlete has been around for a long time, in the last 10–15 years sport psychologists have made a concerted effort to define it and thus make it less elusive and more attainable. At the University of North Texas Center for Sport Psychology and Performance Excellence (UNT-CSPPE), sport psychologists, such as Mishelle Rodriguez, Jay Deiters, Trent Petrie, Scott Martin, and others, have identified five key characteristics of mental toughness—the "5 Cs." Based on their decades of work with athletes, coaches, and sport teams, they suggest that the mentally tough athlete is defined by the following characteristics:

Exercise 13.1 Defining the Mentally Tough Athlete

Take a moment to think about being "mentally tough." You probably have heard that term used by your coaches, teammates, sports announcers, or even yourself. But what does it mean? List 5–10 characteristics that you associate with mental toughness. As you list these, think about how closely they describe you and your approach to your sport.

C—Commitment
C—Confidence
C—Control
C—Concentration
C—Consistency

In the sections that follow, we draw upon their work and define each characteristic. Although we present them independently, you will see from the definitions that there is overlap among them. As you read about each one, think about yourself and your own performances. To what extent are these characteristics present in how you approach your practices, prepare for competitions, and perform when under pressure?

Commitment

First and foremost, mentally tough athletes are committed to their sport. If asked, you would probably say that you are committed—you play on a college team and devote 20 or more hours each week to practicing and competing. But are you really committed? Think for a moment about the pig and the chicken. Both contribute to your ham and egg breakfast, but which one is truly committed and which one is just involved? On which side do you fall?

According to the UNT-CSPPE sport psychologists, committed athletes:

- Know why they play their sport and what they want to accomplish. They have a set of clear values (see Chapter 1) that helps them define their purpose as a person and as an athlete. This purpose, in turn, informs the goals that they set for themselves. These goals, then, guide their daily behaviors; that is, everything that they do, they do purposefully to move themselves closer to reaching their goals.
- Are intense and passionate. They invest themselves completely—physically and mentally—in their practices and competitions. Every day, they push themselves to improve, to test their limits, and to overcome obstacles and difficulties.
- Pursue excellence, not perfection. They understand that there is no "perfect" but strive to be the best they can be in every situation.
- Understand that learning is a process and they are open and dedicated to improving their performances. They are aware of their strengths and do not shy away from understanding their weaknesses; in fact, they embrace these and look to every opportunity to improve on them.
- Are positive, upbeat, and bring energy to their teams.

Confidence

As we discussed in Chapter 1, confidence (or self-efficacy) is something that results from your successes and the fact that you attribute those positive outcomes to yourself: your effort, your preparation, your skills. Confidence, though, is different from arrogance. Where arrogance often is boastful, loud, and variable, confidence is a calm, stable, and enduring belief in oneself. Mentally tough athletes understand this difference.

Accordingly, confident athletes:

- Believe, at a very fundamental and unshakable level, in their abilities and what it takes to perform at their best.
- Understand the importance of goals and use them to direct their energies, monitor their progress, and evaluate their successes.
- Use themselves and their performances, not how they do against their opponents, to gauge their successes.
- Talk positively to themselves as they prepare for and perform in practices and competitions.
- Create positive and self-enhancing (but realistic) images about themselves and their performances.

Control

As an athlete, you probably have heard a coach tell you to "play under control" or to "control" some aspect of your performance. This idea of "being in control" is important and coaches know it is related to success, but what does it really mean?

According to the UNT-CSPPE sport psychologists, controlled athletes:

- Know that they have limited power over the sport environment (e.g., competing in inclement weather, bad refereeing) or their opponents, so they focus on what they can control—themselves.
- Understand that they are in control of their attitude and take responsibility for their behaviors and preparing themselves to be successful.
- Know that mistakes and setbacks are part of performing and develop plans to compensate and adjust when they occur.
- Understand that emotions (e.g., anxiety, joy, frustration) are normal and determine which ones facilitate their performances and which ones interfere.
- Monitor their thoughts and feelings to ensure that they are where they need to be and, if too strong or negative, make changes so as to create an optimal performance.

© Pete Saloutos, 2009 / Used under license from Shutterstock.com

Concentration

As we discussed in Chapter 5, the ability to concentrate and shift attention plays an important role in your academic success. But it also is an essential characteristic in your athletic performances.

According to the UNT-CSPPE sport psychologists, mentally tough athletes:

- Focus on the present moment of practices or competitions. They do not let external factors (e.g., crowd noise) or internal thoughts (e.g., doubts, worries) distract them from what they need to do.

Exercise 13.2 Identifying the Mentally Tough Athlete

Take a moment to review the characteristics associated with each of the 5 Cs of mental toughness. Although there is some overlap in their definitions, together they provide you with a template for identifying a mentally tough performer. Using this template, identify an athlete that you believe personifies each one of the 5 Cs of mental toughness. This athlete could be a professional, Olympian, or collegiate player. You can identify one athlete and use him/her to represent each characteristic or you can identify a different athlete for each one. In addition to identifying the athlete, indicate how he/she represents that characteristic.

                              Name of Athlete   How

Committed -

Confident -

Controlled -

Concentration -

Consistent -

Once you have identified the athlete(s) who represents these characteristics, you have created for yourself a role model who you can emulate as you work to become a mentally tougher performer yourself.

- Let go of mistakes in the moment and come back to them later when it is the appropriate time to evaluate their performances.
- Focus on only what is most important at each point during their performances.
- Know how to shift and maintain their attention on what is important.
- Know how to reestablish focus when it is lost.

Consistency

What makes an athlete or team great? Consistent performances over time! The ability to come out each practice and each competition and perform at the same level is what separates those who are good from those who achieve greatness. Accordingly, consistent athletes:

- Have specific routines that they implement prior to each practice and performance. These routines help them prepare physically and mentally and ready them to compete at their best.
- Have balance in their lives. They are committed to the athlete role, but also have other important aspects, values, and directions in their lives.
- Know that they will make mistakes, but work to learn from them so as to minimize future problems.

To help you think more about and apply the 5 Cs of mental toughness, you may want to complete Exercise 13.2.

Performance: Becoming a Mentally Tough Athlete

Now that you have an understanding of the characteristics associated with being a mentally tough athlete, it is time to evaluate where you are in relation to each "C" and then develop the skills necessary to help you perform at your best. Even if you see yourself as currently being mentally tough, it is likely that you will find areas in which you can improve, and we encourage you to take advantage of the information we present here to do so. If you have a trusting relationship with a coach or teammate, then you also may want to ask them for their honest evaluation of your level of mental toughness. Getting an outside perspective can validate or help you adjust your own assessment of your mental abilities. Don't look back on your collegiate athletic career and wish you had done more (e.g., used sport psychology skills) to be successful. We frequently hear from senior student-athletes that they wished they had taken advantage of, as underclassmen, the applied sport psychology resources that were available to help them become mentally tougher performers.

In the sections that follow, we will take you through a series of exercises that will help you accomplish this evaluation and assist you in developing skills associated with being a mentally tough athlete. But be warned. You will not improve your performances unless you are honest with respect to your self-evaluations and you practice the skills that are introduced. There is no magic wand, bullet, or pill; improvements in your athletic performances will occur only as a result of practicing, practicing, practicing the mental skills we introduce.

Commitment

Mental toughness, in many ways, begins and ends with your commitment. It is the foundation on which the other characteristics rest. Bottom line: If you do not know why you are playing your sport and what you want to accomplish while in college, then it will be extremely hard to be consistent or focused to perform at your best. To begin the process of evaluating your level of commitment, you may want to complete Exercise 13.3.

After completing Exercise 13.3, you now have a sense of your level of purpose: why you play your sport, what you enjoy about your sport, why you don't quit or retire from your sport, and how committed you are to it. The reasons you play can vary from wanting to improve, to winning a conference championship, to keeping your athletic scholarship, to not wanting to disappoint your parents or coaches. Knowing

---

Exercise 13.3 Assessing Your Commitment

Answer the following questions honestly about your current participation in your sport:

1. How did you get started in your sport? How old were you? What did you enjoy about playing?

2. Why do play your sport now? In other words, what are the reasons you participate on your team at your university or college?

3. What do you currently enjoy about participating in your sport?

4. What keeps you from quitting or retiring from your sport right now?

5. On a 10-point scale, ranging from 1, *Not At All Committed*, to 5, *Moderately Committed*, to 10, *Completely Committed*, rate your current level of commitment to participating in your sport.

Exercise 13.4 Identifying Your Sport Goal

1. What do you want to accomplish—individually and/or as a team—during your current or upcoming season? What do you want to accomplish prior to your graduation from college? How consistent are these two goals?

2. To reach these goals, what do you need to do each day (i.e., what behaviors do you need to engage in) to make steady progress? For example, you might need to increase your strength and conditioning training from three to four times per week or watch game film twice instead of only once per week if you are going to become the starting middle linebacker.

Over the next week, monitor yourself with respect to these behaviors. How often are you engaged in them? Based on this monitoring, answer question 3.

3. On a 10-point scale, ranging from 1, *Not At All Committed*, to 5, *Moderately Committed*, to 10, *Completely Committed*, rate your current level of commitment to doing everything you need to do to reach your goals.

   If you found that your commitment to these behaviors and your goals was low, then think about what you need to change in how you approach practice and then work with your coaches or a sport psychologist to make those changes a reality.

---

these reasons can help you determine if you are as committed as you would like. If, after completing this exercise you realize that you are not, then you may want to reevaluate why you continue to play your sport and make the changes that will help you refocus and recommit to your sport. Or, through this evaluation, you may have found that you really are not committed to your sport and your best (and most satisfying) course of action will be to stop playing and focus on other areas of your life that have more meaning. Either choice you make, the key is to match your level of commitment to the time and energy you are putting into the endeavor (be it your sport or something else in your life).

When you know why you are participating in your sport, the next step is defining what you want to accomplish. In other words, your commitment serves as the foundation for your goals—what you want to accomplish in your sport while you are in college. Although you had the opportunity to identify an athletic goal in Chapter 1, you may want to complete Exercise 13.4 to further establish what you want to attain this season.

Commitment also means being able to identify your strengths and weaknesses and then working actively to make improvements. Committed athletes understand that to be successful, they not only need to rely on their strengths, but they need to develop the areas in which they are less skilled. To help you evaluate your strengths and weaknesses as an athlete, you may want to complete Exercise 13.5.

By completing these exercises, you now should know (or have been reminded) why you participate in your sport, what you want to accomplish in your sport, whether or not you are engaging in the

> "Champions are not made in the gym. Champions are made from something they have deep within them—a desire, a dream, a vision."
>
> MUHAMMAD ALI
> *World Heavyweight Boxing Champion*

Exercise 13.5 Assessing Your Strengths and Weaknesses

To benefit most from this exercise, we encourage you to talk about these questions with someone from your coaching staff that you trust and whose judgment you value before you answer them.

1. In your sport, what are your strengths in the following areas?

   a. Physical
   b. Technical
   c. Tactical/Strategic
   d. Psychological

2. In your sport, what are your weaknesses in the following areas?

   a. Physical
   b. Technical
   c. Tactical/Strategic
   d. Psychological

3. Given this assessment, what specifically do you need to do to:

   a. Maintain your strengths?
   b. Improve your weaknesses?

behaviors that will help you reach your goals, and what you need to do to improve your weaknesses and become a better athlete. If you found that, through this evaluation, you are not as committed or involved as you had thought, then you now have the opportunity to either make changes and become more fully invested in your sport or walk away knowing that you no longer are passionate about it. Remember, it is your commitment that provides the foundation for the other characteristics, so make sure you are on solid ground.

Confidence

What you believe about yourself and your abilities is an essential component of your success as an athlete and mentally tough performers are highly confident, relative to themselves and their abilities and how they compare to others in their sport. Confidence, though, does not just happen by accident; it develops out of setting challenging goals, reaching those goals, attributing those successes to yourself, thinking positively about yourself and your performances, and holding positive images in your head about yourself and how you play your sport. For example, if an athlete attributes her success (e.g., winning conference) to how hard she has practiced over the last 6 months, her execution of the game plan, and her conditioning, and she tells herself that this success was deserved, her confidence will likely increase. However, if she believed she won only because the other team did not play well and the refs made a lot calls in her favor, then she is not likely to experience such an increase. You may want to revisit the concepts of learned optimism and explanatory style in Chapter 4 to better understand how it relates to gaining confidence in one's self and abilities.

© Ken Inness, 2009 / Used under license from Shutterstock.com

In the previous section, you had the opportunity to set an athletic goal and determine what you needed to do each day to help you reach it. We encourage you to monitor your progress toward this goal and evaluate how successful your behaviors are in helping you reach it. In this section, we want to focus on your self-talk and the images you carry about yourself and your performances. Basically, your self-talk is that inner dialogue that you have in your head about yourself, your performance, your relationships . . . really anything that is going on in your life. As you probably have experienced, your self-talk can be positive, but oftentimes it is negative as you evaluate yourself much more harshly than you would a teammate or your coach would evaluate you. Would you ever tell a teammate or friend, "You SUCK!"? But few athletes think twice about saying that to themselves. Mentally tough athletes understand the power of this inner dialogue and develop a positive and enhancing, but realistic, way of talking to themselves. In essence, they develop a positive "inner coach" that helps them achieve

---

Exercise 13.6 Evaluating Your Self-Talk

Over the next week, monitor your self-talk before, during, and after practices and competitions (if you have any). After each practice, in a notebook, write down what you said to yourself—both positive and negative. At the end of the week, look through these self-statements and then answer the following questions:

1. List the 5–10 positive statements that you made most frequently to yourself during the last week. For example, you might have said "I'm excited about practice," or "My footwork is getting better, I'm going to keep working on it," or "I'm ready to play and feeling confident."

2. List the 5–10 negative statements that you made most frequently to yourself during the last week. For example, you might have said "I can't execute this play," or "I'll never start," or "I hate practices."

3. Now, for each negative statement you made, write out a positive but constructive statement that you could have made instead. For example:
   "I suck" could become "I'm struggling today, but I'm going to keep trying."

"I hate practice" could be "I've got low energy today, so I'm going to work even harder to get myself up and ready to practice."

As you develop these positive statements, think about what you would say to teammates if they were thinking those things about themselves. Remember, you are trying to develop an "inner coach" that will help you feel more confident, evaluate your performances rationally, help you improve on your weaknesses, and further develop your strengths. Performance excellence is hard enough to attain without having a negative, overbearing critic in your head all day.

Keeping in mind the positive statements you normally make to yourself and the new ones you developed (to substitute for your negative self-statements), work actively over the next week to be more positive and enhancing in how you talk to yourself when you are participating in your sport. At first, being more positive with yourself may feel awkward or uncomfortable, but don't give up. Learning to be a positive, yet realistic evaluator of your performances will go a long way to helping you become a more confident athlete.

---

their goals, remain focused on the task at hand, and feel confident in their abilities. What type of "inner coach" do you have? To help you evaluate your current self-talk, you may want to complete Exercise 13.6.

The images you have in your mind's eye about yourself also have a powerful effect on your confidence and often are related to your self-talk. For example, a volleyball player who "sees" himself shanking a pass may develop negative self-talk, such as "don't serve it to me," or "I'm going to miss it and coach is going to pull me." Such images and self-talk can only detract from performances. To help you become more aware of the images you hold and how they influence your performance, you may want to complete Exercise 13.7.

Exercise 13.7 Assessing Your Sport Images

Over the next week, monitor the images you have of yourself with respect to your general performance or the execution of specific skills. For example, you might have the image of yourself standing confidently at the free-throw line and sinking your foul shots or of yourself dropping a pass from a teammate. At the end of the week, answer the following questions:

1. Describe 5–10 of the positive images you have about your performances and yourself as an athlete. Remember these images can be general (e.g., being confident as you line up to start a competition) or specific (e.g., serving a ball for an ace).

2. Describe 5–10 of the negative images you have about your performances and yourself as an athlete. Be specific and detailed.

3. For each negative image you hold, think about and then describe an alternative positive image that you could substitute. For example, for the image

"being slow out of the blocks," you could substitute seeing yourself "explode out of the blocks with powerful strides."

As you develop these positive images, notice how they are intimately tied to your self-talk. For example, seeing yourself catching a difficult pass from a teammate and eluding defenders is likely to be associated with statements such as "I can make that catch," "I'm faster than the defenders," or "I'm going to score." So, you may want to review your positive self-talk as you create these new positive images.

Over the next week, spend time using these positive images and the self-talk that go along with them. As you walk across campus, before you start practice, while you are icing, or just prior to falling asleep are all times when you might be using this imagery to improve your confidence. Take every opportunity you have to "see" yourself and your performances in a positive light.

Imagery is important not only for developing your confidence, but for learning new skills, mastering plays, reducing anxiety, relaxing, recovering from injury, etc. In fact, imagery is an essential skill that all athletes should master and use as a fundamental building block in becoming a better performer. There are a number of explanations as to why imagery can positively influence performance. Some research has suggested that when we vividly "image" that we can actually increase the activation of neurons in the motor cortex region of the brain. Imaging alone can actually change the physical structure and function of the brain. Other explanations suggest that imagery serves the function of increasing the automaticity of physical movements and elevating athletes' motivation. Whatever the reason, imagery seems to work.

When using imagery, there are several basic things you can do to make it most effective:

1. Whenever possible, conduct your imagery while you are in a relaxed state. Choose a comfortable, quiet (but not so comfortable and quiet that you will fall asleep) location that is free from distractions and breathe slowly and deeply for several minutes until you feel a sense of relaxation. When relaxed, then rehearse whatever imagery scenes you need to.

2. Create images that are as vivid as possible using all of your senses. Imagery is NOT just about "seeing" yourself perform an activity. Imagery is best when you see, hear, feel, touch, smell, taste, etc. For example, if you are a swimmer, then you would include seeing the blue of the water and the black lane lines in the pool, hearing the splash of other swimmers in the lanes beside you, tasting the chlorine in the water, smelling the dampness of the pool environment, and feeling the water as you dolphin kick after a flip turn. The more detailed and involved your images are, the more effective they can be.

3. Try to create images that incorporate internal and external perspectives. Internal imagery is a first-person perspective, what you would see from your own eyes. For example, a diver on the 10-meter platform would see the entire pool area as she looked out but not the water directly beneath them. As she performed her dive, there would be a blur of images as the she found her spot to know when to come out of her tucked position and reach for the water. External imagery, on the other hand, takes a third-person perspective. It is what you would see if you were sitting in the stands and watching yourself perform.

Imagery, like any skill, takes time and effort to master. And, not all athletes are able to image with the same level of ease or clarity. In fact, some athletes have a difficult time creating vibrant, clear, stable images that incorporate all their senses. If that is true for you, you may want to consult with a sport psychologist or counselor at your school's counseling center. They can help you refine your imagery and get the most out of what you can produce in your mind.

Remember, confidence can create expectations that you can strive to fulfill, whereas a lack of confidence can become a self-fulfilling prophecy of spiraling poor performances. If you see something as a barrier or obstacle ("I'll never swim that fast" or "we'll never beat that team"), then you may be doomed from the start. However, with confidence, those same situations can become opportunities to challenge yourself and excel. On which side of this equation do you want to be?

Control

Mentally tough athletes understand that many things in their sport environment—a referee's call, how well their opponent performs, the weather, a problem with equipment—are out of their control. They also know that focusing on things that are out of their control wastes their mental energy and distracts them from their performance. By attending to what they can control—their effort, their motivation, their focus, etc.—they increase their chances of performing at their best. To help you become more aware of what is and is not under your control, you may want to complete Exercise 13.8.

Understanding that you do not have control over everything and then focusing your energy on the things over which you do have influence is a key part of being a mentally tough performer. In completing Exercise 13.8, you may have found that you worry about things over which you have limited influence and this worry disrupts your focus; that is, you become distracted, either by external events (e.g., poor decisions by officials) or internal thoughts (e.g., worry about the weather). When you become distracted, inevitably your performance is negatively affected.

One important area over which athletes have control is their emotions. Emotions can facilitate or interfere with performances. In fact, sport psychologists, such as Yuri Hanin (2000), believe that every individual athlete has a profile of emotions that define their optimal performance state. That is, athletes have certain positive and negative emotions that, when present, help them perform at their best or get in the way and detract from their play. The key, according to Hanin, is to identify which emotions help and which ones hinder, and then determine how intensely they need to feel each one to perform optimally. To help you become more aware of your ideal emotional profile, you may want to complete Exercise 13.9.

> "Mental toughness and the heart are a lot stronger than some of the physical advantages you may have."
>
> MICHAEL JORDAN
> *Six-Time NBA Champion*

Exercise 13.8 What Is Under Your Control?

Take a moment to think about your sport and your performances. In what type of venue do you compete? Do you interact directly with your opponents (e.g., field hockey, basketball) or compete indirectly, such as in swimming? How is your sport officiated? How much influence do officials have over the outcome of competitions? How active can your coaches be during a competition? Can they substitute freely or once a competition begins do they have limited influence? Once you have thought about your sport, answer the following:

1. List 5–10 factors/situations in your sport that could influence your performance but over which you have little or no control.

2. List 5–10 factors/situations in your sport that could influence your performance but over which you have considerable control.

3. Now, take a moment to consider these two lists. About which factors/situations do you tend to worry the most, expend the most mental energy, and/or become the most upset when they occur? Why?

4. What happens to your focus when you worry about the situations/factors over which you have little to no control? For example, do you become distracted by external things, such as the crowd or officials, or overwhelmed by your thoughts, such as when you dwell on a mistake you have made?

Exercise 13.9 Determining Your Emotional Profile

Based on the work of Hanin (2000), you will have the opportunity to become more aware of the emotions you associate with your best and worst performances.

1. Think about a "best performance" you have had when competing in your sport. When we say "best" we are not necessarily referring the performance in which you achieved the highest outcome (e.g., you may have won an important competition, but only performed at a medium level). For "best" think about the process of the performance: when you felt the best, when you were in flow, when everything you did came together. Describe that performance (e.g., against whom were you competing, what were the conditions like for the competition, what were you thinking, how did your body feel).

2. Using the two lists, select five emotions from each that were present for you during your "best performance." These emotions have been designated by Hanin (2000) as either Helpful-Positive or Helpful-Negative. Choose five from each list. If you felt another type of emotion that is not listed here, add it. Remember, these are the emotions you associate with performing at your best.

Helpful-Positive Emotions	*Helpful-Negative Emotions*
Active	Scared
Relaxed	Angry

Calm	Annoyed
Happy	Anxious/worried
Confident	Discouraged
Exhilarated	Uncertain
Determined	Helpless
Excited	Sluggish
Brave	Intense
Satisfied	Jittery
Motivated	Unhappy
Quick	Tired
Other: _____	Other: _____

3. Now, for each emotion that you circled, indicate how intensely you felt it during your best performance on a scale from 1, *did not feel it*, to 5, *moderately felt it*, to 10, *felt it extremely*. Write your intensity rating next to each emotion that you circled.

With this evaluation, you have an idea of the emotions (and their intensity) that you associate with your best performances. You can use this information to begin monitoring your performances to see how closely you are able to approximate this emotional profile. By knowing your ideal emotional state, you can work to achieve it in advance of your competitions so you are at your best when you perform. To learn more about emotional profiling and extend the ideas introduced in this exercise, you may want consult with a sport psychologist at your school.

Ever heard the phrase "always be prepared?" Well, it is something mentally tough athletes do. In being under control, mentally tough athletes plan in advance regarding potential obstacles or setbacks they might face during competitions. They think through every possibility

and plan how they will respond if something occurs. This is also another way that imagery can be utilized. Not only is it important to image successful performances, but it is also important to be able see yourself overcoming obstacles, setbacks, or unexpected factors; for example, the soccer player who has to play on a muddy, poorly maintained field; the quarterback who throws an interception; the basketball players whose teammate is ill and cannot compete; the golfer who has hit a shot in the water and is looking at a triple bogey; or the tennis player who is called for a foot fault. If they had not prepared in advance for how they would handle themselves in such situations, then they might become distracted or overwhelmed. Mentally tough athletes have plans in place for such situations, no matter how small the problem might seem on the surface. They have rehearsed physically and/or mentally how they will handle themselves and continue to perform at or near their best. To help you become more aware of potential obstacles in your sport, you may want to complete Exercise 13.10.

Through the exercises in this section, you have identified the situations/factors over which you have control, the emotions you associate with your best performances, and how you will handle events/situations that could be obstacles (if you are not prepared) to your performances. By focusing on what you can control, moderating your emotional state to align with your profile, and preparing in advance for how you can remain calm and focused when things do not go your way, you increase your chances of performing at your best every time you step out to compete.

Concentration

In Chapter 5 we introduced you to four different types of attentional focus—broad external, narrow external, broad internal, and narrow internal—and described the utility of each one. As we noted in that chapter, your focus will shift naturally between these states. The key is to match the attentional focus to the demands of the sport situation. It is when there is a mismatch, such as when an athlete has a narrow internal focus but needs a broad external one, that performance decrements occur. Mentally tough athletes understand the importance of controlling their attentional focus and develop mental strategies, such as positive self-talk or relaxation, which help them shift to the needed state and maintain it even in the face of obstacles and competitive challenges.

Exercise 13.10 Identifying Potential Obstacles to Your Sport Performance

1. Think about your performances in your sport. What are potential obstacles or typical setbacks/mistakes you might experience? List all that you can think of (no matter how improbable they might seem).

2. Of the potential obstacles/setbacks/mistakes that you identified, select five that you think you might experience when competing. On a piece of paper, make two columns. In one column, list each obstacle. In the second column, list different things you can do to prepare in advance to minimize the event's impact on you. For

example, if you are a golfer and one obstacle was a tee-shot into the trees, you might practice, using imagery, remaining calm while talking positively to yourself, finding your ball, and then making a shot back onto the fairway. In thinking about how you will cope with the event, be as specific as you can be about what you will do. Once you have completed your list of solutions, begin practicing them now so you can handle whatever comes your way.

> "The vision of a champion is bent over, drenched in sweat, at the point of exhaustion when nobody else is looking."
>
> MIA HAMM
> *Olympic and World Champion, Soccer*

Being focused when you practice is related to your level of commitment. If you are not committed to your sport, then you probably will have a hard time being fully present—physically, emotionally, cognitively—during practices. Do you ever find yourself distracted at a practice? Thinking about something else, such as your classes, your boyfriend/girlfriend, or why the coach is not starting you? Mentally tough athletes know that when they are at practice, they are present in the moment, focused on what their coaches are telling them, concentrating on the physical skills they are executing, and committed to becoming the best athlete they can be. They understand that there is a time to "think" and a time to "do," and they keep those separate. At most times during practices and competitions, it is a time to do; thinking will occur during breaks in the action, such as halftime or a time-out, but not when it's time to perform. To help you become more aware of your focus during practices and competitions, you may want to complete Exercise 13.11.

Although the ideal is to eliminate mistakes completely from performances, the reality is that you will make errors from time to time. There is an ebb and flow to performance that mentally tough athletes accept as part of the process to excellence, and understand that getting "hung up" on their mistakes does not help them improve. They understand that, in addition to trying to minimize the errors they make, the key is how they respond when mistakes occur. Mentally tough athletes are able to let go of their errors and bring themselves back to what they need to do in the moment. They understand that focusing on their mistake will only prolong the problem and lead to further performance decrements. Cornerbacks who play on defenses that stress man-to-man coverage know that one of the most important mental skills they need is short-term memory loss after they've been burned by a wide receiver running a hitch and go. When they line up the next series, they need to be focused on the task at hand and not on what happened the last series.

Jay Deiters and Mishelle Rodriguez, sport consultants at the UNT-CSPPE, have developed a system to explain how athletes can respond successfully to the inevitable mistakes and errors that occur during practices and competitions (see Figure 13.1). Athletes practice as much as they do to make their behaviors (their physical responses) automatic; when competing, athletes must be able to *respond* without much (or any in some circumstances) conscious thought. But even

---

Exercise 13.11   Monitoring Yourself During Practices

1. Over the next week of practices, pay particular attention to yourself and your focus. As you do, make notes to yourself about the following situations:

   a. During the 30 or so minutes before practice starts and you are getting ready (e.g., putting on your practice gear, getting treatment from your trainer), where is your focus? What are you feeling and thinking about?

   b. As practice starts, what are you saying to yourself? Where is your focus?

   c. During practice, does your mind wander? To what thoughts, events, etc.? How easy or difficult is it to regain your focus on what you are doing in the moment?

Once practice is over, think about what you can "take away" from that practice. What parts of practice were easier to concentrate on? Were there times during the practice where your focus wandered? Were you able to catch yourself at any times during practice when your commitment waned? Were you able to pull yourself back to present? If so, what technique was effective in helping you do so?

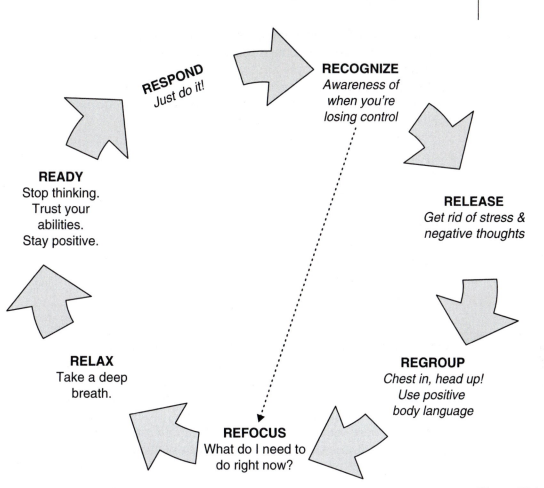

Figure 13.1 Cycle for Recovering from a Mistake

with well-trained athletes, mistakes will occur. When they do, mentally tough athletes *recognize* the mistake and the fact that they are having a reaction, such as becoming upset, to it. Through this awareness, mentally tough athletes are able to *release* the mistake; that is, let go of the negative emotions and self-talk that may have been building up. Then, they *regroup*; they pull themselves back together and project an aura of confidence. Mentally tough athletes often do this behaviorally, such as by keeping their heads up, their back straight (you probably have seen the look of the defeated, overwhelmed athlete—chin down, shoulders drooping). Once they have regrouped, mentally tough athletes *refocus* on the task at hand, bringing themselves back to the present competition and what they need to do right now to perform. Often, such refocusing includes a deep breath, which stimulates a physical *relaxation* and a return to being *ready* to respond. To help you become more aware of how you respond to a mistake, you may want to complete Exercise 13.12.

Exercise 13.12   Recovering from a Mistake

1. Think about your recent competitions/performances and identify a mistake/error that you made and to which you did not respond well (or productively). Describe the mistake and how you responded to it. Be specific in terms of what you did, what you thought, and what you felt.

2. Keeping in mind the Cycle for Recovering from a Mistake, describe what you would do differently if you made that same mistake. Think about each step of the cycle (e.g., regroup, relax, etc.) and discuss what you would do, what thoughts you would want to have, and how you would want to feel.

Maintaining your concentration involves managing your attentional focus and not being overwhelmed and distracted by mistakes that inevitably will occur when you are performing. By keeping your focus in the moment, not dwelling on mistakes, and not overanalyzing situations, you can create a more ideal performance state and increase your chances of being at your best, consistently.

Consistency

Being committed to your sport, being confident in yourself, being in control of your thoughts and feelings, and being focused all set the stage for you to perform consistently. In fact, consistent performances are what coaches strive for because they know if their team or athletes can perform at the same high level time after time (e.g., games, meets, races), then they will win more in the long term. Have you ever heard a coach tell you your play is inconsistent? If you are like most athletes, then you have had that experience.

One of the key strategies for becoming a consistent performer is developing a pre-performance routine. Pre-performance routines are purposefully developed, strategic plans that athletes implement in the days, hours, and minutes prior to their performances. Pre-performance routines also can be implemented during performances, such as when a tennis player is going to serve or a basketball player is going to shoot a free throw. These routines help athletes attain the physical, cognitive, and emotional readiness they need to perform consistently at their best. At its simplest, a pre-performance routine is the set of behaviors, thoughts, emotions, and physical sensations that athletes want to have and engage in prior to competing.

© Gert Johannes Jacobus Vrey, 2009 / Used under license from Shutterstock.com

Pre-performance routines can be created for practices, competitions, and even specific skills (e.g., basketball free throws). We believe there are three primary reasons why pre-performance routines work. First, pre-performance routines contribute to consistency, and consistency usually leads to better performances. Second, routines are something athletes can control and thus provide a sense of comfort and calmness to them. They also can help them get to the level of energy activation that offers the best opportunity to perform well. And third, pre-performance routines increase an athlete's level of commitment through consciously determining how they want to approach a performance instead of leaving the final moments before performance to chance.

We will focus on some of the basic concepts in creating a pre-performance for competition, but these same basic concepts can be used to develop practice pre-performance routines or specific pre-skill pre-performance routines. It's important that we differentiate between pre-performance routines and superstitious rituals. Pre-performance routines include behaviors, thoughts, emotions, and mental toughness skills that we've previously reviewed. The athlete is actively determining what they are choosing to do prior to a competition, and at the same time, allowing for flexibility since they understand that things can come up just before competitions that can throw off their normal way of preparing. With pre-performance routines, athletes consciously plan what they are going to do and then implement those strategies and skills as needed to help them prepare to be their best. In other words, athletes are in control of their pre-performance routines. In comparison, superstitious routines control the athlete. For instance, some athletes might believe that a certain Under Armor T-shirt must be worn for them to play well. If the T-shirt is lost, misplaced, or destroyed, then the athlete is at the mercy of the T-shirt. Or, some athletes might believe that every time they eat a pre-game meal at McDonalds, they will win. But what happens when the athlete's team does not go to a McDonalds before a competition? In this situation, again, the superstition controls the athlete.

There is not a pre-determined time that a pre-performance competition routine must start. Some athletes like to start preparing a few days before the competition, whereas others do not start in earnest until they get to the competition venue. Thus, you need to determine for yourself when it is right to "start thinking about the competition." Athletes need different amounts of time to ready themselves for competition. Some athletes need to focus a lot of attention for longer periods of time to get ready. Other athletes best prepare by keeping themselves distracted and not thinking about the competition until moments before the event. Looking back at your best past performances (as you did in Exercise 13.9) can provide you with some ideas about how much time you need for your pre-performance competition routine. For the purposes of this example, we will break the pre-performance competition routine down to four stages: 1) the night before the competition, 2) the morning of the competition, 3) an hour before the competition, and 4) minutes before the start of the competition. You will notice that as the athlete gets closer to the competition they will be doing and thinking less and less.

During the night before the competition, an athlete might choose to review her game plan for the competition with a coach or teammate and watch some highlight videotapes, or before going to bed she might watch a scene from a favorite movie that reminds her how she wants to feel during the competition (again, see Exercise 13.9). As she lies in bed before going to sleep, the athlete might spend 15 minutes relaxing and using imagery to see herself performing confidently and overcoming obstacles (see Exercises 13.6 and 13.7). The morning of the competition the athlete might choose to take a hot shower to loosen her muscles, and as she showered, again "image" herself performing confidently and adding positive self-statements (e.g., "You are ready, today!"). While eating breakfast, she could listen to songs on her iPod playlist that help her get in the emotional mood she associates with playing her best. An hour before competition, the athlete might want to still be with teammates as they warm up, but as the time to compete grows closer, she may carve out 5 minutes of quiet time where she reminds herself of some simple cues that have helped them in the past (e.g., "Quick feet," "Feel the water, don't fight it," "Keep my hand behind the ball as long as possible"). She reminds herself to have fun because

---

Exercise 13.13   Creating Your Own Pre-performance Competition Routine

Think about some of your best past performances (see Exercise 13.9). How did you approach those competitions? What did you do before those competitions to get yourself ready to perform? As you think about this performance, determine the point when you begin to transition from preparation for competition to it's time to get ready to compete. Use this as the starting point for your routine.

1. Identify three to four stages of your routine leading up to competition, such as the night before, the morning of, and minutes before. What will you do during each of these stages? Remember, you will be doing more in the stages further away from competition and narrowing as you get closer to competition. At the competition, you will mostly want to keep your head out of the way of your body, so it can do what it's been trained

to do. For each stage, write down specifically what emotions you want to be present, what you want to be thinking, what you want to be doing, and how you want your body to feel.

2. Consider sharing your pre-performance competition routine with a coach, teammate, or sport psychologist to get feedback. Based on this feedback, make adjustments to your routine that you think will help you perform better and more consistently.

3. Start practicing using your pre-performance competition routine before upcoming competitions. As you do, monitor how you respond and how you ultimately perform. Make adjustments as needed to help refine your routine.

---

ultimately that's why she plays her sport. Minutes before competition, the athlete takes a few last clearing breaths, puts the competition in proper perspective (i.e., "This is important, but there are still individuals losing their lives to defend this country"), and let's go, trusting the work and preparation she's done so she can compete at her best. To help you create your own pre-performance routine, you may want to complete Exercise 13.13.

Post-Game Review

Coaches, athletes, and even fans would describe great performers as mentally tough. Through this chapter, we have introduced you to what mental toughness is (i.e., the 5 Cs) and given you the chance to evaluate yourself along these dimensions. If you completed the exercises, then you have had a chance to improve your awareness and develop strategies that will help you become a mentally tough performer. Mental toughness, though, will not just happen because you want it to. Just like increasing your physical strength requires time and effort spent in the weight room, developing your mental toughness will take purposeful, targeted practice of the skills and strategies provided through the exercises in this chapter. If you are committed, though, implementing these skills and strategies will be a natural extension of your desire to be your best.

Thinking Critically about Mental Toughness

1. Summarize what you now know about mental toughness based on the information presented in this chapter.

_____

_____

_____

2. What additional questions do you have about this topic and how to use the skills introduced in this chapter?

_____

_____

_____

3. What conclusions can you draw about this topic and how it might help you be a more effective and successful student and athlete?

_____

_____

_____

Achieve IT! Setting a Mental Toughness Goal

1. Based on your self-assessment and your responses to Thinking Critically, select a goal in relationship to becoming a mentally tougher athlete that you would like to achieve this term.

2. Now identify three short-term goals that will help you reach your goal this term.

3. For the short-term goals, identify the attainment strategies you will need to reach them.

4. List any obstacles you might face in trying to reach these goals and identify your plan for overcoming each one.

Don't forget to make your goal visible and tell others about them, so they can keep you accountable regarding what you want to achieve.

Chapter 13 Review Questions

1. Mentally tough athletes are:

    a. Cocky.
    b. Controlled.
    c. Committed.
    d. B and C.
    e. All of the above.

2. Emotions can facilitate and interfere with athletic performances. (True or False)

3. Confident athletes:

    a. Believe strongly in their abilities.
    b. Put down their competitors.
    c. Gauge their success based on their own performances.
    d. A and C.
    e. All of the above.

4. To increase your confidence, you might:

    a. Set and follow through on your goals.
    b. Talk positively to yourself.
    c. Maintain positive images about your performances.
    d. A and B.
    e. All of the above.

5. Juwan is intense and passionate when he competes and knows what he wants to accomplish in his sport career. As a mentally tough athlete, Juwan is demonstrating:

    a. Consistency.
    b. Control.
    c. Confidence.
    d. Commitment.

6. Pre-performance routines are a great way for athletes to develop more control in their athletic abilities. (True or False)

7. Understanding that mistakes are a part of competition and learning how to let go of those mistakes and refocus on the present is an example of which "C"?

    a. Commitment.
    b. Confidence.
    c. Consistency.
    d. Control.

8. According to the Cycle of Recovering from Mistakes, athletes must be able to recognize their error and ultimately refocus on their current performance by letting go of the negative thoughts and feelings they might have concerning the mistake. (True or False)

9. Athletes' attentional focus is static, remaining fixed throughout a performance. (True or False)

10. Which of the following is not a dimension of attentional focus introduced in this chapter?

    a. Broad—internal.
    b. Broad—external.
    c. Narrow—external.
    d. None of the above.

References

American Psychiatric Association. 2000. *Diagnostic and Statistical Manual of Mental Disorders,* 4th ed., TR. Washington, DC: Author.

Anderson, W. A., R. R. Albrecht, D. B. McKeag, D. O. Hough, and C. A. McGrew. 1991. A national survey of alcohol and drug use by college athletes. *The Physician and Sportsmedicine* 19: 91–104.

Bandura, A. 1977. Self-efficacy: Toward a unifying theory of behavioral change. *Psychological Review* 84: 191–215.

Bandura, A. 1982. Self-efficacy mechanism in human agency. *American Psychologist* 37: 122–147.

Bandura, A. 1986. *Social foundations of thought and action: A social cognitive theory.* Englewood Cliffs, NJ: Prentice-Hall.

Berning, J. R. 1988. Wise food choices for athletes on the road. *Sports Science Exchange* 1(1).

Bernstein, D. A., A. Clarke-Stewart, E. Roy, T. K. Srull, C. D. Wickens. 1994. *Psychology,* 3rd ed. Boston: Houghton-Mifflin.

Beswick, G., E. Rothblum, and L. Mann. 1988. Psychological antecedents of student procrastination. *Australian Psychologist* 23: 207–217.

Briggs, K. C., and I. B. Myers. 1976. *Myers-Briggs Type Indicator.* Palo Alto, CA: Consulting Psychologists Press.

Brislin, R., and T. Yoshida. 1994. *Intercultural communication training: An introduction.* Thousand Oaks, CA: Sage.

Britton, B., and A. Tesser. 1991. Effects of time management practices on college grades. *Journal of Educational Psychology* 83: 405–410.

Burns, J., P. M. Clarkson, E. F. Coyle, E. R. Eichner, W. L. Kenney, G. W. Mack, R. Murray, D. Passe, W. Prentice, and C. Rosenbloom. 2001. Why don't athletes drink enough during exercise, and what can be done about it? *Sports Science Exchange Roundtable* 12(1).

Chickering, A. W. & L. Reisser, 1993. *Education and identity,* 2nd ed. San Francisco: Jossey-Bass.

Chickering, A. W., and N. K. Schlossberg, 2001. *Getting the most out of college,* 2nd ed. Upper Saddle River, NY: Prentice Hall.

Clark, N. 1989. Social drinking and athletes. *The Physician and Sportsmedicine* 17: 95–100.

Cohen, D. and T. Petrie. 2005. An examination of psychosocial correlates of disordered eating among undergraduate women. *Sex Roles* 52: 29–42.

Coleman, E. 1998. Carbohydrate—The master fuel. In J. R. Berning and S. N. Steen (Eds.), *Nutrition for Sport and Exercise.* Gaithersburg, MD: Aspen Publishers.

Coyle, E. 2004. Highs and lows of carbohydrate diets. *Sport Science Exchange* 17(2): 1–6.

Davis, M., E. R. Eshelman, and M. McKay. 1995. *The Relaxation and Stress Reduction Workbook,* 4th ed. Oakland: New Harbinger.

Dembo, M. 2000. *Motivational and learning strategies for college success: A self-management approach.* Mahwah, NJ: Lawrence Erlbaum.

Dole, J., G. Duffy, L. Roehler, and P. Pearson. 1991. Moving from the old to the new: Research on reading comprehension instruction. *Review of Educational Research* 61: 239–264.

Eggen, P., and D. Kauchak. 1997. *Education psychology: Windows on classrooms,* 3rd ed. Columbus, OH: Merrill.

Eichner, E. R., D. King, M. Myhal, B. Prentice, and T. N. Ziegenfuss. 1999. Muscle builder supplements. *Sport Science Exchange Roundtable* 10(3).

Ferrante, A. P., E. Etzel, and C. Lantz. 1996. Counseling college student-athletes: The problem, the need. In E. Etzel, A. P. Ferrante, and J. W. Pinkney (Eds.), *Counseling college student-athletes: Issues and interventions,* 2nd ed. Morgantown, WV: Fitness Information Technologies.

Finch, L. 2002. Understanding individual motivation in sport. In J. M. Silva and D. E. Stevens (Eds.) *Psychological Foundations of Sport,* pp. 66–79. Boston: Allyn & Bacon.

Folkman, S. 1984. Personal control and stress and coping processes: A theoretical analysis. *Journal of Personality and Social Psychology* 46: 839–852.

Ford, C. W. 1994. *We can all get along.* New York: Dell.

Frintner, M., and L. Rubinson. 1993. Acquaintance rape: The influence of alcohol, fraternity membership, and sports team membership. *Journal of Sex Education and Therapy* 19: 272–284.

Greenleaf, C., T. Petrie, J. Reel, and J. Carter. 2009. Female collegiate athletes: Prevalence of eating disorders and disordered eating behaviors. *Journal of American College Health* 57: 489–495.

Haldane, B., and J. R. Forster. 1988. Dependable strengths articulation process. [Unpublished training manual].

Hamachek, A. L. 2006. *Coping with college.* Needham Heights, MA: Allyn and Bacon.

Hanin, Y. L. (2000). *Emotions in sport.* Champaign, IL: Human Kinetics.

Hecht, M. L., S. Ribeau, and J. K. Alberts. 1989. An Afro-American perspective on interethnic communication. *Communication Monographs* 56: 385–410.

Hill, D. W., D. O. Borden, K. M. Darnaby, and D. N. Hendricks. 1994. Aerobic and anaerobic contributions to exhaustive high-intensity exercise after sleep deprivation. *Journal of Sports Sciences* 12: 455–461.

Holland, J. 1994. *The Occupations Finder.* Odessa, FL: Psychological Assessment Resources.

Holland, J. 1994. *The Self-Directed Search.* Odessa, FL: Psychological Assessment Resources.

Jackson, T. L. 1991. A university athletic department's rape and assault experiences. *Journal of College Student Development* 32: 77–78.

Judd, T. 2000. What can I do with my anger? [Unpublished handout from Anger Control Training Group].

Katz, R. S. 2000. Helping your clients through grief and mourning. Presentation at University of Washington, Seattle, November 3, 2000.

Kiewra, K. A. 1989. A review of note-taking: The encoding-storage paradigm and beyond. *Educational Psychology Review* 1: 147–172.

King, M. M. 1997. *Handling test anxiety.* Bellingham, WA: Western Washington University.

Knight, J., H. Wechsler, M. Kou, M. Seibering, E. Weitzman, and M. Schuckit. 2002. Alcohol abuse and dependence among U.S. college students. *Journal of Studies on Alcohol* 63: 263–271.

Kuo, M., G. Dowdall, M. Koss, and H. Wechsler. 2004. Correlates of rape while intoxicated in a national sample of college women. *Journal of Studies on Alcohol* 65: 37–46.

Kuo, M., J. Lee, and H. Wechsler. 2003. Trends in marijuana and other illicit drug use among college students: Results from 4 Harvard School of Public Health college alcohol study surveys: 1993–2001. *Journal of American College Health* 52: 17–24.

Kyllo, L. B., and D. M. Landers. 1995. Goal setting in sport and exercise: A research synthesis to resolve the controversy. *Journal of Sport & Exercise Psychology* 17: 117–137.

Lakein, A. 1973. *How to get control of your time and your life.* New York: The New American Library.

Lazarus, R., and S. Folkman. 1984. *Stress, appraisal, and coping.* New York: Springer.

Letteri, C. 1985. Teaching students how to learn. *Theory Into Practice* 24: 112–122.

Lewin, K. 1948. *Resolving social conflicts.* New York: Harper.

Locke, E. A., and G. P. Latham. 1985. The application of goal setting to sports. *Journal of Sport Psychology* 7: 205–222.

Macan, T., C. Shahani, R. Dipboye, and A. Phillips. 1990. College students' time management: Correlations with academic performance and stress. *Journal of Educational Psychology* 82: 760–768.

Maughan, R. J., J. B. Leiper, and S. M. Shirreffs, 1996. Rehydration and recovery after exercise. *Sports Science Exchange* 9(3).

McCabe, S. E., K. J. Brower, B. T. West, T. F. Nelson, and H. Wechsler. 2007. Trends in non-medical use of anabolic steroids by U.S. college students: Results from four national surveys. *Drug and Alcohol Dependence* 90: 243–251.

McKay, M., M. Davis, and P. Fanning. 2009. *Messages: The communications skill book.* Oakland: New Harbinger Publications, Inc.

McKinney, J., J. Dyck, and E. Luber. 2008. iTunes university and the classroom: Can podcasts replace professors? *Computers & Education Computers* 52(3): 617–623.

Middleman, A. B., and R. H. DuRant. 1996. Anabolic steroid use and associated health risk behaviours. *Sports Medicine: An International Journal* 21: 251–255.

Miller, G. A. 1956. The magical number seven, plus or minus two: Some limits on our capacity to process information. *Psychological Review* 63: 81–97.

Murray, B. 1996. Fluid replacement: The American College of Sports Medicine position stand. *Sports Science Exchange* 9(4).

Myers, I. B. 1993. *Introduction to Type,* 5th ed. Palo Alto, CA: Consulting Psychologists Press.

Nicholls, J. G. 1992. The general and the specific in the development and expression of achievement motivation. In G. C. Roberts (Ed.) *Understanding motivation in sport and exercise,* pp. 31–56, Champaign, IL: Human Kinetics.

Nideffer, R. M. 1986. Concentration and attention control training. In J. M. Williams (Ed.), *Applied sport psychology: Personal growth to peak performance.* Palo Alto, CA: Mayfield.

Occupations Outlook Handbook. 2009. Washington, DC: Bureau of Labor Statistics.

Ormrod, J. 1999. *Human learning,* 3rd ed. Upper Saddle River, NJ: Merrill.

Pauk, W., & R. J. Q. Owens. 2007. *How to study in college,* 9th ed. Boston: Houghton Mifflin.

Petrie, T., C. Greenleaf, J. Reel, and J. Carter. 2008. Prevalence of eating disorders and disordered eating behaviors among male collegiate athletes. *Psychology of Men & Masculinity* 9: 267–277.

Petrie, T. A., and H. G. Petrie. 1999. Integrating multiple intelligences and learning styles into college classes. Workshop presented at the College Reading and Language Association annual conference. New Orleans, LA.

Petrie, T. A., H. G. Petrie, L. Landry, and K. Edwards. 2002. *Strategic learning in college.* Denton, TX: RonJon.

Pinkerton, R., L. Hinz, and J. Barrow. 1989. The college student athlete: Psychological considerations and interventions. *Journal of American College Health* 37: 218–226.

Pinkney, J. W. 1996. Coaching student-athletes toward academic success. In E. F. Etzel, A. P. Ferrante, and J. W. Pinkney (Eds.), *Counseling college student-athletes: Issues and interventions,* 2nd ed. Morgantown, WV: Fitness Information Technologies.

Potteiger, J. A., and V. G. Stilger. 1994. Anabolic steroid use in the adolescent athlete. *Journal of Athletic Training* 29: 60–64.

Prochaska, J. O., J. C. Norcross, and C. C. DiClemente. 1994. *Changing for Good.* New York: Avon.

Random House College Dictionary. 1993. New York: Random House.

Riewald, S., and M. Barnes. 2002. Hydration and nutritional strategies for recovery. *Olympic Coach* 12(4): 5–8.

Robinson, F. 1946. *Effective study.* New York: Harper and Brothers.

Schacter, D. 1999. The seven sins of memory: Insights from psychology and cognitive neuroscience. *American Psychologist* 54: 182–203.

Schouwenburg, H.C. 2004. *Counseling the procrastinator in academic settings.* Washington, DC: American Psychological Association.

Schunk, D. 1991. Self-efficacy and academic motivation. *Educational Psychologist* 26: 207–231.

Schunk, D. 2000. *Learning theories: An educational perspective,* 3rd ed. Upper Saddle River, NJ: Merrill.

Selby, R., H. M. Weinstein, and T. S. Bird. 1990. The health of university athletes: Attitudes, behaviors, and stressors. *Journal of American College Health* 39: 11–18.

Seligman, M. E. P. 1991. *Learned optimism.* New York: Knopf.

Sharf, R. S. 1992. *Applying career development theory to counseling.* Pacific Grove, CA: Brooks-Cole.

Sherman, W. M. 1989. Pre-event nutrition. *Sports Science Exchange* 1(12).

Spence, J. C., and L. Gauvin. 1996. Drug and alcohol use by Canadian university athletes: A national survey. *Journal of Drug Education* 26: 275–287.

Steen, S. N. 1998. Eating on the road: Where are the carbohydrates? *Sports Science Exchange* 11(4).

Strong Interest Inventory. 1994. Palo Alto, CA: Consulting Psychologists Press.

Toben, N., and H. Wechsler. 2001. Alcohol and college athletes. *Medicine & Science in Sports & Exercise* 33: 43–47.

Tripp, M., and T. Petrie. 2001. Sexual abuse and eating disorders: A test of a conceptual model. *Sex Roles* 44: 17–32.

Wade, C., and C. Tavris. 2003. *Psychology,* 7th ed. Upper Saddle River, NJ: Prentice Hall.

Wechsler, H., A. Davenport, G. Dowdall, S. Grossman, and S. I. Zanakos. 1997. Binge drinking, tobacco, and illicit drug use and involvement in college athletics: A survey of students at 140 American colleges. *Journal of American College Health* 45: 195–200.

Wechsler, H., A. Davenport, G. Dowdall, B. Moeykens, and S. Castillo. 1994. Health and behavioral consequences of binge drinking in college: A national survey of students at 140 campuses. *Journal of the American Medical Association* 272: 1672–1677.

Wechsler, H., J. Lee, M. Kuo, M. Seibring, T. Nelson, and H. Lee. 2002. Trends in college binge drinking during a period of increased prevention efforts: Findings from 4 Harvard School of Public Health college alcohol study surveys: 1993–2001. *Journal of American College Health* 50: 203–217.

Weinberg, R. S. 1996. Goal setting sport and exercise: Research to practice. In J. L. Van Raalte and B. W. Brewer (Eds.), *Exploring Sport and Exercise Psychology.* Washington, DC: American Psychological Association.

Wittrock, M. C. 1990. Generative processes of comprehension. *Educational Psychologist* 24: 345–376.

Wolf-Wendel, L. E., J. D. Toma, and C. C. Morphew. 2001. How much difference is too much difference? Perceptions of gay men and lesbians in intercollegiate athletics. *Journal of College Student Development* 42: 465–479.

Index